Rediscovering America's Values

"DESERVES A WIDE AND ATTENTIVE AUDIENCE. . . .
The questions the book addresses are so important, and Lappé manages to engage us so thoroughly in the unfolding argument, that we get involved in the running debate. We cheer and hiss as different points of view are put forward. . . . at times one wants to cheer Lappé's ability to reduce the conflict of our time into a clear outline."

Los Angeles Times

"Some of the twentieth century's most vibrant activist-thinkers have been American women—Margaret Mead, Jeanette Rankin, Barbara Ward, Dorothy Day—who took it on themselves to pump life into basic truths. Frances Moore Lappé is among them."

The Washington Post

"A remarkable variety of thought [assembled] in a way which stimulates the reader to inspect his or her basic assumptions about values. It could not be more timely. . . . We must know who we are and what we hold dear or else we fritter away our resources carelessly and decline. . . . An imaginative and creative way to test and renovate our beliefs."

George C. Lodge
Professor of Business Administration
Harvard Business School

"In this book, Frances Moore Lappé provides us with a lively dialogue drawn not only from the Western political tradition but from an emerging consciousness designed to take us safely into the twenty-first century. . . . We find ourselves drawn into the debate and inspired to reexamine our most deeply held assumptions and values."

Frank Roosevelt
Chair, Social Sciences
Sarah Lawrence College

"By writing *Rediscovering America's Values*, Lappé is inserting a fresh voice into the debate where American politics and morality come together."

Oakland Tribune

"No matter what the reader's political stance, this is a vital work, of interest to every American concerned about the future of this country."

The Kirkus Reviews

Rediscovering

America's Values

Frances Moore Lappé

BALLANTINE BOOKS
NEW YORK

Library of Congress Catalog Card Number: 89-92597

ISBN: 0-345-36953-X

Cover design by Andrew M. Newman

Manufactured in the United States of America

First Ballantine Books Trade Paperback Edition: February 1991

10 9 8 7 6 5 4 3 2 1

To Baird, for the philosopher's touch.

Acknowledgments ★

This book, which is written as a dialogue, is also the product of a dialogue, a many-sided one indeed. It carries within it the inspiration, support, and insights of many friends and colleagues. When the book was still the proverbial glint in my eye, the enthusiasm and help of Frank Roosevelt and Nina Rothschild Utne gave me hope in its potential. I am forever grateful to you both.

My earliest musings were allowed to grow in the supportive environment of the Institute for the Study of Social Change at the University of California, Berkeley. I am indebted to its director, Troy Duster, and staff for making possible my nine-month research stint there.

A particular pleasure in writing this book has been my association with outstanding research interns at the Institute for Food and Development Policy—Sheila Crum, Steve Kay, and John Ladd. Your enthusiasm for the project, your meticulous work, your thoughtful suggestions made this a much better book. Your devotion to the project transformed the project from a lonely struggle into a genuine team effort. Thank you.

Other interns also made valuable contributions at various stages of the project. Byron Spicer's attention to the last-minute details was nothing less than heroic.

I also appreciate the work of interns Eben Gossage, Mala Thakur, and Heidi Beirich, and assistants John Torpey and Maggi Despot.

To be able to incorporate feedback from those actually engaging in the dialogue that I hope this book ignites, I enlisted the help of several friends who are professors. Frank Roosevelt at Sarah Lawrence College (economics), Ann Clark at St. Mary's College (philosophy), and Howard Richards at Earlham College (peace studies) each tested the first draft of the book with their students. Your thoughtful comments, as well as the feedback of your students, were enormously useful in completing the project. I am indeed grateful to each of you.

I am also indebted to friends who are also mentors, those whose work has clarified complex issues and helped to inspire this direction in my own work. David Gordon, Sam Bowles, Bert Gross, Kusum Singh, and Harry Boyte, your scholarship, insights, and encouragement have assisted this effort in countless ways. Bob Kuttner and George Lodge must also be singled out for their contributions, as you will see in the references to their work in my notes.

I am grateful also to the many scholars and friends who gave generously of their time to offer thoughtful criticism of all or part of the manuscript: Peter Barnes, Heather Booth, David Crocker, Colin Greer, Herbert Holman, Paul Lacey, Gil

Moore, John and Libby Morse, Howard Naylor, Mark Sagoff, Peter Steinfels, David Shields, Bart Taub, Ellen Teninty, and Bill Wood, S.J. For their critical review on the section on affirmative action, I am particularly grateful to John Powell and Ed Baker of the American Civil Liberties Union; for assistance on the section on employment, my thanks go to Bennett Harrison, Juliet Schor, and Christopher Tilly.

Linda Pritzker, Claire Leverant, John Moore, Joe Jordan, Richard Healey, Gretta Goldenman, Peter Mann, Jonathan Rowe, and Marty Teitel—thanks to each of you for your steadfast encouragement along the way.

My colleagues at the Institute have facilitated this project, so I owe special thanks to Tom Ambrogi, Walden Bello, Medea Benjamin, Marilyn Borchardt, Becky Buell, Lorraine Coleman, Joe Collins, Kevin Danaher, Andrea Freedman, Susan Galleymore, Christopher Kashap, Ann Kelly, Audee Kochiyama-Holman, Marshall McComb, Warren Mills, Ana Perla, Viola Weinberg. I also wish to thank the trustees of the Institute whose enthusiasm for the project helped sustain my energies.

None of my work would be possible without the members and supporters of the Institute for Food and Development Policy. Our special thanks go to the Threshold Foundation, John and Libby Morse, and Nina Rothschild Utne, whose financial support specifically contributed to this work. My special appreciation also to the CS Fund, Harry Chapin Foundation, National Community Funds, Ottinger Foundation, Samuel Rubin Foundation, and Youth Project, whose loyal support has facilitated all of our work.

Among the enthusiasts who got this project off the ground, Joan Raines, my literary agent, is preeminent. Your faith in the project has been a continuing encouragement. At Ballantine Books, Joëlle Delbourgo and Betsy Rapoport contributed excellent editorial guidance. The positive working relationship that you created made even the final, often agonizing stages a pleasure. Thank you for this and for your continuing commitment to the book.

My children, Anthony and Anna Lappé, thank you for your cheerful tolerance of my utter preoccupation and for your belief in the importance of what I am attempting. My husband, environmental philosopher J. Baird Callicott, your contribution is too big and multifaceted to name; you, above all, strengthened my belief in the power of ideas both to limit and to free us. Your clear thinking set a high standard, nudging me out of innumerable mental cul de sacs. I anticipate our continuing dialogue.

Finally, let me underscore that my gratitude for the many contributions of these individuals in no way implies their agreement with my voice in the dialogue. And I, of course, remain solely responsible for errors or oversights.

Frances Moore Lappé
San Francisco

Contents ★

A Personal Foreword   xv

Introduction   3

PART ONE
Freedom: Choice, Opportunity, and Responsibility   19

Freedom From and Freedom To   21
Of Entitlements and Rights   27
The High Price of Neglect   32
Government as Provider or Rule Setter   35
Freedom and Individual Responsibility   39
Freedom and the Responsibilities of Government   46
Freedom and Economic Security   50
Poverty: It's All Relative   51
Freedom as Privacy   54
Security, Risk, and the Work Ethic   55
The Risks of Unintended Consequences   59
What Is the Role of Government in a Free Society?   60
Summing Up the Dialogue   64

PART TWO

What's Fair?   67

Are the Rich Getting Richer?   69
Can Redistribution Ever Be Fair?   71
Is the Market Fair?   75
Fairness: What Works   76
Hope and Fairness as Incentives   79
Incentives at the Top   80
Fair Reward for Sacrifice and Risk?   82
Inheritance Rights, or Wrongs?   84
Inequalities and Self-Esteem   86
Fairness or Envy?   87
Egalitarianism's Slippery Slope   89
Who's Responsible for Inequalities?   91
Equal Opportunities or Equal Outcomes?   93
Affirmative Action or Reverse Discrimination?   97
Fairness, Equality, and Freedom   107
Who Decides What's Fair?   110
Summing Up the Dialogue   113

PART THREE

Freedom and the Market's Efficiency   117

The Market, Competition, and Concentrated Power   119
The Market as Individual Choice   121
The Market and Personal Prejudice   123
The Market and Voluntary Choice   125
The Market: It Works!   128
Efficiency, Size, and Profits   131
Regulation and the Market   134
The Market, Property, and the Environment   141
Market Prices and Resource Use   142
Just Make Them Pay   145
The Market and Resource Depletion   148
Resources for Future Generations   149
Government and Resource Use   152
The Government and/or the Market?   155
Of Interests and Principles   157
Summing Up the Dialogue   158

PART FOUR

Freedom: Property, Power, and Civil Liberties 163

Property: Protection Against State Power? 165
Property: The Right to the Fruits of One's Labor 169
Property: The Incentive to Production 170
Property Rights—Limited or Unlimited? 172
Ownership: Who Makes the Decisions, Who Bears the Consequences? 175
Property: Exclusive or Inclusive? 180
Private Enterprise—What's Private? 182
The Market, Property, and Civil Liberties 184
Economic and Political—How Separate? 187
Summing Up the Dialogue 189

PART FIVE

Freedom and Democracy 191

Democracy: Countervailing Powers or Accountability? 193
Government: Protection Against Power or Participation in Power? 197
Politics Captured by Minorities or Politics as Community Life? 198
Economic and Political Life: The Division? The Interplay? 203
A Democratic Economy? 211
Workplace Democracy: Can It Work? 220
Trade Unions: Help or Hindrance? 225
The Culture of Democracy 227
Democracy and Individuality 231
Summing Up the Dialogue 232

PART SIX

Freedom, Human Nature, and Hope 235

Freedom: Zero-sum? 237
Self-Interest Versus Community Interest 241
Moral Responsibility and the Market 248
A Common Good? 250
Does Capitalism Embody Moral Values? 253
Is Change Possible? 258
The Inescapable Trade-offs 262

Sound Processes or Ultimate Goals?   263
Ends or Means?   265
Summing Up the Dialogue   267

Notes   271

Index   315

A Personal Foreword ★

Because my life's work has focused on world hunger, you might be puzzled to discover my name on this book about America's values. What may appear to be a big leap calls for some explaining.

I grew up in Fort Worth, Texas, in the Fifties, the daughter of a forecaster for the United States Weather Service and a transportation agent for the Corps of Engineers. But my parents' professions influenced my early life much less than their volunteer efforts. When I was four years old, they and their closest friends founded the First Unitarian Church of Fort Worth. My most vivid childhood memories are of being toted to endless committee meetings, playing on the scaffolding as they repainted the church sanctuary, and packing up for family church camp.

The church fellowship provided a forum for my parents and their friends, not only to express their spirituality, but to discuss and participate in the burning social issues of the day. Since my parents' goals included a racially integrated congregation, not surprisingly they faced many obstacles.

Despite the inevitable conflict, my fondest memory of these years is this: I am lying in my bedroom half asleep, down the hallway from the kitchen. It is a Saturday, close to midnight. I can hear my mother's and father's voices, animated, intense, amid a jumble of other familiar voices. Occasionally there is laughter. I can't make out the meaning of much of it, but I love the intensity of this hum from the kitchen. Every once in a while, the percolator goes back on the stove and the familiar smell of coffee drifts in. I love that, too. But mostly I love knowing that the grown-ups are doing what grown-ups do—talking about the big, important things.

They didn't always agree. Not at all. But they were talking about things they cared about deeply—about how to make our world better.

So you see, I grew up in a family that took for granted that one of life's greatest joys is engagement. We assumed that developing one's thinking in lively interchange in order to act responsibly is part of what it means to be fully alive.

Leaving home to go to college in the early Sixties, I was brought up short. Suddenly I had to face devastating revelations about the United States' role in the Vietnam War, and the reality at home of poverty and racism so intense that it exploded in street riots. I was forced to try to become a grown-up myself. I had to discover what *I* believed.

That process led me first to work in the ghettos of Philadelphia and then to a graduate program in social work. Yet I felt deeply dissatisfied. I knew that I wanted to contribute positively, but I didn't know whether my work was helping to alleviate the needless suffering all around me.

So I made a decision. I decided to stop *doing* for a while and to start listening. I wanted to learn, but in a way no formal education offered. I wanted to pursue certain questions for myself, questions so pressing that without their answers, I could not determine the direction of my life.

I soon discovered that to ask the biggest questions, it often helps to start with the most personal. And what could be more personal than food? You don't have to be a genius, after all, to figure out that food is a basic human need, and that if people aren't eating, little else matters.

I wanted to know how close we really were to the earth's limits. I wanted to know why millions were going hungry even amid apparent plenty. While official statistics about national food abundance can easily impress, hunger's message is unmistakable: it means something is terribly wrong. Hunger became my measuring rod. My first test of any economic or political system would be whether or not all its people are eating. This decision and these subsequent realizations have led to almost twenty years of work to understand and to communicate the causes of poverty and hunger.

While my understanding of world hunger has increased, the problem itself has worsened. Today more people are dying from hunger and hunger-exacerbated disease than when I began, despite more than sufficient production for everyone. I refer not only to the dramatic, terrifying famines associated in the minds of most Americans with droughts in Africa or floods in Bangladesh, for I have also come to see the less visible, relentless hunger that kills even more people in countries with so-called food sufficiency, such as India or South Africa, and in countries such as those in Central America where tremendous food-producing resources are tapped for export, not to meet local needs.

As I've lived with such horrifying realities year after year, visiting the Third World myself and witnessing the misery of poverty, one question has increasingly pressed itself upon me: What could be powerful enough to allow us to tolerate, to accept, to acquiesce to, these millions of silent deaths every year? What could possibly explain our ability to condone such a status quo?

I've finally come to believe that there's only one thing powerful enough. *It is the power of ideas*—the ideas we hold about ourselves and our relationships to one another. It is these ideas that allow us to condone, or even to support with tax dollars, that which we as individuals abhor—and somehow to tolerate the discomforting contrast.

I grew convinced that I would never understand the roots of hunger here or in the Third World until I probed my own values more deeply, and those of my fellow Americans. How could hunger exist in a society built upon freedom, fairness, and democracy, I pondered. To find an answer, and even to imagine a nation and world without hunger, I had to define what I really meant by such beautiful concepts to begin with. It was that struggle that gave birth to this book.

Looking back to my childhood helps me to understand more fully why I had to write this book. Maybe for me the book itself is the "hum from the kitchen"—the power of ideas at work. If so, it will help us to engage both our hearts and intellects in rediscovering America's deepest values, values we desperately need in order to face the challenges of the twenty-first century.

Rediscovering America's Values

Introduction ★

To be an American has always meant to take pride in more than the grandeur of our natural endowment, the strength of our armed forces, or the genius of our Nobel laureates. More than anything, we are proud that *America stands for something*, a set of enduring values that have given us a common identity in the midst of incredible diversity—values that have made us one people.

These values are the common language of our commonwealth, without which we could not talk to each other and be understood.

Freedom, democracy, and fairness are certainly three such values, but most of us would also likely agree on a host of other closely connected ones—responsibility, productivity, community, family, and work itself—as central to our national identity.

More than pride, we have gained confidence in believing that these values are profoundly useful to our society, serving both as necessary anchors and as guideposts in the inevitably chaotic and conflictive process of social change. For Americans individually, these values have been crucial as well—allowing us to perceive how our separate pursuits contribute to a purpose larger than ourselves.

Yet, living in the dusk of the twentieth century, I sense that these values have lost much of their power to provide that essential guidance. And just when we need it most! As a people we face daunting challenges—deepening poverty, homelessness unseen since the thirties, educational decline leaving a third of our young people unprepared for productive lives, the loss of middle-class incomes for millions of families, and the loss of middle-class expectations for millions more.

Rarely have we been in more need of firm footing, ground on which to make choices as a people to take us beyond the pain of such difficulties. But I fear that our values now fail to provide this grounding. Have we allowed them to grow hollow and weak? Certainly not from disuse in public discourse but perhaps in part from overuse. Have they become little more than worn-out flags, waved whenever Americans seek public attention, votes, the commitment of others?

Rarely do we stop to probe what we really *mean* by these beautiful words—freedom, democracy, fairness. Yet, if these values are to serve both our personal and social need for direction, it is not enough to pledge allegiance to them; we must actively imbue them with meaning. Indeed we must reclaim and recast the best of America's traditional values if they are to serve our nation's renewal as we enter the twenty-first century.

But how did we arrive at this present painful impasse?

My hunch is that historically we human beings—not just Americans—have been too ready to imbed our values within particular political and economic institutions. In so doing, we've stopped exploring, debating, and defining the values underpinning and justifying those institutions. Have we taken the easy way out, assuming that we need only put in place a particular political and economic formula, follow its "laws," and—voilà! our values would automatically be manifest? In other words, have we allowed our values to be made hostage to economic and political dogma?

Just as we have discovered laws governing the physical universe, it's been too easy to assume that there must be similar laws determining economic and political life, laws we need only obey in order for social problems to be solved, or at least greatly ameliorated.

By the twentieth century such thinking has come to characterize many societies, as in the past many had held to a belief in a divine right of kings. The result is what we've come to think of as the big "isms." Capitalism is the "ism" we know best—a belief that the unfettered laws of the market and private property best serve all concerned. Communism is what we Americans hate most: a belief in state planning and control of economic and political life. And then there is liberalism: the belief that government can soften whatever untoward side effects capitalism brings with it.

But by the closing decade of the century, aren't all of our ersatz economic gods in shambles, or at least in serious trouble? If so, the resulting uncertainty poses not only a social crisis, but a very personal crisis for each of us, since it is in shared dreams that our individual lives are imbued with meaning. They allow us to make sense of the world around us. As our dreams fade, it's not surprising that we are experiencing profound social and personal dislocation as the twentieth century wanes.

Our tendency to accept political and economic absolutes and then attempt to squeeze and contort our values to fit into such dogma has been, I suggest, our very undoing. The challenge of the twenty-first century will be, then, to create a values-based politics, one in which our values provide the moorings. Continually tested against reality, debated, refined, and deepened, our values must become the beacons casting light on the road ahead, so that no preset economic and political absolutes can constrict our vision.

To take on this challenge, however, we must resolutely reject two tempting escape routes.

One is resignation and retreat, trying to imbue our private lives with more meaning to make up for the meaning we have lost in the social arena. Many seem to have chosen this route. Are the "me" generation of the Seventies or the "yuppies" of the Eighties saying, in effect, my interest is *me*— because what else can I count on?

Or, in desperation, we may want to cling more tenaciously than ever to discredited dogma, claiming it was never given a fair chance. In the Eighties, for example, the Reagan presidency could slash welfare and dismantle industrial regulation, claiming that an unfettered free market had never been tried. Few were around to remind us of the misery of workers and farmers in nineteenth-century free-enterprise America.

Both options carry a heavy price. Seeking meaning only through our private pursuits must fail, ultimately, because we are by nature social. In their acclaimed work, *Habits of the Heart*, sociologist Robert Bellah and his colleagues bring to light the unspoken pain many Americans experience because they lack a language to talk about their need for commitments beyond themselves.[1] Turning or returning to old dogma is equally stultifying; we remain trapped among preset formulas, still not free to create new choices.

The alternative path this book suggests requires work, maybe a lot of work—but it is exhilarating work, I am convinced. It means examining the very assumptions on which our old formulas have been constructed.

Quite a challenge—how do we begin?

The format of this book—a dialogue—is itself part of my answer, for I believe that only in interaction with alternative points of view do our own ideas, views, and values take shape. And only through candid confrontation can common meanings emerge. It is thus in dialogue that we discover hope, hope in our very courage to confront opposing ideas. No idea can serve us unless it is freely chosen, and nothing can be freely chosen if we are denied knowledge of alternatives. So I second John Stuart Mill's (1806–1873) challenge to seek out the strongest opponents, for:

All that part of the truth which turns the scale and decides the judgement . . . is . . . known [only] to those who have attended equally and impartially to both sides . . . So . . . if opponents of all-important truths do not exist, it is indispensable to imagine them and supply them with the strongest arguments which the most skillful devil's advocate can conjure up.[2]

It's always tempting to run from opposing points of view. We dread that frustrating moment when, although knowing that we are right, we find ourselves at a loss for words or convincing examples to make our own point of view stick. So we avoid confrontation.

Sure, we can claim that we avoid confrontation because we love harmony. But deep down, isn't the real fear that we might be stripped of those favorite guideposts, however shaky, that we have used to make sense of the world?

The importance of actively engaging ideas that we imagine to be the antithesis of our own lies in more than the primary, personal need for coherence and direction. The implications of such engagement extend outward into our society. Our willingness to confront opposing ideas has implications for our nation's role as a leading force in the world. Historian William Irwin Thompson, warning of a dangerous absolutism within the American historical tradition, observes a "marked ideological tendency . . . to think that there is the Truth, and that all else is heresy and subversion."[3] As a consequence, the dynamic of opposition dies or is smothered within our society, and instead a rigid dualism is projected outward onto the world scene. There, capitalism and communism, good versus evil, are perceived as the only contending Truths.

In so dividing the world, we don't feel the need to investigate and understand other peoples, how they really live and think. Why bother? Don't we already know—they're either like *us* or like *them*. Bound by such rigid thinking, we deprive ourselves of learning through the stunning diversity the real world offers.

If Thompson is correct, we Americans cannot become a positive force in the world until we transcend our absolutism and discover the dynamic of creative opposition through which true self-knowledge progresses.

Each of us carries within us a worldview, a set of assumptions about how the world works—what some call a paradigm—that forms the very questions we allow ourselves to ask and determines our view of future possibilities. It is our personal philosophy. Many of us aren't aware that we have a personal philosophy, especially if it is the dominant one of our society. It becomes like the air we breathe—so taken for granted as to be invisible. The question thus becomes: How do we make our personal philosophy conscious—accessible to our reflection—so that it frees rather than constricts?

Scrutinizing our philosophy is in part self-protection, for if we don't understand our own belief system, we leave ourselves vulnerable. Lacking a framework with which to weigh alternatives put before us, we can easily be manipulated, even against our own interests. More positively, such reflection is essential to our personal development: only if we know what we believe and why can we make real choices, including the choice to change.

My hope in writing this book is that spirited dialogue will bring to the surface the largely unspoken assumptions embedded in our culture. Once brought to consciousness, they can receive uncensored examination.

And how is this to be achieved? Practically, how do we examine the underlying worldviews that so shape our sense of the possible?

To me, the answer lies in probing the social values that comprise our worldviews. Most important are freedom, fairness, and democracy. Others are security, responsibility, opportunity, work, family, and individuality. But while the two voices that follow claim belief in such a similar set of social values, they carry profoundly different understandings of their meanings and how they can be made manifest in American society. What do these voices represent—and what might one learn by engaging these contrasting voices in dialogue?

Ultimately, all political and economic discussion about solutions to any of our core problems boils down to contrasting views on one essential question: How do we conceive our personal nature in relation to the communities we inhabit? Thus the ensuing dialogue reflects contrasting answers to this fundamental question.

One voice expresses the dominant Liberal tradition, a powerful shaper of Western political and economic life since the seventeenth century. We won't let the term "Liberal" confuse us, however. This tradition actually shapes the thinking of today's free-market conservative more decisively than it does today's liberal, although both share many of its assumptions.

Briefly, let me sketch the value assumptions underpinning this mainstay of our common life:

In the Liberal tradition, freedom means individual autonomy. Its positive face is the celebration of individual integrity and expression, giving rise to the concept of inalienable human rights laid out in the founding documents of our nation.

And how is this autonomy to be achieved? Only by making sure that individuals are minimally circumscribed and constrained by society. Thus, to safeguard freedom, our link to one another must always be, in some sense, defensive. As classically expressed by philosopher Isaiah Berlin, freedom is

. . . the holding off of something or someone—of others, who trespass on my field or assert their authority over me . . . intruders or despots of one kind or another.[4]

Berlin's statement is only a twentieth-century version of a long philosophic orientation, most often identified with philosopher Thomas Hobbes (1588–1679), who described our emergence from a primordial "war of each against all."

Hobbes's dictum *homo homini lupus* (human beings are like wolves toward one another) captured our essential nature: to be at each other's throats!

In such a view of freedom, community understandably is perceived as an artificial implant,[5] necessary only to subdue humanity's essentially antisocial nature. As philosopher Jeremy Bentham (1748–1832) explained in the late eighteenth century:

The community is a fictitious *body*, composed of the individual persons who are considered as constituting as it were its *members*. The interest of the community then, is what? The sum of the several members who compose it.[6]

Still dominant today, this understanding of individual freedom and society assumes human character to be, at base, self-seeking. To ignore this too-obvious truth is to court disaster, according to the Liberal perspective, for it leads inexorably to coercive attempts to reshape human character.

Thus, in the dominant Liberal worldview, we cannot create a good society. We can, however, attain the best of all *achievable* alternatives by building on the only trait of which we can be certain—self-centeredness. And we can do so most effectively by wherever possible reducing choices to market transactions, or to economic cost/benefit calculations. Of course, within the realm of the family, church, and community, compassion must be nurtured and expressed. But it is an inappropriate, indeed dangerous guide when applied in the public arena of the marketplace and government.

It's our individual self-seeking that turns the wheels of the economy to the ultimate benefit of everybody, and at the same time we are spared the terribly divisive process of debating *common* choices. Moreover, we can avoid the danger inherent in any process seeking consensus—that the few can impose their choices on the many.

But within this tidy, self-regulating system, don't the resulting extremes in reward—surfeit for some amid destitution for others—cast doubt on Liberalism's sanguine premises?

Here, Western religion has come to the aid of the Liberal tradition.

First, in what has become almost a civil religion, incorporating Judeo-Christian biblical images, the "Hobbesian brutes" of Liberalism are transmuted into decent, self-sacrificing entrepreneurs. Living in the image of God the Creator, entrepreneurs participate in creation through generation of new wealth. Their very success is evidence of their righteousness, since God rewards the righteous, increasing their bounty multifold.

A variant of the Protestant work ethic holds that work is distasteful and hard, but God rewards with prosperity those who stick to it anyway. The bargain is thus a private one between the individual and God, making it quite easy to determine who the economic failures are: they must be the unredeemed, those still caught in original sin who did not keep their bargain with God. The poor, the homeless, the hungry are thus victims of their own sinfulness—they are merely getting their just desserts.

The consequences for human sympathy are obviously profound.

The Liberal worldview has been further buttressed by Western religion's ready acceptance of the notion of the internally divided self, split between body and mind, as conceived by Thomas Hobbes's contemporary, René Descartes (1596–

1650). This mind/body dichotomy eases the way for a parallel division in our lives. Our private lives become the realm of religion and transcendent values; in our political and economic lives, secular rules of the market and property appropriately take command.

In 1926, British historian R. H. Tawney observed this dualism in modern political thought, noting that matters of the soul and affairs of society are conceived as independent provinces. "Provided that each keeps to its own territory, peace is assured," wrote Tawney. "They cannot collide, for they can never meet."[7]

Given these historical roots, it becomes easy to understand why morality today is believed to pertain almost exclusively to our sexual and interpersonal relationships, but not to our responsibility for the economic and political structures we support and live within.

Since the nineteenth century, the Liberal worldview has also incorporated evidence from the biological sciences in its view of human nature. Pure Social Darwinism may be out of fashion, but a belief that the human personality has evolved through eons of competitive struggle (a permutation of Charles Darwin's theories) remains widely accepted. More recently, the emerging field of sociobiology, pioneered by E. O. Wilson's study of the biological determinants of human social behavior, has bolstered a view of essentially selfish human nature. The notion of a "selfish gene"—coined in Richard Dawkins's 1976 book by that title—only confirmed for many that individuals must be seen as calculating organisms, each out only for its own good.

Understandably, from this view of our nature grows a profound suspicion of government and the political process. Government is a necessary evil that restrains us from hurting each other; its power is best kept limited, lest self-seeking individuals use it for their private gain against the citizenry. Prospects for popular democracy appear dim, for democracy presumes citizens acting through government on behalf of the common good, while Liberalism doubts this possibility altogether. Democratic government is a means of protecting individual goods, not a value in itself.

In the Liberal view, the human essence is closely identified with possessions. It is thus acquisitive, and so to stifle individual accumulation is directly to thwart the individual's free development. This human characteristic has a fortuitous side effect for all, however. It drives us to work, to invent, to construct, to transform nature—all to the ultimate benefit not just of ourselves individually but of all humanity. In fact, by developing resources for one's private gain, entrepreneurs are actually making a gift to all mankind. In the seventeenth century, philosopher John Locke (1632–1704) grasped this serendipitous aspect of property rights:

. . . he that incloses Land, and has a greater plenty of the conveniencys of life from ten acres, than he could have from an hundred left to Nature, may truly be said, to give ninety acres to Mankind.[8]

To be sure, fostering such industrious activity requires that society never question the individual's unlimited right to accumulate property, lest we all lose out as productive impetus is undercut.

While this drive for more continually generates new wealth, at any given moment resources are finite. Our acquisitive nature thus pits us against each other in competition for available goods, making inevitable and permanent our conflict over access to finite supply. Freedom, understood as the right to express ourselves through acquisition, is thus by definition a "zero-sum" contest: my freedom cannot expand except at the expense of yours.

With this understanding of our nature, private property and the market are *the* essential institutions to protect the individual's freedom.

Private property, because it provides a source of independence against state power and other individuals.

The market, because it requires no consensus about community needs, while directly expressing individual desires.

In the Liberal tradition, private property and market exchange become sanctified as virtual natural rights, unqualified and absolute—so essential are they to human freedom.

What follows from these beliefs? On the one hand, the assumption that individual self-interest is natural while the community and government are artificial (though necessary) constructs. And on the other, that freedom for unlimited accumulation must be upheld at all costs. Once combined in a single worldview, a certain picture of society snaps into focus.

In it, individuals have prior claim to all goods as they are produced or exchanged, with nothing "left over" for society as a whole. The community has therefore no legitimate claim to resources needed to meet any general demand for economic or social rights—the right to earn a living or to health care, for example.

In the Liberal worldview, to tamper with these institutions is to threaten the very bedrock of individual freedom, which cannot be allowed in a free society. As long as they are intact, individuals must be left free to pursue their own private interests, out of which spontaneously will emerge a workable whole. In other words: Tend to the parts, and the whole will take care of itself. Certainly that process of conscious, group decision-making toward common goals, usually called "politics," is always suspect. By all means, it must be kept outside our economic lives, that sanctuary of individual, private decision-making.

In barest outline then, this is the dominant social philosophy that has long shaped America's search for solutions to its problems. Its striking coherency is in large part thanks to the influence of its most formative thinker, Isaac Newton (1642–1727). Once Newton's concept of universal laws governing the physical universe permeated society, the effect was immediate and indelible. In the eyes of social philosophers, human beings became like atoms of the material world, bouncing about in limited space.

Not surprisingly, the Liberal view is often termed "mechanistic" and "atomistic," because in it individuals become distinct social atoms, each maintaining only external relations with other insular egos. Out of the random collisions of these self-seeking atoms an orderly society takes shape. All human beings need do is discover what philosophers of the seventeenth century called the "gas laws" of human conduct, and fashion institutions according to these laws; everything else will then take care of itself.

Thus, the Liberal worldview—having provided the framework for social debate for three centuries—explains much of our willingness to accept economic and political laws as dogma beyond accountability to consciously evolving social values. Not surprisingly, the result has been increasingly widespread feelings of powerlessness, separateness, and fear.

In so distancing myself from the Liberal tradition, however, I may have left a false impression: that I do not grasp and value its contribution to Western society—its contribution to the concept of innate individual worth and, from that, to our modern concepts of inalienable human rights and civil liberties. I do. My appreciation for the Liberal tradition came home to me very personally upon spending a month traveling throughout rural China in the summer of 1987. Impressed by the remarkable achievements of the Chinese people, I nevertheless felt acutely uncomfortable. The contrast with my own culture's values was too striking. I could detect no presumption of individual rights that we here take for granted; the right to speak out, for example. China's forty years of communism is the usual explanation offered, but certainly as important must be its two thousand years of Taoist, Confucian, and Buddhist traditions in which individuality is not a core value. In other words, China has never experienced developments in social thought even approximating Liberalism.

Thus, my impatience and frustration with Liberalism is not from lack of valuing its contribution to all I now want to promote. Rather, it arises from a sense that we have allowed Liberalism's assumptions to ossify, to become a set of dogmatic, unquestioned beliefs blocking our further growth as a people. Instead of its attention to individual liberty spurring us onward to envision the still greater potential for our culture, we have let Liberalism bind our creativity.

Let me be perfectly clear: The challenge before us is not to reject the Liberal tradition's evident and, to me personally, very precious stress on the value and sanctity of the individual. Rather, I want to build upon all that is most worthwhile in the Liberal worldview, while incorporating the richer, more relational understanding of human nature and society emerging today.

What, then, is the alternative voice you will find in this dialogue?

It is my emerging philosophy, nourished and inspired by a chorus of voices challenging the prevailing paradigm. It grows from my conviction that the framework I've just presented, if it ever did reflect social reality, is jarringly out of sync today; a conviction that unless we develop the insight effectively to challenge its core assumptions, we cannot envision a livable future.

Like the Liberal tradition, this emerging alternative is more than a collection of distinct value commitments. While it does not yet have a historical label, it is nonetheless an interacting and coherent set of assumptions, the roots of which go back many centuries.

First, we human beings are essentially social creatures, fully human only in our relationships to each other. In some sense, this view is even older than the Liberal tradition, identified, as it is, with Aristotle. But surprising to many today might be the discovery that in our philosophic heritage there has been no more eloquent proponent of this social understanding of our nature than Adam Smith (1723–1790). Adam Smith? Yes, the same Smith who is celebrated by today's business leaders for supposedly proving that individual self-interest alone can drive a productive economic system. In his *Theory of Moral Sentiments,* however, Smith describes in sensitive detail our moral ties to each other. He concludes:

It is thus that Man who can live only in society was fitted by nature for that situation for which he was made.[9]

Whereas in the classic Liberal tradition from Thomas Hobbes to Isaiah Berlin, the individual is poised defensively against society, Adam Smith perceived the individual's sense of self and worth embedded entirely *within* society. He thought it quite easy to identify universal human feelings, making possible our capacity to imagine ourselves in each other's shoes.

To Smith, not only do we need each other's approval, but we also need to feel deserving of this approval. All our strivings, according to Smith, whether for wealth or rank, boil down to the same need: "to be taken notice of with sympathy, complacency, and approbation."[10]

Smith held that it is possible to talk sensibly about the well-being of the self only within society. He thus pointedly reconstructed the Christian precept to love our neighbors as ourselves, writing that

. . . it is the great precept of nature to love ourselves only as we love our neighbour; or, what comes to the same thing, as our neighbour is capable of loving us.[11]

If self-love is dependent on community, as Smith so simply states, then surely the selfish and the selfless are impossible to sort out. From this point of view,

Hobbes' "state of nature," in which fully formed human beings once lived as solitaries in a condition of a "war of each against all," is unthinkable. Not only is it impossible to imagine human beings having evolved in the absence of an intensely social environment, but it is inconceivable to consider a fully formed human "person" apart from a social milieu. In this paradigm a more vital sense of individuality emerges: a person's individuality is constituted, not in defensive protection against society, but in that unique mix of relationships she or he bears to family, friends, neighbors, colleagues, and co-workers.

This view of our nature is increasingly confirmed by comparative sociology and anthropology. Indeed, the Liberal paradigm's notion of the autonomous individual now appears as philosophical flight of fancy. Its claim to Darwin's imprimatur is suspect when one notes that Darwin clearly believed that evolving human beings could only have sustained and expanded their societies because of a "moral sense . . . aboriginally derived from the social instincts." Among primeval people, Darwin observed, actions were no doubt judged good or bad "solely as they obviously affect the welfare of the tribe."[12]

In this worldview, once the enveloping social context is perceived as an indistinguishable extension of one's self, it is impossible to think in terms of trade-offs between society's well-being and the individual's unfettered pursuit of happiness. The health of the social whole is literally vital to a socially constituted individual's well-being.

Note the implication: there are no external laws governing our lives together, as in the Liberal tradition; here, we have ultimate responsibility for society—because we *are* society. Suddenly, human beings are back *on* the hook!

From this very different vantage point comes a very different view of the role of government, private property, and market exchange. Since our nature is social, government is no artifice; it is an expression of our social nature. The democratic process of self-government is no longer simply a means but is prized *in its own right:* through it, we make and remake our social reality to ever better serve our needs, and, in the process, remake ourselves.

No longer are private property and market exchange absolutes that exist solely for protection of individual autonomy. Instead, they become mere tools. Removed from the mystique of "natural law," they become devices subordinated to our socially defined needs, including our need for justice.

Whereas the Liberal worldview identifies justice as an artificial device developed to keep transgressions against each other in check, the alternative perspective sees justice emerging directly from human *feelings*—with nothing artificial about it. Justice derives from our capacity for identifying with each other's pain and from our innate need for community. We most fear injustice because it threatens to tear apart community.[13] Justice—a sense that society's rules are just and so applied—is therefore a core value in the alternative paradigm. Again, it was Smith who captured its centrality. He wrote:

[There is] a remarkable distinction between justice and all the other social virtues:
. . . the practice of [friendship, charity, or generosity] seems to be left in some
measure to our own choice, but . . . we feel ourselves to be in a peculiar manner
tied, bound, and obliged to the observation of justice.[14]

Concepts of "rights" change, too. Recall that under the dominant Liberal paradigm property rights are the core defense of the individual's freedom, autono-
mously defined. By contrast, in the emerging worldview, an individual's freedom
is most powerfully threatened by exclusion from society. While property rights
protect our freedom to enjoy what we produce, now equally central to our freedom
is what Professor George Lodge of Harvard Business School calls the "rights of
membership."[15]

Such a concept suggests the right not to be excluded from access to those
resources necessary to sustain healthy life but, more than that, the right to simple
fellowship. For as Adam Smith reminds us, the harshest pain is that of the poor
person who feels pushed "out of the sight of mankind."[16]

In this vein, the meaning of work also changes. Whereas the Protestant ethic
assumes that people labor for fear of punishment, this view suggests that human
beings cannot live without work because it fulfills a need to partake in community
life. The issue of work therefore becomes more than a debate about earning income:
to deprive people of work is to deprive them of an essential rite—and right—of
membership in the human family.

Although the dominant paradigm sees all our resources already legitimately
claimed in individual "property" rights, the worldview I voice in the dialogue sees
our resources differently: it perceives that most wealth generated today builds upon
a common pool of knowledge, invention, and public works developed over countless generations. Thus, no individual or group alive today can legitimately take full
claim; as human beings we each have inherited a share in the legacy.

Perhaps most important is the contrasting view of freedom. Whereas in the
Liberal perspective, freedom means the freedom to acquire both goods and power,
in the alternative perspective freedom is the freedom to develop ourselves through
interaction with others.

More than accumulators of goods, our essence lies in developing our unique
talents. The modern consumer's drive for ever more material possessions in large
part reflects the thwarting of this developmental freedom. Through material acquisitions we seek standing with our peers, it is true, but accumulation becomes
insatiable only when it becomes a replacement for unfulfilled need to develop our
innate gifts—whether they are physical, intellectual, spiritual, or artistic.

And, because our nature is social, freedom must mean joining with others, not
just to develop our own distinct, individual talents, but to undertake common
enterprise as well. Thus the need to feel part of bettering our society derives from
our very nature.

Freedom understood this way is not finite—the zero-sum contest posed by the Liberal paradigm. One person's artistic development need not detract from another's. One's intellectual advances need not reduce the ability of another to develop his or her intellectual powers. Indeed, not only does an individual's developmental freedom not have to limit the expression of others, but the development of each of us in part *depends upon the development of all others*. How can I develop my full potential for physical health unless someone else, with talents in science and medicine, is free to cultivate those talents? Seeing freedom as the mutual expansion of horizons belies the whole notion of zero-sum.

Ultimately, these contrasting worldviews lead to diverging opinions about the very possibility of change, as well as the agents of change. While the Liberal paradigm has presided over unprecedented quickening in the pace of technological change, its stance toward social change is firmly negative: What we have today, flawed as it may seem, is the best we can realistically hope for, we are told. Better not touch bedrock rules governing our social world or we will end up with something much worse.

In the alternative worldview, the opposite assumptions hold: there are no such external rules above human accountability. Accordingly, efforts to achieve broad social goals through government action need not be seen as necessarily coercive and illegitimate. Instead, they reflect traits embedded in our nature. For in every human family, organization, and enterprise, we set goals with others and harness resources to meet these goals. Such efforts by communities and by whole societies may go awry, but the process itself is not suspect; it is essential to fulfilling our nature.

Indeed, our essentially creative nature impels us to apply our ingenuity to social reality. I found inspiration on this point and many others from our nation's founders—those who refused to fit neatly into the Lockean order taking hold in their era. Thomas Jefferson was one such renegade. Suggesting a human capacity for infinite creativity, he wrote:

. . . laws and institutions must go hand in hand with the progress of the human mind. . . . We might as well require a man to wear still the coat which fitted him when a boy, as civilized society to remain ever under the regimen of their barbarous ancestors . . .[17]

In brief, then, these are the two voices you will meet as you proceed through my imaginary dialogue: One is the most persuasive representation of the Liberal perspective that I could muster, gleaned from the seventeenth- and eighteenth-century thinkers such as Hobbes and Bentham, on through to twentieth-century proponents, including Nobel laureate economist Milton Friedman, Harvard philosopher Robert Nozick, and the Hoover Institution's Thomas Sowell.

In presenting this view, I have limited the arguments, almost without exception, to those *actually* appearing in their writings, so as to avoid presenting "straw men" to refute. In a few cases, arguments representing this worldview were supplied by reviewers of the manuscript who share the Liberal perspective. And I have had to learn to live with the consequences—that many of the readers of early drafts of this book found the Liberal voice more compelling than my own!

The other voice in this dialogue is my own. While responsibility for its particular articulation is mine, of course, the philosophy is not "mine." It is inspired, as you have already seen, by Adam Smith and Thomas Jefferson, but strongly influenced by many twentieth-century thinkers as well, especially those mentors and colleagues I thanked in the formal acknowledgments. In addition, my thinking has been shaped by studying the varied forms of American resistance and alternatives to the Liberal paradigm, embodied, for example, in late nineteenth-century agrarian movements and by community-based movements throughout our history.

In my voice you will also find the strong influence of historians R. H. Tawney and Karl Polanyi, as well as political philosophers Sheldon Wolin, C. B. Macpherson, Benjamin Barber, Robert A. Dahl, and Mark Sagoff, among many, many others. Finally, my views have been shaped by Catholic social teaching, as well as by insights into human society now emerging from the ecological sciences via the work of environmental philosophers.

Of course, no one real human being holds all of the views captured in my rendering of the Liberal perspective, just as I am probably the only person who agrees with all the views my voice expresses. My goal is not for readers to agree wholeheartedly with either voice, but to be stimulated, as I have been, by the challenge of dialogue to probe their own belief systems.

Now, you may well ask, isn't the motive of my book simply to lure my readers to trade in one ideology for yet another? Why can't we get away from ideology altogether?

My answer lies in the nature of human consciousness itself: There simply is no unfiltered reality. A worldview, or philosophy, or paradigm, as I variously call it, structures all human experience. We each have a philosophy, whether we know it or not.

That reality we cannot jettison. But we can move away from what I have called "dogma"—a set of beliefs above reexamination—and toward a living philosophy:

A set of working hypotheses, constantly tested against unfolding events and judged for consistency—deepening and becoming ever richer as we age.

While continually shaped by new learning, such a philosophy is grounded in abiding values.

These values are not sentimental clichés. Examining our own life experience, and that of friends and neighbors, and referring to the teachings of our rich spiritual heritage, we can give depth and richness to these values. They can then actively serve us in developing purposeful, satisfying lives.

Let me emphasize: A worldview is a set of *interlocking* ideas. As human beings, we all seek consistency, a coherency in how our values fit together. In this melding, a worldview takes shape. What distinguishes it from dogma is a willingness to examine premises, that is, to probe the component values that undergird our assumptions. A commitment to that process is what motivates this book.

Frankly, my hope in writing this book is to assist us in letting go of a worldview that I believe no longer serves us, a worldview I believe constricts our capacity to find answers to our most pressing problems. My charge will be that this worldview has failed us, both because it profoundly misunderstands our nature and because it is dogmatic, accepting, as it does, certain human-made rules as absolutes.

Of course, I also know that no people will abandon a set of ideas about how the world works until an alternative is in sight to replace it. Indeed, I believe we *can not*. If human beings are social beings, we must have a framework with which to understand our relationships to each other. We cannot therefore step into a "meaning" void.

So it is with a great sense of urgency that I write. Yes, I believe that the worldview I express here is, in one sense, pressing itself on us by fast-changing reality—by unprecedented and, in some cases, irremediable environmental destruction, by growing hunger, mounting population pressure—none of which I believe, practically speaking, can be met by individual, self-interested action. Such problems can only be solved through a political process. Unless we are able to loosen the grip of the Liberal paradigm, its profound suspicion of both our social nature and the political process will hold us hostage. Blocked from joining in common enterprise, we will remain paralyzed to meet these massive assaults on our common life.

That is why I believe the moral struggle this book invites is crucial. Literate or not, we human beings live by ideas. So much so, in fact, that if our ideas are false we may *not* live! Our planet may no longer be able to sustain those values embedded in the Liberal paradigm. I welcome you to join our imaginary dialogue in search of shared values fit for the twenty-first century.

NOTE: To distinguish the two voices, Roman type indicates the Liberal worldview and italics, my own. The marginal quotes follow the same pattern: italics for those supporting my views; Roman typeface for those supporting the Liberal worldview.

Our discussion is about to begin. Can we even agree on a place to start? But where to jump in turns out not to be an issue. Despite our differences, we easily agree that our primary value is the same. Isn't freedom what all Americans want? As individuals we want maximum freedom to live our own lives, and we want to live in a free nation.

Agreeing on where to begin is the easy part, but what do we mean by freedom?

PART ONE

Freedom: Choice, Opportunity, and Responsibility

Freedom From and Freedom To ★

▶ Let's talk very personally, not in grand concepts. When do I feel free? When I get up on a Saturday morning and know I can do anything I want to do. I can lie in bed as long as I please, work in the yard, watch TV. Or, I can leave the house a mess and go to the movies with friends. I'm free because there is no one telling me what to do. I'm left alone—that's the key, isn't it? No interference from others, nobody standing over me.

The freedom to lie in bed on Saturday morning may sound trivial, but I can apply this same understanding to what matters a great deal more to me—the opportunity to strive for any job I want and to move wherever I please. Freedom means no government official or anyone else interfering, telling me which job to take or where to live.

◀ *Sure, lack of interference from others can enhance my freedom, but not always. If lots of people are out of work and I get laid off, too, no one may be "interfering" with me. And that's my problem. I might be left alone by virtually everyone! But how free am I?*

If freedom is the opportunity to make something of myself and provide for my kids, then your concept of freedom—freedom from interference—isn't enough.

▶ Of course it's not enough. It's only the beginning. Aren't there really two basic aspects of freedom—freedom *from* interference and freedom *to* do what we want? The second depends on something quite obvious—income.

The more I earn—and can keep out of the government's hands—the more freedom I have. In our society, money *is* choice. The more money I make, the less I have to worry about paying bills, so I have more peace of mind. I can buy what I like

I am normally said to be free to the degree to which no human being interferes with my activity. Political liberty in this sense is simply the area within which a man can do what he wants.

—Isaiah Berlin,
Two Concepts of Liberty[1]

instead of whatever's the cheapest. With the raise I got last year, I was able to get the additional training I needed. More important, a decent income means I can provide the best opportunities for my kids.

◄ *Certainly in our society we need money to have any choices at all.* But does more money always mean more choice? *Having to make lots of money can actually stand in the way of many career choices. Your definition of freedom could put me in the curious position of saying, well, I can't become what I most want to be—say, an artist, or teacher, or writer, or pastor, or child therapist—because it would interfere with my freedom.*
   Or put another way, to be "free" I might have to work my whole life in a job I hate. What kind of freedom is that?

► I never said that money could buy all the things we value. Many nonmaterial dimensions of life—a happy family, for example—no amount of money can buy for us.

◄ *Below a certain income, though, lack of money can certainly interfere with family life.*

► Absolutely.

◄ *So here's my point: In our society, income is a condition for freedom as choice, but it's not always a means. More income doesn't enhance my freedom if acquiring it precludes my doing what I most want to do with my life.* And, *more income doesn't free me if spending it keeps me on a consumer treadmill.*

► "Consumer treadmill"? That's what you might call it, but to most Americans the accessibility and quality of consumer goods is what makes our society so different from socialist ones. Most Americans wouldn't trade your "consumer treadmill" for their long lines over there!

◄ *Must we choose one or the other? By treadmill I mean that, after a point, consumer buying doesn't relieve me of a burden; it* is *a burden. Incessant advertising tells us we're losers if we don't yet own the latest whatever. Dependent on a constant "material fix," we're hardly freer than addicts in need of an ever bigger hit. Money is certainly a means to that hit, but we hardly think of the addict as free—or happy. In fact, more Americans described themselves as happy in the 1950s, before the consumer binge began.*

▶ Come on now. You enjoy those "hits" as much as anyone. Besides, you've got it backwards. The more money I have, the less I have to pay attention to other people's views. The less controlled I am by public opinion—or even Madison Avenue—the more I can be my own person.

But money is only one essential to freedom. Another is effective government. Without government to protect me against foreign enemies and criminals and to enforce the rules—from traffic laws to contracts—I couldn't sleep at night, get to work on time, or count on any business deal I sign. Without government to establish and keep order, we'd have chaos. No one would be free.

But only one type of government is consistent with a free society—one interfering *minimally* in people's lives. Good government functions like a referee keeping us from hurting each other, and that's all.[3] Remember that in every society it's government bureaucrats—and only government bureaucrats—who have the legal authority to coerce people. They must be restrained. That's why our founders agreed that the "best government is that which governs least."

◀ *None of our founders ever said that! Those are the words of a journalist writing in the nineteenth century, well after our nation's founding.*[4]

▶ They nevertheless capture our founders' intent—their wariness of government and desire to keep it strictly limited.

Our founders understood that unlike the society of voluntary associations, which grows up naturally out of people's desire for community, government is—I hate to say it—a necessary evil to be strictly limited.

◀ *How can you disentangle community and government? From where does government arise if not also from the need for a common life and for a structure in which to debate the shape of that common life? From where, if not in the provision of so many things—from roads to schools to libraries—that as individuals we would find it impossible, terribly inconvenient, or just plain lonely, to provide by ourselves?*[7]

The final cause . . . of men who naturally love liberty, and dominion over others, [is] the introduction of that restraint upon themselves, in which we see them live in commonwealths . . . [It is a way of] getting themselves out from that miserable condition of war.

—Thomas Hobbes,
Leviathan, 1651[2]

. . . a wise and frugal government, which shall restrain men from injuring one another, shall leave them otherwise free to regulate their own pursuits of industry and improvement, and shall not take from the mouth of labor the bread it has earned. This is the sum of good government . . .

—Thomas Jefferson,
1801[5]

Society is produced by our wants, and government by our wickedness; the former promotes our happiness *positively* by uniting our affections, the latter *negatively* by restraining our vices. . . . Society in every state is a blessing, but Government, even in its best state, is but a necessary evil . . .

—Thomas Paine,
Common Sense, 1776[6]

. . . opposed to . . . the secret wishes of an unjust and interested majority . . . the extent of the Union gives it the most palpable advantage. . . . A rage for paper money, for an abolition of debts, for an equal division of property, or for any other improper or wicked project, will be less apt to pervade the whole body of the Union than a particular member of it . . .

— James Madison,
The Federalist Papers, No. 10
1787[8]

[A] government big enough to give us everything we want is a government big enough to take away everything we have.
— Gerald Ford, 1976[10]

An essential part of economic freedom is freedom to choose how to use our income . . .
— Milton and Rose Friedman,
Free to Choose[11]

Our founders' concern was not so much with limiting the powers of government as wisely distributing them among its various branches and between the state and federal levels. What many of them feared was not an unrestrained government, but one unable to resist the demands of the majority, especially those without property.

As to your embrace of society and distaste for government, why can't they be mutually supporting? Our private associations based on tastes and interests naturally tend to be with those with whom we widely agree. But democratic government arises from the need for dialogue beyond these circles in order to pursue the common good.

▶ No, it's precisely such ideas—pursuing the "public interest"—that have created so many of our modern problems. Once you begin thinking this way, you can justify any extension of government. In fact, our society's biggest mistake is that we haven't known when to put a brake on government. We've come to expect it to do more and more for us, to provide security for everyone—to cure all the ills of the human condition.[9] Not only is that impossible, it's dangerous to try, for every accretion of power by government directly threatens our freedom.

In fact, in yearning to make government do what it can't do, we've made government into the greatest obstacle to our freedom.

◀ *How is government an obstacle?*

▶ I'll be very specific. Every time the government takes part of my paycheck in taxes, I am less free. With less money, I can make fewer choices about what I want; the government makes those choices for me.

◀ *Sure, making my own decisions about how to spend my income is one aspect of freedom. But whether I have a chance to earn that income in the first place is even more important.*

I want to come back to this point, but for now let's assume you're right—it's taxes that diminish our freedom. What if tomorrow we canceled all taxes, even the biggest single chunk that goes to the military? Individually, we'd each be roughly 20 percent richer. But how much freer? What constrains me and most of my friends is the lack of affordable housing, medical care, and day care. It's concern about our children because of lousy schools and streets we can't enjoy after dark. The dearth of good jobs is also a big constraint. I don't see how each of us individually becoming 20 percent richer would do much to change any of this.

If personal freedom means being able to design a satisfying life for myself and my family, it's impossible to achieve unless there are real opportunities available if I work hard enough for them—satisfying jobs that pay enough to support my family, housing, medical care I can afford, and so on.

▶ But it's up to the individual to *create* opportunities. They aren't just handed to us on a silver platter. A society is free to the extent that it doesn't actively interfere with a person's choices. And this is true whether or not a person's life circumstances provide many options or only a few. It goes without saying that some people will always have more options than others.[13]

◀ *Individual initiative is crucial, but it doesn't exist in a vacuum. Initiative depends a lot on my assessment of my chances for success, and that depends a lot on how fair my society is.*

But let me understand more fully your concept of freedom as freedom from interference. Do you mean direct, physical interference?

▶ In part, yes. Interference is a law telling me I have to wear seat belts or, as I said, tax laws reducing my income so that I have less to spend as *I* see fit while my earnings go to support things I don't even believe in. It's also government rules and regulations that keep me so tied up in paperwork that it's hard to run my business efficiently.

◀ *But what about the interference in our lives that doesn't result from big or intrusive government but from its failure to protect citizens from harm?*

One young child in four in America now lives in poverty.[14] *A lack of good food interferes with their growth, a lack of good schools stunts their intellects, and a lack of safe streets and parks surely must hurt their social skills. Isn't this interference?*

▶ Government can't possibly protect citizens from all harm!

There is no such thing as freedom in the abstract. . . . Whatever else the conception may imply, it involves a power of choice between alternatives, a choice which is real, not merely nominal, between alternatives which exist in fact, not only on paper.

—R. H. Tawney,
Equality[12]

◀ *Of course. But consider the illogic: Our laws are supposed to protect us from being beaten up on the street. In even the poorest neighborhoods a police force is there to prevent attacks on innocent people. What is the difference between being beaten up and being deprived of good food, good teachers, and a clean bed to sleep in? Both destroy the body and kill the spirit.*

So the most powerful interference in people's lives can be not what government does, but what it fails *to do.*

▶ But as government does more—trying to protect us from all life's hard knocks—it becomes as big and intrusive as an all-powerful parent telling us how to live. Little by little we lose our freedom to ever-encroaching state power.

◀ *Isn't a weak government the greater threat to freedom? It is open to manipulation as well as to the public's embrace of authoritarianism, if made desperate by government's lack of responsiveness to our needs.*

And by the threat of "big government," you can't mean just its budget; with a fraction of the current federal budget, a police state could control us all. After all, computers and wiretaps to track our activities, more riot police and more prisons—all this comes cheaper than the complex supportive services a strong, democratic government provides citizens.

▶ Of course, I don't just mean size! By big government I mean government taking on more and more responsibilities that the individual should shoulder. When I said that freedom meant not just freedom from interference but freedom to do what I want, I stressed that it depended on my own effort and income, not upon government doing it for me.

◀ *Do Americans really fear that government shoulders too many of our burdens?*

▶ Many feel that government *creates* them! And I don't just mean taxes. I mean the volumes of regulations that government forces upon business that you and I pay for in higher prices; along with other government interventions, from rent control to requiring "affirmative action" hiring, that usurp the rights of individuals to make their own decisions.

◄ *I'd argue that many more fear that our government has be-come too distant, out of our reach, answerable mainly to the most wealthy and powerful.*[17] *You see our government* doing too much; *I see our government* answering to too few.

Of Entitlements and Rights ★

◄ *To clarify what I think is government's responsibility, could we return to my point about the parallel between protecting physical security and protecting economic security?*

► There *is* no parallel, certainly where government responsibility is concerned.

◄ *Now wait a minute . . . our legal system is supposed to protect our right to physical security in part because no other right can be enjoyed without it. Why doesn't protection of basic economic security—the opportunity to earn a living and access to necessities like health care—warrant the same justification?*
This view that economic security is essential to freedom isn't new. In this country, it goes back to Thomas Jefferson, who understood that owning a piece of land was critical to freedom because, with a base of economic security, citizens could think independently.
Let's bring Jefferson's insight up to the twentieth century. In 1944, Franklin Roosevelt advocated extending democracy to include economic citizenship. He called for a second bill of rights covering economic life, starting with the right to renu-merative work.[20] *In numerous polls since then, most Americans have endorsed the concept.*[21]

► Your call for the guaranteed right to earn a living seriously overstates the jobless problem to begin with: only about a third of the unemployed have been out of work for a significant period,

No one can fully, if at all, enjoy any right that is supposedly protected by society if he or she lacks the essentials for a reasonably healthy and active life.
—Henry Shue, *Basic Rights*[18]

[P]olitical liberty . . . is a tranquility of mind arising from the opinion each person has of his safety.
—Montesquieu,
The *Spirit of the Laws*, 1750[19]

. . . true individual freedom cannot exist without economic security and independence.
—Franklin Roosevelt,
1944[22]

and for many of them the reason is simply their own unrealistic expectations.[23] They're no longer job-seekers but job-shoppers—not accepting work unless it meets their conditions. Government subsidy now gives them the option, like other "shoppers," not to buy at all, to opt out of the labor market altogether.[24]

And once you begin extending entitlements to include the right to a job, you've created a socialist economic nightmare—lots of job padding, lots of goofing off, lots of inefficiency.

◄ *Actually, official unemployment figures seriously underestimate unemployment, because they don't count in those so discouraged they've stopped looking, and they don't measure the underemployment of growing numbers of part-time workers who really want full-time jobs.*

Anyway, I'm not talking about guaranteeing a person a particular job, but about ensuring job opportunities paying enough to meet personal and family responsibilities.

► But can't you see that our problem now is that one group after another keeps asking for special entitlements—for special help from the government. Farmers demand subsidies; the handicapped demand ramps; working mothers demand child care. With each new entitlement, the freedom of everyone else diminishes because, like it or not, everyone is forced to pay. And with each new entitlement, people become more dependent on government.

◄ *Let me make a critical distinction. Rights aren't a form of charity, given conditionally and demanding subservience from recipients. Citizens establish rights to meet universal needs for protection. Rights require that needs are met with respect because the users of the rights are the citizen/taxpayers to whom the providers are themselves accountable.*

Rights are justified both from society's point of view and from the individual's. A fully literate society, for example, is understood to benefit everyone, so education is made a right. Exactly the same reasoning applies to the opportunity to work.

So when polls record that Americans want health care made a right protected by the constitution, "right" is precisely what they mean. Everyone *needs health care; it is essential protection in enjoying individual freedom and is equally essential to a well-functioning society. I consider it telling that sixty-two*

The important right suggested by [studies of self-esteem] is the right to work. . . . [I]t is the right to consider oneself a functioning member of society . . . the useless person must regard oneself with a degree of contempt. The right to work is . . . more important to most people than the right to express their opinions.

—Robert Lane,
"Government and
Self-Esteem"[25]

other industrial nations consider a child's protection from dep-rivation a right, providing allowances to all families with chil-dren—there's no stigma, no assumption that dependency will follow.[26]

▶ You are quibbling over terms. The point is that entitlements shift the burden of responsibility and cost from the individual to government. Every additional entitlement—or right, if you must—requires that someone else pay to ensure that the entitle-ment is met. By definition, entitlements take away some people's freedom and give it to others. There's no net gain in freedom, and in most cases a net loss.

◀ *To the contrary, protecting basic economic rights vastly ex-pands our freedom.*

▶ Your approach would carry along a lot of people who prefer to live off the work of others—that is, off the public purse.

You also fail to appreciate the longer-term consequences of the direction you're proposing. Sometimes, as individuals and as a society, we have to sacrifice present security for future better-ment.[27] Ultimately your ideas would make us into each other's keepers. If everyone is required to take care of everyone else—in your endless growth of entitlements—government becomes so big, demanding taxes so high, that we have few resources left to make choices in the marketplace.

And it's as consumers, more than as citizens, that we're em-powered to look out for our own interests. As consumers we can vote directly with our dollars; but as citizens individuals have much more attenuated, indirect influence through representa-tives. When you vote, you usually don't get what you thought you were voting for. But when your dollar votes in the market, you get exactly what you voted for, and so does everybody else.[29] So when any function passes from the marketplace into the polit-ical arena, the individual loses power.

◀ *But as consumers our votes are very lopsided—the more money, the more votes. As citizens, at least our votes are theoretically equal. Sure, the wealthy carry much more weight politically as well, but at least a structure exists through which we can work to achieve more genuinely equal representation.* [See Part V for further discussion.]

. . . if you maximize all your "just" social programs, the costs would be so burdensome as to cripple the economy, leading to sharply reduced governmental revenues, and the collapse of these very programs as a result.
—Paul Tsongas,
The Road From Here[28]

▶ Once you enlarge government to solve social problems, there's no turning back. The federal government's role in the economy has multiplied about tenfold during the last half-century.[30] That's an enormous change, and as government grows, not only do you and I have less after-tax income because we have to pay for it, but overall economic growth is stunted so our incomes are threatened. The bigger the government, the more private investment is squeezed out.

The freedom that Americans enjoy depends on a prosperous economy. Most of us would feel robbed of our freedom if government stifled growth and we had to face the scarcity that people in socialist economies suffer under.

◀ *As we jump into the big-government-as-a-drag-on-the-economy debate, let's set the record straight on what is and isn't big about ours. We devote much less of our gross national product to government social programs than virtually any other industrial nation.[32] Government employment as a percentage of the total civilian labor force has fallen since 1970 and, at 14 percent, is now only a few points higher than in the mid-Fifties.[33]*

▶ But much government employment gets disguised by government contracts with private firms; if all these jobs were included, public employment could be five times the official estimates.[34] And any break in the growth in public jobs is probably due only to the tough stand taken in the Eighties against governmental growth.

Look, government spending now accounts for 38 percent of the GNP, up from 23 percent just since 1950.[36] However you look at it, that's an enormous increment in government power:

◀ *Without Social Security, public spending would be smaller now (in relation to national income) than it was in 1960![37] Almost all of the growth has come from Social Security (now running at big surplus), Medicare, federal retirement benefits, interest on the national debt, and—especially since the late seventies—the military. Most of it represents income and health protection. Does this enhance government power or citizens' power to live free from fear of catastrophic loss?*

▶ You seem to forget that we all have to pay for government's growth with our tax dollars, a burden on the family and on the national economy.

◄ *But we Americans are among the least taxed people in the West. If it doesn't feel that way, it's because middle-income earners here carry a bigger share of the tax burden than do their counterparts in many other countries.* [38] *You like to blame "big government," but an unfair tax system must take the blame for much of the burden Americans feel.* [See Part II] *As to the threat that government programs sap economic vigor, during the Sixties when many social programs were launched and grew fast, average family income improved dramatically.* [39]

And to dwell on government as a threat to the economy, you forget that it can't thrive without roads, bridges, and transit to get people to work and goods to market. With bridges collapsing, highways pot-holed, and canals clogged, overspending is hardly our nation's problem! [40]

If government's size is your big worry, why haven't you mentioned that 50 percent more tax dollars are going to the military, just since 1980? Setting aside direct payments to individuals (mostly covered by Social Security receipts), almost half of the federal budget goes to the military. [41] *Since World War II, we've spent $10 trillion on arms buildup. Do you know how much money that is? It's enough to buy every single thing in America, except the land—every safety pin, every light bulb, every factory!* [42] *And since you're worried about too many bureaucrats, why not start with the military? It's the military that employs, directly or indirectly, three-fourths of all federal employees.* [43]

▶ I haven't brought this up because my concern is clearly about the *inappropriate* expansion of government, not its role in protecting national security, which is entirely appropriate.

◄ *And after all this growth do Americans feel more secure?*

▶ By all reports they do, because our recent buildup has brought us closer to parity with the Soviet Union and forced the Soviets into real arms-control negotiations. But that's an entirely separate debate about national defense. It's inappropriate to take it on here.

◄ *Fine, but it's not an entirely separate debate. The massive diversion of resources into nuclear overkill (we're now able to destroy major Soviet industrial centers fifty times over) under-*

mines our economic security. For one thing, when so much of our top scientific and engineering talent concentrates on weapons, it's unavailable to meet the enormous challenges facing our civilian economy. [44]

The High Price of Neglect ★

The issue is not whether or not government will intervene. It will. The question is will it intervene for enhancement and prevention or to respond to breakdown, problems, and deviance alone.
—Alfred J. Kahn and Shelia Kamerman,
Not for the Poor Alone [45]

◀ *In fact, I'd turn your whole argument about the burden of social spending on its head.* Not *providing opportunity for everyone and adequately protecting citizens ends up costing government a bundle in what I call damage control—efforts to salvage or warehouse people after the destructive fallout of poverty.*

Keeping low-birth-weight babies alive whose mothers were too poor to get good nutrition costs government three-quarters of a billion dollars each year. [46] *Supporting just one homeless family in a city shelter can cost over $30,000 a year.* [47] *Billions go to deal with mounting child abuse, spousal abuse, and alcoholism, all problems exacerbated by poverty. Crime costs, too. With already more of our people locked up than in any Western industrial society,* [48] *and one in four urban males now arrested by the age of sixteen, imagine the taxpayers' bill!*

▶ Wait; you can't blame poverty for crime when crime rates didn't rise, and might even have fallen, when poverty was much more widespread—during the Great Depression. Rising crime rates reflect a shift in social mores, the breakup of the family, and the decline in the role of religion. They reflect an embrace of self-expression as a value in itself, further eroding self-discipline. [49] And high crime rates also result from a law enforcement pattern that encourages lawbreakers by making penalties so weak that, in effect, crime *does* pay! [50]

◀ *But violent crime rates in America are several times higher than in other industrial countries, despite much harsher anti-*

crime attitudes and more *severe punishment here. Crime* is
linked to the deprivation of poverty [51]

Poverty's cost to society can also be measured in the loss of
potential wealth. Each class of high school dropouts represents
roughly $240 billion in lost earnings and tax revenues alone. [52]
Joblessness is a huge drain: every unemployed person costs the
government about $25,000 a year in lost revenue and direct
outlays. [53]

▶ Even if you were right, the solutions are much more complex
than anything you've suggested—and much more costly than
you would probably admit. The price tag on all the initiatives
implied in what you've said would drain our tax dollars. Take the
Headstart program for disadvantaged preschoolers. It already
costs almost $2 billion a year; if we tried to reach every needy
child, it could cost five times that much, and that's just one
program.

◀ *Even in a five-fold increase Headstart could be covered by
reinstating only a fraction of the $60 billion lost in the 1980s'
tax cuts for the rich.*

▶ I knew you would answer by increasing our taxes! My point
is that these programs add up to billions of dollars and they
therefore curtail the freedom of everyone who has to pay for
them.

◀ *Okay, let's add up the costs of multiple programs to help a
poor child, all the way from prenatal care, through Headstart,
special help in school, a summer jobs program, and four years
at a public university. The total for one child comes to roughly
$39,000. That's about what the public pays now to keep one
inmate in prison for just seventeen months!* [54]

*I don't deny that ending poverty costs money. But the heavier
drag—on our tax dollars and our well-being—is poverty itself.
We'll see this once we begin to think of poverty in terms of
what is missing. In every poverty statistic are the shadows of
millions of doctors, musicians, journalists, construction workers, artists, engineers, bus drivers, and athletes whose talents
and energies have been stolen from us by poverty. If we can
learn to see our invisible loss, we can appreciate the real burden,
not of ending poverty, but of poverty itself!*

▶ Full employment is central to everything you've advocated. What you haven't put in the ledger at all is the cost of creating jobs and their inflationary effect. In fact, with the broad safety net now established that protects people from unemployment, it takes ever higher levels of unemployment to have the same effects in restraining wages and prices. Economists have long shown an inescapable trade-off between low unemployment and inflation.[55] It's easy to understand: when everyone is working and incomes are going up, demand for goods climbs and so do prices.

◀ *Inflation almost always gets described your way—too much money chasing too few goods. So naturally people think the answer has got to be less money in people's hands—accepting high unemployment and keeping wages down. But the greater problem may be too few goods—that is, the failure to adequately improve productivity (output per worker). If our productivity were growing faster, more income wouldn't mean higher prices because more goods and services would be produced. And higher wages can improve productivity by motivating workers and by pushing companies to modernize.*[56]

[The discussion continues in Part V.]
   During much of the post-war period, some countries with the most extensive social programs and relatively low joblessness— West Germany, Austria, and Norway, for example—have enjoyed the West's lowest inflation rates. Today in Sweden both inflation and unemployment are below 3 percent.[58]

▶ But look at the high unemployment rates in Germany, France, and the U.K. since then.
   Tell me, if your defense of a burgeoning welfare state held water, why are so many people in Western industrial countries revolting against it? Americans want a smaller, less intrusive government.[59] Why? Because most people know that at least half of what the federal government spends is wasted.[60] From Margaret Thatcher's England to the Scandinavian countries, by the Eighties the majority of voters had begun to challenge cradle-to-grave welfarism. So you're now proposing for us the ever-bigger government solutions that other countries have already learned the hard way don't work?[61]

The liberal reward of labour . . . is the effect of increasing wealth. . . . To complain of it, is to lament over the necessary effect and cause of the greatest public prosperity.

—Adam Smith,
The Wealth of Nations, 1776[57]

There is nothing wrong with the United States that a dose of smaller and less intrusive government will not cure.

—Milton and Rose Friedman,
Tyranny of the Status Quo[62]

◄ *Actually, Western Europeans are seeking more efficient ways to continue or extend the protections they have achieved. Almost two-thirds of Britons said in the mid-Eighties that government services should be extended, even if it meant higher taxes.* [63]

► Americans have *never* wanted the bigger governments that Europeans are saddled with—some, like Sweden, with over half their citizens' incomes going to the state in taxes.

◄ *Americans express overwhelming support for government efforts to open opportunities for the poor and the young, and to protect the environment.* [64] *And most say they'd pay more taxes, if it meant supporting better schools and day care.* [65]

The sad irony is that a blind distrust of government leads to heavier public spending; for even when we do establish public provision, we let private interests call the tune. Example: In the U.S., the public covers about half of all medical costs, but we allow the businesses providing the care to maximize profits by maximizing costs charged to the government. So the public gets had; government outlays for Medicare have doubled in less than a decade.

► Any such problems, of course, would never arise if we keep government out of the picture.

Government as Provider or Rule Setter ★

◄ *But many of the changes necessary to ensure opportunities for all Americans wouldn't mean more costly government with more employees. Government's job is to set the rules; some new rules opening opportunities for all would mean more govern-*

ment, but some would mean less government. West Germans
enjoy many more social benefits than we do with fewer government employees per capita. [66]

*Would, for example, creating the opportunity for every high
school grad to get a college education place more burden on
government? All college students could be offered government
loans to be paid back as a percentage of their future earnings.
Covered by a revolving loan fund and paid back through the tax
system, such loans would mean no net loss to the treasury or
added government bureaucracy.*

*And what would happen if we extended the rights our soci-
ety protects so that every high school and college grad
got the opportunity to use that education in a decent-paying
job?*

▶ What would happen? A lot of government make-work custo-
dial and clerical jobs that deaden workers and drain the economy.

◀ *Not necessarily. Jobs in the private sector can be expanded
as well, because their numbers aren't set by immutable economic law. Many choices we make as a society determine the
number of jobs. Let me list a few:*

- *How much federal money goes to build weapons compared to
  more job-creating enterprise;*
- *The availability of affordable credit to small businesses—the
  main source of new jobs;*
- *The length of the work week;*
- *What the tax codes reward—mergers, tax shelters, capital flight—
  or job creation?*
- *Whether government passively pays out unemployment benefits
  or actively helps to match workers to jobs, to retrain and relocate
  workers, and if necessary to subsidize wages.* [68] *(In the U.K., a
  jobless person can use unemployment benefits to start her or his
  own business, but not here.)*

▶ Quite a list you've come up with! To implement it would
require centralized planning and direction of the first order.

◀ *No, but a commitment to jobs would require changing the
rules—who makes economic decisions and toward what end.
Corporations could no longer be allowed to take wealth generated by workers here and use it to transfer jobs overseas. Corpo-*

rations would have to answer to the workers and the community, not just to stockholders.

► Corporations *already* answer to the community and to workers. They must not break contracts or disobey the law. You seem ready to strip corporations of the rights on which the very basis of our economy's efficiency rests! It's because firms are able to move to wherever production costs are lowest that we consumers can have ever-cheaper products and corporations can afford to make new investments benefiting everybody.

◄ *Profitable business depends on a lot more than cheap wages and cheap real estate, which will always be lower overseas or in the poorest states here. Modern plants and an educated, satisfied work force lower production costs. And keeping well-paid jobs here also means more customers here—essential to every profit line. So, holding corporations responsible for reinvesting in modernizing plants in communities where employees themselves have invested lifetimes makes good economic sense.*

You've stressed the value of responsibility coupled with rights. That is what I want more of, too—ownership rights linked to responsibility. [See Part V for discussion of economic responsibility.]

► But you want to put all the responsibility on corporate management and none on the poor or workers themselves.

◄ *To the contrary, I want to enhance workers' responsibility. When more workers take part in making economic decisions, less government is needed.*

If workers are involved in decision-making, wouldn't less government inspection be needed to make sure the employer is protecting workers' health and safety? (With little worker participation on the job, a cutback in government oversight means many more injuries. [69]*) Reducing unemployment itself goes a long way in taking the burden off government for overseeing safety, for the employer knows that if the job is unsafe, workers can just go elsewhere.*

The dumping of hazardous wastes is another example. The more a community is involved in decision-making, the less federal oversight is needed. How many communities would knowingly allow themselves to be used as a dump?

The security of knowing that one is able to find another job also means that the worker is more thoroughly protected against oppression than by any legislation on working conditions.

—Abba Lerner, economist[70]

▶ Aren't you aware that some communities have asked to be used as waste sites? It means more resources coming into the community, more jobs and income. In doing so, they are freely exercising their property rights.

◀ *Others have vigorously protested. Surely, if people knowingly expose themselves to risk it is because they are desperate.*

▶ I see now how very different is our understanding of freedom and human choice. Without unacceptable loss of freedom, it's impossible for society to protect people from risk or to guarantee a person any particular number of choices.

◀ *A "choice" between the economic collapse of my town and its becoming a hazardous dump site is like letting me choose which road to take to the gallows!*

But I want to get back to my main point here—government not as provider but as rule maker. I've emphasized those policies that determine the availability of jobs, but other invisible economic rules determine whether doors of opportunity are open or shut. While you imply the poor are poor because they aren't bringing in income—they're not working and saving enough—in fact wealth is flowing out of poor communities every day!

Unable to finance the purchase of a home, a poor family rents a dilapidated apartment for, say, $400 a month; over thirty years this family pays almost $150,000, but gains no security, no wealth. All of it is lost to that family and to the community, if the landlord invests it elsewhere. In poor communities, income earned by businesses and banks rarely returns to finance housing and new enterprise there; it leaves in search of higher returns. Plus, the poor, because they are poor, often have to pay more than those who aren't. Just one example: Prices in food stores in poor neighborhoods are often higher, not lower, than elsewhere.

So no matter how serious we are about improving job opportunities and education, we can't end poverty unless we also alter the credit and investment policies that drain people's earnings out of their communities.

Freedom and
Individual Responsibility ★

▶ Let's get down to the real-life implications of what you've been saying. Earlier you brought up the plight of poor children, then blamed the government for not intervening to protect them. Before you jump to remedies, you should first ask why poor children's development is thwarted.

The problem is their parents. I just read in the paper that the mayor of New York decided to investigate for himself conditions in the welfare hotels in which the city puts up the homeless at its expense; he met a young man of thirty-one who had already fathered nineteen children! This person fully expected the government to take care of his kids—and that is exactly what we taxpayers are doing.[71]

◀ *Dramatic stories can mask reality: Actually, the number of children per welfare family is very close to the national average.*

▶ Even if you're right, my point still holds: you couch your arguments in the language of fairness, but taking care of such people is patently unfair to taxpayers.

Looking back, you'll discover that the reason for the plight of poor kids boils down to my original warning—too much prior government interference. The parents of poor children are often victims of the government's attempts to do what it just can't do: guarantee livelihood for people.

Welfare programs have removed the incentive for people to work themselves out of poverty. Welfare erodes people's capacity to take responsibility for their lives, and this includes welfare for the middle class as well as for the poor. Government should encourage people to be responsible—for example, by making medical insurance premiums tax deductible—but it shouldn't take over responsibility from the individuals to provide for themselves.[72]

In trying to provide people with economic security, welfare sets a trap that locks families into terrible *in*security, a downward spiral of poverty. From the Seventies, for example, when welfare began to expand rapidly, in northern states at least, a young couple in which the woman became pregnant could do better if they didn't marry and she kept the baby and got welfare. Her welfare would bring in more than if one of them had gotten an entry-level job to support the new family.[74]

◄ *If you say government programs create female-headed homes, how do you explain that before welfare expansion in the Sixties, over 40 percent of poor black families were headed by women? Economic distress, not welfare, was the cause then, as mechanization pushed blacks out of agriculture.[75] Economic distress is the main cause today.*

Do you really believe that government "help" causes poverty?

► Exactly! With the anti-poverty programs of the Sixties and Seventies, we tried to provide more help for the poor, thinking government programs could remove barriers to escape from poverty, and instead we produced more poor. By making welfare more attractive than working, we have inadvertently built a trap for people.[76]

Even though our welfare population has been statistically lifted out of poverty, it has simultaneously sunk deeper into social pathology, including broken families, illegitimacy, and crime.[77] We have increased *twenty-five-fold* the amount of state and federal government funds going to meet the needs of the poor, with $150 billion now spent for such programs. Surely if money and more government help could end poverty, this enormous sum would by now have done the trick! Or at least it would have made a dent in the problem. But poverty has gotten progressively worse.[78]

◄ *If government generosity causes poverty, how is it that we had terrible poverty in America* before *government programs began in the Thirties? And how can welfare cause poverty if most poor people don't even receive it?[79]*

I've heard your $150 billion figure bandied about before. But only 6 percent of that money goes to Aid to Families with Dependent Children—what most people think of as "welfare." Overall, about a third goes to income, food, and housing for the poor and disabled, and a third of it goes to Medicaid, which helps the poor but is direct income for the medical establishment, not the poor. [80]

Rather than generous protection, as you imply, welfare, even with food stamps, has never been enough to bring poor families' incomes even to the poverty line—in most states not even close. [81] *As I said, here less of the gross national product goes to social programs than in virtually any other industrial nation.* [82]

But what are the consequences of your approach? What happens if we assume many prefer dependency and society shouldn't help a single irresponsible person?

Vast resources get used trying to weed out the malingerers, creating bureaucratic nightmares. So worried are we about freeloaders that in South Carolina, for example, the food stamp application is forty-two pages long! [84] *We insist on conditions that defeat our own ends—like denying welfare to two-parent homes, tearing families apart. And, because the sorting out process can never be precise, innocent and vulnerable people get hurt. Finally, the process of screening out the undeserving gives even more power to welfare bureaucrats, which is what you say you fear most.*

But we definitely agree on one thing—welfare can't end poverty for people who want to work. (We can feel proud, however, that government help has cut poverty among senior citizens by two-thirds in only a generation. [86]*) Since most poor people, like most Americans, want to support themselves at a decent living standard,* [87] *our society can't be serious about ending poverty until we shift our national priorities toward creating millions of entry-level jobs with a future, to job training and retraining, to improving schools and recreation in the poorest districts, and to providing quality child care for working parents.*

▶ You seem to have forgotten that government programs *have* provided job training, special preschool programs for poor kids, federal aid to poor school districts. *But none of it worked.* Liberals were surprised because they failed to grasp that in our urban ghettos people are trapped into a culture of poverty that's self-

. . . American "means-tested" programs . . . do indeed debilitate and demoralize . . . It is not receiving benefits that is damaging . . . but rather the fact that benefits are so low as to ensure physical misery and an outcast social status.. . .
—Fred Block et al.,
The Mean Season [83]

Paperwork and red tape are stacked so high that [to get public assistance] people have to be Olympic pole vaulters to get over.

—Director,
Illinois Department of Public
Aid[85]

defeating.[88] The poor refuse to take advantage of such opportunities.

◀ *Actually, even at its height, the federal war on poverty never cost as much as one percent of the federal budget and was scuttled before completing the start-up time needed to test any nationwide program.* [89]

▶ You seem to think I know nothing about poverty. I grew up in one of the poorest neighborhoods in Philadelphia, and when I graduated from high school, no federal program was around to make life easier for me. I had to work hard, real hard, at some pretty grueling jobs to get through college.

Remember that freedom is what we each earn by taking on the responsibilities of adulthood. If the inner city poor won't take advantage of the opportunities out there, there's little the federal government can do. There are plenty of unskilled jobs going begging. At the end of every month, the U.S. Employment Service lists 150,000 job openings. But jobless people don't take them because the wages seem too low compared to the work-free income that government generosity offers.[90]

◀ *Considering the millions without jobs, is that a lot? And are these openings where jobless people are? How much do they pay?*

▶ Your questions deflect us from the real problem that for many people trapped in poverty, it's impossible to take a lousy job and turn it into a stepping-stone to a career because they tend to live almost exclusively in the present. They're unable to make long-term plans, especially those requiring present sacrifice and self-discipline.[92]

◀ *But over four-tenths of poor adults do work, and a third of them work full-time and are still poor.* [93] *Most of the rest have very young children. Evidence of how much people want to work is that when changes in the welfare rules in the early Eighties made it financially better for some poor working people to go on welfare in order to keep medical benefits, many kept working instead, even at a financial loss.* [94]

Low-skill persons usually have little education . . . and many may be of low intelligence. But they are not stupid. Why should they do cumbersome and unpleasant work at low pay as long as society is willing to sustain them at leisure?
—Roger A. Freeman, *The Wayward Welfare State* [91]

▶ Such individual discipline and hard work offer the only escape routes from poverty.

◀ *You don't understand: The crisis is precisely that for many Americans work is no longer an escape route. More than one of three net new jobs—even full-time, year-round jobs—pay poverty-level wages. That's a big turnaround from the Seventies when only one of every five net new jobs paid so little. And part-time jobs—with no benefits or security—are growing twice as fast as full-time.* [95]

▶ The picture you paint is grossly misleading. Our economy has generated millions of new jobs, absorbing the "baby boom" generation into the labor force—a fantastic record compared to job-stagnant Europe. And we've done it without increasing the share of the work force earning low wages. [96]

◀ *But even economists who back up your claim admit that the share of low-paid workers has gone up a third since 1979.* [97]

▶ Over a longer, twenty-year period, though, we've seen a decline in the percentage of workers with low earnings. [98]

◀ *You're right, but what matters most is the direction we're headed now—it's backward, toward more bad jobs.*

▶ Actually, it's the *best* paying jobs that are the fastest growing.

◀ *Jobs like "systems analyst" may be growing fast; but they're a small slice of the job market. Most openings are for jobs like janitor or cashier, paying a few hundred a week.* [99]
But let's get back to the real issue here. How can you insist that work is the escape from poverty if nearly 11 million Americans now work at wages so low that even if they worked full-time, they couldn't pull a family of three out of poverty? That number has jumped from 3 million in 1979. [100]
And for many parents, work isn't an option anyway: the pay is so low that it doesn't cover the costs of day care and transportation. To support my two kids, I would have to earn over $9.00 an hour to make it pay. [101] *That's more than double the minimum wage.*

► But don't you see? You've just admitted the real problem—it "costs too much" to work *only* in comparison to what you could get on welfare. If welfare offered you less, the work alternative would suddenly look a lot more attractive.

◄ *Sure, and my children would go hungry! So I'd turn your conclusion upside down: the problem isn't that welfare is more attractive than work, but that for many work has become unviable as a way to meet family responsibilities.*

. . . Freedom and equality require some capacities *internal* to the individual, and these the mere removal of external barriers can never assure.
    —Lawrence M. Mead,
    Beyond Entitlement[102]

► In saying that people don't take advantage of the opportunities out there, of course, I'm not just telling them to read the want ads! I know that just getting a job, any job, isn't the answer to poverty. People have to make the effort to get training and have a goal before they can hope to succeed. That's what I did, and what every successful individual and ethnic group has done.

◄ *You blame workers who lack motivation and skills; but what if the problem is jobs that lack opportunity? In the vast majority of occupations, workers' earning success turns out to have much less to do with education and formal skills training than with the industries in which they work, and whether they are covered by unions.*[103]
    And it's just these entry-level jobs with middle-income futures, by which so many have pulled themselves up, that have been fleeing the inner city where many poor Americans live. Since the Sixties, millions of city manufacturing jobs have been replaced by service jobs. But they either offer low pay and little future or demand skill and education that poor applicants don't have.[104]

► You insist on taking the individual off the hook, don't you? You refuse to acknowledge individual responsibility. Why don't you mention that fully half of all poor households are single women with children, a pattern many call the "feminization of poverty." The number of families with children headed by single women has increased by three-fourths since 1970.[105] If these women had taken care not to become pregnant, or had gotten and remained married, they could have avoided poverty. *They* made the choice.

◄ *I thought you hated dependency. Now you're telling women to avoid poverty by becoming dependent on men! Besides, in the Eighties, poverty grew fastest among two-parent families.* [106]

► It's obvious that two-income families have a better chance of escaping poverty; that's how most middle-class families are now keeping their heads above water. Why shouldn't the poor be expected to do the same?

◄ *But you don't ask* why *fewer are marrying. It doesn't take a degree in psychology to figure out that a man out of work or with little income isn't likely to think he's marriageable. And by the early Eighties, among nonwhite young adults, for every two women there was one employed man.* [107] *Young black men's real earnings have been cut almost in half since the Seventies. As real earnings of young men of all races have been shrinking, it's no surprise that their marriage rates have been falling, too.* [108]

To blame poverty on a culture of irresponsibility of ghetto life is to forget that over two-thirds of poor people don't live in the inner city. [110] *And since the Seventies, white men are increasingly represented in poverty-wage jobs.* [111]

► But you can't deny that we now have an underclass in this country, people who believe they can do better selling drugs on the street or having babies and living on welfare than by getting a legitimate job.

Don't you see? If the state steps in to take care of such people, they'll never be allowed to learn the consequences of their own actions—they'll never develop the sense of personal moral responsibility necessary to escape poverty. So the problem isn't just the extent of our welfare benefits but the permissiveness with which they're provided. With entitlements must go obligations. This lack of accountability in our welfare helps explain why crime and family breakup are more common among recipients of government help. [112] You can't have freedom without responsibility, and people just haven't been made to learn responsibility.

The number of marriages . . . is greater in proportion to the ease and convenience of supporting a family. When families can be easily supported, more persons marry, and earlier in life.

—Benjamin Franklin, 1751 [109]

The demonstration that [economic] distress is a proof of demerit, though a singular commentary on the lives of Christian saints and sages, has always been popular with the prosperous.

—R. H. Tawney, *Religion and the Rise of Capitalism*, 1926 [113]

Freedom and the
Responsibilities of Government ★

◄ *Okay, let's talk about responsibility. Rights without respon-*
sibility destroy a free society. But shouldn't we start with an
accounting of the gross irresponsibility of our society in violat-
ing the most essential rights of its citizens?

For children born into neighborhoods where inadequate med-
ical care leaves babies dying at double the national average,
where public schools spend only a fourth for each student what
is spent in richer districts, where even substandard housing is
out of reach for many fully employed families, where drug-
pushing and violence rule the streets, you can be sure that
citizens' rights have been violated from birth.

What amazes me is that so many people survive such
assaults to become responsible adults—as most poor people
are.

As long as government is shirking its primary responsibility
to protect life and opportunity, it stands on pretty shaky
ground in castigating citizens' irresponsibility. To legitimately
insist on the duties that come with citizenship—essential in a
democracy—government must meet its responsibilities.

And what you see as irresponsible dependency can actually
reflect parents' attempt to be responsible: some choose welfare
over a low-paying job, for example, to keep medical benefits to
protect their children.

Why focus on the irresponsibility of the poor? Why not try
to root out social irresponsibility among the wealthy? A typical
poor family pays more in taxes than do dozens of major corpora-
tions, which, despite millions in profits, pay none at all. [114] *This*
loss to society is greater than any loss from the nonworking
poor.

▶ If a corporation's gains and losses mean that it pays no taxes one year, that's not bad for society. It means the corporation retains more of its resources to invest in production, benefiting us all.

In any case, you've sidetracked us. You're not denying, are you, that many poor people have opted out of mainstream society to become part of an underclass that's more or less permanent?[115] A new study shows that a third of people on welfare have been there for eight or more years[116]—they're stuck. Even when they're offered jobs, they don't take them; they can do better hustling.[117]

◀ *Even most of those at the very bottom appear not to have given up. The same study you cite shows that most people are on welfare for a short time.*[118] *Nor do most seem to have opted out of society: half of all welfare homes also include working adults,*[119] *and most people who grow up in welfare families don't receive welfare as adults.*[120]

Perhaps most significant, well-managed, subsidized programs to help people get into the work force have paid off.[121] *But the underclass will be permanent and grow if as citizens we do not push for changes in the "rules" I talked about earlier to ensure that more good jobs and child care are available, as well as new credit and investment policies to retain the wealth, needed to improve communities, that poor people are already producing.*

▶ To the contrary, only if we as a society end the permissiveness that characterizes our welfare state and expect the same of the poor that we expect of everyone else is there any hope.

◀ *You're assuming most people prefer dependency?*

▶ I assume that many poor people have *learned* to prefer dependency. In the name of freedom to make meaningful choices you've actually created dependency, but people who are dependent can never be called free.

◀ *Let's say you're right that many parents have learned dependency and that government should do little or nothing. Where does that leave us? One-fifth of all our children live in poverty—two to three times greater than in Scandinavia and 60*

Dependency . . . undercuts the claims to equality made by disadvantaged groups. For how can the dependent be equal . . . with those who support them?
—Lawrence M. Mead, *The Social Obligations of Citizenship*[122]

percent higher than in the U.K. [123] *Can any society afford to write off a fifth of its children?*

▶ Our society goes a long way toward making sure the poor get what they need. We heavily subsidize health care for the poor through Medicaid. And we are putting a record amount into food assistance programs, over $13 billion a year into food stamps alone. That's almost $200 a month for each recipient family—not too bad if you shop carefully.

◀ *Are you kidding? More than half the poor are not covered by Medicaid.* [125] *Almost half of poor kids get* no *welfare help.* [126] *And food stamps provide a measly 40 cents a person per meal.* [127] *I'd like to see you put nutritious meals for your kids on the table for that!*

The best anti-poverty efforts of the Sixties and Seventies suggest that our money couldn't be better spent than on our children. Quality preschools are a good example that you already brought up. Children participating in Headstart have had more education and job success later in life and have been less likely to get into crime. Yes, taxpayers have had to pay, but Headstart saves government roughly five times more than it costs. [128]

If society doesn't uphold its responsibility to children, their development is blocked; they become impaired parents, and there can be no end to the thwarting of human development.

▶ But wait. We began talking about freedom, what it means to each of us. Your points about what poor children need are a separate topic. For emotional appeal, you're using a verbal sleight of hand to blur an important distinction—that between the meeting of material needs on the one hand and freedom on the other.[129]

◀ *I'm not blurring a distinction, I'm making concrete this beautiful abstraction we call freedom, specifying just what it would take to free our children from interference in their development.*

▶ But why do you ask *me* to assume responsibility for every child who needs it? Most poor children live in single-parent households because their fathers have abandoned them. Why should I, the taxpayer, be made the "economic parent" for children whose parents are so irresponsible? The government's proper role is to force these parents to support their own children, not take over the job for them. That means garnisheeing wages, or whatever is necessary.

◀ *Of course parents must be held responsible for their children. But don't fool yourself into thinking that deducting child support from fathers' wages is going to solve the problem. Many such fathers, if the government can find them, are probably out of work or get such low wages that no amount of pressure will do much for their kids.*

▶ If much of the poverty we see today is a result of government's trying to solve people's problems for them, demanding no corresponding change of behavior on their part, of course it will take time to work itself out, probably generations. People have to relearn that they alone can make something of their lives.

By intervening in these children's lives with more assistance, they'll come to assume that the government is there to depend on. They'll have even less incentive to work their way out of poverty.

◀ *But all children are dependent! Do all then learn lifetime dependency? As I've said, children helped by enriched preschools became more self-reliant as adults.*

In truth, most people want to take care of themselves. *If they can't, something powerful is stopping them. Those obstacles, as I've said, are the assaults of poverty from birth that block both development and confidence in one's capacity to shoulder responsibility; all the mechanisms that drain wealth out of poor communities, leaving no basis for growth; and the closing of escape routes out of poverty, including the diminishing numbers of jobs offering middle-class futures.*

Freedom and Economic Security ★

As we deliver economic security, we undercut the implicit assumptions of capitalism, democracy, and individual initiative.
—Lester Thurow,
The Zero-Sum Society[131]

If I knew for a certainty that a man was coming to my house with the conscious design of doing me good, I should run for my life.
—Henry David Thoreau[132]

▶ While you talk about opportunity, you are really saying that government should provide economic *security*. But if government tries to provide economic security for everyone, it removes responsibility from the individual. And only as we're required to shoulder responsibility do any of us develop individual autonomy, which, as I've said, is the basis of personal freedom.

Many well-meaning people want to "help" by doing for other people. If they cooled that emotional response with a little common sense, they could see that "doing for" someone is really taking away their power and potential for self-respect.

◀ *Security doesn't undercut my freedom; it is the very basis of it! Without security what freedom do I have?*

Take job security. With no national commitment to full employment and a growing proportion of low-wage jobs, even if my job is a dead end and ruining my health, I'd be afraid to quit. I'd do what I was told.

I read about Chrysler plant workers in Newark, Delaware, who know for a fact that they are being exposed to poisonous lead and arsenic, but they keep going to work![133] And then there was that New York Times *piece on John Morrell & Company meatpackers in South Dakota. One worker said his wrist was so injured by the assembly line that he can't even carry his kids to bed at night.[134] But he keeps going to work.*

And even workers in less desperate straits know that if they quit, they may not get other jobs paying enough to support their families. Plus, they'll lose medical insurance. Unemployment benefits offer little help: only a quarter of the jobless get them.

▶ Look, everyone doesn't share your values. People who keep working at a job they don't like obviously value security more than freedom. And they value the extra pay they get for risking danger or ill health. That worker in the meat-packing plant could get a cashier's job at the Seven-Eleven and save his wrist, but it would pay less. That's his choice to make.

◄ *If I have to choose between a job that damages my health and another that makes it impossible for me to care for my family, the choice isn't between security and freedom. I have neither.*

► And you're still ignoring the obvious truth that some people simply choose not to work. Unemployment benefits high enough to provide real security would invite more people to slough off.

◄ *Then why isn't unemployment higher where benefits are higher? In the United States, laid-off workers get about half their former pay and only for several months. Several countries with much higher benefits have had lower unemployment. In Austria, laid-off workers get 80 percent of their previous pay for at least a year, but the jobless rate there has been half of ours for many years.* [136]

> *A person whose style of life and family livelihood have for years been built around a particular job, occupation, or location finds a command backed by a threat to fire him indistinguishable in many consequences for his liberty from a command backed by the police and the courts.*
> —Charles Lindblom, *Politics and Markets* [135]

Poverty: It's All Relative ★

► As humane as it sounds, your pursuit of economic security for everyone is ultimately doomed. Why? Because desire for security is insatiable. The biblical insight that the "poor will always be with us" isn't an easy cop-out; it's an inescapable truth because of how poverty is perceived. It's as much a state of mind as a state of income.[137] In large measure it is a relative lack of goods: people will tend to see "poverty" as roughly half or less of the median income at any given time. So the richer we get, the more anti-poverty programs we'll need.[138] There can be no end.

◄ *My concept of poverty isn't mushy. I don't suddenly become poor when I'm the only one left on my block without a BMW!*

> *The poor man . . . is ashamed of his poverty. He feels that it . . . places him out of the sight of mankind . . . [T]o feel that we are taken no notice of, necessarily damps the most agreeable hope . . . of human nature.*
>
> —Adam Smith, *The Theory of Moral Sentiments*, 1790[139]

▶ Poverty is not just about money or consumer goods. After all, in some parts of the world people have much less than even the poorest Americans, yet they feel they're living all right. A set of attitudes, largely about self-respect, defines poverty.

◀ *You're right. Poverty isn't just about lack of money. It means being shut out—the pain of being excluded as a full member of society, and in many ways forgotten.*

▶ But ending poverty is an ever-receding goal as people redefine their needs upward.

◀ *No! Poverty isn't just a relative concept.[140] Poverty is what damages people—it stunts growth and it kills. It can be measured: poor children are three times more likely to die in childhood.[141] Poor children are twice as likely to be stunted physically compared to those from better-off families.[142] Minimally, we could celebrate an end to poverty in an end to these differences in survival and growth among income groups.*

But poverty is also about our relationships with others, for there is a point, not too hard to discern, at which a lack of resources makes it impossible for us to participate in the community and to find meaning in our daily lives.[143] If we can't put a wholesome meal on the table, if we don't have appropriate clothes to wear to that all-important interview, if we postpone taking a sick child to the doctor because we don't know how we can pay the bill, that is poverty.

Let's get clear on one point: In every society, no matter how prosperous, some people just can't work—because of illness, physical impairment, or because they must stay home to care for someone else. Society's help is their sole hope for escaping poverty. Meeting their needs without destroying their dignity is a primary test of any society's humanity. Because Americans so hold to the notion that here anyone can make it who tries, we even seem to blame the incapacitated. How else can you explain why we're stingier in our help for this group than most other Western societies?[144]

There are groups beginning with the family and including neighborhood and church . . . which are duly constituted to render assistance, and in the form of *mutual-aid*, not

▶ No, the explanation is that in America we assume that the family, the community, and our religious institutions—not the state—carry much of the responsibility to care for the sick and disabled. These groups are closest to the individual and can better tailor assistance to meet particular needs. Outside government "experts" could never do as well.[145] History has proven this to be true; all government should do is make sure these voluntary helping structures are strong.

◄ *If private, voluntary initiatives could solve the problem of poverty, why were conditions of the poor even more wretched before New Deal programs established government responsibility? And today in highly mobile America where families are separated by hundreds of miles and many people aren't churchgoers, your ideas are out of touch with reality.*

► They only seem that way to you because government has preempted the provision of services and private initiative has atrophied.[147] This private initiative must be allowed to revive.

◄ *Without a government-protected right to assistance, those unable to be self-supporting are reduced to supplicants pleading for help from relatives or a religious body.*

► Only in rare circumstances. As you replace caring, voluntary associations based on goodwill with government bureaucrats just doing a job, voluntary ties among people, and even our compassion for each other, begin to wither.

And once such organizations decline, nothing is left between the individual and state power.

◄ *Just because people's basic well-being must not depend on the whims of charity does not mean voluntary organizations are any less essential to a free society. They are the buffer between the individual and government, acting as essential watchdogs and advisors to community-guaranteed services, enhancing and personalizing these services. And because government ensures provision doesn't mean government must itself provide. An example: In Florida and Missouri, social service agencies set up a system in which senior citizens can help out their neighbors while accumulating credit to "cash in" for similar help when they need it.[149]*

And, of course, the arts, recreation, conservation, education, and all aspects of political life are inconceivable in a democratic society without a myriad of voluntary associations.

high-flown charity from a bureaucracy. . . . [T]o bypass these groups through welfare aid . . . is . . . an invitation to discrimination and inefficiency and a relentless way of eroding the significance of the groups.
—Robert Nisbet, *Conservatism*[146]

. . . making considerateness, compassion, kindness, generosity, and other virtues pertaining to civilized community life matters of government mandate . . . is a fundamental threat to the quality of human community life . . .
—Tibor Machan "The Petty Tyranny of Government Regulation"[148]

So, private associations can be a vehicle for meeting government-protected rights, can complement government functions—but they are no substitute for government responsibility.

Freedom as Privacy ★

▶ You're ready to extend government responsibility into every arena of our lives. The beauty of capitalism is that it leaves the sphere of the individual inviolable.[150] Your ideas, by so extending state power, would threaten our essential individuality, that private sphere through which we each discover our personhood.

You can see the results in other countries with intrusive government, whether along the Eastern-bloc model or the Scandinavian welfare-state model. There, government comes very close to the "Big Brother" George Orwell warned us against—with extensive information about each person and with power to coerce people to serve its ends, sometimes without citizens even being aware that they are being so directed.

◀ *Dependency is what robs us of privacy. It's being dependent on others for our survival that makes us go along, or reveal things about ourselves, or conform against our will. Such dependency can result from economic powerlessness. What if few good jobs are to be found and I face harassment on my job, painfully violating my privacy? Can I quit without jeopardizing my family?*

And what would be the effect on my privacy if no government-guaranteed help were available so that I had only private groups to turn to? I remember many years ago working with poor women trying to get clothing for their children from a religious agency; before they got help the women first had to endure a humiliating interview and morality lecture.

If we prize privacy as essential to personal freedom and want to reduce vulnerability to coercion, we must establish certain inviolable rights. I would call these our "rights of membership," to be met with no strings attached simply because we are human beings.

Security, Risk, and the Work Ethic ★

▶ But the more we try to protect people from risk and insecurity, the more we also undercut the source of individual productivity, which is so important to freedom. One reason our economy's been so productive is that American society is full of risk-takers. We're entrepreneurs. We're inventors, pushing back the frontiers of knowledge. Did you know that Americans have received more Nobel prizes than any other people on earth?

With the value system you're promoting, people's motivation for risk-taking would be undercut. If we have security, what pushes us to risk?

◀ *But is it insecurity that makes people risk-takers? It might well be the opposite. If I don't have to risk everything—if my family's survival needs are protected—wouldn't I be more willing to take a chance on something new? Without being irresponsible to my family, I could consider starting up my own business, or risk a new, more challenging line of work.*

▶ You seem unwilling to face life's hard trade-offs. Every attempt to provide a floor under people reduces the incentive to do one's best. So the growth of the welfare state has to take a lot of the blame for a waning work ethic, leading to slower growth of productivity—hurting everybody. Plus, the emphasis on security you suggest has contributed to expanded government regulation of workplace health and safety and environmental pollution. So employers end up putting their research and planning effort into meeting these demands instead of improving output.[151]

◀ *Don't worry—the work ethic is alive and well! More families now rely on two wage earners, and Americans report having much less leisure time than in the Seventies.*[152] *Do we have a productivity problem because workers are no longer kept accountable by fear of destitution or because of a lack of accountability elsewhere in our economy? A top-heavy U.S. management structure reduces the share of the work force doing directly productive work; U.S. corporate planners go after short-term profits, buying financial assets and growing by merger instead of by improving production processes. Defense contractors and subcontractors—now over 100,000 corporations—ensure their profits by passing on costs to the government, not by improving productivity. And, rather than U.S. workers having it too good, the decline of wages relative to the cost of new machines lets companies profit without modernizing equipment, necessary to improved productivity. Plus, joblessness itself stifles our economy's productivity.*[153]

Also, if insecurity made people work harder and better, then productivity in a unionized firm should be lower than in a comparable nonunion business, but on average it's higher.[154] *And countries offering more protection to their workers—like Japan, West Germany, or the Scandinavian countries—shouldn't be doing so well.*[155]

▶ The economic stagnation and shoddy workmanship in communist countries derives precisely from the ill-thought notion that government can take over responsibilities that should belong to the individual. There, everyone is guaranteed work, and as a result nothing is well made.

◀ *Productivity problems in communist countries haven't resulted from greater job security per se, but because work effort and quality have been unconnected to reward and because an oppressive political system stifles initiative.*

A floor of economic opportunity under everyone—especially one that ensures protection of children—doesn't undercut work incentives. It makes more people able to work.

Where wages are high . . . we shall always find the workmen more active, diligent, and expeditious, than where they are low . . .

—Adam Smith,
The Wealth of Nations,
1776[156]

► Once citizens take for granted that the state will provide them with health care or a good job, then they'll expect ever more responsibility lifted off their shoulders. Bit by bit, the state becomes all powerful. Citizens lose their freedom, not by brute force, but by their own profound misunderstanding of the meaning of freedom!

Clearly, we both see an important connection between security and freedom, but let's clarify how we differ. Let me repeat: A free society doesn't offer people unlimited opportunity, or even guarantee a certain number of opportunities. In a free society there's always some opportunity open for those who care to make the effort. We all know people who've overcome incredible odds to make something of themselves. They prove my point better than your barrage of statistics.

I believe that government can only protect our physical security and enforce the laws—sales contracts, liability, and so on—making economic life and social life possible. Beyond that, it's up to the individual. Government effort to ensure economic or social security with jobs or health care erodes a society's economic vitality as well as the character of its citizens.

◄ *Oh, that security could be so neatly carved! It's no accident that we use the term broadly, referring to our psychological or financial security, as well as to our personal safety, the safeguarding of our possessions, and our national defense. These many uses of "security" suggest not sloppy language but an awareness of their similarities and interconnections. Earlier, for example, I argued how arbitrary is the line between the maiming of a child by criminal assault and its stunting by malnutrition. How can you claim that society must prevent one but has little or no responsibility for the other?*

► I've been describing what government can do realistically without undercutting other important values.

◄ *But the interplay among these many facets of security means that your neat line between what is and isn't government's responsibility just doesn't exist. Loss of a job—undermining economic security—can literally make one sick—undermining physical and emotional security.[157] It can even precipitate death. Within six months after an auto plant closed near my home, eight laid-off workers had committed suicide.*

In our society it is murder, psychologically, to deprive a man of a job or an income. You are in substance saying to that man that he has no right to exist.

—Martin Luther King,
Jr.[158]

▶ Come on—can we pay people to work at unproductive jobs because they threaten to commit suicide?

◀ *There was no threat! I am simply arguing that economic security can't be separated from our physical well-being. Or what about national security, supposedly assured by our rising military budget? In the international arena a nation's influence depends upon its own economic and social standing as much as its military might. At the same time, such domestic security is precisely what's being eroded by our overemphasis on military buildup.* [159]

So these facets of security that you would separate into two distinct categories are really interacting dimensions of one whole.

▶ Surely you can't expect society to guarantee security in every one of these aspects.

◀ *We can expect it to protect against* harmful *deprivation in each—and that's not an arbitrary line. We can measure it in the high death rates of poor babies, in higher workplace injuries facing low-paid workers, and on and on. Ultimately, it means protecting that level of individual security necessary to participate in community life.*

It is a mistake to base one's hopes for happiness upon the enforcement of security and equality. *In principle*, both desires are insatiable. . . . No individual or society is secure in a world of emergent probability and sin. . . . To exercise liberty is to take risks, to embrace uncertainties . . .
—Michael Novak,
The Spirit of Democratic Capitalism [160]

▶ I couldn't disagree more strongly. Freedom, as I understand it, can't be guaranteed. The fact that some people are exposed to greater risks than others, and that some don't make it, is no proof that we don't have a free society. It's no proof that the opportunities aren't there. If it means anything at all, freedom must mean the freedom to fail as well as to succeed.

The Risks of Unintended Consequences ★

▶ What you fail to grasp is that every government program to solve one problem ends up creating others. All our good intentions bring unintended consequences. Efforts to put an income floor under families sound great, but they end up destroying families. Men's self-esteem is undermined if they no longer feel they're needed to support a family, since government has taken over the job. So, of course, fatherless homes and illegitimacy increase.[161]

◀ *You're still confusing cause and effect—it's unemployment that undermines self-respect and is most associated with family breakups.* [163]

▶ A higher minimum wage is another idea that sounds good until we realize that it will mean employers can then afford to hire fewer workers. The probable result of minimum wage laws has been to benefit low-income female workers at the expense of low-income teenagers.[164]

◀ *Doing nothing can't protect us from the unknown; not acting also has unexpected consequences. So all we can do is search for a direction guided by our deepest values, weighing the historical record. In your example of the minimum wage, the record shows that its enforcement has coincided with great expansion in employment and productivity.*

▶ According to government reports, employment would have expanded more without it![165] And if you are serious about learning from history, you surely would not advocate, as you are now,

. . . like most attempts to pursue an unattainable goal, the striving for [social justice] will also produce highly undesirable consequences, and in particular lead to the destruction of the indispensable environment in which the traditional moral values alone can flourish, namely, personal freedom.
—Friederich A. Hayek,
" 'Social' or Distributive Justice"[162]

a broadening of the welfare state when it's being rejected in the U.K. and elsewhere as unworkable.

◀ *Labeled accurately, ours isn't a "welfare state" anyway. It's a "social security state" or a "military state." Here we haven't achieved even the basic protections to health and to child welfare, nor help for job seekers, that most Westerners call a "welfare state."*[166]

▶ Now it sounds like you would take us even farther than the European welfare state, adding to government responsibilities. Your ideas would extend government even deeper into economic life, toward the communist or socialist model which restricts freedom.

◀ I reject all models, *certainly the state-controlled model of communist countries. It isn't guided by a democratic process but by an elite party hierarchy. I reject the welfare state model as well,* if *it means handouts instead of economic rights and top-down government action excluding citizens in economic decision making.* [Discussion continues in Part V.]

What Is the Role of Government in a Free Society ★

▶ Of course, but don't you see that what you think is the solution is precisely our problem? You may not think that you are advocating any worn-out models, but as you expand government's role it is shaken loose from constitutional restrictions. Already each year Congress passes about a thousand new laws.[167]

◀ *Three a day? Congress is busier than I thought!*

▶ As a result of such unrestricted government, people are unsure of just what government will and won't do. The result is instability and a reduction in business investment.

Without constitutional boundaries strictly limiting government's role, everyone starts seeking favors from government. Entrepreneurs will seek tariff barriers to protect themselves, farmers will seek subsidies, educators will plead for more funds for public schools, and magazine publishers will demand cheaper postal rates![168]

◀ *Your ideal of constitutionally restricted government, the "night watchman" state, would, it seems, reduce government's role in everything from job training to environmental protection, to food and workplace safety, and on and on. Am I right?*

▶ For the most part, absolutely.[169] Although government should help the elderly and the handicapped generously. (Let me be clear, though; the purpose here is not to redistribute income but simply to assist those who cannot provide for themselves.[170]) Otherwise, freedom is smothered. People stop relying on their own value system to decide what is right and assume that government policing action will enforce decent ethical standards. And the only kind of competition we then end up with is competition for government favors.

◀ *Okay, let's take your advice and restrict government to its military and police functions. Why couldn't a powerful minority simply use these functions to protect its own privileges? Sound familiar? Doesn't this pretty well describe what government amounts to in dozens of countries from the Philippines to Haiti?*

So the first test of a free society isn't how limited its government's functions are but who controls the government. *Because political and economic life are always intertwined, government, whatever its size and functions, will represent the public interest only if the economic and cultural underpinnings of democracy are strong.*

▶ Don't you understand that a key virtue of democratic capitalism is that it separates the economy from the state?[171] Attempts to end poverty by government intervention, as you advocate, threaten to weaken this all-important separation. The programs generated end up creating a new class of social service professionals and government do-gooders who have a permanent stake in big government—and in bigg*er* government. They become part of an elite in our society who want to make the world over according to *their* ideals, rather than allowing the more democratic process of the marketplace to determine social outcomes.[172]

You are asking government to do what it cannot do. Government programs will inevitably be the tool of private concerns.[173] Welfare programs, for example, invariably get distorted by the interests of a bureaucracy whose workers tailor programs to maintain their jobs doling out the benefits. Almost half of the welfare budget is eaten up paying bureaucrats.

◀ *It's clearer now why we're often talking by each other. You see government as some* thing *outside of ourselves—a thing with its own momentum that we have to beat back in order to remain free.*

▶ You could put it that way to make sound extreme what is merely prudent: with its monopoly on legal coercion, government should make any reasonable person wary of too much of it. As national authority increases, individual freedoms must shrink.

◀ *But your view of government as alien and threatening becomes self-fulfilling, if it reduces our confidence as citizens to use government to serve our values. It's only been because we have seen government as a vehicle for expressing our values that we have been able to free ourselves from such blights as child labor and racial discrimination.*

So far we've differed on government's responsibility in protecting our well-being . . .

▶ That's right. And I've made clear that beyond empowering it to protect physical security, giving over responsibility to government actually robs us of personal freedom to learn how to take care of ourselves, which is the ultimate freedom.

◀ *But we've neglected another essential role of government in a free society. It is to create citizens.*

The individual freedoms destroyed by the increase in national authority have been in the main the freedom to deny black Americans their elementary rights as citizens, the freedom to work little children in mills . . . the freedom to pay starvation wages . . . the freedom to . . . pollute the environment—all freedoms that, one supposes, a civilized country can readily do without.

—Arthur M. Schlesinger, Jr.,
The Cycles of American History[174]

► I'm not sure what *you* mean by citizen, but to me it means someone who understands that his or her duty is not not only to obey the laws of our country and remain loyal, but to contribute rather than just take. Government can only create such citizens indirectly, by not taking upon itself what citizens should do for themselves and by attaching obligations to every government benefit so that citizens learn responsibility.

◄ *But a democratic society is more than a collection of people developing their individual talents and shouldering responsibility. It is also the dynamic of the common life itself, in which citizenship means joining in public dialogue to uncover and give shape to our common values and to decide how to act upon them.*

Citizenship, understood this way, sees democracy as a value, not just because it protects the individual's well-being, but because it promotes a public arena of deliberation over common concerns, an interchange that is itself morally transformative, inseparable from our individual moral development.

What is it, after all, that distinguishes democratic government from totalitarianism?

► Beyond the obvious economic and political dimensions, freedom of thought and expression, of course.

◄ *It's easy to passively permit citizens to have their own views. Something much more difficult is required of democratic government. It must actively enhance the social competence of citizens to participate in shaping community life, fostering the widest range of viewpoints, assisting citizens in overcoming racism and other prejudices that block communication, and generally building enthusiasm for public discourse. It must encourage even more forums in which citizens can freely participate in the ongoing dialogue of democracy.*

► What are you talking about? Of course our government does this. Public education is key, and a bigger share of American young people are in high school and go on to higher education than in most other industrial countries,[176] reflecting our country's deep understanding of the importance of education in a democracy. We also keep government out of communications so

A government cannot have too much of the kind of activity which does not impede, but aids and stimulates, individual exertion and development. The mischief begins when, instead of calling forth the activity and powers of individuals and bodies, it substitutes its own activity for theirs.

—John Stuart Mill,
On Liberty, 1859[175]

that public debate will not be controlled by Washington. We have a free press that's unsurpassed . . .

◄ *No. Public education remains a low priority. And how can democratic dialogue thrive as long as access to the public through most media outlets is costly and mostly sold to the highest bidders? As long as wealth plays such a pivotal role in selecting candidates for public office? As long as foreigners are kept out of the country if their views displease Washington? As long as we lack forums locally and nationally for citizens to debate and shape the direction of economic and social policies?*

▶ We disagree even more than I had supposed. In our society, the structures of democratic government have been in place for two hundred years through which each citizen can participate. It is up to the individual to make use of those channels or not.

[The discussion of democracy continues in Part V.]

Summing Up the Dialogue ★

WHAT IS FREEDOM?

▶ No one interfering, telling me how to live or how to use the income I have earned.

Making my own choices, and living with the consequences, so that I can go as far as my abilities allow.

◄ *Having real opportunities to develop my fullest potential and to participate with others in making our society better.*

The security of knowing that my family and I are protected from catastrophic loss.

ON WHAT DOES FREEDOM DEPEND?

▶ Largely on myself—my own effort to earn an income, allowing me many choices.

On my willingness to sacrifice now in order to build for the future and to take risks.

On government effectively protecting me, both from foreign enemies and lawbreakers here at home.

◀ *On my initiative, on my willingness to risk and sacrifice, and also on whether society protects opportunities for everyone to develop their capacities and to participate in community life.*

On a democratic government protecting all citizens from harm that stunts growth and causes premature death; a government actively promoting both citizen competency and participation.

WHAT MOST THREATENS FREEDOM?

▶ An expansive government, exceeding its constitutional bounds, that taxes away our incomes and takes over what is really the individual's responsibility.

◀ *Job insecurity, low pay, declining schools and neighborhoods, and environmental degradation reflecting unaccountable economic and political power that deprives citizens of a say in how society is run.*

WHAT'S THE SUREST PROTECTION OF FREEDOM?

▶ Government limited both in size and powers, especially in economic matters best left to the marketplace.

A citizenry of self-reliant individuals who do not ask government to take over what are appropriately their own responsibilities.

◀ *A citizenry enabled, by sound education and access to the widest possible views and information, to participate in public life—in the workplace, the community, and the nation.*

A citizenry committed to ensuring that everyone has some economic power, so that those with disproportionate economic muscle can't use it to control government and public decisions for their narrow gain.

HOW DO WE EXPAND OUR FREEDOM?

▶ By greatly curtailing government's powers, especially in economic matters, and strengthening its capacity in defense and in the maintenance of civic order.

By freeing citizens from dependency and the government from an economic burden by cutting back government supports for the nonproductive.

◀ *By expanding our democracy to protect economic rights, the right to earn a living, and the right to security from deprivation.*

By expanding opportunities for citizen participation in shaping public life.

PART ★ TWO

What's Fair?

[There is] a remarkable distinction between justice and all the other social virtues . . . the practice of [friendship, charity, or generosity] seems to be left in some measure to our own choice, but . . . we feel ourselves to be in a peculiar manner tied, bound, and obliged to the observation of justice.

Adam Smith,
The Theory of Moral Sentiments, 1790[1]

Are the Rich Getting Richer? ★

▶ You've led us into a discussion of democracy, but I'm not ready to go on—I just can't let stand some of the implications of what you've said about poverty and the responsibility of government.

For you it seems to be an article of faith that the rich are getting richer and the poor, poorer. But if we look at the big picture, the striking feature of American society over the last two hundred years is that everyone's gotten less poor, and we've seen steadily decreasing disparities in how people live.

◀ *It's hard for me to conceive of a contrast in "how people live" any more stark than that between a family coping with rats and falling plaster in a Chicago slum and a family coping with a raft of servants on their estate in Westchester County!*

▶ Come on now, the progress is undeniable. Just to remind you of one obvious example—the "Okies" that Steinbeck and others so poignantly described are no more. Even the poorest families today have TVs, refrigerators, cars, lots of things only the wealthy could afford just a generation ago.

How has this been achieved—by governments deciding what people are entitled to? *No*, but by capitalism's productive success in bringing the price of goods within the reach of an ever larger portion of the population, turning luxuries for the rich into necessities for everyone. And this remains the only solution to poverty today: economic growth bringing with it rising real wages.

You insist on painting such a bleak picture, but a federal study in 1988 concluded that median family income has grown 20 percent since 1970—not bad considering our many economic setbacks and intensifying international competition during this period. And this study doesn't even include in-kind transfers like food stamps. Its conclusions are hardly consistent with your gloomy views.[2]

◄ *But almost half the gain you find so encouraging had occurred by 1973. And most of the small gain after that reflects income improvements for the elderly, mostly a result of Social Security, not market-generated income. Young people and poor families with children became worse off. Most frightening: the report says that four out of ten young families with children are now living at half the poverty level or below.[3]*

► Because it's obvious that the past fifteen years have been exceptional, what's most important is to look at the big picture. And when we do, what's so striking is the consistency in the distribution of income in this century. The gap between rich and poor is definitely less than it was in 1929.[4]

◄ *Again, it is due to government "transfer payments" that income distribution has not gotten much worse. Without this subsidy, in the post-war period the poorest Americans would have seen their incomes cut in half.[5]*

While government "transfer payments" have helped mask growing disparities, even they haven't prevented the gap between rich and poor from growing.[6] Because so many new jobs pay poorly and tax changes have benefitted the well-to-do, the share of after-tax income going to the richest fifth of Americans grew markedly after the late seventies—they now receive half.[7] Over this period, most Americans watched their incomes stagnate or shrink—but not the super-rich. For the 1 percent at the top, after-tax incomes shot up by two-thirds.[8]

► Income and wealth distribution data often seriously misstate issues by throwing Americans of all ages into one statistical pot. They mask the fact that people have varying incomes and assets over their lifetimes. By taking only a static picture of one year, your data overstate income differences.[9]

Plus, if you added in the full cash value of all the benefits the poor get, as I mentioned, you would find that there are at least ten million fewer poor people than you imagine. But you don't seem to want to hear the good news.[10]

◄ *Actually, official figures greatly understate poverty. If the definition of poverty had been kept at what most people think of as deprivation—that is, measured as it was in 1960, at half or less of the median income—then ten to fifteen million more Americans would be judged poor today.*[11]

But let's forget statistics for a moment. And let's say you're right, that the concentration of income isn't getting worse, or that I've exaggerated. The question still remains: Is a distribution of income defensible that leaves some without homes or even adequate food? Is it consistent with a free society?

Can Redistribution Ever Be Fair? ★

▶ Even to raise this question means that you think the current distribution requires justification. I don't. The current distribution of wealth and income results from a multitude of voluntary transactions by individuals over time. They are, after all, the voluntary acts of consenting adults! They should not have to be justified to observers like you who weren't party to these transactions.[12]

You seem to imagine that some things have just come into being and that who is entitled to them remains an open question. In fact, when things come into the world, they're already attached to people who have legitimate entitlement to them.[13] They either made them or bought them with money they or their forebears earned.

If someone works hard for something, how can you justify taking some of it away to benefit somebody else who didn't work for it? "Redistribution," as you call it, by its very nature is unfair.

◀ *Redistribution is going on all the time—it's hardly something social reformers dreamed up! Everyday, rules governing taxes, credit, interest, employment contracts, access to education, and so on shift income and potential income among Americans.*

For example, the Federal Reserve's policy of high interest

The major objection to speaking of everyone's having a right *to* various things such as equality of opportunity, life, and so on [is that] . . . No one has a right to something whose realization requires certain uses of things and activities that other people have rights and entitlements over.

—Robert Nozick,
Anarchy, State, and Utopia[14]

Few of us believe in a moral code that justifies forcing people to give up much of what they produce to finance payments to persons they do not know for purposes they may not approve of.

—Milton and Rose Friedman,
Free to Choose[15]

rates launched in 1979 greatly enhanced the earnings of the wealthy from interest on their financial assets. In 1982, this bonanza for the rich totaled over $300 billion a year, roughly equal to all the government's other income-transfer programs like Social Security and welfare combined. [16] *But who fretted about whether the rich were "truly needy"!*

The soaring national debt is also redistributing wealth: interest payments on the national debt, mainly going to the well-to-do and federal retirees, reached over $140 billion a year by the late Eighties. [17] *And changes in tax laws have shifted over $100 billion from the bottom 90 percent of the population to the top 10 percent over the last decade.* [18]

The tax deduction for mortgage interest is another example of this invisible aid to the nonpoor—benefits accruing to the middle class are worth ten times more than benefits the poor receive from public housing. [19]

But let me give you a more personal example. Inflation in the housing market in the Seventies increased my net worth about $50,000 in four years. Wealth shifted toward me, a homeowner, and away from my friends who were renting, and saw their rents climb. I certainly didn't work hard for my windfall; I didn't work for it at all!

▶ Now, surely your book writing must have earned you some income, part of which you made an effort to save in order to buy your home. And the market rewarded you for it. You really needn't feel so guilty. That's perfectly fair.

◀ *Developments in society as a whole increased the value of my home, so why should I reap all the gain? But my point is that quashing redistribution toward those at the bottom doesn't prevent its going on daily in the other direction, regardless of effort or contribution. Is that fair?*

▶ But you have still not faced up to the real ethical problem: taking something from someone who's earned it and giving it to someone who hasn't.

◀ *"Earned" implies reward for effort. But of the richest Americans, only about one in eight got their wealth as entrepreneurs starting from scratch. More than half simply inherited their wealth or reaped windfalls in lucky investments.* [20]

► Surely you're not attacking the right to pass on a legacy of one's accomplishments through inheritance! But I'd like to come back to that point. And you're sorely mistaken if you think that making profitable investments is a matter of sheer luck—it requires considerable insight, skill, and experience to know the market well enough.

But my essential point is that your goal of trying to equalize incomes violates most Americans' innate sense of justice, since the fact of great inequalities in effort and talent is so obvious to everybody.

◄ *Who's talking about leveling incomes? I'm suggesting that differences must be kept within a reasonable range.*

► Reasonable to whom? To you?

◄ *No, not just me. The gap between the income of the top and bottom in the United States is among the most extreme in the world.*[21] *A U.S. corporate executive makes about forty times more than the typical manufacturing worker—a gap that has widened by a third just in the 1980s (In Japan the gap is only seven-fold).*[22] *Lee Iacocca makes the median annual income in three hours' work! I think most Americans would consider that unreasonable.*

► You're mixing apples and oranges. The executive is likely to be in his fifties, but a worker is typically much younger, maybe in his twenties. Older workers usually earn more than younger ones. As I already said, over whole lifetimes these differences even out considerably.

◄ *If you were right, in retirement we should all be in about the same boat (or yacht!). But differences in wealth among older people are extreme.*[23]

► But we already do dampen extremes in the United States. The rich pay a bigger share of their income in taxes. In fact, the top 20 percent of taxpayers shoulder well over half of all federal taxes.[24] And through welfare payments, the government transfers wealth from the better off to the poor. We've gone as far—or some would say, farther—than we can go without grossly penal-

The transformation in the distribution of our national income [toward greater equality] . . . may already be

izing exceptionally successful individuals and without hurting our society's growth potential.

◄ *That taxes significantly redistribute income is simply a myth—they don't.* [26] *The wealthy pay such a big chunk of all taxes simply because they have so much more money than the rest of us to begin with. Considering all types of taxes, the richest Americans now pay almost no greater share of their income in taxes than do those at the bottom, violating any principle of "equality of sacrifice." And in social security taxes, the rich pay* half *the share of their incomes that middle-class Americans pay.* [27]

Government payments, on the other hand, do narrow the gap between rich and poor; but remember that two out of every three dollars the government pays to individuals, including Social Security, are not targeted to the poor. [29]

► But there is yet another sense in which redistribution policies are unfair. All government income transfers use up resources. They take time, money, and human effort. So they necessarily diminish society's total output, reducing growth. The poor are hurt the most by economic stagnation. In other words, since it's only through economic growth that we can reduce poverty, income transfers from one group to another end up hurting the poor no matter who is supposed to benefit.[30]

◄ *Actually, government transfer payments seem to stimulate growth,* [31] *probably because they get money into the hands of those most likely to spend it on goods that create jobs.*

But I challenge your very premise—your assumption that without imposed government redistribution, somehow the more natural laws of the market would determine our well-being. Who our parents happen to be, what kind of education is available to us, where we live—all this greatly affects the income and wealth we each end up controlling. Plus, aside from the market, I've just noted a whole slew of rules and policies; few of us think of them as "redistribution," but they nonetheless shift income and wealth among us. An obvious one I haven't mentioned is the setting of national budget priorities. Take just one example from the last decade: The choice for a massive military buildup was a choice against, say, a transportation or an education "buildup." So income growth shifted to

counted as one of the great social revolutions in history.
—Arthur Burns, former chairman, Federal Reserve Board[25]

The subjects of every state ought to contribute towards the support of the government, as nearly as possible, in proportion to their respective abilities; that is, in proportion to the revenue which they respectively enjoy under the protection of the state.
—Adam Smith, *The Wealth of Nations*, 1776[28]

investors and workers in 35,000 firms and their subcontractors making weapons for the government, especially the top ten which make a third of all weapons. With billions in new weapons orders, the return on their stocks has been well above that on commercial stocks. [32]

So, your assumption all along that if we could just get rid of government redistribution to assist the poorest, then the market could determine our fate, is grossly misleading.

▶ Look, your righteous indignation is itself based on a false premise—that the rich get richer by robbing the poor. The economic pie is constantly growing—*that's* why their wealth is growing, and the poor can participate in that growth, too. Nothing is stopping them.

Is the Market Fair? ★

◀ *Nothing, that is, that you seem to be able to see, but I want to go on, for to condemn as unfair using government to ensure wider dispersion of income and wealth suggests that you think the market's distribution is fair. What if the market rewards a teacher working fifty hours a week with $20,000 and a real estate agent working thirty hours a week with $60,000? Why is that fair?*

▶ It's not supposed to be. In a market economy, a person's financial success is determined by his or her value to others.[33] The real estate agent is providing a service that people value more highly, and they show it by paying more. So she or he gets more.

I can think of a lot more extreme examples than yours. The Boston Celtic's Larry Bird makes at least ten times more each year than even the most esteemed professor at Harvard. You might not like it because you value education, but the market doesn't allow you to impose your values on others.

[The fundamental issue] is whether it is desirable that people should enjoy advantages in proportion to the benefits which their fellows derive from their activities or whether the

Within our market economy, people are rewarded according to their productive contribution to the economy[35]—the prices their services command.

> distribution of these advantages should be based on other men's views of their merits.
> —Friedrich A. Hayek, *The Constitution of Liberty*[34]

◄ *Productive contribution and what the market rewards are hardly the same. More and more corporate chiefs have discovered that they can make profits without producing anything.*[36]

Just owning farmland during the Seventies made more for investors than farmers could earn through hard work by growing food.

► You take the notion of reward based on productive contribution too literally. Those who are producing what the rest of us want to buy—even if it's a pet rock or false eyelashes, or even if it's not producing anything tangible, but rather conserving a scarce resource—are making a productive contribution to the economy. They are stimulating growth of the GNP.

Of course the market isn't "fair." People are unequal—nature made us that way. If *life* isn't fair, how can the market be?

Fairness: What Works ★

◄ *To me, rewarding people's effort and the care they take on the job would be fair. Everything else seems to depend on our genes—the ultimate lottery.*

► But how could society or even employers decide who is more diligent?

◄ *It would be impossible. Of course I'm not advocating it.*

► So are you then saying that a fair system would reward people according to their needs?

◄ *For the essential protections of life, absolutely. Beyond that, no. It's impossible—how could needs be determined? I'm agree-*

ing that a truly fair system of rewards is out of our reach. But that admission isn't the end of the subject; it's only the beginning. It suggests we should start with different questions: not what is perfectly fair, but which attainable system of rewards serves the well-being of the whole society? And which hurts any person unnecessarily or unduly?

▶ So we can agree that what we're really talking about is "what works"—not some unreachable ideal.

◀ *Yes, but it's no trade-off, for the more fair a society is, the better it works.*

▶ Not if, as you would have it, making a society "more fair" means limiting people's opportunities for reward in order to avoid what you call "extremes." Workers would have less incentive to do their best—that clearly *won't* work! Understand, of course, unlimited rewards benefit even those who themselves don't receive the fattest paychecks or the nicest perks. It's the incentive for all of us of knowing the sky's the (only) limit that makes a society prosperous.

The wealthiest Americans open opportunities through their investments for the rest of us.[39] The less industrious and less well off benefit from the productivity and innovation of others whose efforts get stimulated by these big incentives. That's how we've achieved the prosperity we enjoy today.

◀ *Isn't this the thinking behind what's called "trickle-down" economics?*

▶ It's been called a lot of things, including "supply-side" economics, because the approach recognizes that producers must have the wherewithal to generate supply if consumers are to enjoy the fruits. The results of this approach benefit everybody.

◀ *Benefit everybody? In 1986 the four hundred richest Americans, who own much of the nation's productive capacity, increased their net worth by over 40 percent,[41] but real weekly earnings of production workers rose by less than 1 percent. A "trickle" is right!*

Incentives are crucial—that's exactly why reward and effort can't be divorced if we want to achieve a productive society. Today, in too many cases, there is no connection.

Society may subsist, though not in the most comfortable state, without beneficence; but the prevalence of injustice must utterly destroy it.
—Adam Smith,
The Theory of Moral Sentiments, 1790[37]

The prosperity of the middle and lower classes depends on the good fortune and light taxes of the rich.
—Andrew Mellon,
Nineteenth-century industrialist[38]

[T]he injustice of paying unmerited rewards to individuals must be traded off against the injustice of depriving society of available benefits by not paying enough to provide incentives to their production and full utilization.
—Thomas Sowell,
A Conflict of Visions[40]

In 1982, Union Carbide's earnings fell 52 percent, but the company's chairman got a hefty raise. [42]

▶ Hey, wait. Eighty-two was a bad year for most companies. You can't blame the CEO!

◀ *Okay, take the last decade. On average, salaries, and bonuses of chief executives tripled, while corporate profits grew only 8 percent, and in many of the biggest firms, investment actually fell.* [43]

▶ Don't worry; the market forces people to pay for their mistakes. If these raises are in fact bad decisions from the point of view of the company's productivity, the company won't prosper, and soon a T. Boone Pickens will be eager to buy it up cheap.

◀ *Still, there's a yawning gap between performance and reward. And rewards need not be excessive in order to serve as incentives for those at the top. In real purchasing power, U.S. chief executives earn roughly twice their counterparts in Japan and five times their Swedish counterparts, but the performance of Japanese and Swedish corporations surpasses many of ours.* [44] *Neither do big wage differences among workers appear necessary to high productivity.*

▶ Yes, and because Sweden's high taxes reduce the incomes of top executives by half, so many of the most talented Swedes are fleeing to Switzerland and other countries where they can hold on to more of their income. All your approach has accomplished is to increase their incentives—not to invest, but to leave!

◀ *The country seems to be doing very well without them. My point is that for an economy to function well, incentives must be there throughout society, not just for those on top.*

A just society is not one in which the allocation of wealth, opportunity, authority, and status is equal. Rather, it is one in which the inequalities are reasonably related to reasonable social goals.
—George Will, [45]
"In Defense of the Welfare State"

Hope and Fairness as Incentives ★

◀ *And hope is a most potent incentive. It's hard to hold on to, though, if the system doesn't seem fair. Youngsters feeling trapped in the ghetto have to believe that staying in school and working hard will earn them a chance to build a better life.*

It's telling that polls now show that the percentage of Americans, especially students, who agree that hard work always pays off has fallen markedly.[47] Where is the source of hope for poor children today? Few can now pay for college.[48] Doesn't this jeopardize our society's productive future?

A belief in the fairness of rewards is especially crucial when times are tough. There's been a lot of handwringing about the need to increase America's competitiveness by getting workers to work harder and smarter. In manufacturing, productivity growth has indeed been dramatic—up almost a third since 1979. But what happened to real hourly compensation? It went down.[49] Meanwhile, the number of corporate executives taking at least a million dollars in annual compensation has jumped fifty-five-fold since 1981.[50] So why would workers continue to knock themselves out, knowing that their bosses were making a killing while the workers were making all the sacrifices?

If workers don't think the setup is fair, output is bound to suffer. Two-thirds of a broad sample of American workers admitted sloughing off on the job. One-third admitted to stealing at work. Researchers said that the workers' feeling that the company was unfair to them was a large part of the explanation.[51]

▶ Evidence like this suggests a very different conclusion to me. It suggests a serious weakening of society's moral fiber, which has never recovered from the attack on the authority of religion and family values in the sixties. I think we're also seeing a decline of the work ethic because Americans have had it too easy for too

When a Negro youth can reasonably foresee a future free of slums, when the prospect of gainful employment is realistic, we will see motivation and self-help in abundant quantities.

—Bayard Rustin, "From Protest to Politics: The Future of the Civil Rights Movement"[46]

long. We had an extended period of prosperity after World War II because we had so little real competition; the economies of our major competitors had been destroyed by war. We got spoiled by being on top too long. Let's not excuse workers' indiscipline by blaming it on "exploitation." That's too easy.

◄ *Your "we've had it too good" argument is hard to make stick when the real incomes of most families have declined or stagnated in the last decade, despite many more two-earner families.* [52]

> The moral justification of the market process rests [not on a just pattern of results but] on the general prosperity and freedom it produces.
> —Thomas Sowell,
> *A Conflict of Visions* [53]

► But you haven't listened to me. Fairness—the lack of which you've been complaining about—isn't the central value of capitalism in the first place. Rather, capitalism's remarkable accomplishment is in generating goods and services, which offer prosperity and freedom instead. And that's why Americans like it so much.

Incentives at the Top ★

> It should be the policy of governments . . . never to lay such taxes as will inevitably fall on capital, since by so doing, they impair the funds for the maintenance of labor, and thereby diminish the future production of the country.
> —David Ricardo,
> *On the Principles of Political Economy and Taxation*, 1817 [56]

► Your approach—moderating differences in reward—would kill the proverbial goose that lays the golden eggs. If the wealthy couldn't reap unlimited benefits, why would they bother to invest? If you try to tax away the resources of the wealthy, they'll just spend more time and attention trying to avoid taxes. So the rich actually pay more taxes where their rates are low, for they will then move out of tax shelters and into productive endeavors that generate taxable income. [54]

And, if you tax the rich heavily, where do you think that funds for investment will come from? The rich are much more able to put their money into investments that in the end make everyone better off. [55]

◄ *High taxes don't necessarily deter investment.* [57] *Japan, with high investment, makes corporations carry a much heavier tax burden than is typical in the industrial world.* [58] *And why as-*

sume that more wealth in the hands of owners of productive assets will automatically mean more funds going to business investment? What did corporations do with the hundreds of billions in tax benefits they got in the early Eighties? Business promised a boom in investment; instead its rate of increase slowed. [59]

▶ In suggesting we reduce the income and wealth of the wealthiest Americans, you forget a simple economic fact: the well-off can best afford to save—obviously because the poor and most middle-income people have less discretionary income. And it's savings the economy needs to increase investment.

◀ *If true, then why do any number of industrial nations with less extreme concentrations of income also have a better savings record than we have?*[60] *In part the answer is that, in several countries, national pension funds as well as household savings are much more effectively used as capital sources available to firms.* [61]

But in part the answer is that efficient production depends on more than investment capital. Consumer demand is what most stimulates output, as I've said. But demand is stifled where income and wealth are highly skewed.

▶ Come on now; dollars plunked down in the market stimulate supply, whether they be a rich man's or a poor man's.

◀ *No, dollars spent on a Renoir and dollars spent on a new refrigerator do* not *equally stimulate the economy.*

But I want to get back to your point—unlimited reward as the necessary incentive to industrious activity. The irony is that the unlimited reward ends up creating the opposite of initiative: as it accumulates, wealth itself gets rewarded[62]*—return for putting one's money in safe investments and doing nothing! And income from wealth is going up twice as fast as income from work.*[63] *What does that suggest about the vigor of our economy?*

Fair Reward for Sacrifice and Risk? ★

▶ Don't let appearances confuse you. Just because a person isn't physically laboring doesn't mean he or she is doing nothing! Investment income is the reward for doing something very important—for putting your wealth at the disposal of society rather than just hoarding it under your mattress or indulging in luxuries. So it is a reward for sacrifice.

◀ *Sacrifice? It might be hard for many Americans to be moved by the millionaire's forbearance in putting off that second BMW or third home!*

▶ You're being snide—return on investment is also a reward for risk. Without the chance of big returns, who is going to take a big risk?

◀ *Risk? A person with $20,000 in a no-risk security can earn in a year of doing nothing what it takes a production worker three months of effort to earn.* [64]

▶ There is just no such thing as a no-risk investment. Even government bonds aren't without risk: historically, many governments have defaulted.

◀ *But how big are such risks compared with those facing people with no investment income? For them, being laid off means losing a livelihood, and perhaps a home.*

▶ But if there were no return for investing money, why would anyone save? Where would investment capital for economic growth come from?[65]

◄ *You've got me wrong. Of course, the use of capital must carry a price. The problem arises when the price paid accrues to a narrow and distinct group of investors. Absentee investors drain wealth out of the communities producing it. The priorities of investors, not the needs of communities, come to determine the economy's direction. Under these conditions, return on investment accelerates both concentration of wealth and localized economic decay. And the problem gets compounded whenever investment income is taxed more lightly than work-earned income, as has often been the case.*

So we need both effective taxes on income from wealth and mechanisms for closing the gap between workers, communities, and investors. But how? Owning shares in one's own workplace closes that gap—it makes workers also investors. If workers had more say over the trillion-dollar pension funds that are nominally "theirs," these funds could also become a major source of capital for community development. What are called "community development loan funds"—now thirty of them nationwide—offer a return to their investors but use their fast-growing capital only for local economic development.[66] Community-controlled banks, like Chicago's South Shore Bank, use their capital for lending to local businesses. [See Part V for further discussion.]

▶ What you describe is a totally insignificant part of the American economy, and for a very good reason. Your suggestions could not be implemented on a large scale without sapping the vitality of the capitalist system. They would discourage investors and entrepreneurs. Capital must be free to move to wherever returns are highest, unprejudiced by people's sentiments and narrow concerns about their own particular communities.

The fact that workers and investors are distinct groups of people is an asset, not a problem! What makes capitalism work so well is that it unites knowledge and power. It's the very same people who conduct successful entrepreneurial experiments that reap the lion's share of the rewards and that's good, because they are therefore able to direct the future course of that enterprise.[67] Your ideas would rip apart that vital connection between these "doers" and the resources they need.

Your prescription for a good society would also mean

. . . no one surely would gladly accept the disappearance of all the activities which find their market in [higher] classes. . . . The production of all first-quality goods would cease. The skill they demand would be lost and the taste they shape would be coarsened. . . . Who could buy paintings? Who even could buy books other than pulp?

—Bertrand de Jouvenel, *The Ethics of Redistribution*, 1952[68]

the disappearance of many of our finest cultural activities. Without those enjoying considerable disposable income, who would subsidize the works of great artistic and intellectual merit?[69]

Inheritance Rights, or Wrongs? ★

I'm disturbed, not only by the potential impact on economic efficiency and on culture of what you are saying, but with the moral implications as well. Could you really justify taking wealth that someone has earned so that they can make life easier for their children and deny them the right to pass it on? You're ready to rob people of one of the greatest satisfactions that a free society can offer. Historically, this tradition has been central in maintaining strong family bonds, the very basis of our civilization. Our current inheritance laws already threaten this important family-centered right.

◀ *Don't misunderstand me. There's a big difference between leaving a gift to your children when you die and setting them up so they need never work again! Taking care of one's children forever is not (I hope) the greatest satisfaction of parents; it is seeing one's children grow into capable adults, able to support themselves.*

Yet, less than 2 percent of all estates pay any inheritance taxes at all. Today estate and gift taxes contribute next to nothing to federal government revenues.[70]

▶ I fail to see what's different about a child's inheriting a magnificent voice from his or her parents—enabling that person to make a lot of money—and inheriting wealth directly. It makes no sense that you would challenge one and not the other.[71]

◀ *The reason you're unable to perceive the difference is that you do not acknowledge something called power. Inheriting*

. . . we do not protest the unequal advantage given . . . by virtue of genetic transmission of qualities of strength and acuity; why, then, should we protest the inheritance of cultural-material qualities . . . which are equally a part of what we think of as family and ancestry?

—Robert Nisbet, *Conservatism*[72]

talent means being equipped—if one exerts the effort to develop the gift—to earn acclaim and maybe income. But inheriting enormous fortunes accumulated over generations means one is set up, with no effort, to wield power over others and, potentially, in arenas money shouldn't govern. (I want to return to this point.)

In other words, in any society, hereditary wealth creates a serious threat to democratic life: The emergence of an aristocracy—people in powerful positions simply because of who their parents happened to be—is exactly what our forebears fled. If it's impossible to inherit huge sums, there's less need to redistribute the wealth of the living to make sure opportunities remain open to all. It's a lot more efficient.

▶ Your attack on inherited wealth is actually, I fear, a subterfuge for something else. Your interest seems to be, not to tax away a person's wealth upon death to redistribute to the poor, but to tax it away so as to enlarge the power of the state. Talk about redistribution of wealth is actually talk about redistribution from the citizenry to the public treasury. That way, people who think they know better than the rest of us can decide what to do with our money.[74]

◀ Some of our government's most significant actions on behalf of greater equality of opportunity didn't enlarge state power or bureaucracy in any significant way. I'm thinking of the Homestead Acts and the Federal Housing Authority, both putting property within reach of ordinary citizens. Today, if the rich were simply taxed at the same level as the Seventies—a step in the direction I'm talking about—one third of the federal deficit would disappear.[75] Would you call reducing the deficit a plot to enlarge state power?

There is . . . an artificial aristocracy, founded on wealth and birth, without either virtue or talents. . . . and provision should be made to prevent its ascendancy. . . .
—Thomas Jefferson, 1813[73]

Inequalities and Self-Esteem ★

When everyone, or almost everyone, has some thing or attribute, it does not function as a basis for self-esteem. Self-esteem is based on *differentiating characteristics;* that's why it's *self-*esteem.

—Robert Nozick,
Anarchy, State, and Utopia[76]

▶ Practically all the proposals you've made would diminish the differences among people. You may not be advocating an economic leveling, but your idea of "limits" does shrink the possibilities for differences in wealth. Some people argue that reducing the wealth of those at the top will make the rest of us feel less inferior and enhance our self-esteem. But in lessening differences in wealth you would actually be robbing people of an arena in which to gain self-esteem. After all, we all judge ourselves in the ways we differ from others. We take no pride in being able to read if everyone else can, too!

Even if you successfully mitigated differences in wealth, people would only seek other ways to distinguish themselves from others. You would have gained nothing in improving people's self-esteem.

◀ *The direction I am suggesting allows more people to develop their innate gifts. Differences in achievement in the great array of human talents would not diminish but flourish.*

▶ You forget: We achieve self-esteem not just by being different but by being different in a certain way—by being better. Differences in wealth (and therefore possessions) are a primary way people make a public statement that their achievement is better than their neighbors'.

◀ *People gain self-esteem not just by being Number One but by experiencing their own progress, by feeling they are living up to their own potential.*[77] *In fact, we often seek out people precisely because they are better then we, so that we can improve our skills, knowing we'll never surpass them. Self-esteem derives, not only from individual achievement, but from feeling that one is contributing something special to a group enter-*

prise—a family, a team, a work group—heightening self-esteem. Extreme differences in reward can undercut such common effort. We also gain self-esteem by earning the acceptance and respect of others.

Monetary rewards and self-esteem are not necessarily connected. A person who has worked hard to develop a talent can have tremendous self-esteem, whether it's financially rewarded or not. The professor, the musician, and the amateur athlete may have low or no pay but solid self-esteem because they and others value the quality of their work. On the other hand, if you have money without earning it, wealth can lower your self-esteem.

Fairness or Envy? ★

▶ Don't you see that underneath the high-sounding arguments for greater equality lies a pretty ugly emotion: envy. Your arguments open the door to precisely the kind of leveling of people's incomes that you say you are not advocating. But once you unleash poorer people's envy, allowing it to dictate policy, there would be no end to the drive to pull those higher up down to their level.

Why do inequalities in income, or in positions of authority within a company, gall people so much?

◀ *They don't!*

▶ Oh, but they do. She or he may not admit it, but it's the recognition that the reward is deserved that injures a co-worker's self-esteem. Just knowing of someone else who has accomplished more or risen higher makes a person feel less worthy.[79] In my teens I worked in a light bulb factory one long summer. How many times, when someone got praise from the supervisor, did I hear a co-worker murmur under his breath, "I *hate* him!"

I have no respect for the passion for equality, which seems to me merely idealizing envy.

—Oliver Wendell Holmes[78]

◄ *Sure, we've all felt threatened by the success of others, especially when pitted against each other for the few good jobs. But what makes people downright angry is undeserved reward. If I saw the manager goofing off, doing a sloppy job so that the department worked badly, that's when I'd get mad, furious that she's making lots more than I do, when I could do better than she does. You underestimate people's innate sense of fairness.*

You also underestimate common sense. Few worker-run businesses rush to flatten wages. Worker-owners often pay top managers well in order to attract the best, knowing that they will benefit, too. Many worker-owners assume that rewarding the additional responsibility and skill required by top management does make sense to a point. But salary differences of three-to five-fold are a lot different than gaps of forty-fold, which we have today.

Contemporary populism, in its desire for wholesale egalitarianism, insists in the end on complete leveling. . . . Its impulse is not justice but *resentiment.* The populists are for power ("to the people") but against authority—the authority represented in the superior competence of individuals.
—Daniel Bell,
*The Coming of the
Post-Industrial Society*[80]

► The picture you're painting is totally detached from reality. Just look at what happened in communist countries like the USSR or China. Once fervor for so-called equality was let out of the bag, people wanted to do away with all differences. In China, first landlords were brutally wiped out. Later intellectuals and top managers were told they had to go into the countryside and work with the peasants—to learn they were no better than anybody else. Lives and talent were wasted. The country was set back a full decade or more.

◄ *Any reasonable idea taken to extremes becomes unreasonable. Your argument has been used against virtually every democratic advancement. In fact, the societies you cite haven't leveled incomes but have only reduced income differences compared to what we have here. To the extent that extreme leveling was social policy, it did not come from the pressure of ordinary people.*

► You're wrong. People *are* eager to challenge differences in reward because they make those lower on the ladder feel bad, as I said. I know—I've experienced it in my own business.

◄ *Actually, most Americans want to believe there is some logic to the present distribution of income. If one acknowledges that rewards are unfair, it's easy to feel one's efforts are for naught. So most people try to rationalize the present system of rewards*

and blame themselves, even if it is grossly unfair to them.[81]
*This self-blame, not "envy," is our biggest problem, if it means
we go along with a status quo that hurts so many people,
including ourselves.*

▶ You forget that Americans have never wanted to do away with
rich people. Except among intellectuals, there's very little passion for reduced discrepancies in income and wealth.[82] What
American would deny Muhammad Ali, Robert Redford, or Barbara Walters their millions?[83] Everyone imagines that someday
they themselves might be rich. And they enjoy the vicarious
pleasure of seeing how the rich live.

◀ *Can you really have it both ways? Can you argue that envy
would drive people to level everyone's income and at the same
time hold that Americans love having super-rich people so they
can fantasize getting rich themselves? Have you considered that
fascination with the rich may serve as a substitute for hope? It
increases as people's economic conditions worsen because all
that remains is fantasy—watching the "Lifestyles of the Rich
and Famous" on TV.*

Egalitarianism's Slippery Slope ★

▶ You say that you're not talking about leveling, but the spirit
of what you say is just that. I would call it "egalitarianism."
Maybe you're not advocating a total leveling, but you are for
moderating the peaks and valleys. You're convinced that a less
skewed distribution of income would make people happier because they would see society as more fair.

But people aren't like that. Focusing on our differences in a
vain effort to diminish them ironically ends up exaggerating
them in people's eyes. So as the actual differences in income
diminish, the perceived differences do not. In fact, as inequality
decreases, resentment increases.[84]

So what's fair is totally subjective. Today there is actually much less inequality than one hundred years ago, but then people perceived society as more equal.[85] In other words, once people decide that they can deliberately make their society "fair," there is no end to the interference in people's lives. If you could wave a wand and reduce all differences in wealth by half, the remaining differences would bother some just as much as the current ones. Shrink the differences by half again? The same result: Some would insist that fairness had still not been achieved. People are never satisfied with the distribution of income.[86] This is the "slippery slope" that terrifies anyone who thinks seriously about what follows from trying to impose any particular notion of fairness.

◄ *Your "slippery slope" is a legitimate fear only if people were bothered by differences in reward per se. But, as I've said, most people aren't. It's the* unearned *rewards that irk. And it's the excesses of wealth when others go without food or shelter that disgust so many Americans.*

► But you do not understand the "slippery slope" concept. The more equal things become, the more the little inequalities will bother people. They'll loom just as large. People will feel no progress.

◄ *Of course our idea of "what's fair" changes. One hundred and fifty years ago many people thought that slavery was fair. Seventy-five years ago many thought that denying women the vote was fair. Yes, our standards rise to reflect deepened sensitivities, but people do see the progress. Just because women who take for granted the right to vote are now fighting wage discrimination doesn't mean we don't see progress!*

Who's Responsible for Inequalities? ★

▶ All your arguments against the wealthy presuppose that the rich are rich because they have ripped off the poor, an assumption running through your entire argument.[87] I don't agree that most people have gotten wealthy through exploitation. They're wealthy because they have developed their own talents and economic resources more fully.

It's obvious that human talent and ability fall along a bell-shaped curve. Most of us are clumped in the middle ranges, with fewer at the very top and at the very bottom. Since that's how nature made us, it's not surprising that in a free society, distribution of income and wealth falls along a similar bell-shaped curve.[88]

◀ *Your single bell-shaped curve is simply fantasy. For each of the countless human talents and abilities, there may be such a curve. Depending on which talent is being measured, each of us would land at different spots on many different curves. So how could you say which ability-curve determines income? The range in income among fully employed white men is only about one-fifth as great as among the rest of us.[89] Does this mean that among white men differences in ability are more narrow? Of course not. It suggests that many forces beyond our individual mix of abilities determine incomes.*

▶ You want to duck the fact that much of the inequality we see is the responsibility of individuals themselves. Some simply prefer to take a chance at a risky career and then live with the possibility of failing rather than choosing a surer, lower paid job. Some people don't want to make the effort to become rich. I am

not criticizing them; it's just that they want different things out
of life. They have other values. That's fine.

Inequality results from such choices that people themselves
make. And it results from differences in taste. Consumers' tastes
expressed in the market reward some people and not others. And,
of course, plain old luck plays a part, too.

Given all of our individual differences and that elusive thing
called luck, it's not surprising that few societies have ever been
successful in significantly reducing inequalities in income and
wealth, no matter how hard they've tried. To try to make up for
all our natural differences is futile.

◄ *But so much of the enormous income differences in our society reflect, not the distribution of innate qualities, but the
distribution of power to secure resources, especially jobs and
education, which itself depends greatly on who your parents
are, what race you are, where you live, and so on. [91]*

*Of course people differ—in abilities and in how much making
money matters—but this hardly explains the extreme differences in assets that leave some families with hundreds, even
thousands of times more than others. These extremes are
created by the underlying economic rules we live by that multiply the wealth of some and foreclose opportunities for others;
rules that drain wealth out of poor communities while it accrues beyond any useful function in wealthy communities.*

*So debating whether "the rich" are ripping off "the poor" is
a distraction if it prevents us from seeing that the rules are
unfair; and it's these rules that need addressing. They're destructive both because they leave some people out—some literally out in the cold, homeless and hungry—and because they,
very practically speaking, just don't work to create a livable
society.*

*And your suggestion that no society has succeeded in reduc-
ing income differences is simply untrue: The gap between rich
and poor in our society is among the most extreme in the
world. [93]*

Equal Opportunities or Equal Outcomes? ★

▶ But this country has the greatest equality of *opportunity* of perhaps any country in the world. A person can begin at the very bottom of the ladder and rise as far as his or her skill and determination will permit, with no rigid caste or class barriers to overcome, as in most other countries. And opportunities to enter high-status jobs have improved for each generation for at least the last forty years.[94]

What you're really advocating is equality of *outcome*—equalizing what people end up with, not opportunity, as you claim.[96] Regardless of the absence of legal restraints, unless competition ends up with a certain result—without what you call "extremes"—then by definition the process isn't fair in your eyes.

Even to come close to the realization of such a vision, we'd have to downplay the natural differences among people. How else could I, for example, expect an equal chance to become a great cellist or chemist compared to someone who has outstanding musical or scientific talent, when I have neither? It's absurd!

◀ *Of course equal opportunity doesn't mean the equal prospect of achieving any given result! It simply means that each of us must have as much opportunity to develop our particular gift as anyone else with that gift.*

▶ Once you discard the market as the mechanism for allocating rewards, then social issues become a matter of coordination by "experts." You yourself admit that most people aren't calling for more equality. So it would have to be imposed.

Some select third parties would have to agree on what constitutes need or proper reward. Society faces so many conflicting

We are the land of big dreams, of big opportunities, of fair play . . . the American people realize that we are a very special country for anybody given the opportunity can make it and fulfill the American dream.

—President George Bush[95]

Equality as a process characteristic means application of the same rules to all, without regard to individual antecedent conditions or subsequent results.

—Thomas Sowell, *A Conflict of Visions*[97]

It might be possible (though certainly very difficult) for government to equalize incomes, but not equality of opportunity, for that would require eliminating inequalities of beauty, strength, health, intelligence, size, and talent.

—Jeane J. Kirkpatrick, *Dictatorships and Double Standards*[98]

values that consensus is not possible.[99] So decisions must be left to the market, whether it seems "fair" or not.

◀ *I'm not for imposing particular outcomes, but to achieve equality of opportunity takes a lot more than an absence of legal restraints. Equality of opportunity would require that the minimal conditions necessary to develop one's unique talents and to participate in community life be available to all. This is impossible without a floor and a ceiling in the distribution of income. Let me explain why.*

The opening or closing of opportunity begins in infancy and childhood. So without a secure economic floor under families, millions of children are denied opportunity from birth. To have a fair chance in life, each child minimally would have to have good nutrition, education, and medical care. That one-fourth of young American children live in poverty, and 12 million children go hungry,[101] proves how frightfully far we are from achieving equality of opportunity.

▶ But to put a floor under everyone also means supporting those who will not work; that means we will inevitably be carrying along some people who are just lazy. That's certainly not fair to the rest of us.

◀ *You're right; there is always this risk. Against it, we must weight the alternative risk: the much greater damage to society of stunting our youth before they've even been given a chance.*

But the argument for a floor under everyone goes beyond this very practical point. All our nation's varied religious traditions agree: Every *human being is innately worthy of respect. Isn't the inherent worth of the person in itself enough to justify a floor of decency to make opportunity real?*

▶ But people cannot achieve dignity if they're taken care of. In fact, taking care of people robs them of their opportunity to achieve the dignity to which every human being is capable.

◀ *I'm saying that in our religious faiths dignity is innate, not earned. In any case, I've never advocated "taking care of people." That's not what people want, except the minority in every society who are incapacitated.*

> . . . a democratic conception of equality. . . . is the affirmation of equality of being and belonging. . . . It stresses the greatest possible participation in and sharing of the common life and culture while striving to assure that no person shall determine or define the being of any other.
> —John H. Schaar, "Equality of Opportunity and Beyond"[100]

> We have become the first society in history in which children are the poorest group in the population.
> —Senator Daniel Moynihan, 1985[102]

► Equality of opportunity doesn't mean promising anybody anything; it means that society doesn't prevent people from taking advantage of the opportunities available to everyone.

In defining equality of opportunity as a right to something, you forget that to ensure such a right requires resources that other people already have rights to—they've either bought them, acquired them through investments, or inherited them. These particular rights to things leave no general rights of the type you are talking about, like a "floor of decency," to use your words.[104]

◄ *Those rights you treat as virtually God-given in fact reflect choices society makes about which claims it will back up: a billionaire's right to returns in the stock market supersedes a poor child's right to medical care. What predetermines which claim takes precedence? Nothing. The choice depends on how our society defines freedom—in other words, what we as a people value.*

Plus, your view that after individuals make their claims, there's nothing left to meet a general right to social protection ignores the extensive, common domain of human invention, knowledge, technology, and services which no one or no group of people living today can take full credit for and without which our individual incomes could not be made or enjoyed. Surely this common legacy makes us each legitimate claimants to at least minimal access to resources.

► Of course property rights represent a choice. They are the choice that our society has made for a very good reason. To introduce any other distribution principle is to dissolve everyone's sense of security: If we accepted your views, anything one owns could be claimed by someone else as what they've decided they need to ensure their "basic needs" or to ensure themselves "equal" opportunity, or to stake their claim in some "common legacy."

◄ *Absolutely not. To establish the principle that human beings must be ensured basic needs, what I call "rights of membership," doesn't obviate claims people have to property. That's absurd. It simply adds an obligation to our common life: that we construct the rules in such a way that no one is left out, left without resources to earn a living or to thrive even if they cannot work. Yes, it means a tempering of prop-*

Capitalism delivers many good things but, on the whole, economic equality is not one of them. . . . Rather, capitalism has always stood for equality of economic opportunity, reasonably understood to mean the absence of official barriers to economic opportunity.

—Irving Kristol,
"The Capitalist Concept of Justice"[103]

erty rights but hardly an abrogation. [See Part IV for a discussion of property.]

▶ In addition to a threat to property, which is so essential to security, your ideas about equal opportunity are utterly unrealistic—unless, that is, you are willing to intervene in family life. One critical determinant of a child's future success is who her or his parents happen to be, as you yourself acknowledge.[105] So, if you want to equalize opportunity, you are going to have to equalize parenting. That means intervening directly in family life. Are you willing to do that?

◀ *You seem to argue by extremes to avoid acknowledging how much we can do without sacrificing other values. Good health care, good day care and preschools, and solid education—all this society can ensure without interfering in family life. The conflict is not between two goods—protecting child welfare versus protecting family integrity—as you would pose it. The conflict is between allowing wealth itself to be our society's guide or standing firm that protecting life comes first.*

▶ I am hardly arguing by extremes. I am merely trying to get you to see the logical implications of your wish list. Similarly, you mentioned a ceiling, didn't you? How can you talk about opportunity and justify capping a person's achievement? Telling someone that she or he can only go so far but no higher violates the very spirit that made America great.

◀ *I am not talking about capping achievement. The capacity to develop one's talents is unlimited. But accumulation must be restrained in a fair, workable society for many reasons. Some resources—farmland, for example—are finite. We can't make more. So one person's unfettered acquisition directly limits opportunities for many others. Our founders feared the consequences of precisely this unlimited accumulation.*

But there's another reason a fair society would want to limit accumulation. As I argued earlier, wealth conveys power. Limits on accumulation help to reduce the likelihood that money will govern arenas of life which should be ruled by other distribution principles, such as equality in each citizen's political influence, or in access to education or health care; or, in the arts, ability alone as the entree to training and exposure.[107] The

What I want to see above all else is that this country remain a country where someone can always get rich.
—President Ronald Reagan, 1983

The great objects should be to combat the evil [potential within a political system]: One. By establishing political equality among all. Two. By withholding unnecessary opportunities from the few to increase the inequality of property by an immoderate, and especially unmerited, accumulation of riches.
—James Madison, 1792[106]

. . . the rights of any man which are morally justifiable on any egalitarian principle are only those which allow all others to have equal effective rights; and that those are enough to allow any man to be fully human.
—C. B. Macpherson, *Democratic Theory,*[108]

more extreme the concentration of wealth, the harder it gets to keep money's influence out of arenas it shouldn't dictate. Moderating the wealth of those at the top is not likely to interfere with their development, but only with their acquisitions. Such moderation is, however, required to allow the development of all others. [109]

Affirmative Action or Reverse Discrimination? ★

We need something more than an economic floor and ceiling to achieve equality of opportunity. Where whole groups of people have been consistently denied opportunity in the past, equality of opportunity requires public policies to enable these groups to catch up.

This means affirmative action—vigorous programs by employers and educators to recruit, train, and promote minority group members and women.

▶ Now that you've brought up affirmative action, I see that you're ready to jump on any bandwagon adorned with a liberal banner. Policies that differentiate among people based on race or gender are both impractical and dangerous. No one who claims to believe in fairness can embrace such an idea.

First of all, affirmative action is based on the false premise that an uneven distribution of races among all types of jobs proves past discrimination. It doesn't. A racial group ends up concentrated in certain lines of work for many reasons, including its average age, location, education, and culture. [111]

◀ *You beg the question of why the race or ethnic group was concentrated by education or location in the first place! But the telling evidence of discrimination is that certain racial groups*

Freedom is not enough. You do not wipe away the scars of centuries by saying: Now, you are free to go where you want, do as you desire, and choose the leaders you please. You do not take a man who for years has been hobbled by chains, liberate him, bring him to the starting line of a race, saying, "you are free to compete with all others," and still justly believe you have been completely fair. Thus it is not enough to open the gates of opportunity.
—President Lyndon B. Johnson, 1965 [110]

and women are overrepresented in low-status, low-pay work and grossly underrepresented in professions wielding the most influence in society.[112] *And the earnings gap between women and men hasn't lessened in thirty years: women still earn only two-thirds as much as men.*[113]

▶ *What?* There are four times as many blacks in management as there were in the Seventies, and women have made great strides. Women's earnings now exceed three-quarters of men's earnings, if you compare men and women working full-time with comparable educations.[114]

◀ *That's a big "if"! And blacks control only one-twelfth the average wealth of whites.*[115] *That's an enormous handicap for blacks, who also hold but a minuscule share of top professional posts.*[116] *Now, with financial aid cutbacks and declining inner city schools, the gap is widening: The share of black high school grads who go to college, which a decade ago had almost reached the level of whites, has now dropped by a quarter.*[117]

If we don't take corrective action now, it would take hundreds of years before we could overcome these disparities, if then. In the meantime, enormous human potential is lost to our whole society. Mistrust, anger, and guilt compound.

▶ And that's precisely why we have outlawed discrimination, but affirmative action goes further, threatening a central premise of a free society: All any person should be able to expect is equal treatment under the same rules that apply to everyone else.[118]

◀ *We all want a society in which the law applies equally to everybody, but the wide social and economic gap between minorities and whites perpetuates prejudice, making the goal of equal legal treatment unattainable. Blacks arrested for felonies get sentenced to prison much more often than whites and are kept there longer; in fact, such disparities in treatment by race reach all the way to death row.*[119]

. . . government intervention . . . [would] have to continue forever to secure proportional [racial] equality in the desirable

▶ It is not just within a system of justice that everyone must be subject to the same rules in a free society. You brought up hiring and school placements. Here we've long respected the simple principle that the most qualified person has a right to a position. But you're arguing that one should give a black person or a woman a job in part just because of her color or gender. This is nothing more than reverse discrimination, which the Supreme Court condemned in the landmark Bakke case.

◄ *Your notion of a person's right to a certain job or school placement just isn't how the real world works! Most often a broad range of people meet the qualifications, so luck plays a big part, along with personal connections—"it's not what you know but who you know," your looks, the boss's hunch. Special preferences go to veterans and workers with seniority. And when children of alumni and star athletes get preferences, few of us complain.*

So affirmative action doesn't violate any absolute principle or right; it adds a positive *guideline into what is a mixed bag of reasons that people get jobs. In fact, many companies report that complying with federal affirmative action requirements has not meant compromising what were fair and open personnel practices; it's meant standardizing procedures to everybody's benefit. To comply, they've had to eliminate nepotism and personal networks in hiring, advertise openings more widely, improve complaint procedures, and more carefully specify criteria for promotion. The results feel fairer to everyone, so worker morale goes up, many report.* [121]

► You focus on possible benefits, but they are far outweighed by the costs. Perhaps the most serious cost of affirmative action that all society is bearing is the lowering of academic and professional standards through obligatory acceptance of weaker applicants.[123]

◄ *Affirmative action does not suggest that anyone hire or admit an unqualified person, but where qualifications are met, to give preference to the underrepresented group. That's all. And where's your consistency? You don't seem too troubled that preferences given to athletes, veterans, and alumni's children are diluting standards.*

► But you can't get around the fact that your notion of affirmative action means denying someone else the job or school placement in part due to her or his color. That's patently unfair! The most qualified person, the candidate with the strongest educational record and highest test scores, deserves to get the position.

occupations. This kind of intervention would . . . drive a wedge between individual merit and economic and professional success . . .

—Richard Posner,
The Economics of Justice [120]

. . . *affirmative action and equal opportunity compliance literally caused many of our [personnel] practices to be questioned and resulted in standardized policies which benefitted all employees.*
—Johnson & Johnson, Inc.[122]

◀ *Is it that high scorers deserve to be rewarded? After all, high grades and test scores depend in large part on one's home environment, schooling, and inherited traits, for which the individual can take little credit. A low scorer might have worked much harder. Rather, we reward high scores because we assume it best serves the whole society to have people in positions for which they show talent.* [124]

So, even what we think of as rewarding individual merit is actually premised on a social good—just like the principle of affirmative action. Thus, "merit" changes as perceived social needs change. Remember the post-Sputnik era? Suddenly, students with aptitude in science appeared to have special "merit." No one questioned their preferential treatment, in scholarships, for example. If a healthy, racially plural society is even more important, is it not equally appropriate to take race or gender into account in order to meet that goal?

▶ But on a deeper level, once you've established affirmative action as a legal concept, you've replaced the notion of the rule of law, which is above human tampering, with the notion that individuals have the wisdom to adjust rules to particular cases. I just don't think we do. In a search for illusory social justice, we destroy the rule of law. Once we start fashioning different rules for different groups, we'll generate a whole new set of injustices—there can be no end to it. Most important, it destroys the right of every individual to be treated as an individual, not as a member of a group.

Affirmative action has to be enforced by the courts, and the courts must apply laws equally to all, requiring absolute "color blindness." It's the equal application, not the consequences of the law, that a free society must be concerned about. The courts can't make sociological judgments about motives and effects—that's not their role.[125]

◀ *There is no neutral "rule of law." All laws advantage some more than others. The desirability of every law depends on its purpose and effect. Segregation laws, for example, were upheld for years as race-neutral—weren't whites excluded from black schools as well? In 1954, when the Supreme Court finally struck down these laws, it had to look past their formal color-neutrality to consider their intent and effect. And today, color blindness can mask the perpetuation of racial subjugation.* [126]

▶ But why should a particular white person be denied a job for which he or she is better qualified in order to pay for the sins of our forebears? Injustice to correct injustice must defeat itself—as they say, two wrongs never make a right.

◀ *I'm not arguing that whites should pay for prior evils. We're all—blacks and whites—paying now in lost human potential and in mutual distrust that holds back our whole society. The challenge is how to heal society for everyone's gain. Besides, we often embrace rules that serve the common good, knowing full well they could penalize us as individuals; rules such as those establishing a minimum age to serve in public office, school guidelines to achieve a wide geographic mix of students, or laws requiring educational credentials to practice medicine.*

▶ And many people are fighting a number of such rules as unacceptable abridgments of our liberty.

◀ *But why don't most Americans perceive such rules as threats to liberty? Because it's clear that these rules, like affirmative action policies, are not made on the basis of prejudice to hurt any group. They serve larger, positive purposes.*

▶ Whatever you say does not change the fact that "affirmative action" means discrimination on racial grounds. To the qualified person passed over, there may be no other equally desirable job opportunity. Whole careers can be at stake. No wonder the white person who is discriminated against is angry. No wonder the whole concept generates a backlash.

◀ *A critical distinction must be made: Racial discrimination damages people by communicating to them that they are unworthy, lesser human beings. Affirmative action, like my other examples, carries no such message. Yes, the hopes of the person who doesn't get the position are dashed, but no more than if the opening had been eliminated in a budget cut-back or if the employer had decided a midwesterner would be a better sales rep in the Kansas market than the New Yorker who loses out.*

As to backlash, the majority population's reaction to affirmative action isn't fixed. In a big turnaround from the Seventies, Americans now overwhelmingly support it.[128] *And this despite the attack on affirmative action during the Reagan presidency.*

We have created two racial and ethnic classes in the country to replace the disgraceful pattern of the past. . . . The two new classes are those groups that are entitled to statistical parity . . . on the basis of race, color, and national origin, and those groups that are not.
—Nathan Glazer,
Affirmative Discrimination[127]

Maybe it's because Americans can see the positive results: Where affirmative action has integrated police forces in minority neighborhoods, for example, better community relations improve public safety for everybody.[129] *Many corporations, including giants like Equitable Life Assurance, Hewlett-Packard, and Control Data, report that what most determines workers' acceptance of affirmative action is whether the company's leadership is firmly behind it. Executives from these companies say they back affirmative action because it brings new talent, an improved working environment, and heightened public good will toward the company.*[130]

▶ In citing exceptional cases, you also ignore the impact of affirmative action on the very minority individuals and women you want to help. Not only can it undercut the morale of employers and white male employees, but it can hurt even minority and female employees and students who have to live with the backlash.[131] Just imagine how your own self-esteem would suffer if you thought you got a job because of your color, not because you were the best applicant. You would be pretty angry, I'm sure, if you suspected that co-workers assumed you were less qualified, even though you knew you were head and shoulders above all other candidates.

Once a person gets a chance through affirmative action, he will live or die on performance.
A. Barry Rand,
black executive at Xerox[132]

◀ *With entry-level jobs and those with on-the-job training—in fire departments, for example—who's more qualified upon hiring (other than passing physical tests) is largely a moot point. In fact, in most jobs, it's what you learn on the job that counts.*

▶ You're belittling a problem that is quite real. A study of thousands of workers in the largest corporations found that the majority of whites thought minorities got their jobs because of their race, not their skills.[133]

◀ *That's a problem for the* white *workers. Sure, some minority members or women suffer from fear that somebody thinks they didn't deserve their job, but I'll bet the more typical feeling is: "It's about time!" When I get asked to lecture and I learn that I'm in special demand because I'm a woman, I'm not insulted. I'm delighted to be able to help right the balance for women.*
And if self-doubt from insecurity about why you got hired is such a problem, why haven't white males been plagued by

similar self-doubts, fearing that it's their gender, color, or the "old-boy network," not their real abilities, that got them the job?

Most important, any stigma felt by particular individuals has to be weighed against the continuing, broader stigma attached to all minorities as long they remain so excluded from the more prestigious positions. [134]

▶ There you go again, so willing to sacrifice the individual to some nebulous social goal, although now you are sacrificing the minority individual.

◀ *Not at all, for without affirmative action, the individual "stigmatized" by it might never have gotten the job in the first place. Plus, your charge ignores the existing sacrifice of so many due to blocked opportunities that affirmative action could open.*

▶ I am not just referring to the effects of affirmative action on minority individuals. I'm also talking about an overall demoralization of entire minority communities. If you grow up expecting special compensation, you won't try as hard as you otherwise might. Skills will not be developed by a group that is told by programs such as affirmative action that skills are not the real issue.[135]

◀ *That's exactly what discrimination, not affirmative action, has done! It's told minorities that their skills and hard work didn't matter. It has suffocated ambition. Affirmative action holds out the opposite message: Doors* will *be open if you work hard.* [136]

▶ But minorities develop an underlying anxiety that they don't merit positions and honors. To justify affirmative action, especially in admission to elite institutions, it's necessary to argue that almost no blacks would make it to such heights without special compensation—what does that do to the self-respect of blacks? If achieving equality really means gaining respect, then a policy maintaining any group in the position of supplicants to benevolent whites can hardly contribute to that goal.[137]

◀ *Self-respect comes from living up to one's full potential, which is what affirmative action allows more people to do. It doesn't undermine self-respect unless one believes our society to be a single-standard meritocracy in which affirmative action is the exception. As I've said, most Americans know that's not how things work in our society.*

▶ Theories often sound beautiful, but frequently they create more problems than they solve. Affirmative action is a classic example: it just doesn't work. After years of programs imposed by affirmative action, there's virtually no hard evidence that it's made any difference; that any social, economic, or psychological gains have been made by blacks due to this strategy. Minorities experienced job and income gains mainly during the Sixties and early Seventies, before affirmative action programs got underway.[138]

◀ *Where implemented vigorously, affirmative action has worked. In firms with government contracts, which are required to have affirmative action plans, minority and female employment has risen much faster than in noncontracting firms.* [139]

▶ But affirmative action has degenerated into a spoils system among competing racial and ethnic groups. We've ended up with a quota system, with numerical targets reducing people to numbers—in effect, guaranteeing not equal opportunities but equal *results.*

◀ *Of course affirmative action must entail some counting! Comparing the number of minority members or women selected with the size of the qualified pool is the only way to determine what a fair balance would look like. From there, one can set reasonable targets. These need not become rigid quotas; but without such benchmarks by which to measure success, affirmative action becomes a meaningless shibboleth.*

▶ But affirmative action also fails the "fairness" test because it ends up assisting the already-privileged members of minority groups and women, who might be getting into professional schools at higher rates. Affirmative action can do little for the ghetto kid who needs help the most. Typically, it's better-off minority members who end up getting special consideration at the expense of poor whites who are actually more disadvantaged but happen to be the wrong color.[140]

◄ *Not necessarily. Significant numbers of minority students admitted to medical schools in the Seventies came from under-privileged backgrounds.* [141] *And advances even for the more privileged minority members develop role models benefiting others in the group. But your basic objection stands; that's why the best approach to affirmative action is to target job training and educational opportunity to all those who have been economically disadvantaged, with additional consideration for racial minorities and women within this group.*

► But you're still ignoring the enormous costs involved in implementing affirmative action. Besides the suffering caused by the backlash and the dilution of standards to accommodate the less qualified, there's the real dollar cost of the red tape involved in government enforcement of affirmative action. The five hundred largest government contractors estimate that they spend $1 billion annually to comply with federal affirmative action requirements.[142] So how can you argue that the whole society gains by affirmative action? We all have to pay that billion dollars yearly in higher prices.

◄ *Affirmative action is not problem-free; its implementation can no doubt be simplified. I want to stress only that it is essential to heal our society, it has worked, and it is now threatened. The Justice Department's attack on affirmative action, along with cutbacks in college financial aid, is closing doors, especially for minority young people, and threatening to undo the positive changes we've seen.*

The [affirmative action] programs I once enjoyed that allowed me to get where I am—are extinct.
—Gail L. Brooks, radio station executive, former welfare recipient[143]

► All your talk about contributing to society's well-being masks the fact that, in reality, we are only individual people. Using one person to benefit someone else does not respect him or her; that person receives no overbalancing good from his sacrifice. So it can't be justified by any theory of justice that I can accept.[144]

In fact, your ready embrace of social engineering frightens me. Just look down the road. Once you condone distinctions based upon people's color or gender, the sanctity of constitutional protection against discrimination is lost. The practice could easily be turned around to discriminate against any group for virtually any reason.

◄ *Your objection would apply if affirmative action were disconnected from its underlying positive purpose—to heal and strengthen the whole society. Many policies or practices can be used for either good or evil. (The government's keeping Social Security records on every citizen is an example.) But we use them as long as we have confidence that in a democratic society we can prevent abuse.*

► But you've evaded the central problem: Once you condone different treatment for different individuals, the whole idea of equality before the law goes out the window.

◄ *Equality before the law is our* mutual *goal. To introduce affirmative action is to spread opportunity in order that equal treatment before the law—which we do not have now—can be realized, to move us toward a society in which affirmative action will be unnecessary.*

► But once you introduce such a principle, there's no turning back. Racial preference programs will not self-destruct! Just like other government-benefit programs, they develop their own constituencies that will make sure they're extended.[146]

◄ *To continue, affirmative action will depend on support from more than the minority "constituencies" who benefit directly. It can't continue without the active cooperation of the majority population, too. And why should they support it once racial and gender disparities are behind us? It wouldn't make sense.*

But don't get me wrong. Affirmative action can have only limited effect until we're committed to protecting the economic rights of every American. Affirmative action can succeed in healing our society only as the doors of opportunity, now blocked by poverty, open for all Americans.

. . . discrimination on the basis of race is illegal, immoral, unconstitutional, inherently wrong, and destructive of a democratic society. Now this is to be unlearned and we are told that this is not a matter of fundamental principle but only a matter of whose ox is gored.
—Alexander Bickel,
The Morality of Consent[145]

Fairness, Equality, and Freedom ★

▶ What bothers most me is that you won't admit that talk about fairness is actually a guise for a program of forced equality.

◀ *You're wrong! I've been arguing that much inequality today is forced upon people. But let's take fairness and equality separately—they're distinct, albeit overlapping, concerns. Fairness is a primary value in and of itself. And it is also functional: no society can work well if people don't believe the rules are fair.*

▶ Of course, but fairness necessitates inequalities, I think that most Americans would agree. People are so different in their talents and ambition that differing rewards are most appropriate and fair.

◀ *I agree, to a point, as I've said. But when reward becomes detached from effort and sacrifice and when the differences in reward become extreme, we all suffer. The roughly five hundred individuals and families, which* Forbes *magazine identifies as the wealthiest, own assets sufficient to give them control of 40 percent of all private business capital. They're not accumulating wealth just for the pleasure of consumption—for billionaires to consume their own wealth they'd have to spend over half a million dollars a day!—but for the power it confers.*[146] *Such great power in so few hands belies a free society.*

From the earliest days of our nation, it was also understood that when differences in wealth are so great that people in different classes no longer come into contact, they have no common experience from which to arrive at a common agenda. So democracy itself is in jeopardy. This point is so important, I'd like to take it up in more depth. [See Part V.]

▶ You are rewriting history. The push toward egalitarianism that your views reflect was invented by intellectuals of the twentieth

Future consumption is not the motive that leads to large accumulations of wealth. . . . Great wealth is accumulated to acquire economic power. Wealth makes you an economic mover and shaker. . . . It allows you to influence the political process . . . and remold society in accordance with your views.

—Lester Thurow,
Massachusetts Institute of
Technology[147]

century because of their own feelings of emptiness. It is really elitism in disguise. Intellectuals cannot tolerate the democratic society with its common tastes, its lack of overriding purpose. Filled with anxiety, they call for greater equality.[148] It is the working people who have been most resistant to this kind of self-serving egalitarianism.

◄ *The desire for greater equality—a twentieth-century idea? Throughout human history, people have devised means to avoid or reduce extreme inequalities. Three thousand years ago in China, so concerned were people about concentration of land holdings that each young man was given a certain amount of land, which upon his death was returned to a public body for redistribution. The founders of our nation were repelled by the extreme inequalities in Europe and strongly desired to avoid them here.*

But yes, I agree. The debate about equality has never been central in America. We've bathed ourselves in a mystique of equality that never really existed. Even in the colonial era, nearly one-third of even the white population had no property, and in some southern states the vast majority of people were without land.[149] A belief in "mobility"—that anyone who really tried could make it—has substituted for the goal of equality.

But if many Americans have never identified with the idea of equality, in large part because it has been wrongly interpreted to mean forced leveling, there is an unwavering commitment to fairness. Almost two-thirds of Americans perceive the current distribution of wealth as unfair and want it to be more equally distributed.[150]

► In opinion polls people say all sorts of things that have little relevance to what they would actually do if they had to face up to the real-life consequences. Your ideas can sound appealing to those who don't understand their implications because you avoid the hard question—*how?* How do you plan to go about making people give up their incomes? There is no way to do it without confiscation, which is another word for theft.

It is . . . one of government's most important tasks to prevent extreme inequality of wealth, not by taking treasures away from those who possess them, but by removing the

◄ *In large part the "how" isn't redistribution after the fact; it's making that kind of redistribution unnecessary. First, this means ending the redistribution now going on in the direction of the better off, all the public policies I talked about that favor wealth.*

▶ But your definition requires constant government intervention—that's why it is so dangerous. Mine does not.

◀ *Why do you hate only the interference of government and not the continuing interference of deprivation itself? Besides, maintaining your definition of freedom also requires continual government involvement, but to protect and enhance the interests of the better off.*

▶ You refuse to face the ethical problem in any "solution" that involves confiscating people's property.

◀ *And you forget what you yourself stressed earlier: new wealth is being continually generated. Our nation's real wealth has almost quadrupled since World War II. Imagine how different our society would look today if, say, half of the new wealth had gone to the poorest fifth of our people and communities. So, in large part, the challenge isn't how to take away wealth from anyone, but how to make sure new wealth goes to ever greater numbers of Americans. Achieving this doesn't necessarily require more government intervention, as I explained earlier; it requires a change in the rules: much fairer taxes, a higher minimum wage, policies to encourage unions and worker ownership, tax and credit incentives for creating jobs and affordable housing. It also requires a shift in how government spends: away, for example, from a wasteful approach to military spending driven by the Pentagon and a noncompetitive arms industry and toward education and other programs opening doors for young people.*[153] *And it requires a change in how decisions get made: more decision-making power in economic life for workers and communities. [See Part V.]*

As such changes enable people better to protect their own interests, they need government protection less. Remember that minimum wage laws, rent control, subsidized housing, and so on, are in part to offset the effects of huge income disparities that impair the market's function. As differences moderate, less correction by government would be needed in the market itself.

means of accumulating them from everyone; nor by building poorhouses, but by protecting citizens from becoming poor.
—Jean-Jacques Rousseau, *Discourse on Political Economy*, 1755[151]

Every form of social justice . . . tends toward confiscation, and confiscation, when practiced on a large scale, undermines moral standards, and in so far, substitutes for real justice the law of cunning and the law of force.

—Irving Babbitt[152]

▶ You're confusing cause and effect. It's the government's interference in the market that has caused the problems in the first place. But let's come back to this [*See Part IV*]; I want to get down to a more basic difference between us.

Who Decides What's Fair? ★

The fact is that government cannot produce equality, and any serious effort to do so can destroy liberty and other social goods.

—Jeane J. Kirkpatrick,
*Dictatorships and Double
Standards* [154]

▶ All attempts to deny our natural inequalities end up in oppressive rules to try to mask our inevitable differences. I would go even further. I don't think an economy—a system for producing and transferring goods and property among people—should have a pattern with an overarching aim, like fairness, in any case.

What matters is whether the economy is constituted of individual aims that are themselves reasonable and make sense to most people. And that's for the most part what we have in a capitalist system of exchange. Goods are transferred according to how much individual people perceive they will benefit from them, as I said earlier. Capitalist society works because people accept this logic, even though it may not result in an ideally just pattern of distribution. We accept it because its principle of exchange makes sense. [155]

◀ *But in a capitalist economy, goods aren't distributed according to perceived benefit. The benefit a poor family living in a two-room slum apartment would derive from a house in the suburbs is unarguably greater than the benefit a wealthy family could derive from a second or third home. But guess who gets the house? The principle of exchange is not who can most benefit—or even who perceives themselves benefiting most— but who can best translate their need or desire into purchasing power.*

This isn't arbitrary, as you say—there is a principle at work: money talks. But does the fact that a principle guides a system justify it?

▶ My point is that the market distribution of rewards is less unfair than any alternative. Trying to make it fair ends up causing worse problems, like your notion of using the government to take from some to give to others.

Your schemes mean someone has to decide what's fair. But an individual can make his or her best contribution to society by sticking with the duties of a special institutional role. It's not the businessperson's job to decide what's fair but what will make a profit; it's not a judge's role to decide what's fair but what's passed down in the law. Outcomes must be decided by institutional processes like the market and the law; otherwise, individuals, with all our prejudices and vested interests, dictate for others what is right and wrong.[157] *[See Part III.]*

Your primary value obviously is equality, while mine is freedom.[158] Perfect justice of the type you are seeking must mean perfect tyranny, because the only way it could be achieved is by the extension of political power into every arena of life to make sure that "social justice" had been realized.[159]

◀ *No, my primary value is also freedom. But it cannot be realized without fairness, and fairness entails the mitigation of extreme inequality. Fairness does not conflict with freedom, it is the very basis of it—freedom understood as the freedom to develop fully our unique human potential.*

▶ Your last statement is most revealing. Once you define freedom for something—it's purpose or pattern—you can't possibly realize it without imposing it. Every conception of "social justice" has to mean someone's conception, some particular version that must be imposed on others.

There's no way to achieve it without redistribution entailing unconscionable interference in people's lives. By its very nature, freedom can't be freedom for something predetermined by someone else.[161]

◀ *Your definition of freedom also carries within it a predetermining purpose or pattern, only you are blind to it because it represents rules you unquestioningly accept; rules, for example, giving owners of economic assets great decision-making freedom but little such freedom to those owning few or no assets.*

. . . the concept of "social justice" is necessarily empty and meaningless. . . . any particular conception of "social justice" could be realized only in such a centrally directed system. . . . [T]he impersonal process of the market . . . can be neither just nor unjust, because the results are not intended or foreseen . . .
—Friedrich A. Hayek, " 'Social' or Distributive Justice"[156]

The passion for equality . . . is always dangerous to liberty because it is a passion for power: the power to impose one's ideal of justice-as-equality on other people.
—Irving Kristol, "Thoughts on Equality and Egalitarianism"[160]

▶ But the market is less dangerous than government butting in with its value judgments as to who should get what.

◀ *But the market does butt into our lives if it prices life's necessities out of reach. It also operates on rules made by human beings. In that sense, it is no different from rules narrowing extremes in income. They all result from human choices.*

▶ Of course, but the point is, *whose* choices? Those of a few or all of us? Over time, the voluntary choices of people are going to overturn any egalitarian distribution pattern that people like you try to impose through government.[162] So "social justice" (or fairness, as you like to call it here) must mean the government is constantly choosing, interfering to prevent certain exchanges or to redistribute goods—in any case, overriding voluntary choices of people in the market. That's why I reject the very concept of "social justice," which is what you are really talking about.

◀ *But is it the voluntary actions of people that lead to increasing concentration of wealth? Or is it the dearth of voluntary choices? Earlier I argued that when good jobs are scarce and unemployment is high, a person may take a job in a nonunion plant at the minimum wage. "Voluntary" implies choice, but for this person there's little choice.*

My goal is to increase our voluntary choices. The more society can reduce the power differential among citizens, the more choices will be real choices, that is, voluntary—and to the advantage of all parties.

▶ Moving in your direction requires individuals making decisions about what others need and, ultimately, to authoritarianism. This, I cannot accept.

The law and government can have no views on how well off particular people should be. Of course, this produces economic inequality, but the only alternative is a subjective approach—considering each individual's circumstance—and then society is no longer subject to the rule of law but to the fallibility of human beings. That's when you've opened the door to oppression. So, for all its deficiencies, we must stick with an economy governed not by people but by the market alone and the law protecting people's property.

. . . [N]o end-state principle or distributional patterned principle of justice can be continuously realized without continuous interference with people's lives.

—Robert Nozick,
Anarchy, State, and Utopia[163]

By equality, we should understand, not that the degrees of power and riches are to be absolutely identical for everybody; but that . . . in respect of riches, no citizen shall ever be wealthy enough to buy another, and none poor enough to be forced to sell himself.

—Jean Jacques Rousseau,
The Social Contract, 1762[164]

. . . any policy aiming directly at a substantive ideal of distributive justice must lead to the destruction of the Rule of Law.

—Friedrich A. Hayek,
The Road to Serfdom, 1944[165]

Summing Up the Dialogue ★

IS REDISTRIBUTION EVER FAIR?

▶ No,
   . . . the present distribution of property reflects legitimate exchange and inheritance.
   . . . it means taking what some have earned and giving it to others who have not earned it.

◀ *Yes,*
   . . . it goes on continuously in every society; government's job is to ensure that it serves the good of the whole society.

IS THE MARKET'S DISTRIBUTION FAIR?

▶ No, but that's the wrong question; the market rewards people according to how they serve other's perceived needs, so it works to the benefit of all.

◀ *No, but it's the only practical device for distributing goods and services. Since it is simply a device, however, it can and must be guided so as to prevent extremes in reward that undermine a healthy society.*

SHOULD THE MARKET DETERMINE REWARDS?

▶ Yes, because any direct attempt to determine outcomes leads to authoritarianism.

◀ *Within limits, yes, but if it is allowed to generate extremes, it undermines our values, even life itself.*

IS THERE A TRADE-OFF BETWEEN FAIRNESS AND PRODUCTIVITY?

▶ If by fairness you mean preventing people from rising as high as they can go, then yes. It's the possibility of unlimited reward that is the greatest motivator to productivity.

◀ *No, productivity in fact hinges upon fairness, because hope of a fair return for one's effort is the greatest motivator.*

WHAT ACCOUNTS FOR INEQUALITY?

▶ The natural differences among individuals, including not only their talents but the different value they assign to making a lot of money.

◀ *Innate differences and tastes can explain moderate differences in wealth but not the extremes we have today; they result from economic rules that deny economic rights, reward wealth over work, and allow wealth to accumulate over generations.*

WHAT IS EQUAL OPPORTUNITY?

▶ Allowing each individual to achieve whatever her or his talents and determination permit, without legal impediment.

◀ *Allowing each person to fulfill her or his innate potential and to participate in a community life in which the development of each person's talents benefits all others.*

HOW DOES SOCIETY ENSURE EQUALITY OF OPPORTUNITY?

▶ By ensuring that the same rules apply to all, and that the doors are open to anyone who makes the effort. Anything more than this is actually an attempt to secure equality of outcome—a type of social engineering.

◀ *Three ingredients are essential to make equal opportunity real: a floor of economic security under all citizens, grounded in the right to earning a living; a ceiling on accumulation of income-producing property; and affirmative action for groups hurt by discrimination.*

IS THERE A TRADE-OFF BETWEEN FREEDOM AND FAIRNESS?

▶ Yes, because "fairness" implies a judgment about who should get what, decided by some higher authority. Enforcing that judgment requires continuous interference in the voluntary transactions of consenting adults. This is the very opposite of freedom.

◀ *No, because fairness is the very bedrock of a free society. Without fairness protected by government—the connection of reward to effort and opportunity for every citizen—people are not free to develop their innate gifts.*

PART THREE

Freedom and the Market's Efficiency

The Market, Competition, and Concentrated Power ★

▶ It's been obvious in talking about what's fair—or not fair—in our society, we've had to touch on what are *the* most essential ingredients of a free society: the market and private property. Nowhere in the world do we find freedom without these two economic institutions.

Take the market. Perhaps its greatest service to freedom is that it prevents the concentration of power, and thus greatly limits people's capacity to hurt each other.

◀ *With just one hundred U.S. corporations—a tiny fraction of 1 percent of all firms—controlling over 60 percent of industrial assets, power in our market economy seems pretty concentrated to me!*[1] *A handful of firms in loose monopolies—what economists call oligopolies—now control more than half the markets of all manufacturing industries.*[2]

▶ But there's still competition, actually more today than in the past. A century ago, with poor transportation networks, local monopolies were quite common. During the twentieth century, firms have grown bigger, it's true, but so have their markets, canceling out monopolistic effects.[3] Monopoly is rare nowadays except for the biggest one of all—the government.

Industry concentration is no evil. Evidence suggests that as concentration increases, so does productivity, while prices fall.[4] Concentration of power implies the ability to dictate terms, to defy competition, but the fact that some of the biggest firms have recently been in trouble and even gone belly up, means that they're hardly free of competitive pressure. Tough new competition is now coming from abroad. This, combined with government deregulation, means that our economy is probably more competitive now than at any time during the modern era.[5]

> [A monopoly] will compete against the threat of future rivals. Its monopoly can be maintained only as long as the price is kept low enough to exclude others. In this sense, monopolies are good. The more dynamic and inventive an economy, the more monopolies it will engender.
>
> —George Gilder,
> *Wealth and Poverty*[6]

. . . [because] advertising intrenches monopoly by setting up a financial barrier to the competition of new and small firms . . . an appropriate remodeling of the system with respect to merchandising would do more than free wasted resources . . . it might remove one of the main factors working to destroy real competition in industry.

—Henry Simons, founder, Chicago School of Economics, 1948[9]

. . . if you have absolutely unrestrained competition in the marketplace, pretty soon you'll wind up with no competition at all, and I think we may all be getting carried away again, like we did in the robber baron days.

—Lee Iacocca, Chrysler Corporation, 1987[13]

The rare company which is able to retain its share of the market year after year and decade after decade does so by means of productive efficiency—and deserves praise, not condemnation.

—Alan Greenspan, Chairman of the Federal Reserve Board[15]

◄ *What you call competition I call terminal competition—it terminates in the oligopolies now dominating our economy.*[7]

They can keep prices up by unspoken agreement not to underprice each other. They can block out competition by expensive advertising—how many can afford the $20 million or so that Proctor & Gamble can spend to launch a new product? And they can squeeze competitors off the store shelf by proliferating new products, furthering the myth of a diversified economy. Just five firms control 90 percent of the breakfast cereal market by selling us 108 brands of cereal![8]

► Industry concentration doesn't mean higher prices; as corporations grow, their costs per unit go down and they can lower prices.[10] And advertising doesn't block competitors entering a market. What to you is a negative—the proliferation of new products—is really a service big firms can best provide: increasing variety that consumers obviously appreciate or corporations wouldn't profit by their innovation.[11]

◄ *My point is that the market itself doesn't guarantee dispersed economic power. After a point, big simply begets big, beyond any limit justified by efficiency.*[12]

► In a free economy, if a corporation can hold 40 or 50 percent of a market, that's quite a feat! It takes unfailing business sense, relentless effort, and continuous improvement in the goods or services for sale.[14] It's no proof of undue power or a threat to competition. Remember, it only takes two firms to make a competitive market. Your suspicions about monopoly would lead to punishing success!

When a company does hold on to a market unfairly, it's usually because of government intervention. You blame the power of advertising that big-budget companies have, but the necessary precondition of monopoly is what economists call "closed entry"—the barring of competing producers—and only government can accomplish that. Government—its licensing, franchises, and other restrictive devices—is *the* source of monopoly power, not the market.[16]

◄ *You're saying that without government there would be no problem of undue corporate power in our society?*

► Precisely.

◄ *But even if your economics were on target, you again ignore power: the tremendous power big corporations exert over workers and the communities in which they operate. To workers, they can simply say: Accept the wages I offer, or I'll take my plants elsewhere. To a state, community, or whole nation they can say: Reduce my taxes, or I'll locate elsewhere. To the government they can say: Bail me out, or I'll go bankrupt, upsetting your whole economy. So workers accept wage concessions, communities offer all sorts of inducements, and Washington offers billions in bailouts to a Continental Illinois or a Chrysler. The power to hold hostage is no insignificant power!*

► The problem you've put your finger on isn't too much corporate power; it's an inappropriate conception of government's role. If we didn't allow economic intervention by government—bailing out companies, for example—the problem wouldn't exist in the first place. And as far as corporate power vis-à-vis workers, the flexibility it gives corporations is absolutely essential to keep U.S. firms alive in today's competitive global economy.

But let's get back to the market itself. It serves freedom in more ways than by just preventing the concentration of power.

> *. . . the modern corporation wields economic and social power of the highest consequence for the condition of our polity. Let us resist this conclusion, or belabor it, no further. Let us accept it as our first premise.*
> —Judge Abram Chayes, "The Modern Corporation and the Rule of Law," 1959[17]

The Market as Individual Choice ★

The market is also inherently more democratic than any type of government allocation of resources. The very premise of the market system is that no one is capable of knowing what will make others happy. Individuals can decide what they want according to their own tastes. In the market, we all get to vote; no one is telling us what our tastes should be.[18]

Of course, many intellectuals don't like it because they don't approve of popular tastes—snowmobiles, video parlors, prime-

> [The market is] a system of proportional representation. Each man can vote, as it were,

time soap operas—how tacky! But such snobbery is *their* problem, not the market's.

So the greatest thing about the market economy is that no one stands over people deciding how much each person should get. As soon as you get government involved in deciding how to distribute goods, the structure of society becomes authoritarian.

◄ *The market has many virtues, but it is hardly "democratic": the more money you have, the more votes you get. What's so democratic about that? The market is a device and only that. Yes, it can serve freedom, but it needs help.*

Let me explain by telling you about a debate I had with Milton Friedman, author of Free to Choose *and other books extolling the free market's virtues. The market, he says, gives people what they want instead of what someone else thinks they want. It serves freedom by responding to human preferences.* [21]

► That's unarguable. And it's why today so many nations are embracing Friedman's basic theories.

◄ *But does the market necessarily respond to our preferences? I told Dr. Friedman that in studying world hunger most of my life I had noticed a salient fact: while a universal human preference is to eat, at least half a billion people living in market economies are going hungry! The market isn't responding to their preferences.* [22]

So I made a simple observation. Because the market can only respond to money, it can respond to people's preferences only on one condition: that purchasing power is widely dispersed. Where purchasing power is narrowly held or very lopsided, what happens? Here in the U.S., hunger pushes up the rate of infant deaths, while demand for caviar at Bloomingdale's was up 40 percent last Christmas.

In other words, if it is for enhancing freedom by responding to our preferences that we prize the market, then as citizens we must establish the conditions necessary for it to do its job. We must ensure the widest dispersion of purchasing power so that the market can reflect people's preferences.

► What you fail to grasp is that the market itself best promotes such wide dispersion of purchasing power because it stimulates growth in which all can prosper.

◄ *I'm puzzled. You reject so adamantly the authority of government in the economy, and then turn around and take the authority of the market as absolute. In its impact, it can be as coercive as the harshest state edict. The market is always forcing some businesses to fail, some workers to become unemployed, and some tenants to be forcibly evicted. The market—an abstraction—can't willfully do anything. But its effect can be as devastating if the market prices food out of people's reach, if it forces the sale of a homestead that has been in a family for generations.*

. . . the price system is, and ought to be, a method of coercion.

—Paul A. Samuelson, "Modern Economic Realities and Individualism," 1971[23]

The Market and Personal Prejudice ★

▶ But the difference is enormous! The authority of government is really that of a self-serving minority. The market, however, is an impersonal mechanism that can't hold grudges, prejudices, or put people in jail.

◄ *But it can put people on the street. And how can anyone who believes in human freedom take as absolute any principle other than the protection of life itself?*

▶ I don't take the market as absolute. But to the extent that market mechanisms are set aside, economic power is centralized in government, and this is the greatest threat to our well-being. Economic life guided by the marketplace allows no room for the petty prejudices of individuals.

When I buy something I have no way of knowing the race or creed of the person who made it.

No one who buys bread knows whether the wheat from which it is made was grown by a Communist or a Republican . . . a Fascist, or . . . a Negro or a white. . . . an impersonal market separates economic activities from political views and protects men from being discriminated against . . .

—Milton Friedman, *Capitalism and Freedom*[24]

◄ *You might be right if we ordered everything out of the catalog! But much of "the market" is exchange between* people. *It can't protect us against their biases. Blues artists Sonny Terry and Brownie McGee captured this obvious truth in their lyrics in "On the Road Again": "I don't sell no black gas here," says the gas station attendant.* [25] *Segregated housing; preferential prices for "preferred customers"; nepotism; women paid less than men for the same work—the market protects us from none of this.*

You fear government as the agent of prejudice, but in our society, citizens need to use government to protect against such prejudice. Ultimately, federal troops were needed to protect the right of blacks simply to sit at a lunch counter in the South. It's been in public, not private, employment that minorities have achieved the greatest progress. The civil service, precisely because it is publicly accountable, has had to uphold a high standard in eliminating bias. [26]

▶ But prejudice is a defect of people's character and a failing of our culture, not a shortcoming of the market.

◀ *Of course bias isn't the fault of the market. The market is simply no protection against it.*

▶ But the more that market values hold sway, the less prejudice you'll see. [27] The gas attendant would of course sell to Sonny and Brownie, because he'd be interested in making the sale!

The market's very impersonality makes it liberating.

◀ *But does it also liberate us from responsibility? Let's say I make cigarettes and promote them through the market to people who die of cancer; or I make infant formula and distribute it through the market in poor countries without safe water, where babies die if their mothers shift from breastfeeding to formula; or I make anti-personnel weapons, sell them to arms merchants abroad, and they end up used in massacres of civilians. Am I responsible? No, I can say to myself, I just responded to a market.*

▶ You *aren't* responsible. Relax! The person who is responsible is the one who created the market by demanding cigarettes, baby formula, or anti-personnel weapons in the first place.

But you still have not fully grasped the most significant value of the market mechanism: that no one stands on high telling people what they should want or what's too dangerous or too immoral. That's the real danger once you shift production and distribution decisions from the individual in the market to government planners. If you're outraged by individual prejudices, remember that in the market at least one prejudiced person can hurt relatively few people. Make that prejudiced person "economic czar," and you'll see much greater injustice.

The Market and Voluntary Choice ★

◄ *My purpose isn't to replace the market but to allow it to function better. But first we must see it for exactly what is, a useful tool—and one whose usefulness in providing real choice can easily be subverted.*

It's subverted to the extent that the number of corporations in any one product line is so reduced that they no longer compete in pricing or quality; they compete for store shelf-space by coming up with novel, eye-catching packages or slight variations in order to proclaim "All New!"

The market's usefulness in letting us make independent choices is subverted to the extent that information about products is limited to a few companies' products and to what they choose to tell us about them. That's what happens when advertising is concentrated: a handful of firms control virtually all TV advertising. And we all have to pay. Just in the costs of TV and radio ads alone, Americans pay $1,000 per family each year in higher prices. [28]

▶ There's an enormous difference between persuasion and coercion. In a market system, advertisers seek to persuade, of course, but consumers are left to choose.[29]

. . . that despised demon, advertising, is educating the middle and working classes into the tastes for goods and services thus far reserved for the upper class. "Higher" tastes are being diffused much more broadly than ever before.

—Robert Benne,
The Ethic of Democratic Capitalism[30]

Profits may be obtained either by producing what consumers want or by making consumers want what one is actually producing. The possibility of . . . manipulat[ing] demand is, perhaps, the greatest source of diseconomy under the existing system.

—Henry Simons,
founder, Chicago School of Economics, 1948[31]

Mass demand has been created almost entirely through the development of advertising . . . Advertising ministers to the spiritual side of trade. . . . It is a great power . . . part of the greater work of the regeneration and redemption of mankind.

—Calvin Coolidge,
1926[33]

◄ *Call it what you will, but advertising powerfully shapes our choices. In the Forties, few Americans were clamoring for cholesterol-ridden, grain-fed meat. Instead, when grain-feeding became profitable, advertisers convinced us that marbled meat was high-status. Did American drivers demand big, gas-guzzling, polluting, tail-finned cars in the Fifties? Or were they just a lot more profitable for automakers than compacts? And what farmer would have chosen to make his farm dependent on a host of chemical agents, some threatening his family's health, unless chemical-industry TV ads had been hitting him daily?*

And now that medical evidence on the effects of smoking is indisputable, how many nonaddicted people would choose to smoke without ads repeatedly associating smoking with sexy "lifestyles"? The latest rage among young men is chewing tobacco, as harmful as smoking—a deliberately created demand if there ever was one!

► No one is forcing people to buy any of the things you mentioned. I find your distrust of the consumer's intelligence downright insulting to people. If consumers buy things for psychic satisfaction instead of their practical usefulness, who are you to say they're not getting their money's worth? If advertising enables the purchaser of a cosmetic, for example, to believe she is more beautiful as a result of buying it, advertising sure seems like a good worth paying for to me![32]

◄ *And if the product shortens a person's life?*

► That's an individual's choice—only the individual should decide whether he or she wants to give up something that provides pleasure now on the mere chance of living longer. Some people might decide that a shorter, more pleasurable life is better than a longer, less pleasurable one.

Advertising is essential to the market system because it gives consumers information so that they can make their own choices. Sure it stimulates demand, but that is good for economic growth from which we all benefit.

◄ *But as long as access to television and other forms of costly advertising is itself merely a commodity sold to the highest bidder, consumers won't have the information necessary to make informed, unmanipulated choices among products.*

Imagine the incentive to invention and entrepreneurialism if newcomers in a field weren't deterred by knowing that big-name advertisers had the market sewn up.

And don't forget that the market power of the biggest corporations influences more than our consumer choices. Corporations now devote about a third of their (tax deductible!) advertising dollars, not to selling products but to buying ads to sway our views on public policy.[34]

▶ If we were to remove advertising from the market, we'd still have the same problem: if dollars don't decide, someone has to. That means an advertising authority deciding who can get access to the airways and newspapers.

◀ *Not at all. That's our present problem—only a handful of people making those decisions on the basis of their wealth.*

Why not limit any one firm's access to television so that more firms have a chance? How about a progressive tax on advertising expenditures once they exceed a certain percentage of a corporation's total budget?[35] *Why couldn't a certain portion of TV advertising time be set aside for new products from young companies—to break the monopoly power? In other words, we can imagine many possible rules for distributing advertising that would diminish rather than enhance the control of a minority—what you rightly fear.*

▶ But you've still missed the essence of what makes the market system democratic. It's that in the market choices are *voluntary.* Individuals decide themselves what jobs to take, what to buy or sell. The very fact that these millions of exchanges, all reflecting individual choices, take place daily in a market system demonstrates how the market enhances our freedom.

> . . . if an exchange between two parties is voluntary, it will not take place unless both believe they will benefit from it.
> —Milton and Rose Friedman,
> *Free to Choose*[36]

◀ *Because an exchange takes place in the market is no proof that it is voluntary. Even that I benefit does not mean that I go into an exchange voluntarily. If I'm without food to feed my kids, I would take a job at the minimum wage. Sure, I would benefit compared to letting my family go hungry, but it is not a voluntary choice, since the alternative—starving—is unthinkable.*

The only way that the market can actually reflect voluntary choices is for people to have economic security. Security is the basis of free choice, as I have said all along.

The Market: It Works! ★

▶ I don't want to repeat my argument that freedom doesn't guarantee us a certain number of choices. I'd like to make an even more obvious observation. Remember: "The proof of the pudding is in the eating." That old adage is the strongest argument in favor of the market system—it works![37] In any statistical ranking of nations by accumulated wealth or per capita income, those that have fostered capitalism always sit at the top.

It's the ongoing economic growth that a market economy generates which has made possible our unprecedented standard of living.

◀ *But what if growth in the GNP results from our spending more on medicine, lawsuits, weapons, burglar alarms, and bottled water? Growth sounds great, but it might really mean that we're more ill, in more conflict, more frightened, and more polluted!*

The capitalist achievement does not typically consist in providing more silk stockings for queens but in bringing them within the reach of factory girls in return for steadily decreasing amounts of effort.

—Joseph Schumpeter,
Capitalism, Socialism and Democracy[38]

▶ No measure of well-being is going to be perfect. But the GNP does measure the expansion of goods and services. If having choice is a big part of what it means to be free, as you just said, certainly the market/private property system has resulted in greater freedom of choice—a proliferation of goods, far beyond what our forebears could ever have dreamed possible.

And please don't misunderstand. I'm not saying that capitalism means freedom simply because it gives us twenty varieties of toothpaste to choose from.

The productivity that characterizes the market system liberates people on a much deeper level. It allows work hours to be progressively reduced and work made less grueling. As a result we have more free time to do with as we please.

◀ *"Less grueling, more liberating?" But what about the increasing number of people staring at video screens all day, timed to* meet hourly quotas, with every stroke at the keyboard, or every call taken, monitored by computers?

And if ever-greater efficiency drives our system, why do Americans report that they have eight hours less leisure time per week than in the Seventies?[40] And how come it takes two incomes to provide a middle-class living standard that one breadwinner could provide twenty years ago?

▶ I am talking about a general trend, obviously. The problems we face in today's economy are largely from international competition, much of it related to foreign governments' subsidies; such problems are certainly not the result of the market system itself. Capitalism has a built-in push for economic efficiency far greater than any system that tries to impose efficiency from the outside.[41] And its efficiency has been *proven.*

◀ *What I'm suggesting would stimulate efficient output, not undercut it. What, after all, stimulates production? In large part it's "demand"—customers with the income to buy. When income distribution is lopsided, demand suffers. A million dollars flowing to a wealthy person might buy one palatial home. As a result, wealth shifts from one rich family to another rich family. But that same sum earned instead by twenty-five families would buy washing machines, clothes, toys, sofas, TVs. Producing these thousands of items would contribute to many more jobs and multiply much more wealth throughout the economy.*

And there's an international parallel. You blame foreign competition for our problems? Sluggish international demand hurting our economy reflects an extreme version of our domestic problem: the majority of people in so much of the world are too poor to be customers for our exports and are forced to bid down our wages.

▶ But you have been talking about curtailing the market's free reign and now you're extolling its valuable function. You can't have it both ways! You can't attack the market and try to tamper with it on the one hand, then turn around and praise it, claiming to use its virtues.

◀ *That is precisely what we can and must do! We can "tame" the market. We can allow it to do what it does best, while*

As production becomes increasingly complex, working people actually become less and less skilled. . . .
Lower-level work becomes increasingly that of feeding information into computers and then doing tasks as prescribed by the computers.
. . . . Many workers come away from work believing that they are not capable . . .
because their work gives them no opportunity to . . . develop their abilities . . .

—Michael Lerner,
Surplus Powerlessness[39]

guiding it where necessary and substituting different distribu-
tion principles when the market is harmful. In other words, as
citizens we set the moral context in which the market func-
tions.

In distributing goods, the market is tops; although, as I've
said, if it is to reflect people's needs, widely dispersed buying
power and widely accessible product information are both es-
sential. But in distributing survival necessities, the market can
be downright dangerous—as well as wasteful.

Consider the provision of health care. Provided as a matter of
right through public funding and oversight, efficiency goes up
and costs go down. Ours is the only Western industrial country
without a national health plan and we spend the highest per-
centage of gross domestic product on health care. [42]

▶ But if government gets involved, competition is killed and
quality suffers. All my friends in London complain no end about
the long queues and inferior care they have to put up with in
their national health system. And many health professionals
there are now trying to introduce more market features into
health delivery.

◀ *But remember—you said it: The proof of the pudding is in the*
eating! Countries with national health plans typically have
lower infant death rates and longer life expectancy than we
have here. [43]

Making health care a right doesn't have to kill competition.
Why not a government-protected right to health care with con-
tracts awarded to health providers for certain services based on
quality of care, efficiency, and effective community oversight?
The principle of a government-protected right combined with
delivery by competing local providers incorporates the market's
advantages, but it doesn't abdicate public responsibility. In-
stead of just government-run day care, why couldn't day care
co-ops get government backing?

▶ Your proposals are light-years from what Americans want or
are willing to pay for. Most Americans understand that anything
that takes responsibility from the individual and puts it onto
government means inefficiency and waste. Not to mention the
erosion of individual integrity when we let others do for us what
we know we should really do for ourselves. Why should child

care be a government responsibility? If both parents choose to work, it's their responsibility to make sure their children are cared for well.

◄ *Most Americans don't agree. In fact, when it comes to health care, most feel so strongly that the vast majority supports a constitutional amendment to make it a right.*[44]

► That's not surprising, but people don't realize that you can't allow government control in one sector of the economy and keep it out of others. You risk the gradual erosion of confidence in the market altogether.

◄ *Because a society chooses not to distribute health care according to the market, it doesn't follow that it will next remove cars and stereos! It's not difficult to perceive that there are classes of needs essential to survival that are unconscionable to meet by distribution according to income.*

Efficiency, Size, and Profits ★

► The danger is too great. Once you introduce the notion of nonmarket distribution, you open the door to government interference in business, which will undermine the confidence of businesspeople and decrease efficiency.

In fact, you seem ready to block mergers and break up big companies, directly undermining efficiencies of large scale, particularly important in light of today's global competition.

◄ *Today's largest corporations are hardly paragons of efficiency, any way you measure it—by operating efficiency, innovation rates, or response to a community's needs. Above a modest size, resources devoted to R&D decline as corporations grow.*[45] *Subsidiaries that have been sold back to their former*

Few of our gigantic corporations can be defended

managers and freed from their conglomerate parents have shown marked efficiency gains. [46]

on the ground that their present size is necessary . . . their existence is to be explained in terms of opportunities for promoter profits, personal ambitions of industrial and financial "Napoleons," and the advantages of monopoly power.
—Henry Simons, founder, Chicago School of Economics, 1948[47]

► What you are saying makes no sense at all. A corporation would not grow, mergers would not occur, unless there were competitive advantages in doing so.

◄ *Corporations do seek advantages by mergers, but advantages not necessarily related to improving productivity.* [48] *Buying up another company is a lot easier than building a market from scratch. IRS rules also make mergers attractive: corporations can deduct the multimillion-dollar expenses of takeover battles as well as the interest on the debt they incur. The latest twist, so-called junk bond financing, allows corporate raiders to borrow the entire amount needed before even beginning a raid. In the "merger mania" of the Eighties, corporate managers have also responded to pressure from money managers for the short-term profits that mergers can bring.*

. . . conglomerate mergers make the market more competitive. They so do primarily by improving efficiency in the use of our capital and labor. . . . Surges in merger activity are manifestations . . . of vigorous competition.
—Professor Yale Brozen, University of Chicago[49]

► Actually, a high rate of merger activity suggests intense competition and is thus a healthy sign. As long as there is competition, and certainly there is now with so much competition coming from abroad, the discipline of the market will force enterprises to be efficient through cost savings—expanding our consumer choices with new and better products.

◄ *It's not efficiency but profits that determine business survival.*

► But efficiency is what turns a profit.

◄ *Not necessarily. An employer can divide a complex job into a lot of mindless ones, then replace skilled workers with unskilled workers, who come cheaper. Overall more hours of work go into the job—which I'd call inefficient. But the employer still profits.* [50]

► With lower labor costs, consumer prices could be lower; and even in your example, workers would gain—after all, more could be employed.

◄ Consumers gain only if the employer passes the savings on to them. And the logic of such "cost savings" leads to poorer workers—hardly a strategy for prosperity!

Most important, the goal of profit-making doesn't necessarily spur efficiency, because the accountability of major corporations is so weak—management is accountable only to itself and the biggest shareholders. So businesses discover ways to profit by evading the market's discipline. And the bigger they are, the better they get at it.

► What are you talking about? U.S. corporations have never been hit by such competitive pressure.

◄ And how have they met it? In recent decades, many have flourished by abandoning industrial investment in favor of expansion by merger, nothing contributing to "efficiency." In fact, most mergers have led to declining economic performance.[51]

► Mergers, even so-called hostile takeovers, contribute to a healthy economy in part by keeping management on its toes. Corporation acquisitions often add new capital and new management talent, resulting in a bigger, healthier enterprise.[52]

◄ Corporations also do well living off noncompetitive government contracts[53]—only about a tenth of government defense contracts are competitively bid.[54] And corporations thrive by legal tax evasion: at least forty-four of the nation's top corporations pay no taxes and enjoy millions in tax rebates.[55]

► You're blaming corporations? Noncompetitive bidding is the government's inefficient way of doing business. And corporate taxes are made to be avoided—they are counterproductive to begin with. Shareholders pay taxes on dividends, so making corporations pay is unfair double-taxation.

◄ Corporations can also profit by pushing their costs off onto the community. It's not hard to profit if a corporation can simply dump its toxic waste instead of spending the money to dispose of it safely. The chemical industry economizes by emitting a third of its wastes uncontrolled into the environment—over eighty million metric tons a year.[56] And automakers *saving themselves a bundle by reducing the resiliency of car bumpers, for example, while the costs—billions in repair bills— are foisted on consumers.* [57]

Within concentrated industries, corporations can most easily profit by passing along costs to consumers, instead of improving efficiency. The Federal Reserve's past chair, Arthur Burns, complained that he couldn't bring inflation under control in the late Seventies because in concentrated industries—transportation equipment, metals, machinery, and the like—prices were up four to five times as much as in the more competitive industries. [58]

So efficiency and profit-taking aren't necessarily linked. If the discipline of the market is to work, we must make corporations accountable to the community's interests and to the national interest.

Regulation and the Market ★

▶ "Accountability" is only your code word for government planning.

. . . as the United States draws off its limited engineering resources into the defense sector . . . [it] is in danger of ending the twentieth century as the leading producer of ICBMs [missiles] and soybeans, while the Japanese monopolize the production of everything in between.
—Chalmers Johnson [60]

◀ *No, but what you don't see is that planning is happening every day. We can't escape it; the only question is who is doing it. To further military and space projects, the Pentagon and NASA supply half of all research and development funds used by U.S. industry.* [59] *That's hardly a supply-and-demand model at work. That's government planning, diverting away from our civilian economy resources that are so desperately needed.*

And corporations plan their own aggrandizement. In the Forties, GM bought up electric streetcar companies, scrapped the streetcars, and resold them to companies who signed on to buy only GM buses. Soon the efficient trolley car had virtually disappeared, and in its place the polluting bus. That's planning, too. [61] *So the issue isn't whether we plan; it's whether we devise mechanisms for involving citizens and communities, making more broadly accountable what's going on all the time.*

▶ There's your favorite code word again! What you really mean by planning is the nightmare of a government-controlled economy in the service of private interests. That process began to evolve here in the United States in the nineteenth century with government regulation of the marketplace. The Interstate Commerce Commission, launched in 1887 to protect farmers and manufacturers from unfair rates, soon became the captive of railroad interests. In this century it succumbed to the growing power of the trucking industry. In fact, regulation is a prime example of how government ends up serving private interests.

In a competitive economy, without government interference, the problems that have led us down the hazardous path of increasing market regulation would not occur in the first place.

Recent developments have proven once and for all, let's hope, the anticompetitive nature of market regulation. When Washington finally cut back the regulation of markets in the late Seventies and early Eighties, competition got a big boost. Productivity went up, prices went down. In fact, we can thank deregulation of oil and transportation for much of the overall decline in inflation. Since the late Seventies, airline fares have dropped 13 percent in inflation-adjusted dollars.

◀ *Your suspicion that government regulation can serve vested interests is surely justified; but your rigid antigovernment stance leads you to throw the baby out with the bathwater! Because government economic regulation has often stifled competition does not mean that throwing it out is going to solve the problem.*

After deregulation, industries quickly started congealing. Since the late Seventies, in the airlines alone there have been twenty mergers. In airlines and railroads, six companies now control virtually the entire market of each industry. [63] *I depend a lot on the Minneapolis/St. Paul airport, and now one airline controls almost three-fourths of the flights there. If consumer choice is essential to competition to keep prices low, frankly I'm worried!*

Deregulating the structure of an industry can't work over the long haul to increase competition unless government continues to protect the market against monopoly power. If government

Government . . . can do little more than register the shifting balance of forces in the community; regulatory agencies become prizes in the struggle for power. That interest or group of interests which captures control of them impresses its policy upon them . . .

—Arthur F. Bentley,
The Process of Government,
1908[62]

is incapable of serving broad public interests, a competitive market itself becomes inconceivable.

▶ You're assuming that without some magic number of competitors there's no competition. You're flat wrong, as I've already said. If after deregulation fewer companies remain in a given market, it's because they have demonstrated their superior capacity to serve the public, once freed from government constraint.

◀ *It's beyond me how you can so fear government power but remain sanguine about the increasing power of a few private players.*

▶ You keep forgetting: Government, and only government, has the power of coercion—of law—behind it. It is infinitely more dangerous than any private entity.

◀ *And you forget that a democratic government is open to public scrutiny and is required to answer to public needs; a private entity has no such accountability. To me, it's unaccountable power, whether called public or private, that is dangerous.*

▶ So far we've talked only about government's control of the structure of markets, but in this century government has extended its oversight into almost everything—from workplace safety to the quality of goods themselves. In the Seventies alone, three powerful agencies, the Environmental Protection Agency, the Occupational Safety and Health Agency, and the Consumer Product Safety Commission, were born. So, all told, twenty-seven regulatory agencies now tell business what it can and cannot do. During the Seventies, the budgets of these agencies soared fivefold before the Reagan presidency began to check their power.

Protecting the consumer is the rationale for this activity, called "social regulation," but in most cases the consumers' interests suffer. Just a few examples: Excessive government regulations have added $10,000 to the price of a modest three-bedroom home.[64] Thousands have died—perhaps unnecessarily—because rules enforced by the Food and Drug Administration, supposedly to protect us against untested drugs, have instead prevented patients from getting the medicine they needed in time. These deaths might never have happened if the new drugs had been allowed on the market earlier. This loss of life is greater than any potential harm from the marketing of unsafe drugs.[65]

Growth of the *Federal Register*, which contains all federal regulations, mimics the proverbial snowball! Each year tens of thousands of pages are added. In 1970 it grew by 20,000 pages; in 1980 it increased by over 87,000 pages. By now, it must be growing by many more pages each year.[66]

◄ *Your dramatic numbers tell us nothing. The* Federal Register *also contains notices of hearings and proposed rules; only those regulations approved become part of the* Code of Federal Regulation, *now contained in roughly 200 books. If standards protecting 240 million Americans from everything from faulty bridge construction, to nuclear accidents, to toxic wastes, to hazardous X-ray machines, could fit on one bookshelf in my cramped office, is this excessive?*

As one who admits having trouble completing a tax form, I'd be the first to advocate simplification. But a marked increase in regulation since World War II should surprise no one. Let's face it, the world is *vastly more hazardous.*

► Actually, the more complex society becomes, the more we must rely on the marketplace. As the complexity of modern society increases, individuals become even less able to master the knowledge required to make decisions for the whole society.

Moreover, businesses might be forced to spend millions to comply with an entry of just two or three lines in these tomes of government rules. Do you realize the cost you are paying for all this? Compliance adds as much as $200 billion annually to the cost of doing business in this country. Just doing the paperwork, including tax forms, required by federal regulations uses up over a billion work-hours a year—representing a "disguised" federal work force of over 500,000 full-time employees.[67]

◄ *It's fairly easy to estimate the cost of enforcing regulation. It's trickier to total up the cost of insufficient regulation. How would you assess the costs of thousands of deaths from asbestos exposure or mining accidents? Or the deaths of babies before regulation of crib design reduced accidental strangling? Or the lives destroyed in the Love Canal and other toxic waste debacles? And added to this immeasurable cost to individuals is the drain on the public purse from insufficient regulation: taxpay-*

ers must now foot the multibillion-dollar bill for toxic cleanup.[68] And it will cost billions more to bail out those savings and loans now collapsing due to mismanagement and fraud after deregulation of that industry.

Remember, too, that if government doesn't protect citizens, the problems don't just go away. Anyone who can will act in self-defense, after the damage is done. Since the mid-Seventies, product liability cases in federal courts have soared 1,000 percent,[69] an increase for which the Reagan era attack on regulation must shoulder some responsibility. If relaxing regulation means billions then get eaten up in unproductive litigation, have we gained anything?

▶ Yes, because the alternative, letting government regulate complex business activity, not only wastes time and money, but it stifles the independent judgments of the entrepreneur and is therefore a direct restraint on the freedom of the businessperson.

◀ A restraint on freedom? Not to have to worry about whether the food I buy is contaminated with pesticides would certainly feel liberating to me. And wouldn't the field worker feel freer knowing hazardous farm chemicals were banned? Hm . . . is regulation restraining? Or is it freeing? Maybe the answer depends on where you sit.

▶ Regulation is not merely a limitation on the entrepreneur; it is an affront to individual liberty as well. Someone without a lot of money might very well want, for example, the option of choosing a cheaper washing machine that is less reliable. Regulation forecloses that choice if it mandates standards that price the machine out of a person's reach.

So even social regulation hurts the consumer. Established interests use it also to guarantee themselves customers, bar competition, and keep prices up. Regulations requiring inspections of automobile lights, brakes, and other equipment have had no detectable effect on reducing accidents but give garages a degree of monopoly power, compelling consumers into more extensive repairs than they might otherwise choose. Certain professions have demanded licensing standards so stiff that many competent practitioners are locked out.[72] Established day care operators now lobby for standards that would make in-home and much needed child care alternatives illegal.

> . . . because regulation uses the coercive power of government to alter outcomes, it diminishes individual liberty: people are persuaded by the threat of sanctions to act differently than they would otherwise prefer.
> —Jeane J. Kirkpatrick,
> *Dictatorships and Double Standards*[70]

> *The shepherd drives the wolf from the sheep's throat, for which the sheep thanks the shepherd as* liberator, *while the wolf denounces him for the same act as the destroyer of liberty. . . . Plainly the sheep and the wolf are not agreed upon a definition of the word liberty . . .*
> —Abraham Lincoln, 1864[71]

Besides, it's not the government's job to protect us against all life's harms. If freedom means anything, it must mean the freedom to make bad decisions. Otherwise, why not just transfer all power to those who think they are wiser, allowing them to make decisions for us? That's really what regulation is all about.[73]

◄ *Most of the standards set by regulation are needed precisely because as individuals we have no way to choose. How can I choose a safer power plant or cleaner air? Without government standards, how can I even choose pesticide-free food? I have no lab to test its toxicity.*

► You are evading responsibility. It's your job as a consumer to boycott unsafe foods and the field worker's to refuse employment where conditions are hazardous. The government's responsibility is to make sure that information about hazards is available, but the rest is up to the individual. A free-market economy must presume responsible consumers.

And in the workplace, government protection of workers against unscrupulous employers who cut safety corners may be a noble concept, but an employer who is that unprincipled surely can find ways to evade government regulations. So the taxpayer spends a lot of money paying inspectors . . . and for what? The worker's real protection is a healthy economy in which he or she can simply quit an unsafe workplace and take another job. It's precisely this burgeoning economy that government regulations undercut.

Besides, government regulation can't get rid of the unscrupulous among us. There will always be those who will attempt to deceive customers, but they will be driven out in a competitive market. Regulation doesn't eliminate such businesspeople; it simply gives them a new resource to manipulate in their interests.[76]

◄ *Wait. You can't argue that regulation is both onerous to business and at the same time a mere instrument of business. Old-style regulation of industries such as railroads and trucking did benefit the established players, as you pointed out; so they didn't complain. It's only been since citizens began to demand protection of their interests that industry has discovered the evils of regulation. Perhaps they've found that social regula-*

. . . the consumer has been exploited by special interest groups seeking to improve their own economic position behind the veil of government regulation.
—Richard B. McKenzie,
Bound to Be Free[74]

The sovereign is completely discharged from a duty . . . the proper performance of which no human wisdom or knowledge could ever be sufficient; the duty of superintending the industry of private people . . .
—Adam Smith,
The Wealth of Nations, 1776[75]

tion, *reflecting broader public concern, is not as easily manipulated.*

▶ Let me correct you. Much social regulation that industry resists is not an expression of broad public interest, as you claim, but of special interest groups such as environmentalists who claim to wear the public mantle.

◀ *You've touched on some real problems, but your narrow antigovernment stance blinds you to how regulation can also abet American industry. Our businesses cannot compete today if they produce shoddy products compared with those made in Japan or West Germany where governments enforce higher quality standards.[77]*

While we can agree that much regulation has been ineffective, it has also been grossly inadequate because of the power of corporate interests to defeat or co-opt it. So we must go to the roots of the problem. One is the narrow governance structure of corporations that allows disregard for the public interest. [See Part V for a discussion of alternatives.] But just as great an obstacle may be our society's deep ambivalence about the role of government in economic life. As long as government lacks a clear mandate and practical channels to frame, through public dialogue, consistent policies serving the national interest, government will produce regulations and policies that are after-the-fact, piecemeal, often contradictory, and sometimes disastrous. The cost of decommissioning used nuclear power plants, developed with considerable government "oversight," is expected to reach one trillion dollars over the next thirty years![78]

▶ The only alternative is a central planning process that would more thoroughly usurp, not create, the "public mandate," as you call it. The public mandate can best be realized through individuals expressing their views in the market.

What ultimately defeats your attack on the market is the evidence we see of its abundance all around us—abundance that only exists in market economies.

The Market, Property, and the Environment ★

◄ *The market's success measured by volume of output can be dangerously misleading. It is blind to the costs of natural resources, which don't have prices. If we treat soil and water as "free," the market can't help us sustain our natural resources, much less protect the environment.*

► You've hit on a real problem, but it isn't in the market system; it's that certain resources are used like a medieval "commons"—a free good available to all, so no one has the incentive to economize. Logically, each person seeks to get as much as possible from the common resource before everyone depletes it by overuse.

Overuse of resources arises largely because property rights haven't been clearly enough defined. Where rights to a stream, say, are privately held, the owner can sue a polluter for damaging his or her stream. Establishing clear property rights to resources currently beset by overuse or underproduction would virtually eliminate these problems.[80]

The great virtue of property rights is that they create self-interested monitors of our environment. That's why today no "owned" creatures risk extinction. No "owned" forests risk destruction. Of course not, for sensible people would never kill the goose that lays golden eggs when it is *their* goose![81]

◄ *But in today's corporate world, owners of resources have little in common with your lucky goose owner. A corporate executive must show a profit this quarter to the board of directors, so can he or she be concerned with the long-term prosperity of "their" goose—the corporation? Even many business leaders blame lack of American competitiveness on just such shortsightedness.*

> Ruin is the destination toward which all men rush, each pursuing his own best interest in a society that believes in the freedom of the commons. Freedom in a commons brings ruin to all.
>
> —Garrett Hardin, "The Tragedy of the Commons"[79]

There's another fallacy in your goose analogy. An owner will kill and sell his golden-egg-laying goose, if alternative fowl producing even bigger golden eggs are waiting to be bought with the proceeds. And in the real world, such alternative fowl abound! Entrepreneurs who own a lucrative resource can simply destroy it by overuse, and then invest their windfall elsewhere.

▶ But a system of well-defined property rights works better than any conceivable alternative. One reason is that property rights are combined with a price system.

Market Prices and Resource Use ★

▶ To bring that point home, let's look at a current resource problem: forest management. "Privatizing" the national forests would greatly improve their management.[82] Why? Because the market and only the market holds every private owner accountable to the rest of society for making the best use of a resource, in this case, the forest. The owner has to outbid everyone else for every alternative use that is foregone (or destroyed) on the land.[83] Private ownership rights, transferable through the market, hold the individual owner responsible for allocating a resource to its highest valued use, thus maximizing the individual's and society's wealth.[84]

Without such enforceable rights, resources are used by individuals who don't have to outbid others—leading to substantial waste. If users don't have to pay, they won't use the resource efficiently.[86] Lands managed by the Bureau of Land Management suffer precisely from this problem. Cattle and sheep owners overgraze government land at fees below what they would pay on private land.[87]

Private property is always more productive than public property . . . The *only* way to improve the productivity and efficiency of public lands is to privatize them.

—Steven Hanke, former staff economist, Council of Economic Advisors[85]

◀ *It's not so simple—private ownership hardly guarantees care. A big conglomerate bought Pacific Lumber Company a few years ago and today is sawing down one thousand-year-old red-woods to pay off its debt. On our privately owned farmland, overuse in the Thirties contributed to the Dust Bowl disaster, and serious soil erosion continues still.*

Neither does public ownership necessitate waste and destruction. The Forest Service, in contrast to private timber companies, has limited timber sales to levels that can be sustained perpetually—at least until the Eighties, when Reagan-appointed administrators began pushing for more sales.

▶ The U.S. Forest Service? You must be kidding. Its management of our forests is an abomination. Every American would benefit if we sold off this land and used the proceeds to, for example, help reduce the huge federal deficit.[88] The Forest Service has logged wilderness areas using inefficient methods that would fail the cost-versus-revenue tests of Weyerhauser.[89] In fact, its policies cost taxpayers hundreds of millions of dollars every year in lost income from timber sales.[90]

◀ *One reason is that government has let the timber industry influence its priorities. So now your solution is to sell off public lands to that same industry? You've conveniently forgotten that it was the destruction of forests by lumber barons at the turn of the century that led to public ownership to begin with![91]*

To you, highest value use equals highest market *value use. But people have values that can't be priced in the marketplace. Americans have supported laws to protect endangered species and wilderness areas, though the highest market value would derive from their continued demise.*

In your scenario, every appropriate use of a resource will be backed up by bidders in the marketplace. But what if the best use has no bidders, or only relatively poor bidders?

▶ If people aren't willing to pay for using a resource in a particular way, then by definition it can't be the best use. Whoever values conservation must pay for it. If not, they have no legitimate grounds on which to attack those willing to pay to use the resource.

A good example is the Nature Conservancy. It's a private, nonprofit group that values land preservation and wants to protect endangered species. Instead of lobbying and forcing others

In principle, the ultimate measure of environmental quality is the value people place on these . . . services *or their willingness to pay.*
—A. M. Freeman, Robert Haveman, Allen Kneese, The Economics of Environmental Policy[92]

to sacrifice, it raises money to bid for land in the open market to be put to what it considers best use: preservation.[93]

◄ *Okay. Let's apply your approach. Imagine the economic wealth that could be generated if hydroelectric dams were built to flood the Grand Canyon floor. What a boon to Arizona's economy! Just think of all the new jobs created to build the dams and the increased power and irrigation potential.*

Now compare, dollar for dollar, the value of the Grand Canyon just as it is, even with all the money visitors spend each year multiplying through the local economy. I bet it wouldn't come close to the potential wealth generated by the dams. Yet, I'll also bet that no matter how big the difference, you wouldn't find many Americans who would agree that the dams represent the "best use" of the Grand Canyon.

► What you're saying shows how dishonest people can be. If you aren't willing to compensate the economy of Arizona, say, to the level of economic benefit that would derive from the dams, then you can't ethically stand in the way of development. How can people claim to value something they aren't willing to sacrifice for? Willingness to pay is a concrete statement of what we value.

◄ *Americans* have *repeatedly shown themselves willing to pay for environmental protection—we've voted for clean air laws knowing that ultimately we pay the passed-along abatement costs.*

But you're right, I would back laws to protect things that I wouldn't or couldn't pay for by outbidding others in the market. I may very well vote to deny a wilderness area to developers even though I'd never go there myself and wouldn't pay a penny to compensate a would-be developer.

► I find your stance ethically indefensible. You sit on your high horse, forcing others to pay for your values.

A contradiction between principles—between contending visions of the good society—cannot be settled by

◄ *Some values just cannot be settled through the market. To make my point concrete: During the Civil War, abolitionists fought for a legislated end to slavery because they believed slavery was wrong. The economic cost of ending slavery fell primarily on southern plantation owners, not on those fighting for emancipation. Yet few would argue that abolitionists should have abolished slavery simply by paying a fair-market price for all slaves and then freeing them.*

It is because some values transcend the market that people establish a polity, an arena of common life in which decisions are made through debate about what is right and what is wrong, not just how much something costs.

asking how much partisans are willing to pay for their beliefs.[94]

—Mark Sagoff

Just Make Them Pay ★

▶ Not only do I think consumers must pay if they want to protect the environment, but I also believe that the market system can and should be modified to make producers pay, too, for a failure to protect the environment. Corporations, for example, must be taxed according to how much they pollute the environment. They are then forced to incorporate into their costs of production the pollution damages which historically have been mere "externalities"—economists' lingo for the side effects of doing business that somebody else had to pay for, either in nuisance or ill health, for example.

The government's current approach—trying to legislate the actual levels of permissible pollution discharged—is inefficient. Instead, taxing polluters in what are called "effluent fees" efficiently allows the market to determine the appropriate level of pollution.[95] The same system could even work for cars: drivers could simply be taxed according to how badly their cars pollute.[96] Or, we could institute "pollution entitlements" to companies that they could trade in the free market.[97]

Effluent fees and taxes or such "entitlements" make it possible to determine the cost-benefit ratio of every effort to reduce pollution. Since we can't eliminate all pollution, we need ways to measure what the optimal level is—the least pollution we can have without its being too costly to achieve. If a company must spend fifteen dollars to eliminate ten dollars of pollution damage, then pollution has obviously been reduced too much.[98] But if the government dictates the level of permissible discharge, we'll never know whether we're spending too much—the optimal level can never be determined.

◄ *Your cost-benefit ratio assumes that the damage of pollution can be assigned a dollar value. How do you price damage to human life? Or the destruction of resources that today may have no economic value but are irreplaceable?*

Under your tax scheme, a prosperous company could afford to pollute, whereas a poor company could not pay the pollution tax. But by supporting legislation with absolute pollution standards, Americans are saying that, no matter how much one is willing to pay, certain actions are wrong.[99]

► My point is precisely that we must get better at assigning legal culpability and that is best done through clearly defined property rights. As I've said, if each person's rights to a stream are clear, owners cannot pollute or they will be prosecuted.[100]

◄ *It's not so simple. In an ecological context, linear chains of cause and effect don't exist. Eighty percent of Nebraska's wells, most used for drinking water, are now polluted by nitrate from fertilizer runoff.*[101] *In such circumstances, it's impossible to determine even roughly which use of* whose *property accounts for how much of any given harm.*[102] *So how is it possible to assign legal liability after the fact?*

Your solution—just making sure that private parties pay for dealing with the pollution they cause—can reduce pollution but can't solve the problem. Where it matters most, it would cost too much. To eliminate the more than two and a half million tons of toxic chemicals produced each year by the chemical industry would consume more than the total annual profits of the top thirty chemical companies![103] *Impossible. So to be serious about solutions, we must be able to choose alternative technologies in order to avoid pollution in the first place.*

Consider water pollution. Despite more than $100 billion spent to enforce the Clean Water Act and significant progress, the quality of most rivers has not improved and groundwater is increasingly contaminated.[104] *The reason is no mystery. The manufacture of almost every petrochemical product results in toxic waste; and some of these products, such as plastics and pesticides, are themselves pollutants. Yet the petrochemical* *industry has shifted almost every aspect of our economy from dependence on biodegradable paper, leather, and glass, to polluting but more profitable plastic, and has made our food system dependent on polluting chemicals as well.*

▶ "The industry" has not done any of this to us! We buy all of those products. To any extent that what you are saying is true, *we* are responsible. Americans have demanded the convenience of plastic and big cars as well as cheap and blemish-free food that requires heavy doses of pesticides.

◀ *You assign to consumers responsibility precisely for what as consumers we cannot choose: the technology of production. With our purchases we make a very limited statement: whether a given item serves our immediate and individual benefit. The market doesn't encourage us to weigh that advantage against the host of disadvantages that arise if many others buy the product. First, the market doesn't give us that information; and second, it offers little hope that our individual "yea" or "nay" is going to make any difference.*

▶ You're wrong. Economists know that those consumer "votes" make a difference. That's why they refer to consumers exerting market demand to which producers must respond.

◀ *But producers can override consumer "demand" if it means more profits for them: because big cars brought more profit per car, U.S. automakers kept making big, polluting, gas-guzzling cars in the Sixties even when consumers began turning to smaller imports.* [105] *But my central point is this: As consumers we don't experience ourselves demanding anything, only choosing among what has already been produced. As consumers we feel we have no power over the process of production itself.*
   But we're capable of more: If we knew we could choose clean, healthy water and air, and we could avoid destroying the protective ozone layer and heating the planet in the "greenhouse effect," and be free of nuclear hazards, don't you think we would?

▶ I don't have to answer. Your question is being answered right now. Consumers could avoid buying polluting products, but they don't. They are voting with their dollars, recognizing that life always involves trade-offs between competing goods. Things aren't as bad as you paint them, in any case, and most people realize that. Moreover, many people will choose the conveniences that modern industry offers over a pristine environment.

◀ *Much more is at stake—our planet's health and our children's future. It depends upon whether we as a people make a critical distinction. The market, relying upon millions of individual cost-benefit choices, is superb for distributing goods. But the core decisions about technologies that affect the well-being of all of us, whether we buy a given product or not, must be seen for what they are: not private decisions to be made for us by small, self-appointed bodies of corporate leaders, but decisions so broad in their impact that democratic principles must apply. This means rethinking the governance of corporations, insisting on mechanisms for public accountability in the choice of technologies. [Parts IV and V pursue this question further.]*

And, we must be realistic about the market's additional limitations. By itself, the market can't answer other ethical questions, such as whether a resource should be used at all or how much should be left for future generations.

The Market and Resource Depletion ★

▶ You're wrong. The market's ability to take the needs of the future into account is one of its greatest advantages. The market system makes possible credible projections about future prices. If tighter supplies loom ahead, then prices climb. Higher prices reduce demand, thus protecting the resource as it becomes more scarce.[106] A prime virtue of the private property/market system is its ability to alert us to impending scarcity.[107]

◄ *Alert us? The market can just as easily deceive us. It can reflect current supply unrelated to impending scarcity. Today, a couple dozen Third World countries are exporting virtually irreplaceable tropical hardwoods, but only ten are expected to have anything left to export by the turn of the century. The end to this bonanza is already just around the corner, but the market price of this wood gives us no clue.* [108]

Or take American agriculture. A big boom in farm exports in the Seventies got lots of applause. What Americans didn't know was that the export push so taxed the land that soil erosion in some areas hit Dust Bowl proportions. [109]

Resources for Future Generations ★

► You're assuming that we shouldn't use up natural resources, I suppose, because you think they will be more valuable to future generations than the things we can make of them today. But it's precisely because our grandparents used up resources that they were able to build the stock of capital which allows us to enjoy the standard of living we do. [110]

What if past generations thought like you? What if they had not used resources for fear of depleting them? Much of the stocks of resources we enjoy would never have even been discovered. If our forebears had listened to warnings of conservationists about the threatened exhaustion of the coal supply, for example, industrial development would have been drastically retarded. [112]

It's in using resources that new discoveries are made. Cadillacs aren't what deprive future generations; they are among the incentives promoting the discovery of new knowledge and its use. [113] The known reserves of almost all natural resources have increased, not decreased, as demand for them has risen—it's like a store's inventory that goes up as the store's sales volume increases. [114]

So, in any meaningful sense, our natural resources aren't finite.

> The conservationist who urges us to "make greater provision for the future" is in fact urging a *lesser* provision for posterity.
> —Anthony Scott,
> *Natural Resources: The Economics of Conservation* [111]

Take copper, for example. Since there's no method of ever knowing how much is available and there's always the possibility of discovering how to create copper or its economic equivalent, why think of its supply as finite and try to limit its use?[115]

Future generations will be richer than we are. Expecting us to refrain from using resources in order to aid them is asking the poor to give to the rich![116] The best thing we can do for future generations is not to leave them maximum natural resources but a stock of manufactured goods and natural resources that have the greatest value.[117]

◀ *There's not much sense arguing. That humans will just go on discovering (or inventing alternatives to) needed raw materials is your statement of faith, but one based on but a sliver of human experience. Generously estimated, the period since the beginning of the industrial revolution represents about 1/2,000th of human existence. Isn't it rather presumptuous to indulge ourselves on the faith that this explosion in resource use can go on indefinitely? A minimal ethical sense would require that we see ourselves as stewards of the richness we've inherited.*

▶ To the contrary—we would be doing future generations a disservice *not* to operate on the presumption of infinite possibility.

◀ *But our world is not simply an assortment of substances—oil or copper or bauxite—for which we may or may not find substitutes for. Our world is made of immeasurably rich interacting systems that we cannot, in any practical sense, recreate, for they have evolved together over eons.*

Today's commercial logging and other developments are destroying tropical rain forests in which live at least half the world's species.[119] In the process, species are being made extinct at rates that may rival the die-off of the dinosaurs. We cannot create a rain forest or a species.

▶ Sure, some people believe that trees are a unique national treasure and that all species have a right to exist (would you include the malaria-carrying mosquito in your concern about species preservation?). But these questions have nothing to do with the role of the market and the question of resources needed

---

Each epoch has seen a shift in the bounds of the relevant resource system. Each time, the old ideas about ''limits'' . . . were thereby falsified. Now we have begun to explore the sea . . . and . . . the moon. Why shouldn't the boundaries of the system from which we derive resources continue to expand . . . just as they have expanded in the past?

—Julian Simon,
The Ultimate Resource[118]

We abuse land because we regard it as a commodity belonging to us. When we see land as a community to which we belong, we may begin to use it with love and respect. There is no other way for land to survive the impact of mechanized man.

—Aldo Leopold,
A Sand County Almanac,
1948[120]

by future generations. They involve personal religious values or are simply matters of aesthetic taste.[121]

◄ *Do you consider survival a matter of taste?*

► Oh, you really are a doomsdayer, aren't you?

◄ *No. Doomsdayers forecast; I'm looking at the evidence. We humans are members of an immensely complex ecology which our actions are destroying. Chlorofluorocarbons from industrial processing are generating a measurable hole in the protective ozone layer of the upper atmosphere. The combustion of fossil fuels, along with the burning of tropical rain forests after the hardwood is removed, is contributing to rising carbon dioxide levels heating the whole planet—the so-called greenhouse effect. Yes, we might devise substitutes for energy sources and industrial minerals, but we cannot recreate the earth's atmosphere and climate.[122] Without international governmental accords that strictly limit atmospheric pollution, catastrophe lies ahead. The drought of 1988 may only be our first taste.*

The world is . . . one's extended body and one's body is the focus on the world . . .
—J. Baird Callicott, *In Defense of the Land Ethic*[123]

► You are overblowing many of these problems. For all we know, a warming of the planet could help fend off the next ice age. If a pollution-free environment is something people are willing to pay for, private enterprise will respond with the technology to achieve it. That's how we've made so much progress in reducing pollution.[124] The market protects the interests of future generations better than the government can. The public sector has no interest in looking to the future, but participants in the market do. The speculator—so often maligned—actually performs a service for the future by outbidding others who are merely seeking resources for *present* use.[125]

The speculator . . . acts as a middleman between the present and the future.
—Richard L. Stroup and John A. Baden[126]

◄ *Are you serious? A speculator's time frame is hardly intergenerational. The very definition of a speculator has come to mean someone who buys, only to resell the moment a good profit looks likely.*

Government and Resource Use ★

▶ So, what's your alternative—government planning? Setting artificially high prices for scarce resources? Once the public sector gets involved, it does the opposite, disguising oncoming scarcities with production subsidies.

Government intervention in energy markets has tried to keep energy costs low, smothering innovations in alternatives to what the government is protecting. Government has subsidized nuclear power to the tune of about $40 billion. Federal subsidies for electricity have inhibited the development of alternative energy sources.[128] In fact, government subsidies have favored nonrenewable energy sources ten to one.[129]

Both our pollution and any overuse problem, as well as our future energy needs, can best be met if government limits its role. Yes, government must force producers to pay for any pollution they cause. And it should establish clearer ownership rights to water and even airspace where feasible. But that's it. If government stopped getting in the way of the free market, solar, wind, and thermal energy technologies would grow even faster—if they're truly more cost-effective.

◀ *If the market always worked to reward cost-effectiveness, I'd agree with you. But it doesn't. A simple case in point: When the person choosing the technology and the long-term user are different people, the pressure to achieve cost-effectiveness is lost. Almost half of all furnaces, washers, air conditioners, and the like, for example, are bought by contractors, not consumers directly. The contractor profits by keeping initial costs down, not by considering long-term energy efficiency. And, why would developers build solar homes? Solar heating can reduce energy costs considerably over time but are somewhat more expensive to build.*

Your claim for the market is that it links decision-making and responsibility. But very often it doesn't. That's when government's responsibility to the public interest begins.

Because regionally owned utilities, for example, are accountable to the public, they have taken the lead in encouraging energy conservation, while private utility companies have resisted conservation because it can mean decreased sales. [130]

In serving the public's interest in conserving energy and avoiding hazards, government's legitimate role is to assist the market: it can set energy-efficiency standards. (If all refrigerator makers had been required to meet the efficiency of an already available Whirlpool model, we could now be saving energy equal to twenty-four coal-fired generating plants!) [131] *It can inform the public of the cost-effectiveness of alternatives. Government revolving funds can make capital available to energy-efficient inventors and developers—how else can alternatives compete when private electric utility companies have $25 billion to invest annually in new plants?*

And to conserve nonrenewable resources, government can intervene in the market to keep them priced at the cost of the best renewable substitute, thus stimulating development of those substitutes. [132]

▶ Based on its lousy record, what makes you think that government efforts could be positive? Recall what happened when government stepped in to keep oil prices down and to ration oil when the Iranian revolution cut our supplies in the late Seventies. Those maddening lines at the gas stations could have been avoided if prices had been allowed to rise and pull in additional supply. Government's attempts to correct market irregularities have been neither efficient nor equitable.[133]

◀ *What about national security—do you condemn the government's role there also?*

▶ Of course not! From the very beginning of this discussion I've made clear that national defense is one necessary function of government.

◀ *Government's initiative in spurring development of safer, cleaner, less vulnerable energy sources is just as essential to our security, both directly and indirectly, by freeing us from dependence on foreign sources.*

▶ You are again playing with the multiple meanings of words. Security, as you've used it here, is an entirely different matter.

◀ *No. Because of the extreme centralization and complexity of our current energy technology, our nation is indefensible. A handful of people could "turn off" our entire nation.* [134]

▶ This is beginning to sound familiar! Government can't get involved in every aspect of security. Government subsidies have been the major culprit in getting us locked into these centralized, often less efficient energy patterns to begin with.

Government is always vulnerable to the power of special interest groups. You would have it protect resources directly. But let me give you an example illustrating why that can't work. Take water for irrigation. Irrigators in the western states, organized into potent political pressure groups, have gotten high government subsidies for irrigating, reducing the price of water and therefore increasing demand and waste much above what it would be unsubsidized. [135] And reliance on government overlooks the environmental degradation generated by government agencies themselves. [136]

We come back to our basically different assessment of government, don't we? I don't believe it can reflect the "common good." The key obstacle is the separation of authority from personal responsibility, almost universal in the public sector. Government employees don't have their own savings or even salaries on the line as do people in the private sector; they don't have to live with the consequences of their decisions.

You're naive to believe that regardless of government's failures, government control provides the chance for more equitable influence over resources, at least in a democracy. In a representative democracy, voters can't be informed enough, or keep representatives accountable enough, to do a better job than markets in determining resource use.

Self-interest governs bureaucrats' behavior. In that sense, they're no different than anybody else. What's different is that bureaucrats aren't just making decisions about their own money; they're making decisions about everyone's money. They have strong incentives to increase their agencies' authority by spending more and more of it.

The idea of public interest becomes a fiction used to describe an amalgam which is shaped and reshaped in the furnace of [interest group] conflicts.

—Arthur F. Bentley,
The Process of Government,
1908[137]

The ability to influence government is probably no more (and arguably less) equally distributed than the money income which can influence market decisions.

—John Baden and Richard Stroup, "The Environmental Costs of Government Action"[138]

Of course, I don't think the market system results in perfect solutions to environmental problems, but that doesn't mean collective action would be better. An imperfect market is in most cases the preferred alternative.[139]

The Government and/or the Market? ★

◀ *To you, the market and the government are opposing and mutually exclusive principles. But without effective government, the market cannot function. It's government's responsibility to prevent economic monopoly and to ensure dispersed purchasing power so that the market can function, so that customers will be there to drive it.*

There's a fundamental contradiction in your belief in market competition on the one hand, and your skepticism of democratic government on the other. It's not possible to conceive of a competitive economic system unless one can conceive of a democratic government to keep it that way. And one can't conceive of a democratic government without civil servants accountable to the public.

And it's citizens' and government's responsibility to create new, effective forums to discuss and determine community needs in order to plan responsibly for our future. Government involvement in our complex economy is inevitable; the only question is whether it will be constructive or shortsighted, reflecting only narrow interests.

The market and government aren't interchangeable ways of making decisions. They are two different realms of our lives in which we make decisions based on different criteria. As consumers and sellers we often act, naturally enough, to maximize our private gain; but as citizens, we can act on our principles.

Fundamentally, there are only two ways of coordinating the economic activities of millions. One is central direction involving the use of coercion—the technique of the army and of the modern totalitarian state. The other is voluntary cooperation of individuals—the technique of the marketplace.

—Milton Friedman,
Capitalism and Freedom[140]

The road to the free market was opened and kept open by an enormous increase in continuous, centrally organized and controlled interventionism . . . Laissez-faire was planned.

—Karl Polanyi,
The Great Transformation,
1957[141]

As a consumer, to take a trivial example, I might be too lazy to recycle glass bottles; but as a citizen I'd vote for someone advocating mandatory recycling.

▶ If individuals feel strongly enough about something they should be willing to use their dollar-votes to make their point in the marketplace. They can choose to boycott, choose to recycle, choose to buy from firms they think are better for whatever reason. That's one great advantage of the market system. We as individuals can express our views. You want the government to be a parent, forcing you—and, of course, others—to do what you aren't disciplined enough to do by yourself!

◀ *No, that's not it. Thinking about it, I realize that if I failed to recycle it would not be out of laziness; it's that I would know my individual decision would have little impact—so why bother? Whereas if everybody is doing it, my individual effort* will *matter, and, what's more, systems will be set up to make recycling practical. As citizens, we can organize our common lives to make it practical to do what as individual consumers we wouldn't do—but what in our hearts we know is right.*

If we had only interests and no principles, we wouldn't need a polity at all; we could get by with just an economy in which all transactions—from education to law enforcement to saving endangered species—are left to the market. Indeed, if you were right, there could be no such thing as a civil servant. Motivated only by rational self-interest, officials would just respond to bribes of one sort or another. [142]

Market-like arrangements . . . reduce the need for compassion. . . . Harnessing the ''base'' motive of material self-interest to promote the common good is perhaps the most important social invention mankind has yet achieved.
—Charles Schultz,
The Public Use of Private Interest [143]

By relying on market arrangements, we can live more comfortably with our pluralism, and thereby resist the temptation to impose a specific value system on our people.
—Robert Benne,
The Ethic of Democratic Capitalism [146]

▶ Fortunately, most differences of opinion *can* be reduced to differences of interests. That means they can best be settled with a cost-benefit approach through the market, as I have argued.

Political decision-making is enormously time consuming and contentious. We must economize on its use. [144] Otherwise people just throw up their hands in disgust at the bother of it all! Because we can rely on the market to settle differences, we can live together much more harmoniously. The market requires no concensus, so it reduces strain on the social fabric. [145] The more decisions have to be made politically, the more divisive society becomes, as it is forced to haggle over who gets what. [145]

◄ *We use the political process to establish the ethical boundaries in which the market is allowed to function. Because trading with the enemy is outside that boundary, many Americans were justly appalled that during World War II our government failed to block Standard Oil from doing business with the Nazis.* [147] *As a polity, we also proscribe the selling of babies, and we curtail trade to South Africa because Americans believe apartheid is immoral. Limiting the market to protect the environment is, similarly, a statement of values.*

. . . the market needs a place, and the market needs to be kept in its place. . . . The tyranny of the dollar yard-stick . . . given the chance . . . would sweep away all other values, and establish a vending-machine society.
—Arthur M. Okun,
Inequality and Efficiency [148]

Of Interests and Principles ★

▶ You've found a nice way of talking about a minority being able to impose its values on everyone else by simply skirting the most impartial standard there is: economic efficiency. Any time you remove a decision from the marketplace and give it to government, inevitably a few people end up deciding for everybody else.

So, wherever possible we must rely on people's good sense about their own interests. And certainly the resource issues we've been discussing lend themselves well to reliance on that motive. You assume that people can be motivated by a sense of what is in the common good, and, what's more, agree on it! Just think of the unending conflict within our society over issues like school busing, welfare policies, or nuclear power, not to mention the preferred trade-offs between convenience and pollution, and you'll see how unrealistic your ideas are.

◄ *The problem is precisely that most Americans have had no opportunity to participate in dialogue about any of these choices or to devise alternatives. Pursuing the common good doesn't mean quashing our own interests in favor of others, only that we're able to sense that our well-being and self-respect are linked to those of others.*

It's nothing superhuman. It's as basic as what our children

[In halting production of chlorofluorocarbons] I know I'm doing something that's important, and it felt good.
—Joseph P. Glas,
E. I. du Pont de Nemours
& Co. [149]

expect from us; they admire us, we hope, not for how we further our own private agendas, but for doing "what's right." When Du Pont finally decided to stop producing ozone-damaging chlorofluorocarbons, the executive in charge said that what pleased him most was the praise he got from his children! Pride, in ourselves and in our country, is a powerful motivator.

Summing Up the Dialogue ★

DOES THE MARKET ALLOW UNDUE CONCENTRATION OF POWER?

◀ *Yes. Within a market system unchecked by a democratic polity, those with the most economic strength easily expand beyond a size that efficiency could justify. Big simply begets big. The economic clout of large corporate entities then translates into political power as well, making government vulnerable to their demands.*

▶ No. The free market itself ensures competition, which places limits on power. Mergers of companies that lead to competition by a small number of firms is itself a sign of a healthy push for greater efficiency. As long as there are two firms in a market, competition is adequate to protect consumers. Only government interference creates monopoly power, and the market system itself keeps economic power safely separated from political power.

DOES THE MARKET ENHANCE FREEDOM?

◀ *It can, but only to the degree that purchasing power is widely dispersed so that all are free to participate in the market; that reliable information about marketed goods is easily accessible;*

that competition is protected by a democratic polity; and that the most essential human values—including the protection of life—are not reduced to market exchange values.

▶ Yes, because it doesn't allow individuals to inflict their prejudices on others and because it responds to individual preferences with no authority telling us what we want. Moreover, by expanding our choices as consumers, the market's impetus to efficient production enhances freedom.

DOES THE MARKET SYSTEM ENSURE EFFICIENT PRODUCTION?

◀ *Only if the polity protects competitive markets so that economic concentration, and the political power accompanying it, do not allow firms to thrive by manipulating demand and passing on costs to consumers and taxpayers, rather than by improving efficiency.*

▶ Yes, because the competitive pressure to earn profits forces firms continually to improve efficiency by lowering costs in order to stay in business.

IS THERE A ROLE FOR GOVERNMENT IN THE MARKET?

◀ *Yes. On the consumer side, government must protect wide dispersion of wealth and income so that individuals can express their preferences in the market; on the producer side, government must prevent concentration that undermines the market's chief virtue—competition.*

▶ No, with very few exceptions. Government action to correct the market's flaws only undermines it, for government action typically serves the interests of self-interested bureaucrats. The only alternative to the market is authoritarian planning; we all know the consequences of that.

CAN THE MARKET PROTECT THE ENVIRONMENT AND CONSERVE NATURAL RESOURCES?

◄ *No, for many reasons:*

· *Private owners won't protect a resource if they can deplete it and move on to higher profits elsewhere.*
· *Certain values, such as clean air or wilderness, are impossible and inappropriate to price.*
· *The price mechanism does not reflect the depletion of resources well enough to prevent it.*
· *Incentives for choosing lowest cost, renewable energy sources are missing when those who select technologies are more interested in lowest* installation *costs than lowest long-term* use *costs.*
· *Once inefficient or dangerous energy technology has powerful economic interests behind it, government must actively encourage alternatives to enhance our security.*

► Yes, to the extent that either is necessary, but:

· Private owners in a market system will protect resources best because it's in their own long-term interests to do so.
· Forcing producers to pay for pollution damage, not mandating given levels, is the best way to achieve lowest cost pollution control.
· The wilderness should be protected to the extent that those who value it are willing to pay to remove land from development.
· The unfettered market will force new discoveries benefiting future generations much more than any effort at conservation of resources.
· If renewable energy sources are truly more efficient, they will succeed in the market without government help.

ARE SOME TYPES OF GOODS INAPPROPRIATE TO DISTRIBUTION BY THE MARKET?

◄ *Yes. That which is necessary to life itself—health care, for example—cannot be left to market distribution without violating the sanctity of life. The disposition of other goods of innate worth—clean air and wilderness, for example—must be deter-*

mined by the polity on the basis of other values, not willingness or ability to pay.

▶ Of course we do not permit the selling of babies or dangerous drugs, but in most instances market distribution is superior. That's true even in the provision of health care or in the disposition of wilderness lands because market distribution produces the most efficient and highest value use.

PART FOUR

Freedom: Property, Power, and Civil Liberties

Property: Protection Against State Power? ★

▶ In talking about natural resources, we've already had to touch on the role of private property, but it deserves a lot more attention in any discussion of freedom.

Private property rights give people latitude to do some things by restricting what everyone can do. If I own something, no one else can tell me how to use it or intrude upon it. Almost paradoxically, property rights give us freedom by setting limits on our behavior.[1] As an institution, the right to own private property helps ensure the security that you've stressed from the beginning is so essential to freedom. In the seventeenth century, civil government as we know it came into being precisely to protect the individual's right to own property, thus shielding people from the arbitrary actions of kings and land barons.

◀ *Wait a minute! Property rights do serve as protection, but only for some people. With the backing of the state, property rights have been used throughout history as much to deprive people of resources as to protect people from infringement by the state.[3]*

Property rights didn't protect the security of the English peasant; instead, the lords used property rights as an excuse to seize for themselves common land that had long been the bulwark of the peasants' security.[4] When western colonizers introduced private property into the Third World, they put new state power behind those already in control, further weakening the security of the majority.

And today, private landholdings in much of the world reflect centuries of outright seizure by the most powerful. Can poor peasants defend their property claims against big landlords backed by police power? Can they hire lawyers to uphold their property claims in court?

The great and *chief end* therefore of Mens uniting into Commonwealths, and putting themselves under Government, *is the Preservation of their Property.*

—John Locke,
"The Second Treatise of Civil Government," 1690[2]

Civil government, so far as it is instituted for the security of property, is, in reality instituted for the defence of the rich against the poor, or of those who have some property against those who have none at all.

—Adam Smith,
The Wealth of Nations, 1776[6]

. . . The freedom of property from the indefinite despotism of sovereignty, is the best security to be found against those unjust laws . . . and against that despotism of majorities . . .

—John Taylor,
1820[7]

[Because] inequality produc[es] so much misery to the bulk of mankind, legislators cannot invent too many devices for subdividing property . . .

—Thomas Jefferson, 1785[8]

▶ You are raving about distortions—about violations of property rights. Obviously, in those countries in which property rights are not respected, might does make right. These examples tell us nothing about the value of the institution as such. Property rights are established precisely to avoid these transgressions. The more property rights are respected, the less possible it is for people to be abused. This distribution of property among people—and away from the state—has been for centuries the most effective device for keeping state power in check.[5] That's why the right to own private property is essential to freedom.

◀ *But in much of the world, the threat to freedom isn't intrusive state power, as such; it's the power of the biggest property owners to enlist the state behind their interests.*

My point is that private property rights can be used for good or for harm—to expand or to restrict freedom.

▶ Of course there's no automatic link between property and freedom. Property rights must be respected first!

◀ *But respected by whom? Property relationships are a reflection of the power relationships in any society, defining who can do what to whom (and get away with it!). That's precisely why many of our forebears feared that if property were allowed to move into the hands of a wealthy minority, the economic security—the freedom—of the majority would be in jeopardy. They believed that property can serve liberty only when dispersed, when all people have access to it as a base of independent power over their own lives.*

▶ No. What our founders understood and feared most is *government*—because it can be used by ruling groups against the majority.

◀ *Some feared most the majority itself! But my point is this: What distinguishes* democratic *government is precisely that it can counter elite rule by ensuring that property doesn't end up in only a few hands. That's the challenge that every free people must understand. Thomas Jefferson did.*

He and other founders recognized that economic power always translates into political power. So, once we allow concentrated control over property, an economic elite will be able to use the state for its own ends.

► You can't seem to get my essential point: Private property is the necessary counterbalance to government power. And because the system of property is coupled with a market economy, there's built-in protection from the concentration of economic power that you so fear.

◄ *But private property can hardly counterbalance government if concentrated ownership of property gives a few undue influence* within *the political system.*

► But you're assuming undue economic concentration behind your undue influence. You haven't proven either. Many of our founders understood that the market itself does not tolerate concentration; that's its beauty, as I explained in the previous chapter. The protection against an economic elite is our market system itself, its competitive structure, if we just let it work. And largely it has worked.

[The] balance of power in a society, accompanies the balance of property and land. The only possible way, then, of preserving the balance of power on the side of equal liberty and public virtue, is to make the acquisition of land easy to every member of society . . .
—John Adams, 1776[9]

◄ *You already know how strongly I disagree, so I won't bore you with my objections. But many of our founders understood that the importance of owning property wasn't just that it could shield people from government intrusion. They argued that if citizens owned productive property—meaning farmland in their era—they wouldn't be economically dependent on a boss or landlord. With such security, they could act independently. Without it, they could be manipulated.*

While our founders certainly didn't imagine women or blacks to be capable of such independence, many assumed—or hoped—that the problem for white men and their dependents was taken care of by the good fortune of our geography. "Our" plentiful land (once native peoples were killed or pushed aside) could provide every deserving American male with ample property to establish economic independence.

Unfortunately for us, though, our forebears failed to build into the structure of our government a means to prevent what they feared. So, two hundred years later their worst fears have come true: the richest 10 percent of Americans own 86 percent of the country's net financial wealth![12]

. . . a power over a man's subsistence amounts to a power over his will.
—Alexander Hamilton,
The Federalist Papers, No. 79, 1787[10]

What should we farmers be without the distinct possession of the soil? [This farm] . . . has established all our rights; on it is found our rank, our freedom, our power as citizens . . .
—St. John de Crèvecoeur,
Letters from an American Farmer, 1782[11]

► You're exaggerating, just like you did with your income figures earlier. The picture is quite different if you take all assets into account—including people's homes, for example—not just stocks, bonds, and other financial assets.

◀ *Financial assets are resources we can use. That's why I chose them. Owning my house provides some long-term security, but it can't help my family's current financial problems unless I sell it or use it as collateral; that's just too risky for most people. But let's look at all net assets; the top 10 percent still hold almost 60 percent.* [13]

. . . neither the state governments nor congress have a sovereign power over property; . . . neither of them has any right at all to create modes for transferring it artificially from one man or one interest to another . . .

—John Taylor, 1820 [14]

▶ I don't see the problem. Many of those on that top rung have accumulated wealth over lifetimes of work. And I don't think our founders would have seen a problem either.

You are terribly confused about what our founders thought. They feared all-powerful government more than they feared any concentration of private power. And a government that involves itself in redistribution is by definition all-powerful.

We do have widespread property ownership in America, just as our founders envisioned. First off, corporate taxes represent a form of government ownership. Many Americans own stock directly, and well over half of us also own the homes we live in. [15]

◀ *By the Eighties only one family in ten could afford a first home.* [16] *But our homes aren't what I've been talking about anyway. As I said, owning my home means a big mortgage, which doesn't go far in making me feel secure. Our founders understood that it is* income-producing *property that provides economic security. And that's the sort of property I've been talking about—not our homes, lawn chairs, or hair dryers, but property that produces wealth and generates income, that can support us if we lose our job or some other catastrophe hits. Less than one in ten Americans owns enough of that kind of wealth to provide a meaningful economic cushion.* [17] *More than half of Americans are net debtors: we have no financial cushion at all to fall back on.* [18]

Income-earning property is a bulwark of liberty only for those who have it!
—Charles Lindblom, *Politics and Markets* [19]

In today's world, our definition of "property" should include job security itself and adequate pensions—in other words, all the bases for an individual's claim to participate in economic life and to be protected against catastrophe.

Property: The Right to the Fruits of One's Labor ★

▶ What you're suggesting—significant interference with the institution of property—would no doubt destroy it. I'll explain why in a moment, but first I want to lay out more clearly why private property is so central to liberty. Without it, no one is guaranteed the fruits of her or his labor. Without legal claim, backed by patent laws and the courts, anyone could seize the property that I have developed. Freedom must mean the right to enjoy what I produce.

◀ *In today's economy, in which ownership and work are largely distinct—some own and many work—do property rights guarantee to those who work the fruits of their labor? No, only to those fruits that property owners decide are theirs! That's why we see big raises for corporate executives while workers sacrifice.* [21]

▶ You're more sophisticated than that! You're taking "work" too literally. Those who hold ownership rights work. They contribute the entire structure that makes the "workers'" contribution possible—risk, inventiveness, and initiative, as well as the machines the workers use. Under capitalism, workers get a return proportional to what they contribute—that's perfectly fair.

And how would you get around this division between workers and owners, anyway? Are you suggesting that we all become proprietors of little farms or shops, so that we each control the entire output of our work? You would push our economy backward a few centuries, and, besides, most people would not want the headaches.

The principle of individuality, or to use a less winning term, of selfishness, lies at the root of all voluntary human exertion. We toil for food . . . for property . . . because we know that the fruits of our labor will belong to us, or to those who are most dear to us.
—James Fenimore Cooper, 1838 [20]

With some, the word liberty may mean for each man to do as he pleases with himself and his labor; while with others, the same word may mean for some men to do as they please with other men and the product of other men's labor.
—Abraham Lincoln, 1864 [22]

◀ *Obviously. But we can bring the key insight of many of our founders up to date. Their insight, I repeat, was that property served freedom by providing security and thus independence. In their time property meant ownership of farmland or a small business; how can we translate that into the context of an industrial economy?*

Relinking property and freedom would mean, as I've suggested, establishing the opportunity to work as a citizen's right—the right not to be excluded from access to economic property needed to earn a living. [23]

Property: The Incentive to Production ★

The institution of property, when limited to its essential elements, consists in . . . a right to the exclusive disposal of what he or she have produced by their own exertions, or received either by gift or by fair agreement . . . The foundation of the whole is the right of producers to what they themselves have produced.

—John Stuart Mill,
Principles of Political Economy, 1848[24]

▶ But your entire approach would undercut one of the most important aspects of property rights: the notion of exclusive use. The whole point of ownership is the privilege of using one's property as one sees fit, for one's own gain. Because of this privilege, people know they will benefit from what they produce. So they work harder, and, in the end, everybody benefits as more and better goods are produced. As an incomparable incentive to production, property rights are a boon to freedom.

In this sense, an entrepreneur's industrious development of the resources he or she owns becomes a gift to the whole society. An entrepreneur must suppress his or her own desires in order to respond to the desires of others.[25] Often conservatives get attacked for being more concerned about the individual than society's well-being, so I want to make myself especially clear on this point: I'm not defending property rights because they elevate the individual's interest over the common good; I'm saying that protecting property rights is essential to the society at large.[26]

◄ *I want to clarify something, too. When you talk about the capitalist contribution to society at large, the common good, you mean contribution to its material prosperity?*

► That's exactly right—and its spirit of creative enterprise.

◄ *But I mean something more by the common good—a democratic process we as citizens can all participate in shaping. It's that process that becomes inconceivable once we permit the concentration of economic power you're defending.*

► I'm not defending the concentration of economic power, but since people differ widely in their abilities, naturally some will acquire more than others. That goes without saying.

Any attempt to impose equality—even your notion of a right to participate in the use of economic resources—places constraints on the free reign of property owners. It would kill the incentive of property owners to contribute for everyone's good.

We can see this principle operating today in our own economy. I'll take a small, commonplace example: What happens when do-gooders try to protect renters and punish "greedy" property owners through "rent control," which limits the landlords' right to charge what they think is fair? Immediately, upkeep declines and the number of rental units available to the poor decreases as many property owners abandon their buildings. So we see the terrible upsurge in homelessness.[29]

In other words, the result is just the opposite of what the do-gooders expected because they, like you, fail to understand the importance of property rights in motivating people to invest and make an effort. They also miss the simple economic fact that if rents are set below the market value, landlords will not have the money with which to maintain their rental property.

Or take a practical example from abroad. In many agrarian societies, large farms have proven by their very growth to be the most productive. But at the hint of "land reform" landowners, naturally enough, stop investing and production starts sliding downhill. Just look at what's happening in the Philippines. What are the Philippine coconut plantation owners doing in response to fear that their land might be taken? They've threatened not just to slow production but to chop down the coconut trees—critical to the whole country's export income—if the government

. . . he that incloses Land, and has a greater plenty of the conveniencys of life from ten acres, than he could have from an hundred left to Nature, may truly be said, to give ninety acres to Mankind.

—John Locke,
The Second Treatise of Civil Government, 1690[27]

. . . it is from the nature of things impossible to uphold the freedom of contract and the right of private property without at the same time recognizing as legitimate those inequalities of fortune that are the necessary result of the exercise of those rights.

—Supreme Court,
Coppage v. *Kansas*, 1915[28]

. . . if property were overthrown with the direct intention of establishing equality of fortune, the evil would be irreparable: No more security—no more industry—no more abundance; society would relapse into the savage state from which it has arisen . . .

—Jeremy Bentham,
Principles of the Civil Code, 1802[30]

tries to seize their land. Clearly, property rights must be inviolate if you expect people to go on producing.

◀ *Your examples are powerful evidence of why tightly held economic power so threatens our freedom.*

In your first example, you didn't ask why there was a problem to be corrected in the first place! Why wasn't the market working to keep rents within reach and to force property owners to compete for tenants by maintaining their properties? The problem wasn't rent control robbing owners of incentive; the problem was that too many people couldn't afford to pay the rent. Establishing a right to earn a living—today's equivalent of having one's own homestead in Jefferson's day—would enable the housing market to work better. Renters could afford to pay for housing and could threaten to move out if irresponsible landlords didn't do their job.

And your example of the Philippines landowners? It demonstrates the danger of letting a few have so much power. About 70 percent of the people who work in agriculture don't own any land. While the majority of Filipinos go hungry, the big landowners can keep the entire economy hostage! Just as giant corporations can do here, threatening not to invest without massive government concessions to their profit demands. (And, by the way, you're wrong about small farmers in the Third World. They produce by far the most per acre.[31])

Property Rights— Limited or Unlimited? ★

▶ Property rights, as I've been arguing, are a means to achieve security from the state, to enjoy the fruits of one's effort. And they're an incentive to production. All these are essential aspects of freedom in any society, destroyed once we begin setting limits and qualifications on property.

◄ *I disagree. It is precisely when property rights are made absolute and unlimited that they threaten our liberty. Jefferson, for one, believed that the only way to protect people's natural right to the means of subsistence was to make property a civil right, that is, one subject to government action, accountable to the public interest. Let me put it more simply: In order for everyone to enjoy the right to subsistence, no one must have the right to unlimited property.* [32]

That's why Benjamin Franklin argued that a person's claim to property wasn't unlimited, but defensible only as long as it didn't interfere with the common good.

And because Thomas Jefferson thought that through inheritance, property would come to serve the dead instead of the living, he believed that every generation had the right to decide for itself the best redistribution of property. [35]

► But why then would a farmer care for his land if he couldn't be sure to pass it on to his offspring? He would just run it into the ground before he dies.

◄ *Certainly we can devise inheritance laws that would allow children of farmers to farm without also permitting them so many advantages that they emerge as landed aristocracy.* [37] *Jefferson's concern was that land not come into a few hands so that each new generation would have a chance.*

► But you can't have it both ways! You can't say that property rights are essential to the protection of our freedom because they give people security and then turn around and say that property rights can be violated in some sort of redistribution for the sake of freedom of others. You have to choose. The only way that property rights can really protect people's freedom is if they are inviolate—above tinkering to meet other ends.

Otherwise, the majority can always claim that it's in its interest to seize the property of the minority—even if that accumulated wealth is essential to the productivity the majority itself depends on! [39]

◄ *Where productive resources are finite—farmland is one example—one person's unfettered accumulation means over time that many are left with too little even to meet essential needs. We see this pattern in the Third World, and increasingly in the*

Whenever there are in any country uncultivated lands and unemployed poor, it is clear that the laws of property have been so far extended as to violate natural right.
—Thomas Jefferson,
1785[33]

Private property, . . . is a Creature of Society, and is subject to the Calls of that Society, whenever its Necessities shall require it . . .
—Benjamin Franklin,
1789[34]

. . . "the earth belongs in usufruct to the living"; . . . the dead have neither power nor rights over it. [Upon death] the portion occupied by an individual ceases to be his . . . and reverts to the society. . . . [T]he child, the legatee or creditor takes it, not by any natural right, but by a law of the society. . . . Then no man can by natural right oblige the lands he occupied . . .
—Thomas Jefferson,
1789[36]

The moment the idea is admitted into society, that property is not as sacred as the laws of God, and that there is not a force of law and public justice to protect it, anarchy and tyranny commence.
—John Adams,
1787–88[38]

United States—now the top 7 percent of all farms control more than half of the nation's farmland. [40]

▶ Once again, I question your limited view of resources. Only in the short run do they appear limited. In the long run, they are not limited, as I argued earlier. New wealth-generating property is being created every day, so one person's accumulation doesn't have to mean concentration of or interference with anyone else's. That's one of the greatest features of a dynamic capitalist economy.

◀ *But you forget one important point about all this new wealth: Control of it will at best be proportional to the control of present wealth unless we as a society make our economic rules more fair. Today, the richest 10 percent of Americans control almost three-quarters of all corporate stock.* [42] *They are positioned not only to maintain that same degree of control over newly generated economic assets, but to increase their share. And that's what they are doing. Today income from property ownership is rising twice as fast as income from work.* [43]

Wealth begets wealth. That's why Thomas Jefferson, for one, believed a free society must commit itself to ensuring citizens' access to economic resources. His view was based not just on the right of everyone to survival, but on a certain view of the human essence—that human freedom must mean each person's right to full development of his or her innate gifts.

So, the danger of unlimited property accumulation isn't just that many are left without basic economic wherewithal. Unlimited accumulation means that some people gain enormous power over other people. The consequences for freedom are profound; if a few control most of the resources, at some level everyone else has to answer to them—it's that simple. [44]

Private property, in every defence made of it, is supposed to mean, the guarantee to individuals of the fruits of their own labour and abstinence. . . . [When this guarantee] . . . reaches a certain height, [it] does not promote, but conflicts with, the ends which render private property legitimate.

—John Stuart Mill,
The Principles of Political Economy, 1848 [41]

The rich are not rich because they eat filet mignon or own yachts . . . The rich are rich because they can afford to buy other people's time. They can hire other people to make their beds, tend their gardens, and drive their cars.

—Christopher Jencks et al.,
Inequality [45]

Ownership: Who Makes the Decisions, Who Bears the Consequences? ★

▶ Think about the implications of what you've been saying! Your arguments amount to the prime rationale for public ownership of all productive property: public ownership is the only way to include everyone's interest, according to many people. After all, in communist countries isn't the state supposed to represent "the people"?

In reality, of course, a minority—a political elite—does well for itself while claiming to act in the name of the people. Common ownership is always a myth—it's a cover for the few to exploit the many. When responsibility is widely shared, no one really feels responsible. Everything falls apart. Remember the medieval commons I mentioned earlier? That's one reason why nothing works in socialist countries. No one is put on the spot. But with private property, everyone knows who to blame—the buck stops with the owner.

◀ *The vast bulk of the productive wealth in this country is owned by investors. And most shares are held by a tiny, privileged minority. How is this so very different from decision-making by an elite in the communist system you condemn?*

▶ Ownership in the United States is *not* by an elite. In fact, practically everyone in America is an owner of our nation's productive wealth. Over a trillion dollars in pension funds—owned by American workers—are invested throughout our economy. And most of us put our money in banks that then lend it to

When everybody owns something, nobody owns it, and nobody has a direct interest in maintaining or improving its condition.
  —Milton and Rose Friedman,
    Free to Choose[46]

corporations. To whom are our banks accountable? To us, the depositors. So, even if we don't own stocks directly, we are owners. And it's to stockholders that corporate executives must be responsible.

◀ *Your world exists only on paper, not in real life! If ownership means anything, it must involve control. I can't even get my bank to straighten out a mistake it made with my automatic teller card. And you're telling me that my checking account makes me an owner of the firms it lends to! And pension funds? Most workers have no say in how their retirement savings are invested. Overwhelmingly, employers select pension-fund trustees.* [47]

▶ Your critique misses the point: Stockholders approve major management decisions. So there is widely dispersed control, allowing millions of Americans to participate in ownership in our economy.

◀ *But most Americans—over 80 percent of us—own no stock at all.* [48] *Ironically, the more widely dispersed is stock ownership (and most big corporations have tens of thousands of shareholders), the more likely it is that whatever control stockholders do have is exerted only by the few who own big blocks of shares.* [49] *Upwards of 80 percent of all daily stock market trades are for large institutions like insurance companies and pension funds that allow the individual holder no control.* [50] *So, it's long been conceded that most firms are controlled by management, not by stockholders or their boards.* [51] *In effect, corporate management is accountable to itself.*

▶ But this is changing. It's a new ball game now that professional money managers control the huge institutional funds you just mentioned, now that brokerage fees have been deregulated, and now that new financial mechanisms have been devised for individuals to gain a block of shares big enough to take over a company. Now, a few smart, aggressive individuals can seize control of even the biggest U.S. corporation if its management has not been serving its stockholders well. They're often derided as "corporate raiders," but these folks are breaking the grip of the self-serving managing class you criticize—they're forcing corporate executives to be responsible to their stockholders' interests. [52]

◀ *Corporate raiders may force management to get the highest short-term return for stockholders. But is this the same as serving the nation's interests?*

▶ Of course it is. Keeping the corporation accountable to the shareholders—bringing them the best return on their investments—creates a tough taskmaster for corporate leadership. And it means the corporation is kept responsible to the nation's needs. After all, the value of its stock reflects the overall health of a company. Shareholders use the new wealth that effective corporations help them to acquire—they buy and invest with it, spurring the economy to everyone's benefit.

◀ *But in today's world, a stock's value may not reflect the true health of the company; and getting the highest immediate return to stockholders may not be what our economy as a whole needs. To meet shareholders' demands and fend off corporate raiders, firms slash research budgets and forgo long-term investments and risks that could benefit the whole country.[53] Under these conditions, your easy assumption of common interests between shareholders and the nation as a whole is a myth.*

And as foreign nationals buy up more U.S. corporations—including mainstays like CBS Records, Firestone, and Double-day—the divergence of interests widens still further. More important, as U.S. corporations shift operations overseas, they can do quite well while the U.S. economy is hurting badly. There are now so many U.S. corporations manufacturing goods in Japan for export back here that imports from U.S. companies account for fully 40 percent of our trade deficit with Japan![54] Washington points the finger at unfair foreign competitors, not our own unaccountable corporations. Yet their takeover frenzy in the Eighties, racking up massive corporate debt, brings more economic instability, not improved productivity.

▶ It's always easy to criticize, to find fault with what is. And that's all you seem to do, because you don't want to face the only alternative—state control of economic life.

◀ *The direction I advocate isn't state ownership of the economy, although key services run by public agencies have been shown to serve the public better. Public utilities are a good example: They provide cheaper energy, spending much less on administration than private utilities.*[55]

But if widespread state control of the economy doesn't make sense, neither does its control by wealthy investors. As systems, both come to be controlled by elites—one political, one economic. So the question is, how do we go beyond both?

▶ You may not admit that your ideas lead to state ownership, but that's precisely where government intervention would take us. Ultimately, your path would both consolidate state power and dilute individual responsibility. It's the exclusive ownership rights within the capitalist system that best link authority and responsibility—it's the best system for coupling decision-making and cost-bearing.[57]

◀ *We seem to be talking right by each other. Linking decision-making power with the responsibility to deal with the consequences of decisions is exactly what I'm talking about—about making owners more responsible to all of us touched by their decisions, and about expanding ownership so that more people are responsible. In other words, my goal is to strengthen accountability, not dilute it.*

Then it wouldn't be possible for a huge corporation to get government tax breaks and make its workers accept pay cuts with only the vague promise that it will update aging plants, and then turn around and use its increased profits not to revive a failing industry, but to invest in speculative financial ventures.[59] *Here, accountability is a joke.*

To strengthen accountability, we aren't left simply to choose between ownership by absentee shareholders or by remote government bodies.

▶ And where is a "better way" working? Or where even tested?

◀ *There's no one model. That's my point: We must leave behind the whole notion of models. But a first step is to let go of the fiction that ownership and financing are the same thing. Shareholders can then be seen as what they really are,* mere investors.[60] *And then we're free to begin thinking creatively about varied forms of governance of corporations—seeking not a given model but ever better ways to link decision-making responsibility and cost-bearing, strengthening accountability* so that economic decisions affecting everyone involve workers and the community as a whole.

In the Basque region of northern Spain, for example, the most productive industrial complex has long been owned by the workers themselves. [61] In other instances, union reps serve on corporate boards. And in others, governments share some key responsibilities with corporate management. The Swedish government, for example, requires corporations to engage in long-range planning to keep both unemployment and inflation low. [62] And it works.

▶ But once government dictates corporate plans, you might as well have government ownership. At that point, the difference becomes only a matter of semantics.

◀ No, these examples reflect an evolution in our understanding of ownership of productive property. If we all depend upon it, such property can't carry with it an absolute notion of ownership but ownership as a cluster of rights and responsibilities. This transition is in some aspects actually a return to an earlier understanding. Well into the nineteenth century it was understood that a corporation was chartered to serve the public interest—as a privilege, not a right. [63] Its charter could be withdrawn if that interest were not served.

So I'm not talking about ending private property but removing its destructive features—the power it bestows on some over the well-being of others—while strengthening its usefulness in giving people security.

▶ But effectively you are ending private property, by removing the privileges associated with it. Without the privilege of conducting business as you, the owner, see fit, why bother with the headaches of ownership in the first place?

◀ The privileges of some people would be reduced but for many others, greatly enhanced, if you consider that more people would participate in the privileges linked to ownership.

[The discussion continues in Part V.]

When . . . one devotes his property to a use in which the public has an interest, he, in effect, grants to the public an interest in that use, and must submit to be controlled by the public for the common good, to the extent of the interest he has created.
—Chief Justice Waite, Munn v. Illinois, 1877[64]

Just as we are reluctant to abandon the property rights fiction, we are equally reluctant to forgo the erroneous belief that our franchise was somehow ordained by God. . . . It was not God, but the people who granted us permission to function, and not for our benefit, but for the public's . . .
—Donald S. MacNaughton, Former CEO, Prudential Insurance Co., 1972[65]

Property: Exclusive or Inclusive? ★

▶ But if property is not an exclusive right—the right to exclude the claims of others—then it loses its meaning altogether. From John Locke to the present day, it's been understood that private property is liberating precisely because it means that the individual owner doesn't have to answer to others.

◀ *In the seventeenth century, when much of the natural world was untouched, it made perfect sense that Locke would see as liberating the individual's right to appropriate any product of nature that one transforms through work into a useful object.* [66] *Wherever this justification for the individual's claim to the fruits of his or her labor protected people from the demands of the more powerful, it was liberating.*

But today, when virtually everything in nature is already claimed, this exclusive idea of property has the opposite effect. Instead of ensuring people access to life-sustaining resources, it deprives people of that access. To bring Locke's goal up to date, property rights, rather than meaning the right to exclude people, would have to mean the individual's right not be to be excluded from resources necessary to sustain life. [67]

▶ So I would have the right to walk onto a farmer's land and take what I please—he would have no right to exclude me—since, after all, farmland is a productive resource. Or I could walk into the auto assembly plant near my home and demand to "participate"!

◀ *Of course not. I am talking about a socially protected right to the opportunity to earn a living, just as our right to get an education is protected.*

▶ But you talk as if property were just land, water, and minerals as in Locke's day—nature's bounty, freely available. Today most property isn't created by nature. It is intellectual, technological, and organizational property generated by people. Their rights aren't based on just adding their labor to something in nature, as Locke would put it, but on the fact that they invented, organized, or developed something. This kind of property isn't finite, as I keep telling you. No one has to be excluded because everyone can help make more of it and have a claim on what they create.

◄ *Your description of modern-day property makes my recasting of property rights even more appropriate. You stress that property today is the product of people more than "nature." I would add that today's property is the product of* many *people, most of whom are no longer living. Every invention, every new technology, is built on millions of insights and breakthroughs—not to mention hours of labor—by those who have gone before. So all the tools we depend on to earn a living—from an electric light or telephone, to an improved variety of wheat seed, to a laser printer, to a computerized machine tool—are not solely products of our own hard work or bright ideas. Plus, one's ability to generate new wealth depends upon the maintenance today of innumerable social supports. Could we even get to work without highways and bridges? Would we have the skills to apply without public schools? Would we even be here if not for public health initiatives that freed us from most periodic epidemics?*

So the changes since Locke's time are all the more reason to see today's productive capacity as a social product to which we each have some claim.

The goods of this world are originally meant for all. The right to private property is valid and necessary, but it does not nullify the value of this principle. Private property, in fact, is under a "social mortgage," which means that it has an intrinsically social function . . .
—Pope John Paul II,
On Social Concern [68]

Private Enterprise—
What's Private? ★

▶ In blurring the lines between public and private you open the door to a unitary system in which there is no distinction between the two. This is dangerous. For freedom to thrive there must be a private sphere into which the public interest does not intrude, for it's here that we each develop our own morality and individuality.

◀ *Your mistake is lumping today's corporate world together with other "private" matters. Don't you find it a bit baffling that we in Western societies could leap from private property, conceived of as an extension of self and family, to private property as run by giant bureaucracies with outside investor "owners"—all without appearing to notice a change!*[69]

▶ Not at all. The transition took place because it worked—it led to unparalleled productive capacity. The corporation came into being almost overnight, out of both necessity and opportunity. In the nineteenth century there were large pools of capital and the possibility to take advantage of unprecedented economies of scale. Even though the corporation has brought such abundance, oddly enough, it's never been popular. Attacks like yours are hardly new! They seem to reflect a deep suspicion of authority itself.[70]

Having perhaps benefited briefly by corporate organization, America might now be better off if the corporate form had never been invented or never made available to private enterprise.
—Henry C. Simons, founder, Chicago School of Economics[71]

◀ *It's not authority I suspect but a fantastic sleight of hand! The myth of the modern corporation as "private property" disguises its profoundly undemocratic control. As I just said, the corporation was conceived as a servant of the public good, chartered by the local government to undertake road and water* projects from which the community would benefit.[72] Then, in the nineteenth century, it acquired legal protection as an individual, but without liability to the real people behind it. In 1886, corporations claimed the fourteenth amendment—enacted to protect the constitutional rights of blacks—as their own. Gaining constitutional protection as "persons," corporations furthered the myth of their private nature, avoiding democratic control. The corporate structure then spawned enormous bureaucracies that powerfully affect our daily well-being,[73] all while claiming constitutional protection as persons. So by 1986 Dow Chemical could claim that the Environmental Protection Agency, by simply trying to monitor compliance with the law, was violating its constitutional protection as a "person" against unreasonable search and seizure.[74]

When a structure so transforms itself, don't we need to rethink its original justification and ask whether it still serves its intended function?

When we were a nation of small farmers and self-employed business people, the family often was the business. And it still makes sense to think of family-owned, community businesses as private economic units. But today, only one hundred corporations control almost two-thirds of industrial assets.[75] At the current rate, by the year 2000 just two hundred corporations will own over half of the assets on the entire planet.[76] Surely such extensive control is not a private affair.

▶ Such projections are ridiculous. They hint at some sort of global monopoly—almost a conspiracy! But the great increase in international competition has been the striking feature of the post-war era.

More serious, however, than your false alarm is the drift of your thinking about property: you would abolish the distinction between public and private, as I just said. Why is this such a danger to freedom? Because it would collapse the wall between the sphere of life in which you have to do as you're told and that in which you can do as you please.[78]

◀ Just the opposite. My vision—broadening accountability in economic life—would expand the arena in which we don't have to just "do as we're told." Making large economic bureaucracies more accountable would not mean fusing the public and private sectors. It would more accurately reflect what is and isn't "pri-

> The government of a firm can have more impact on the lives of more people than the government of many a town, city, province, state.
>
> . . . . [P]eople who are compelled to obey public governments ought to control those governments: no taxation without representation. Should this reasoning not apply also to the government of a large economic enterprise? If not, why not?
>
> —Robert A. Dahl, The Dilemmas of Pluralist Democracy[77]

vate'' in today's world. It would allow more people more power over their private lives by ensuring them a greater voice in life-and-death economic matters.

▶ Your ideas about property are neither fair nor workable. Before going further, we need to address a closely related issue. Touching on many aspects of freedom, we've left one gaping hole—basic civil liberties, which include free speech, free assembly, and religious freedom.

The Market, Property, and Civil Liberties ★

◀ *Very true. The civil liberties we enjoy make us in the United States among the privileged in this world.*

The correlation between free economies and political and civil liberties is almost perfect.
—Lay Commission on Catholic Social Teaching and the U.S. Economy[80]

▶ Right. They exist only in a few dozen countries, and it's no coincidence that they're all capitalist.[79] Property rights, the market, and civil liberties grew together. The right to the exclusive use of property has been the basis of free expression, for no one—no government official—can tell you what to do. And it's the ethos of the market—the free exchange of goods—that makes the control of ideas very difficult. Just look at what is happening in Eastern Europe and other state-controlled economies today. With the introduction of at least some market distribution, we see the glimmering of free expression also.

Wherever there has been the kind of sweeping restructuring of wealth that you're advocating, civil liberties are just as much a victim of the process as the wealthy themselves are.

◀ *Private property and the market are no guarantors of civil liberties; many capitalist countries are among the world's worst violators of human rights: we need only think of Chile, El Salvador, South Korea, or South Africa. In fact, capitalism has coexisted throughout most of its history, not with democracies, but with governments ruled by emperors, kings, military strongmen, and outright despots.*

▶ An important distinction must be made. Capitalism has coexisted with authoritarian societies but never with totalitarian ones like the Soviet Union and China, in which the government not only denies citizens the right to participate but tries to control everything they think and say.

◀ *Isn't fascism a totalitarian system? Yet it emerged in capitalist Germany and Italy.*

But your argument is off the point, anyway, for none of the changes I advocate would threaten civil liberties. The contrary is true. In fact, many industrial countries have gone a lot farther than we have to reduce extremes in wealth, to end poverty, to protect workers' economic rights—all while enjoying civil liberties very much like our own. I'm thinking of the Scandinavian countries, West Germany, the Netherlands, and Austria, for example. [82]

In most cases the struggle to achieve economic rights—the right to union protection, for example—has helped strengthen, not weaken, civil liberties. Workers have had to press and extend the right to free speech and assembly in order to achieve their goals. [83]

▶ But what about the Third World? To carry out the reforms you imply means severely infringing on some people's property rights. Of course, they'll kick and scream—wouldn't you? The new rulers will restrict their rights to speak out against what is being inflicted upon them. Look at Cuba or Nicaragua today.

◀ *In the Third World, it would be hard to make the case that more equitable access to resources is accompanied by greater infringement of civil liberties. You mention Cuba and Nicaragua. But think of Chile, South Africa, Guatemala, and Pakistan—they're all countries where no real reform in access to resources has been permitted, but abuse of civil liberties is just as or more severe than in the countries you mention. The violators are those determined to block the reforms.*

... the diffusion of wealth and power and status in a market economy ... creates the "social space" within which civil and political liberty can flower ...
—Irving Kristol,
Two Cheers for Capitalism [81]

Obviously, social gains [in education, health, and protection from unemployment] ... are not a substitute for the essential citizen liberties .... In reality, those liberties have been the instrument by which the [social] advantages ... have been won, and have themselves in turn, been not a little strengthened by them.
—R. H. Tawney,
Equality, 1952 [84]

In the Third World, the choice isn't between a status quo protecting free expression and economic reforms that end up gagging people. As long as a privileged group lives in luxury while their neighbors are starving, we can be pretty sure that poor people will resist and that their civil liberties will be violated.

In any case, it's unreasonable to draw sweeping conclusions from Third World societies with no prior history of protection of civil liberties. In the end, whether changing the rules to allow redistribution of access to resources also must entail the denial of civil liberties is not for us to prejudge for other people. Civil liberties—and democracy, more broadly speaking—can only be protected if citizens demand them for themselves. What we do know is that the more our government intervenes— either to shore up an oppressive government or to overthrow a reform government—the more likely it is that civil liberties will be curtailed. [85]

▶ But our government *can* successfully use its influence to bring about greater democracy and civil liberties in Third World countries. Just look at Central America. There are four democratically elected governments today where only one existed just a decade ago. The U.S. can take a lot of credit.

◀ *But do elections necessarily reflect democracies guaranteeing free expression, even in the narrowly political sense?*

▶ Yes, because people have a choice. They can express themselves, often for the first time.

◀ *But are elections democratic if held after opposition leaders proposing reform have been assassinated or driven from the country because they threaten the interests of the wealthy?*
What I'm getting at is that democracy, including civil liberties, can't be separated from economic life. Free expression requires not only certain political institutions but certain economic realities as well. In the Third World this is easier to see. If you have no schooling, no land, no livelihood, how much "free expression" can you enjoy? Your voice doesn't carry very far. You must take whatever job is offered and shut up no matter how much a boss violates your rights. If this is true, then extending access to land and to education, for example, is

not simply a social or an economic reform but an essential step in fulfilling any honest definition of civil liberties.

You suggested earlier that property rights protect free speech because they give people an independent base, free from government. But it's not just government that can stifle free expression. Economic insecurity undercuts free expression here in the United States, too. We don't protect the right to the opportunity to work, joblessness is high, and many jobs pay poverty wages. These aren't just economic facts, they affect one's free expression. How free am I to complain against mistreatment on the job if few well-paying jobs are out there? Or imagine working for an arms contractor. Despite moral qualms about the arms race, might I feel compelled to push for more military spending to protect my job and my family's income?

Economic and Political— How Separate? ★

▶ Your ideas about poverty, the market, and now about property would subordinate economic life to political institutions. This leads precisely to the kind of unitary, totalitarian system that capitalism thankfully avoids. Capitalism maintains the distinction between economic and political life *on principle*—on the principle that a plurality of interests and rules best prevents the concentration of power. Once work life and social services become dominated by the political process, diverse power is held in a few bureaucratic hands, exactly the concentration you claim to loathe. And this is the problem of socialism: economic and political convergence in a single power structure. That's why there are no civil liberties in socialist countries.

In other words, keeping economic power strictly outside government and within the market is vital to freedom because government, complete with police powers, exercises authority over the whole person, whereas in economic life, each employer has limited authority over only one aspect of our lives—our work.

◄ *Perceiving economic power as so much less threatening than state power, you forget that in political life we who live in political democracies have won certain rights protecting us against arbitrary state power—these rights we have yet to win in regard to corporate power. In this sense, we are less protected in our economic lives.*

Civil liberties don't exist in communist countries largely because a single, political elite dominates both political and economic life. But one could well argue that in capitalism both aspects of life are dominated by an economic elite. Going beyond both means dispersing power more broadly by making control over productive property more accountable and dispersing income so that the market can respond to human needs.

So my views wouldn't tie political and economic life together—they're inevitably intertwined. This being true, we'd better be sure that the economic conditions for real political freedom are in place, that is, the widest possible dispersion of economic power in the form of job opportunity, income, and wealth. This is the only way to prevent what many of our founders feared, the subversion of political democracy by concentrated economic power.

▶ And I'd say that once you try to address economic questions through political mechanisms, you've already lost the battle against concentrated power.

I hope we shall crush in its birth the aristocracy of our monied corporations which dare already to challenge our government to a trial of strength, and bid defiance to the laws of our country.
—Thomas Jefferson, 1816[88]

Summing Up the Dialogue ★

WHAT IS THE LINK BETWEEN PROPERTY AND FREEDOM?

▶ The institution of private property protects citizens against intrusive government power.

It provides a stimulus to investment, freeing the whole society from scarcity.

It allows people freely to enjoy the fruits of their labor.

◀ *There is no automatic link between property and protection against the government: the wealthiest property holders can use the power of government for their own ends.*

Home ownership and income-producing property provide economic security, the basis of free choice. So when property concentrates in few hands, freedom for the majority diminishes.

UNDER WHAT CONDITIONS CAN PROPERTY SERVE FREEDOM?

▶ When the government cannot interfere with the right to accumulate property.

When owners have exclusive rights—except to do harm to others, of course—to use their property as they see fit.

When property is privately held so that responsibility for its use is clearly defined.

◀ *When everyone has access to productive property necessary to earn a living.*

When accumulation is limited so that the few do not gain power over the many.

When ownership is understood as a cluster of rights and responsibilities, so that those making decisions about the use of property have to live with the consequences, and those who have to live with the consequences participate in the decisions.

WHAT IS THE LINK BETWEEN PROPERTY, THE MARKET, AND CIVIL LIBERTIES?

▶ The private property/market system creates an open environment, not controlled by central power, in which civil liberties best flourish.

Challenging this system results in assaults on civil liberties by those imposing their new order.

◀ *Where property is permitted to accumulate in few hands, civil liberties are undermined regardless of what the law says. Citizens made dependent and economically insecure have no voice, or a weak voice, in affairs of the body politic.*

Throughout history, citizens' efforts to make the property/ market system more fair have resulted in a continuing expansion of civil liberties.

PART ★ FIVE

Freedom and Democracy

Democracy is perhaps the most promiscuous word
in the world of public affairs.
—Bernard Crick, *In Defence of Politics*[1]

Democracy: Countervailing Powers or Accountability? ★

◀ To talk meaningfully about the market and property, we've already had to touch on many aspects of democracy. Now we need to define what we mean by democracy in the first place.

This has got to be easier than talking about property! At least there's widespread agreement in this country about what democracy means. It is representative government—leaders elected from among a number of candidates, not just appointed by a single party as in communist states. The essence of democracy is selecting good leaders.

As I pointed out much earlier, the market guarantees our freedom in economic life. And in parallel fashion, the "market" in our political life—competing parties and candidates—guarantees freedom by offering us real choices.

◀ *But appearances can deceive. Some countries have had dozens of political parties as well as elections, while power remains in the hands of a small group, often of military strongmen. Elections and multiple parties can actually disguise the fact that leadership answers to a privileged minority.*

So let's not confuse political mechanisms with a core principle of democracy—the accountability of decision makers to all those who must live with their decisions. With this principle, we can cut through appearances. Take a real world example: If in Central America or the Philippines, a government refuses to stand up against the minority interests of wealthy landowners in order to enforce a law allotting idle land to hungry families with no land, then it isn't accountable to the majority who are landless. Elections may have been held. There may be many parties. But we can be pretty sure that the landless weren't fairly represented.

Let's take another example here at home. Most Americans

> . . . the concept of competition for leadership. . . . [may be usefully compared with] the concept of competition in the economic sphere . . . in political life there is always some competition, though perhaps only a potential one, for the allegiance of the people.
> —Joseph Schumpeter, *Capitalism, Socialism and Democracy*[2]

believe health care should be a citizen's right,[3] *but tens of millions of Americans aren't covered, and Washington has yet to come up with a plan to put health care within everybody's reach.*

▶ There will never be a one-to-one correlation between majority opinion and government action. That's out of the question. Every item would have to be decided by referendum!

In fact, one of the greatest threats to democracy is precisely your idea that democracy means government should be continually obedient to eruptions of popular opinion. Representative democracy means that those who are to govern, once elected, must rely on their own judgments.

Popular opinion is easily manipulated. This fallacy that government must reflect popular opinion leads officials to try to shape the very opinions that they're supposedly responding to. "Affirmative action," for example, could only have been dreamed up by government officials who wanted to impose on others their own social philosophy. They then did a fine job selling the policy by convincing people that minorities couldn't make it without special (and unfair!) advantage.

Worst of all, popular opinion is like a sand dune, taking its shape from whatever wind happens to be blowing through the marketplace of ideas. That's why popular opinion must be refined through the political community—elected government—before it is to be taken seriously.[5]

◀ *But your view can easily become an apology for despotism. Dismiss public sentiment if you will, but to the extent that government isn't responding to the long-expressed priorities of the majority, democracy is in doubt, and citizens must ask: To whom is government really listening?*

▶ Government must consider minority interests, too. All we can reasonably demand of a democratic government is that it remain true to its constitution and that all power not rest in the same hands.

So my view of democracy is more sober than yours—it's the absence of tyranny. Certainly I am not naive enough to think that we could do away with a governing elite, a social stratum with experience in public life.[6] But democracy ensures that

Of all the heresies afloat in modern democracy, none is greater . . . and potentially more destructive of proper governmental function than that which declares the legitimacy of government to be directly proportional to its roots in public opinion.
—Robert Nisbet, "Public Opinion Versus Popular Opinion,"[4]

[T]hought must be given to generating a satisfactory (let us not flinch from the phrase) governing class. That here must be such a class is, I think, beyond peradventure.
—George Will, *Statecraft as Soulcraft*[7]

there's not just one center of power—as in totalitarianism—but several.

Our constitutional structure of checks and balances separating the executive, legislative, and judicial branches of government, has never been surpassed as a model for avoiding tyranny. Its dispersion of power in several centers makes it relatively immune from takeover by an economic, political, or other elite group.

◀ *Your theory of countervailing power begs a crucial question: Are these "powers," no matter how many, broadly accountable?*

▶ Elected government with a structure of countervailing centers of power is simply a mechanism; it doesn't guarantee accountability. In fact, it can't guarantee any particular outcome. It can, however, prevent tyranny by either a minority or a majority.

◀ *There's another vision of democracy with roots in our history as deep or deeper than yours. In it, democracy is not competing centers of power at the top but a structure in which each of us has some—in which no one is left with none at all!*

▶ In our system, every person *does* maintain some degree of power. Since every citizen can vote, each of us has some power—if we choose to use it.

◀ *Let's test your view that our democracy leaves no one powerless. You'd agree, no doubt, that, first and foremost, all living creatures want to eat and to feed their offspring?*

▶ Of course.

◀ *Then, if millions of people in our country are going hungry—or if even a few are—is this not proof that they have been stripped of all power? In the language of rights, they've been denied their right to life itself.*

▶ Absolutely not. The extent of hunger in America is grossly overstated. But if anyone is hungry, it means only that they have not used the power that they have in a free-market democracy to get a job and provide for themselves.

The accumulation of all powers, legislative, executive, and judiciary, in the same hands, . . . may justly be pronounced the very definition of tyranny . . . the preservation of liberty requires that the three great departments of power should be separate and distinct.
—James Madison, *The Federalist Papers*, no. 47, 1788[8]

Wherein the will of everyone has a just influence . . . the mass of mankind . . . enjoys a precious degree of liberty and happiness.
—Thomas Jefferson, 1787[9]

Recent changes in the American economy and public policies have produced a situation virtually unprecedented in modern times: An economic recovery that is having little impact on the nation's 20 million hungry citizens.
—Physician Task Force on Hunger, *Hunger Reaches Blue Collar America*, 1987[10]

◀ *I might agree if we were talking about something less basic to survival. Even education. People might well choose not to use their right to public education and instead teach their children at home or drop out of school themselves. But eating? If people are hungry, it is not by choice!*

Hunger within a political democracy suggests to me only one conclusion: Unless democracy is extended to make economic rights as basic as civil liberties—as I argued earlier—a minority can easily be made powerless to secure the necessities of their own development. Your notion of countervailing centers of power might prevent tyranny by a visible few, but it can't prevent this invisible tyranny of economic powerlessness.

Your definition of democracy is inadequate to protect life.

▶ But you've shifted the ground of our discussion from political power to issues of economic power. If someone is not eating, that's an economic or psychological problem, not a political one. People must solve their economic problems for themselves—mainly, by getting jobs.

◀ *What if I can't find a job that pays enough to provide for my family? What if I can't work? To be meaningful, rights must be connected with power. It's only because no one has to pay tuition that we view education as a citizen's right. Our rights are what we have the power to do, whether rich or poor. If people are hungry, it's because we have not yet made the right to life inviolable. To do so, minimally we would have to expand our rights to include the opportunity to earn a living, health insurance, and decent provision for those unable to work.*

So political democracy actually rests on an economic foundation—a citizenry with economic security who are therefore able to think and act independently. This insight goes back to at least the seventeenth century. Then, it was believed that those without wealth, who had to work for others, could not think for themselves. For this reason, they were excluded from the democratic franchise.[13] But today our solution must be the opposite: to extend economic rights as the basis for an independent citizenry, the only safe foundation for political democracy.

▶ As I said when we began, in a free society, government can't guarantee economic rights. Must I repeat this point? To ensure economic rights would entail a bigger, more intrusive state.

With more power removed from the individual and given over to government, citizens would lose more than they would gain. *[Part I more fully discusses the appropriate role of government.]*

Government: Protection Against Power or Participation in Power? ★

▶ Just as freedom is at risk, so democracy is endangered when government tries to guarantee people's security through forced redistribution of wealth. Necessarily, this means violating property rights.

And if by democracy we mean the opposite of authoritarian rule by a few, then democracy depends on a limited role for government. Government, by definition, involves a relative few making decisions for the many.

Nobody likes government. It traps us in a curious paradox: we need it to protect our interests while at the same time it is the greatest threat to our interests! That's why we cannot allow ourselves the temptation of believing government can solve all or even most of our problems.

◀ *But why is it that so many Americans perceive government as a threat? Because they feel it is outside their control. So, just limiting government's size is no solution. We have to ask: How can government become a vehicle through which citizens can participate in shaping community and national life?[16] In answering, Americans can reclaim insights of many of our nation's founders. Jefferson, among others, believed government was not just a vehicle to defend ourselves against power but an avenue to participate in power.[17]*

Growth in government means a movement away from private decisions, which require unanimous agreement but affect relatively few people, to collective decisions, which, although they affect many, can be made by a small group.
—Richard B. McKenzie,
Bound to Be Free[14]

A democracy, then, has for its characteristic object and effect, the securing its members against oppression and depredation at the hands of those functionaries which it employs for its defence . . .

—Jeremy Bentham,
Constitutional Code, 1830[15]

In ancient times liberty had meant the right to participate in government; now [in early America] it meant freedom from government—was that progress?
— James MacGregor Burns, *The Vineyard of Liberty*[18]

Where every man is a sharer in the direction of his ward-republic, or of some of the higher ones, and feels that he is participator in the government of affairs, not merely at an election one day in the year, but every day . . . he will let the heart be torn out of his body sooner than his power be wrested from him by a Caesar or a Bonaparte.
— Thomas Jefferson, 1816[23]

▶ What you are hinting at is naive. Representative government has always and will always mean a leadership group making decisions. So a primary challenge of democracy is to ensure that that leadership group is of the highest quality.[19]

◀ *As isolated individuals it's impossible for citizens to participate meaningfully in shaping public choices. You're right. But as part of organizations—religious, ethnic, union, civic, school, and so on—millions of Americans effectively engage in developing public policy. Citizens' movements have ended slavery, gotten the vote for women, won the eight-hour day, and ended child labor. Just in the last three decades, citizen action for civil rights and environmental concerns, just to name two, has significantly shaped public life.[20]*

Today citizen action is addressing key economic concerns. In Montana, environmental, labor, farm, and other groups facing their state's deteriorating economy have undertaken a series of citizens' training sessions to analyze alternative policies to pave the way for a common vision for economic recovery.[21] In Baltimore, church groups, business leaders, and the public schools have developed what they call a "commonwealth agreement" in which they pledge to work together to ensure every high school graduate a job with opportunity.[22] In Catholic parishes across the country, congregations are discussing how to act on the 1986 bishops' pastoral letter on the economy, which calls on citizens to help end poverty.

Politics Captured by Minorities or Politics as Community Life? ★

▶ But your notion that democracy means getting citizens more involved ignores a most obvious feature of human behavior: citizens have little incentive to work for what is in the general interest. Since one's single vote has little impact, it's rational for a citizen to get no more deeply involved in politics than voting occasionally for a party label or even just by whim.[24]

I'm not being cynical or judgmental, but why should people give up their leisure to work in a process that is difficult to grasp, probably a grand hassle, and returns little to them? In fact, most Americans are unable to say how government affects their lives at all.[26] A study in 1972 showed that the proportion of Americans who spent any time on political participation during the week of the study was less than 1 percent![27] Surely participation hasn't risen in the Eighties.

◄ *Involvement in official politics may be low, but if politics means citizen action, it's way up.*

► But my point is this: Without much incentive to get involved in details of public issues, average voters understandably take up those ideas that are "in the air." And, unfortunately, the idea that has been in the air for some time is that if something is bad—junk food in the schools or poverty in the Third World—our government ought to suppress it, and if something is good—saving an endangered species or better housing—government ought to promote it. And anyone who dares oppose it is made to feel selfish and mean-spirited. No wonder people are susceptible to your ideas and government keeps getting bigger and bigger.

But who decides what's good or bad to begin with? A few self-selected people who press their own agendas. But that's only part of the problem. Precisely because most citizens don't see it's in their interest to go to the trouble to get involved, those who do take on a particular cause have disproportionate influence. Legislators are understandably more responsive to the pressure of these special interest groups than to the general interest of average voters who are—quite rationally—apathetic.[28]

So, what your idea of greater participation amounts to is giving more room to lobbyists and what I would call "hobbyists," those who identify with some cause—whether consumer safety or a speedy cure for the disease that killed a family member or whatever—and want government to solve it. The result isn't more democracy; it's rule by minorities.[30]

There is no real solution because the problem lies in human behavior itself and the nature of political life. But we can minimize the threat to general well-being and have more democracy by constitutionally limiting the functions of government. Cer-

Acquiring and acting on information about public issues has a low payoff because it is a "public good." . . . If an average voter should go to the trouble . . . most of the benefits, in the form of sounder policy, would accrue to others . . . He has little incentive to work for what is in the general interest.
—Leland B. Yeager, "Is There a Bias Toward Overregulation?"[25]

. . . the effective operation of a democratic political system usually requires some measure of apathy and non-involvement on the part of some individuals and groups.
—Samuel Huntington, "The Democratic Distemper"[29]

tainly we can keep it out of economic life, which will always be inherently more democratic than government because it is driven directly by our individual "dollar votes."

◀ *To you, political involvement is only a cost that citizens weigh against an improbable return to themselves. But like other voluntary activities you yourself extolled earlier, political activity offers the rewards that many Americans yearn for— fellowship, satisfaction in teamwork, new skills, and knowledge of new issues. And it offers heightened self-respect gained in taking a principled stand. Self-respect in no longer feeling like a passive victim of outside, distant forces is a powerful reward.*

To you, democracy is a means toward some other end—like protecting my property or my individual rights. To me, democracy is in itself also of value: its commitment to participation, self-government, and action from principle—not just interests—means that democratic life offers essential channels of human development. So, democracy isn't just about the making of public policy; it's also about the making of citizens.[31]

▶ You make the political process sound like some sort of human development crusade! That's not what it's about. It's not through government but through private associations and interpersonal commitments that individuals develop.

◀ *And you confuse cause and effect: the reason most Americans remain so detached from political issues isn't inherent in political life; it's that core determinants of our well-being—both the corporate engine of our economy and the money system—are kept largely outside the bounds of citizen deliberation. So, if my family's main worry is job security and being able to afford a home of our own, what good is it to join with others to advocate full employment or lower interest rates, since I can't see how the polity itself can bring them about?*

Your "rational" citizen's apathy may be rational, but only to the degree that the underlying antidemocratic structure of our economic life remains unchallenged.

▶ What are you talking about? Of course the government is not allowed to dictate employment opportunities or provide a home for everyone in a privately run economy.

[Democracy is people] acting together [to] define the ideal aims of the common life. . . . Through acting with others to define and achieve what can be called good for all, each realizes part of his own meaning and destiny.

—John H. Schaar, "Equality of Opportunity and Beyond"[32]

◀ *"Privately" run? The continuing fiction that giant corpora-tions are "private"—in the sense of being exempt from public accountability—is itself a reflection of the power of wealthy individual and corporate interests to influence public policies.*

▶ And you complain because you have no say in monetary pol-icy? Well, if the monetary system were controlled by Congress, the result would be a nightmare of financial instability!

◀ *Our monetary system—controlled by the Federal Reserve—has since the nineteenth century been so shrouded in mystery and so removed from public debate, that most Americans have no idea what it is. Yet within the Federal Reserve's governing structure are the very same banking interests it is supposed to monitor.[33] So where's this "countervailing power" you say is the essence of democracy?*

No wonder more and more Americans believe the issues that most affect their daily lives—security and opportunity—are outside their control.[35] So even voting can seem pointless. A smaller percentage of eligible U.S. voters—barely more than half—vote than for virtually any elected government in the world. In most western European countries, 80 to 90 percent of eligible voters vote.

▶ In fact, voter turnout is up compared to earlier in this century. But you seem to be hinting at some sort of "participatory democ-racy" completely unfit for the complex, high-speed world we live in. People don't have time to get involved in community life. Besides, our communities are just too big for town meetings and face-to-face decision-making.

◀ *The scale and pace of modern life don't rule out community involvement as democracy's base. We all live within political jurisdictions small enough to allow us to get involved. And some of today's advances in telecommunications—community-controlled cable TV, for example—could make it easier for peo-ple to help set their community's priorities. To repeat: The real problem is that core determinants of our well-being are outside the democratic process.*

▶ You refuse to see that the "democratic process" you so roman-ticize is really a battle of minorities, each with its own ax to

[The Federal Reserve system amounts to] a dictatorship on money matters by a banker's club.

—Wright Patman, former chair of the House Banking Committee[34]

Many public policies are better explained as the outcome of pure power struggle—clothed in a rhetoric of public interest that is a mere figleaf—among narrow interest or pressure groups.

—Richard A. Posner, "The DeFunis Case . . ."[36]

grind. The most passionate, the most vocal, maybe the most unscrupulous will always be best at capturing the ear of the representative who in theory represents all of us.

◄ *Obviously, it can be that—but* must *it be? A great deal turns on what we as citizens come to believe is possible. The democratic process need not mean isolated individuals or groups battling to impose their fixed views on everyone else. What distinguishes a democratic process is that through it people change themselves—so democracy isn't simply about casting votes and using our dollars to register our preset opinions and wants, or simply to react to preset choices served up to us. Joining with others to solve common problems, weighing the consequences of our choices, citizens together help to create new options.* [37]

In this understanding of democracy, citizens' relationship to "politics" changes. It is not just lining up at a polling place every few years.

Let me give you one example. Since the 1970s, seventeen "citizen participation districts" in St. Paul, Minnesota, with elected, volunteer leaders have been involving citizens directly in allocating public improvement funds for everything from trees to traffic lights.

► I can imagine the endless fights among the neighborhoods over who's going to get how much of the government's largesse, and even bigger headaches for the city officials.

◄ *Neighborhoods come to better understand each others' needs, say those involved. Yes, it's taken more time, but to a lot of people in St. Paul it must be time well spent, because these groups are now taking initiative in everything from day care, to recycling, to neighborhood responsibility in caring for the elderly.* [40] *And the hassled bureaucrats? They probably feel some relief, too; with citizens sharing in responsibility for decisions, they don't have to take all the heat.*

► Community self-help is terrific. It's what I've advocated all along. But your repeated complaints about economic decision-making suggest you really have something else in mind. Suggesting that citizens use the political process to make economic decisions ultimately means political interference with the

Voting suggests a group of people in a cafeteria bargaining about what they can buy as a group that will suit their individual tastes. Strong democracy suggests a group of people in a cafeteria contriving new menus, inventing new recipes, and experimenting with new diets in the effort to create a public taste that they can all share . . .
　　　　　—Benjamin Barber,
　　　　　Strong Democracy [38]

Democracy is not brute numbers; it is a genuine union of true individuals. . . . the essence of democracy is creating. The technique of democracy is group organization.
　　　　　—Mary Parker Follett,
　　　　　The New State, 1918 [39]

. . . democracy developed precisely in the same Western countries in which modern capitalism unfolded. And modern democracy was clearly one of the historical achievements of the bourgeoisie, the rising capitalist class.
　　　　　—Peter L. Berger,
　　　　　The Capitalist Revolution [41]

prerogatives of private businesses. Your ideas thus blur the all-important line I've tried to get you to see—that between economic and political power. Capitalism maintains that line; you want to dissolve it. But this separation is vital to a democracy. By separating economic power from political power, in a very real sense capitalism gave birth to modern democracy.

In totalitarian systems, politics and the economy are united. In democratic capitalism they are separate spheres.[42] Independent economic power can keep a check on government power.[43] Yes, some minimal government regulation is necessary, but beyond that we don't have politicians interfering in economic affairs—and to the extent we do, our economy suffers.

> . . . the free market provides an offset to whatever concentration of political power may arise. The combination of economic and political *power* in the same hands is a sure recipe for tyranny.
>
> —Milton and Rose Friedman,
> *Free to Choose*[44]

Economic and Political Life: The Division? The Interplay? ★

◄ *But economic and political life are unavoidably linked. For one, those with greater wealth have more political influence, especially in competing for public office: the biggest spender is four times more likely to win.*[45] *The overwhelming majority of elected officials come from the wealthiest 5 percent of the population; most U.S. senators are millionaires.*[46]

► You've hit on yet another inescapable trade-off within a free political system—the fact that those with more money can offer more support to their favorite candidates. Of course, that gives them more influence, but those with less money to contribute can compensate by giving more of their time.

This trade-off is unavoidable simply because the alternative would mean untenable restrictions on First Amendment liberties that Americans are unwilling to accept. Campaign giving is simply one form of participation in politics that a democracy should be wary of discouraging. In electing the president, we've already placed limits on an individual's campaign contribution and on the total that candidates who accept public funding can spend.

These limits directly inhibit free speech, but the Supreme Court accepted them as necessary in order to prevent an even more serious danger—the potential of unfair influence on elected officials by the biggest contributors to their campaigns. But the Court rejected limits on how much presidential candidates can spend of their own money and on what Americans can spend independently; that is, if they have no dealings with the candidate.[47] There's no justification for these further limits.

◀ *No? On the heels of these decisions, in the 1980 presidential race,* twenty-seven times *more so-called independent money went to Reagan than to Carter, evidence that "money votes" are way out of line with citizen votes.*[48]

We can close the loop-holes and extend the system of public financing tied to contribution limits—to all major contests. Otherwise, the rising price of a congressional campaign (up six-fold to $3 million in just a decade) will continue to eliminate good potential candidates. And incumbents can store up "war chests" for future races, intimidating the competition. In recent years at least four congresspeople, with hundreds of thousands of dollars on hand, ran for re-election unopposed. Their money no doubt helped scare off challengers, killing the competition that democracy depends on.[49]

▶ You've got it completely backwards. Rising campaign expenditures aren't bad, they're good! They're dramatic evidence of the health of our democracy, hardly a sign of citizens being shut out. In fact, more citizens giving more money reflects greater interest in and commitment to the political process. Campaign financing reforms have so limited individual contributions that candidates must solicit help from more citizens. Over half of all contributors give $100 or less.[50] And many more citizens are involved in lobbying in Washington today than ever in the past. In fact, the top-spending lobbying organization in Washington is Common Cause—a broad-based "citizens" lobby on a wide variety of issues.

◀ *It's not citizen involvement but the four thousand special-interest Political Action Committees (PACs) that increasingly determine the political process. Last year, members of the House likely to run for reelection got almost half their funds from PACs.*

▶ I certainly don't understand why you are so down on PACs. I thought you believed in participation! PACs represent a broad cross-section of interests—from business to labor to all sorts of peace and ethnic groups, many of whom were never active in the political process before.[51]

◀ *I now see how your earlier definition of the political process—the vying of interest blocks for the official's favor—becomes self-fulfilling. With PACs as primary actors, that's exactly what it becomes. PACs aren't a form of citizen participation. Citizen participation means joining with others to debate issues, to seek high-caliber leaders who share one's political values, and to keep those leaders accountable. PACs do none of this and PACs care about none of this. They are money-blocks—primarily for the banking, real estate, insurance, and oil industries, and for labor unions—with fixed and often narrow agendas. Their interest is not in choosing the superior candidate, not in debate, or even persuasion. They simply want to make the representative feel dependent enough on their money to sway their votes.*

Six to one, PAC dollars go to incumbents in order to curry favor with those most likely to win. And if their candidate loses? Well, PACs often turn around and offer the winner a big gift—surely proof that their interest is in gaining influence, not in the candidate's philosophy or public record.[53]

> When these political action committees give money, they expect something in return other than good government.
> —Senator Robert Dole[52]

▶ Attempts at campaign spending reform in many countries have hardly solved the problem and have in some ways made it worse. Spending controls have ended up benefiting the incumbents and the established parties. The experiences of West Germany, Austria, Finland, and several other countries suggest that the very complexity of the procedures has increased the political party's dependence on hired professionals and downplayed the role of volunteer activists. It's made the party system more rigid, not opened it up.[54]

◀ *You ignore the positive lessons. Great Britain effectively limits campaign spending;*[55] *and nearly every other major democ-*

racy limits candidates' access to TV and distributes it equitably.[56] Until we have the courage to eliminate the power of wealth in elections, we'll have what one long–time investigator calls "the best congress money can buy."[57] A democracy can't allow free political speech to be reduced to some sort of freedom to spend. That we've never guaranteed!

▶ But the freedom to spend our money as we please—a basic part of freedom of choice—*is* essential in a free society. And when virtually every form of public speech requires the expenditure of money, restricting a person's contributions is directly limiting their freedom of speech.[58]

◀ So why not go to the root of the problem—making sure that as much as possible exercising free speech doesn't require expenditures? After all, the Bill of Rights doesn't say that we have freedom of speech as long as can pay for it. It says we have free speech, period.

In a democracy, free speech means more than self-expression without fear of reprisal. It means the right to help freely shape the decisions we all have to live by. Democracy therefore depends on citizens having access to the widest possible viewpoints with which to interact in order to act responsibly. If this is the very foundation of democracy, then not just campaigns for public office but all venues of civic discourse must be open, not limited to the highest bidders, or contingent in any way upon wealth.

The opinion page of the newspaper is a small example. If Mobil Oil and other companies can buy a big chunk of The New York Times opinion page to tell us what to think on public policies, democracy is being violated. We're letting money buy political influence. Let's move in the opposite direction: establishing many more opportunities in all media—radio, TV, the press—for citizens to express themselves freely. And I mean freely, without paying.

▶ Look, instead of crying foul, you—along with others who believe as you do—could buy space yourself. I've seen ads there paid for by nonprofit groups for causes you yourself espouse. And I really don't see what is so different about Mobil's comments on the opinion page and that of the invited contributors. They're probably just as self-interested as Mobil, some also motivated by profit. The only difference is that Mobil had to pay—so what?

If you remove the market from its function in distributing access to the media, what will you put in its place? Either government or unaccountable individual editors decide. What's more democratic about that?

◄ *We have always limited "the freedom to spend" to make a public good available to all. We don't let the Rockefellers buy Yellowstone, for example, because we believe that all Americans should be able to enjoy this national treasure. (But we did let them spend $20 million to get Nelson, Winthrop, and Jay elected![61]) In a democracy, shouldn't means to influence public opinion be considered a public good—to be kept open to the public? Once agreeing on this principle, we would discover many ways to open debate. And, yes, to answer your question specifically—allowing editors to seek a variety of views is more democratic than selling off the opinion page!*

► But your analogy of the national park is misleading. Keeping it open to the public is simple, but eliminating wealth as a factor in influencing public opinion would mean endless restrictions. The better off will always be more able to influence politicians and use the media to their advantage. Trying to do the impossible would mean ever more interference with personal freedom.

◄ *Because a principle is never perfectly realizable is no excuse for doing nothing. And one thing we can do is to protect citizens' access to the widest possible range of viewpoints and outlets for expressing their views by reversing the movement toward media monopoly—media outlets controlled by fewer and fewer people.*

► What do you mean? We probably have the freest press in the world! We're one of the few countries in which the government does not heavily control the media.

◄ *Government can control information and stifle free expression without owning the media—by greater secrecy (reflected in the expanding CIA budget), by not-so-subtle intimidation (like the FBI's surveillance of groups opposing U.S. policy toward Central America), and by barring dissenting voices from*

make sure that nobody who wanted to speak was prevented from doing so by being hit over the head, locked up, tortured, or shot.

—G. Warren Nutter,
"Income Redistribution"[60]

If the influence of economic inequalities on politicians—an influence that is indirect as well as direct—were ever to be eliminated, the required coercive restrictions on free expression and association would be quite enormous.

—James S. Fishkin,
Justice, Equality, Opportunity and the Family[62]

our country. [63] *To expose this kind of control, we need competitive news sources—with no vested interests. And that's what we are fast losing.*

And government control is not the only threat to free public discourse. Control of news outlets by powerful economic interests also poses a threat. Despite tens of thousands of media outlets—from newspapers to TV stations to motion pictures—most are now owned by just twenty-six corporations, down by almost half in less than a decade. [64]

▶ There is no evidence that such ownership patterns have in any way compromised the American media. In fact, the greater resources of these large corporate owners have made possible more citizen access to information—through expensive satellite hookups and other innovations beyond the budget constraints of smaller firms.

◀ *If you don't think ownership influences content, then why fear government ownership? You're arguing out of both sides of your mouth!*

▶ Come on now . . . twenty-six corporations as owners is not the same as *one* government agency in control. There's still competition, and that's what we're talking about.

> It is normal for all large businesses to make serious efforts to influence the news. . . . Now they own most of the news media that they wish to influence.
>
> —Ben Bagdikian,
> *The Media Monopoly* [67]

◀ *Competition within a geographic market is what counts, and in many cities there's now only one major daily. A free media also means an* independent *media. A few decades ago most newspapers were owned independently; but now three-fourths are owned by outside corporations. [65]*

And the twenty-six corporations controlling American media also invest in agribusiness, airlines, nuclear power, and banking, among many other things, whose profits are all affected by public opinion and public policies. For these parent corporations to ensure that their media subsidiaries don't damage their other interests is, after all, only good business. [66]

But I certainly agree that measures to protect and enhance free civic speech will have limited impact as long as we tolerate such enormous concentrations of wealth to begin with.

▶ It seems that you just can't get away from this, can you! You see the world through one, and only one, lens.

◄ *No, but it is a useful lens, when you consider that Washington lobbyists spend more influencing representatives than the American people spend paying their salaries![68] Who has the bucks will not only influence who the candidates are, but how votes go in Congress.[69]*

Just an example: Between 1981 and 1986, PACs representing the electric, coal, and automobile industries against clean air legislation donated more than $15 million to congressional candidates. They appear to have gotten what they paid for: within a key House energy committee, only one of the ten members receiving the biggest contributions from these PACs cosponsored a 1986 bill to control acid rain pollution; of the ten members receiving the least PAC help all were cosponsors. So the law was stymied despite overwhelming support among Americans for tougher clean air legislation.[70]

▶ Your picture is entirely too simple. In many instances, Congress has voted against the interests of, say, large corporations. In 1987, the government succeeded in fining oil companies billions of dollars for what it considers violations of price controls during the seventies. Aren't oil companies the most powerful of all American corporations? And what about the 1986 tax bill? It ended many tax breaks for corporations—good evidence that the Fortune 500 hardly call the shots.

◄ *Yes, and at the same time Congress slashed corporate tax rates to the lowest in the industrial world.*

▶ A wise move on sheer economic grounds. But, in general, I would not argue with your basic point: Money talks. It's always true to some extent. But you've ignored the most obvious—and perhaps the only realistic—remedy.

The more power government has, the greater prize it is, the more people will attempt to seize its channels for their private designs. Any illegitimate use of government by private economic interests is rooted in a preexisting illegitimate power of government: the power of government to enrich some at others' expense.[72] We can best address the problem by expunging this prior evil: the less extensive we allow government powers to become, the less interested in controlling it will be those with wealth to throw around.

That's why I advocate what one might call the night-watch-

We can have democracy in this country or we can have wealth in a few hands, but we can't have both.
—Justice Louis D. Brandeis, 1941[71]

The minimal state best reduces the chances of such takeover or manipulation of the state by persons desiring power or economic benefits . . .
—Robert Nozick, *Anarchy, State, and Utopia*[73]

man state, government restricted primarily to law-and-order functions.

◀ *But these powers are potentially the most threatening to individual liberty! If you believe that citizens are capable of keeping security functions—armed and necessarily secretive—under democratic control, surely you must concede the possibility of keeping the less easily abused economic and social functions of government responsible to the public interest.*

> Men born to freedom are naturally alert to repel invasion of their liberty by evil-minded rulers. The greater dangers to liberty lurk in insidious encroachment by men of zeal, well-meaning but without understanding.
> —Justice Louis Brandeis, 1928[74]

▶ No, to the contrary. The threat of government intrusion here is actually greater: while citizens are on guard against state police powers, they more readily allow do-good social planners to steal their freedom without full awareness of what they are losing.

But the real point is that you don't grasp the built-in protection of the public interest within our economic system—countervailing powers. Since government and business are not merged as in the communist system, power is more dispersed. The trick is to keep it separate. The greatest danger here is not too much business influence in government, as you charge; it's the other way around—too much government control of business. The market and firms participating in the market serve, as do other voluntary groupings, to empower individuals against intrusive state power.[75]

◀ *But your "countervailing powers" only seem to go one way! You stress only the need for independent economic interests to check government's power, but not the need for a strong, democratic government to check economic power. Our government can't effectively counter the power of private business interests because we're trapped by the myth that they're "private" and because the role of wealth within our political system itself stymies fair citizen participation.*

> The problem with defense spending is to figure out how far you should go without destroying from within what you are trying to defend from without.
> —President Dwight Eisenhower[76]

Perhaps the biggest danger in this dual trap is what President Eisenhower warned us against: a military–industrial complex that usurps political power. The top ten corporations in the Fortune 500 are all major weapons or petroleum suppliers to the Pentagon, able to bring tremendous economic and political clout to get congressional and military support for their weapons programs. They shape the military policy of the nation. It's too bad your fixation on government's threat blinds you to such a dangerous usurpation of public power.[77]

▶ No, I understand the threat of private interests using government for their own ends. But since this is inescapable, the answer, as I've already said, is obvious: Provide fewer vehicles through which economic power can have influence. The government regulatory agencies are one example. If you're worried about private interests capturing the public bodies supposedly established to monitor them, get rid of the regulation, or at least greatly reduce it.[78]

◀ *From the frying pan into the fire! I'm not eager to take that jump. Instead, we can attack the root problem: we've confined America's democratic principles, including the accountability of decision makers, solely to political life.* That *we can change.*

A Democratic Economy? ★

▶ What are you suggesting—that workers have "voting rights" on the job? It's absurd. Our economic system *is* democratic. People do not have direct control over the economy through their representatives, thank God, but through our consumer dollars we exert decisive control.

◀ *To call our economic system democratic because our dollars vote is a travesty when some Americans have one thousand times more of this "voting power" than others, and as few as four thousand individuals control half the nation's industrial assets.*[79]

▶ You love to point an accusing finger. But a business, no matter who owns it, is always at the mercy of consumers; it must respond to what we consumers want or it will surely fail. The fact that thousands of businesses go under every year means that the consumer remains sovereign.

Our economy is also democratic because it is based upon giving people the widest possible choice. Striving to make profit for themselves, businesses are at the same time providing Americans with choice unparalleled anywhere in the world.

Finally, our economy is democratic because Americans have the right to organize economic life without government telling us what to do. In a free-market democracy anyone can start a business, buy and sell, without interference.

Our nation's founders never meant for the democratic principle of one person, one vote to apply in private affairs, where it is inappropriate. In the family, schools, and business, authority is based on other principles. In these social institutions, authority reflects differing levels of knowledge, experience, and responsibility.

◄ *Lumping big business together with other "private" matters is a little outdated and artificial, isn't it, given the enormous size and influence of corporations in our lives?*

► We just went through this, so let me just say that whether you call economic life private or public, the notion that non-owners should have decision-making rights along with owners is patently unfair. Under capitalism, workers get a return proportional to what they contribute. Owners are rewarded for contributing risk, inventiveness, and initiative, as well as the machines the workers use. Workers are rewarded for the value they add. Owners shoulder the responsibility. They should be able to make the decisions because their stake in the enterprise is so much greater. That's perfectly fair.

◄ *This sounds familiar! Yours is precisely the argument used for centuries against citizens' right to vote, and against equal voting power regardless of wealth. Many argued that those without property had no stake in society, so they shouldn't be allowed to determine its direction. The more wealth you owned, they reasoned, the more you had to lose—so you were entitled to a bigger say in public affairs. In fact, many Western countries weighted voting rights by property ownership well into the twentieth century.*

► Just because the argument against one person, one vote was false in relation to public life, where it's obvious that everyone's stake is equal, doesn't mean it's false when applied to business life, where the stakes vary so greatly.

. . . big corporations . . . command more resources than do most government units. . . . [T]hey do not disqualify themselves from playing the partisan role of a citizen . . . and they exercise unusual veto powers. . . . The large private corporation fits oddly into democratic theory and vision. Indeed, it does not fit at all.
—Charles Lindblom, *Politics and Markets* [80]

. . . it is dangerous . . . to alter the qualifications of voters . . . New claims will arise; women will demand a vote; . . . and every man who has not a farthing, will demand an equal voice with any other, in all acts of state
—John Adams, 1776 [81]

◄ *I'd turn your "stake" argument on its head. A worker with few resources has much more to lose than does the wealthy stockholder. After all, if the business goes under, the stockholder loses an investment, but the worker loses his or her livelihood and maybe a home, too.*

Even the term "investment" can mislead. Do most stockholders throw in their fate with a company to make it go? No, they buy and sell stock with concern for the highest return, not the fate of the company.

▶ Your critique misses the point. First of all, most businesses are proprietorships and partnerships—they *are* worker-owned. Mostly they're small shops and firms of doctors, lawyers, and the like. Why is the worker-owned setup appropriate only to such firms? Because of the "free rider" problem. Where profits are evenly split, one partner can do less and still benefit from the hard work of others. With just a few worker-proprietors, this isn't such a problem—they can monitor each other's efforts closely.

But in bigger organizations, this monitoring breaks down, and the free-rider problem gets out of hand. That's why a professional class of managers, separate from owners, is needed to oversee performance. And that's also why the principle of remuneration must shift from equal division to a division of rewards according to contribution, as we have in major corporations today.

Moreover, because corporations are "giant," as you call them, doesn't mean they're not democratic. As I pointed out before, thousands, even millions, of shareholders own most of these giants. They approve major management decisions, so democratic control is intact.

◄ *But most Americans own no stock whatsoever. Of the one-fifth who do, a small percentage own most of it.* [83] *And what's so democratic about a structure in which the stockholder's power is based on the number of shares owned, not on the democratic basis of one person, one vote?*

As I argued earlier, the corporation is losing legitimacy because it's no longer clear to whom it is responsible beyond management itself. [84]

Corporate executives give themselves big raises, even when the company is doing badly. [86] *Where's the democratic control there? And legitimacy based on the idea that serving stockholders is equivalent to serving the nation is falling apart. As I said*

[C]orporations still like to sustain the legend that their legal owners are "shareholders," people who . . . share in the company's fortunes for better or worse. In reality, the fate of corporate management is ultimately decided by a motley group of speculators. . . . They do not "invest" in a company but are rather in the business of trading in its securities.

—Irving Kristol,
Two Cheers for Capitalism [82]

The problem is deciding who the hell the corporation is responsible to. I can't ask my shareholders what they want. . . . my shareholders change so damn fast I don't even know who they are.

—Andrew C. Sigler,
Chairman, Champion
International [85]

before, the nation needs long-term investments, but stockholders demand immediate returns, and stockholders want returns from lucrative overseas investments, but Americans need jobs here.

The corporate form has clearly torn away from its moorings—its legally structured responsibility to community interests—while growing ever more influential in our lives. No wonder so many Americans have lost confidence in big business.[87]

▶ You may have lost confidence, but not most Americans. In any case, you're falsely characterizing corporate America. Millions of small proprietorships—the vast majority of all corporations—still fit the private enterprise model. They generate most of the innovation and new jobs.[88]

[GE's] directors were in every case selected by the officers . . . We had then, in effect, a huge economic state governed by non-elected, self-perpetuating officers and directors—the direct opposite of the democratic method.
—T. K. Quinn,
former General Electric
executive, 1953[91]

◀ *Yes, but they are not the backbone of our economy. Roughly two thousand large, publicly held corporations control most of the productive wealth and make decisions determining our nation's future—they are the core of our economic life.*[89] *And the original justifications of their power—ownership and control by enterprising entrepreneurs rewarded for their risk, backed by people throwing in their lot with the company—all this no longer applies. The large corporation has transformed itself into what some scholars call a one-party system of private government.*[90]

▶ That's wild! You're ignoring the many constraints government already places on corporations—from workplace safety to corporate taxes.

Besides, you offer no realistic alternative. Are you ready to break up big corporations and take us back to the eighteenth century? In a complex industrial economy, competing in global commerce, large enterprises are essential.

◀ *No, I'm talking about making corporations legitimate participants in a democratic process.*

▶ You're just using the language of democracy in the economy as a code for public ownership, or constraint of businesses by government, which would amount to the same thing. Already government regulation of business is costing the economy at least $100 billion every year.[92] More regulation is the surest way to undermine our chances to compete successfully internationally.

◄ *You are still trapped in old dogma: that there can be only two economic models—"free market" capitalism, as we know it, or Soviet state-planned economy, as we fear it. Your fear of the second prevents you from seeing that the very system you are defending is in many ways similar!*

► That's utterly absurd. Ours is a consumer, market-driven system and theirs is a top-down, state-driven system.

◄ *But neither is democratic.*

► You can say that only because you refuse to admit that our economy responds to the individual consumer's wishes. Nothing could be more democratic.

◄ *Rather than repeating all the reasons why I disagree, I want to take a fresh look at what might be ingredients of a democratic economy.*

► Oh, you have it all worked out, do you? A blueprint to offer us?

◄ *Hardly! But I do see certain principles that would help us move toward more democratic economic life. For one, large corporations would reestablish their lost legitimacy through responsibility to community needs. Because a corporation's only responsibility now is to make money for shareholders—a small minority of us—companies, or whole industries like the oil business, for example, seek to increase their value by takeovers instead of through productive investments.*

A federal charter for corporations operating nationally would become the corporation's "birth certificate" in which corporate responsibilities in serving the nation are spelled out. Key information about expansion and contraction plans—including plant closings—would be public, since they obviously affect everyone.[95] Parallel charters with communities in which the corporation operates would specify additional responsibilities.

Such a charter of corporate responsibilities could, for instance, greatly reduce pollution, thereby lessening need for gov-

. . . we stress the advantages of the free enterprise system, we complain about the totalitarian state, but in our individual organizations . . . we have created more or less of a totalitarian system in industry, particularly in large industry.
—General Robert E. Wood, former chairman of the board, Sears, Roebuck and Company[93]

It has become cheaper to look for oil on the floor of the New York Stock Exchange than in the ground.
—T. Boone Pickens, corporate "raider"[94]

ernment regulation. The charter would stipulate: Either the corporation recovers its used products and wastes and renders them ecologically benign itself, or it pays fully for it to be done. (An example? Those who profit from auto-making would also shoulder responsibility to dispose of junked cars.[96] Imagine the impetus to produce easily reusable or degradable material!

Within this framework, capital investment could be made more responsible to community needs. Government could reward companies with tax breaks, conditioned on their putting capital aside to be used for job-generating investments to avoid layoffs during recessions.[98] Another aspect of more democratic control of capital involves pension funds—now worth $1.3 trillion. They are the biggest single source of equity capital, but the beneficiaries—workers—have virtually no say in how they are managed. Allowing workers more control could help shift these funds into more productive, job-generating investments.[99]

In a democratic economy, governance of the large corporation would also become more broadly accountable. Once we as a society see this need, there will be no shortage of ideas on how to achieve it. George Lodge of Harvard Business School proposes one possibility: Why not, he asks, have long-term employees elect corporate boards from nominations by the CEO, an appropriate government group, and the long-term employees themselves?[100] Such constructive suggestions deserve national dialogue—that's what I'm advocating, not a blueprint.

▶ Each of these suggestions destroys the very heart of economic freedom. You are using the police powers of the state to direct economic activity. And this would result in incredible inefficiencies. Requiring corporations to notify workers and the public of impending plant closures actually ends up causing plants to close. It increases the cost of doing business. And being forced to announce a shut-down publicly makes it a fait accompli, when otherwise the situation might still have been turned around. Another good idea gone awry![102]

Of course, corporations must behave responsibly in their communities, but there's a world of difference between voluntary acceptance of social responsibility and compliance by government edict. If it means anything, economic freedom must include entrepreneurial freedom, the right to guide one's own enterprise as one sees fit. Whatever nice name you give it, if government is telling corporations what to do, we're one step closer to state ownership of the economy.

◀ *You still can't break away from either/or. To render large corporations legitimate participants in a democratic process, government does not have to own them. In most instances that isn't helpful. Government's role is to establish a corporation's function (to provide a service, not just to make money!) and a framework of responsibilities to match the corporation's power.*

▶ But who is to make these determinations? Since government decides what's needed, you've automatically consolidated power at the top.

◀ *No! The appropriate responsibilities of corporations need not be determined by officialdom alone. Citizens must be involved in assessing needs and establishing priorities. Unfortunately, however, belief in the market as the sole legitimate source of such information and in the myth of the "limited state" have left us woefully undeveloped in channels for citizens to take on such responsibilities.* [103]

But it's beginning to change. In San Antonio, Communities Organized for Public Service—perhaps the nation's largest community organization—has helped reshape the city's long-range development plan away from real estate-favored investments and toward neighborhood and environmental needs. [104]

In Burlington, Vermont, municipal government working with citizens set up a broad-based Local Ownership Project stimulating locally controlled economic development, stressing worker-ownership. [106]

▶ In your Vermont example, you're trying to make something sound new and original that is no different than the old, discredited notion of letting government decide what people need and then allocating resources. In all such socialist experiments it's been a proven loser—inefficient, wasteful, and, ultimately, unworkable. No government planning procedure imaginable can match the efficiency of the market as a spontaneous coordinator of decentralized decisions.[107]

◀ *Your fear of alternatives blinds you to inefficiency in what you defend: in the U.S. we consume twice as much fossil fuel*

We're teaching people about what politics is really about—public discourse, negotiations, how to argue, when to compromise, not just the quadrennial electronic plebescite we usually call politics.

—Ernesto Cortes, Jr.,
Communities Organized for
Public Service[105]

to produce a given output as Japan or Italy; gridlock on our highways wastes everyone's time; suburban sprawl wastes irreplaceable farmland; unplanned dumping of toxic materials (now in 25,000 sites around the country) destroys health and means huge cleanup costs. Is this efficiency?

▶ You want to see waste? Need I remind you again of all the waste in communist economies built on similar ideas about state planning?

◀ *Why let the USSR model so limit your vision? What I am describing is the opposite—not top-down planning but citizens' involvement in setting community priorities so that both government and the market can respond. Planning isn't something that socialists thought up! It's going on in every corporate boardroom; let's bring that process out from behind closed doors into the democratic process. In other words, I'm suggesting that a democratic economy means, first, the linking of corporate power to community-defined needs.*

There's a second feature of a democratic economy that I've already touched on: citizens' responsibility to set the value boundaries in which the market functions, deciding what's too essential to life to be left to the market alone. I've said that the opportunity to work and health care are that important. Another example: Nebraskans voted some years ago to safeguard family farm agriculture by effectively barring nonfarm corporations from the market for farmland. They didn't destroy that market but they made sure their values defined it. [108]

▶ They *did* destroy the market, undermining the family farm instead of protecting it. If nonfarm corporations are barred from the market for farmland, land prices will be lower than if they had been allowed to bid for land. All family farmers in Nebraska will suffer—their property will be less valuable, so they'll be handicapped in getting operating loans.

◀ *There's no clear evidence that land values have fallen. The point is, however, that Nebraskans put their commitment to family farming above their pocket books. But you've brought up the critical importance of competition, another key to a democratic economy.*

▶ Of course, that's what I've been saying all along. And competition is the hallmark of the U.S. economy. New companies are being formed daily, and others are going out of business in an on going competitive process that spurs creativity.

◀ *But what you call competition I earlier called "terminal competition" because it terminates in shared monopolies, undermining efficiency. Competition isn't "natural," after all; it will always be killed by those who'd rather buy up competitors than compete with them. So the sustained competition required in a democratic economy must be nurtured by a democratic polity. That's what Nebraskans are saying; if Prudential Insurance and other corporations continue to buy up farmland, before long it will be monopolized by the few with the most money, not competitively bid for among family farmers with the most skills.*

Nurturing competition in the national economy wouldn't mean blindly enforcing old antitrust concepts. The meeting of community needs would become a key standard by which proposed mergers would be judged. [109]

▶ Even if such a vision were desirable, it isn't possible—government oversight comes to mean government intervention to serve narrow interests, not the broad public interest. As I explained before, the history of regulation demonstrates that it comes to serve the very interests it's supposed to be regulating.

◀ *Protecting competition would mean less need for economic regulation. Without such a policy, after deregulation companies quickly merge, and with less competition more government oversight is needed to protect the consumer's interest.*

But I want to move on. I've stressed linking corporate power to community need and the responsibility of citizens to set value perameters for the market, including the need to sustain competition, but there's a third dimension of a democratic economy: it's in our workplaces themselves.

Workplace Democracy: Can It Work? ★

What then is [the employer's] power to manage and assign workers to various tasks? Exactly the same as one little consumer's power. . . . The single consumer can assign his grocer to the task of obtaining whatever the customer can induce the grocer to provide at a price acceptable to both parties. That is precisely all that an employer can do to an employee.
—Armen A. Achian and Harold Demsetz,
American Economic Review[110]

. . . *being the managers rather of other people's money than of their own, it cannot well be expected, that they [managers of joint-stock companies] should watch over it with the*

▶ Hold on, now. Arguments for a "democratic workplace" are based on an obvious fallacy. They assume that owners somehow have unfair power over workers and the community, but you have provided no evidence to prove it. Power means the capacity to reduce someone else's options. But employers have only as much power over workers, in that sense, as consumers have over employers.

Since capitalists can't reduce workers' preexisting options, they have no power over them.[111] So your aim of applying principles of political democracy to the economy is based on a false premise.

Moreover, the intrusion of democratic principles into the workplace—leading to more cumbersome decision-making and divisiveness—would undermine efficiency and thus reduce the consumer choice that Americans expect. I don't think Americans would opt for a little more say on the job, or somehow more input into economic decisions, if it meant more expensive goods and less choice in the marketplace. To most Americans, this would mean shrinking their freedom, not increasing it.

◀ *Why assume that a workplace divided between owners and workers is superior? Efficient work depends on motivation, and many aspects of such a divided workplace kill motivation and generate waste.[112]*

Where workers and owners are distinct—and often opposing each other—many more managers are needed to watch over workers. In U.S. manufacturing, there are over forty administrators for every one hundred production workers.[113] That's four times more than at the turn of the century, and considera-

bly more than in many other industrial countries. Doesn't this reduce efficiency because a smaller proportion of workers are doing directly productive work?

▶ Compare that to the untold hours of meeting time wasted in worker-owned businesses committed to your "democratic decision-making"!

◀ *Wouldn't workers strive harder to be efficient if they carried more responsibility and knew they would share directly in the rewards? In the late Seventies, G.M. considered its Hyatt-Clark subsidiary in New Jersey an albatross and was ready to shut it down. Instead, in 1981, the union local bought Hyatt-Clark, and since then some divisions of the plant have doubled, even tripled output per worker.[115] It's hardly surprising that typically the more the workers own of a company, the greater its profitability.[116]*

Excluding workers from decision-making also means forgoing hands-on input from the very people who know most about doing the job better. Not very efficient.[118] High personnel turnover is also terribly inefficient—all that investment in training goes walking out the door. Since they feel more loyalty to the firm, worker-owners are less apt to leave.

▶ But capitalism is driven by serving the interests of shareholders and consumers. A plant or an industry cannot operate in the interest of a permanent and distinct set of workers and still serve the interests of consumers.[119]

◀ *In fact, with more worker-owned firms, consumer satisfaction might be greater. If as owners workers produced shoddy goods, could they face their neighbors? As it is, over a quarter of American workers admit they wouldn't buy the products they themselves make![120]*

▶ Another drawback is that worker-owned firms would not contribute to creating badly needed new jobs. It's only logical that workers in such firms would be very reluctant to let new workers come on board in order to minimize the number of people with whom they would have to share profits.[121]

◀ *Why wouldn't worker-owners, just like capitalists, see that new workers could enhance profits, stimulating income greater*

same anxious vigilance with which the partners in a private copartnery frequently watch over their own. . . . Negligence and profusion, therefore, must always prevail . . .

—Adam Smith,
The Wealth of Nations,
1776[114]

. . . co-operation [worker ownership] . . . would make it [the workers'] principle and their interest—at present it is neither—to do the utmost, instead of the least possible, in exchange for their remuneration.

—John Stuart Mill,
Principles of Political Economy, 1848[117]

than the cost of their added salaries? Some evidence suggests faster job growth in worker-owned firms. [122]

▶ But, regardless of your arguments, the record of worker-owned businesses demonstrates the instability of the structure. In recent years, a lot of companies bought out by workers have flopped—Iowa's Rath Packing Company is just one of many disasters—and workers have lost a lot in such desperate experiments.

◀ *Most worker–owned businesses are thriving.* [123] *Remember, a reason for failure might that the business was already in big trouble, and that's why the owner sold it to workers in the first place. But this isn't the typical case.*

▶ Worker cooperatives are nothing new, yet, after hundreds of years, they are a minuscule fraction of all firms. There are less than ten thousand firms with any real degree of worker-owner-ship in the entire country—less than one-half of one percent of all firms. There must be important lessons in all of this history. If they were as efficient as those organized and run by capitalists, they would have beat out the capitalist competition long ago. Indeed, if workers sharing in ownership were really more profit-able, then it would be in the self-interest of the capitalist firms to convert.

◀ *You insist on seeing life in narrow, economic terms. In so doing, you ignore the reality of power. Sharing ownership means sharing power. How many owners are willing to do this, regardless of the economic advantages?*

Plus, for worker-ownership to develop, workers must have credit. But laws in capitalist countries have been designed to support the division between owner and worker, and banks have been reluctant to lend to worker-owned businesses.

▶ But workers didn't have to wait for banks. Union treasuries have long had enough money to launch worker-controlled firms. And workers could always pool their own resources and start businesses themselves. But they haven't—why? Largely for one reason: They don't want to carry the risk. Understandably, they'd rather push it off onto the entrepreneur. Such specializa-tion in risk-bearing is only one of the many advantages in the capitalist system. [125]

The form of association . . . which if mankind continue to improve, must be expected in the end to predominate, is not that which can exist between a capitalist as chief, and workpeople without a voice in the management, but the association of the labourers themselves on terms of equality, collectively owning the capital with which they carry on their operations, and working under managers elected and removable by themselves.

—John Stuart Mill,
Principles of Political Economy, 1848 [124]

◄ *Risk aversion isn't the problem. A worker in a capitalist firm often faces more risk than the investor. The biggest obstacles to more worker participation and ownership are the power held by current owners, workers' lack of capital, the myths you're repeating here about their impracticality, and workers' own lack of confidence—bred by the current work structure—in their capacity for self-government in the workplace.*

► Are you suggesting that ordinary workers have the knowledge to make business planning decisions? To run a firm themselves?

◄ *Look, we assume an average person has the intelligence and good sense to raise a child, serve on a school board, or decide life and death questions on a jury—but not to make policy decisions at work or in the community's economic development? Where's the consistency?*

Sometimes it is said that man cannot be trusted with the government of himself. Can he, then, be trusted with the government of others?
—Thomas Jefferson, First Inaugural Address, 1801[126]

► Your comparison is grossly misleading. Business decisions require specialized knowledge, not just good sense!

◄ *Of course. Economic life based on democratic values would not eliminate the key role of specialized knowledge. Nor would it mean decision by committee, or everybody's hand in every pot. Worker-owned businesses are learning that management is a talent like any other. What would change most is responsibility: to whom do managers and those with specialized knowledge answer? To themselves (since most stockholders now serve as rubber stamps) or to workers within guidelines responsible to the community?*

In a democratic economic enterprise, experts are no longer on top—they are "on tap."
—Hubert Humphrey

► But most people just don't want the burden of participating in decision-making. That would mean having to put out more energy on the job. Most Americans would rather save their energy for their leisure time with their families. For Americans, it's our leisure pursuits that offer the most life satisfaction.[127]

On the job, pressure to "participate" can feel as oppressive as the pressure of an overbearing boss! It means more meetings, more debates, more hassles. Everyone knows that at work it's often easier, and much more efficient—ultimately, more liberation!—just to let one person make the decisions.

◄ *Psychologists tell us that those who have the least self-direction on the job suffer the most job stress. And you've neg-*

lected to ask why many people have so little energy on the job to begin with. Many feel their views are not sought or respected. Their jobs feel like dead ends. No wonder they lack enthusiasm. [128]

A U.S. Chamber of Commerce poll showed that over 80 percent of the work force wanted greater participation in decision-making on the job. Another survey concluded that two-thirds of American workers would prefer to work in an employee-owned business. [129]

▶ But the efficiency of an economic *system* is more than just the separate workings of each workplace. The system's efficiency hinges in large measure on the "mobility of capital," as economists call it. Investors shift resources to where greatest profits are to be found—this is how new industries get started. It's the very heart of capitalism's dynamism.

The whole idea of putting workers instead of investors in charge of capital undermines this process—the ongoing destruction of low-productivity plants and their replacement with high-productivity plants. Workers wouldn't allow capitalism its naturally creative course, in which some firms must die for others to emerge.

With worker ownership, those workers in fear of losing out could stymie the whole process from which society benefits. Capital would be stuck—because it's tied to the workers. In response to a changing economy, worker-owners would not be likely to change or drop a line of production, if it's all they themselves know how to produce.

◀ *Why assume that capital flowing unrestrained toward highest profits is so efficient? Billions going into mergers bring big profits to some but little or no improved output, as I said before.*

And part of why "capital mobility" appears as an unmitigated good is that firms don't shoulder the social costs of plant closings in one community and start-ups in another. We citizens pay for much of that—in unemployment benefits and welfare costs; in building new schools, sewers, and roads where new plants are built, and so on. Let's add in the full costs and then talk about the efficiency of "capital mobility"!

And why assume worker-owners would resist change? With

livelihoods at stake, why wouldn't they be just as eager as investors to adapt to changing demand? During the economic downturn of the Eighties, worker-owners in northern Spain, for example, retrained themselves and retooled plants. [132]

Trade Unions: Help or Hindrance? ★

▶ But you've led us into a debate about worker ownership as if the issue were actually on the national agenda. In fact, we're headed in the opposite direction. Concern today is about the problem of too much worker power. Workers covered by union contracts on average make a third more than their nonunion counterparts. The function of unions is to force employers to pay workers more than they would be worth, judged by the market alone.

So union members form a privileged elite themselves, with the power to demand high wages and push the consequences off on consumers who are usually poorer than they are themselves.

Unions' demands have helped price U.S. goods out of international markets, contributing to our huge trade deficit. And now these workers are screaming that they deserve protection from imports.

Because unions have shown they can't handle power responsibly, their power is dwindling.

◀ *In fact, in this country good and rising wages have often gone hand in hand with high productivity and competitive prices.* [135] *And today, the cost disadvantage that U.S. auto manufacturers suffer relative to Japan's automakers is due more to the cost of management—inefficient procedures and superfluous layers— than to labor costs.* [136]

People who lack the capacity to earn a decent living need to be helped, but they will not be helped by . . . trade union wage pressures, or other devices which seek to compel employers to pay them more than their work is worth.

—James Tobin, former member, President's Council of Economic Advisors[133]

. . . [trade] protection . . . is a subsidy by the median American workers who earn $10 an hour or less compared to the aristocrats of the labor market who under collective bargaining earn over $20 in the auto and steel industry.

—Paul A. Samuelson, 1983[134]

Union workplaces are generally more productive than comparable nonunion firms. One reason is that workers covered by unions don't quit as often—less turnover means more efficiency. [137] In countries where 80 to 90 percent of the work force is organized, strikes are much less frequent than in less organized economies. [138]

▶ You are conveniently forgetting the cost of union work rules that have been a major brake on technological innovation. Unions do everything they can to save jobs, not produce more efficiently. One study in the Fifties showed that the restrictive rules imposed by unions in the building industry were costing home buyers as much as 7 percent of the purchasing price.[139]

◀ *Arguing over whose studies to believe won't get us very far. So let's say you are right—that unions have slowed technological change or pushed wages up faster than productivity. What's the answer?*

▶ American workers are already providing the answer. They are fed up with the corruption of union leadership, the self-centeredness of their demands, and their combative tactics. They are choosing not to join. Only 17 percent of the work force is in unions, and that share has been falling for many years now.

◀ *In part you're seeing the effects of a decade-long assault against unions by employers with government backing. But undermining unions is cutting our own throats. Why not further the positive contribution of unions and reduce the drawbacks?*

Take job security. It's been a major goal of unions, and now many well-managed companies are coming to see that job security improves productivity. If workers know their jobs aren't on the line, they will welcome new technology. Or take consumer safety. A friend of mine is an airline mechanic. Recently he blew the whistle on a serious oversight in the maintenance routine. Without a union to help protect his job, would he have spoken out?

Or consider productivity again. As it is, most workers say they aren't working up to capacity. [141] Less than one in ten thinks increased productivity from more effort would benefit them—so why try harder? Unions can help solve the problem

With strong [union] organization, established workers . . . are in a position to . . . capture for themselves the full advantage of favorable changes affecting their industry. . . . Ethically, they should share their gains with . . . consumers . . . and with outside workers. . . . But no group will practice such sharing if it has the power to prevent it.

—Henry Simons, founder, Chicago School of Economics, 1948[140]

by bargaining for wages and bonuses linked to profits and productivity. [142]

So, while you're right that worker ownership is so far a minuscule part of our economy, much of what's positive about worker ownership applies to workplaces with effective trade unions.

Unions are also demonstrating that workers have the capacity to participate in management decisions. In 1988, for example, Pan Am unions more accurately projected the company's losses than did top management and helped oust the chief executive they felt was responsible for the airline's problems. [143]

The most important function of the union movement has not been economic but political—making the worker an equal to the employer, not economically, of course, but as a human being.

—Guy Tyler,
"What Do Unions Really Do?"[144]

The Culture of Democracy ★

▶ And this is a very dangerous precedent, indeed, having a powerful interest block like unions dictating business policy. But we've strayed from the topic of democracy: our form of government and whether it makes sense to apply rules of political life in economic life. It doesn't.

◀ *But in just talking about formal rules we miss what may be even more important—people's attitudes, habits, and assumptions about their responsibility in society that make up what might be called the "culture of democracy."*

▶ Extremely important, I agree. Many societies have constitutions with beautiful language about individual rights, but these rights are just ignored. And few people complain. The reason we have a democratic society is only that people expect and demand standards of honesty and legality. Without that, no number of laws could make us a democratic culture.

◀ *But I also see a threat to this democratic culture. It relies on people's good faith—on citizens abiding by the rules, not out of*

. . . democracy is unstable as a political system, as long as it remains a political system and nothing more, instead of becoming, as it should be, not only a form of government, but a type of society. [This] involves . . . the resolute elimination of all forms of special privilege. . . . and the conversion of economic power, now often an irresponsible tyrant, into the servant of society . . .

—R. H. Tawney,
Equality, 1952[145]

fear but from a desire to contribute to a well-functioning society. This good faith is lost if the rules don't seem fair; and if the powerful can break the rules . . . and get away with it. (If a General Dynamics can cheat the public for years, get its wrists slapped, and go right on raking in billions in defense contracts![147])

▶ As a democratic culture, we're head and shoulders above just about any other country in the world. In most, bribery and income tax evasion are a way of life.

◀ *And where are we headed? Most Americans now believe that those with more power try to take advantage of them, that hard work doesn't necessarily pay off, and that "the rich get richer."*[148] *These beliefs don't come out of thin air.*

▶ We all have a tendency to blame others for our disappointments. It's human nature.

◀ *Rather, it's that many Americans feel betrayed. Workers have taken wage cuts to keep their companies alive only to see top management give itself a big raise. We've seen corporations get big tax breaks, then fail to invest in revitalizing American industry; others dump toxic wastes and hide the dangers; some hundred officials in the Reagan administrations have been indicted or charged for misusing their positions for private gain. Seeing all this, why not look out for Number One?*

▶ The truth is that both government and corporations were much more ruthless and corrupt one hundred years ago, or even fifty years ago, than they are now. Just consider the "bosses" that ran whole cities. You have no perspective. I hate to say this, but to the degree that people do have the beliefs that you claim they do, it's largely because naysayers think and talk as you do. You sow mistrust of our economic and political system and then wonder why people have such negative attitudes!

◀ *Would that so many people read my work!*

▶ I'm serious—I'm talking about a whole class of people—academics, writers, media professionals, human services bureaucrats, and others who make a profession out of bemoaning the shortcomings of American society. They project their own discontent onto society and fancy themselves to have the answers for others. But, of course, if we solved any of the problems they proclaim, they'd be out of work!

◄ *Feelings of powerlessness arise from people's experience, not from what someone tells them to think.*

Many Americans now say they fear even writing their representative to express an unpopular view.[149] *Yet citizens' confidence to confront both political and economic power lies at the very heart of democracy. The isolated individual, whether as voter or as consumer, is pretty powerless. That's why democratic organizations within the workplace and community are vital to a democracy, for in them citizens gain confidence in themselves as molders of social and economic policy.*[150]

But this doesn't just happen; it requires positive stimulation. That's why government should be encouraging unions, for example, instead of setting roadblocks in their paths.

Democratic culture can thrive only if citizens see themselves as capable adults able to shoulder responsibility. So, as long as our work lives are based on opposite presumptions, democracy is diminished.

▶ What are you talking about? Employers *must* assume workers are capable adults. Work life is built on voluntary contracts between informed adults, and most jobs, especially in today's high-tech economy, entail considerable responsibility. What you are saying demeans American workers.

◄ *But opposing principles do govern our lives: the principle of self-government rules our political lives, while the structure of our economic lives remains autocratic—the boss decides. Surely it's naive to divide our lives into separate parts, governed by opposing principles, and expect one to have no effect on the other!*[153]

If in the workplace we are expected just to take orders, how can we as citizens believe we have the capacity to hold legislators accountable to us, to question their judgment, to challenge them if they violate our trust?

When workers take more responsibility, their lives outside work change, too. After Proctor & Gamble's plant in Lima, Ohio, instituted greater worker participation, more workers got involved in community projects and ran for elected office.[155]

. . . government [must] *prevent statism by enhancing the social competence of citizens. . . . Government can do this by enhancing . . . the vigor of those intermediary institutions which shape, support and inspire individuals, drawing persons out of the orbits of individualism and into social relationships.*

—George Will,
Statecraft as Soulcraft[151]

We are going to have to . . . stop treating [workers] *like children, or, even worse, like machines with nothing to contribute to their jobs but their bodies.*

—Rex Reed,
a former vice-president,
AT&T[152]

[Americans] *. . . live out their working lives, and most of their daily existence, not within a democratic system but instead within a hierarchical structure of subordination. To this extent, democracy* [is] *necessarily marginal . . . to their daily lives.*

—Robert A. Dahl
"On Removing Certain Impediments to Democracy"[154]

. . . the understandings of the greater part of men are necessarily formed by their ordinary employments. The man whose whole life is spent in performing a few simple operations . . . has no occasion to exert his understanding. . . . Of the great and extensive interests of his country he is altogether incapable of judging. . . . The uniformity of his stationary life naturally corrupts the courage of his mind . . .

—Adam Smith,
The Wealth of Nations,
1776[157]

On the negative side, when people are cut out of economic life, political life suffers: among Americans out of work, only half as many vote as among those employed.[156]

▶ Be that as it may, your basic assumption about conflicting principles is false: both the economy and our political system are actually based on a parallel principle—democracy understood as the maximization of our choices. In the economy, it's choice among products; in political life, choice among candidates with differing political philosophies.

◀ *A culture of democracy isn't a collection of individual choices, it's a process that depends on people being able to talk to each other—and be understood—so that we can devise policies we can all accept as fair. Recall when in the early Eighties President Reagan said—no doubt sincerely—that we needed no more anti-hunger efforts because the only hungry Americans were those who didn't know how to find help? To families living on the minimum wage, Reagan must have sounded like a creature from outer space! This social distance, making communication impossible, is one reason that Thomas Jefferson, along with others in his day, believed that free institutions could survive only if there were rough equality in how people live.*

▶ Your notion that people with very different lifestyles and personal values will somehow be able to talk with each other and arrive at a "common good" ignores political reality. Democracy allows and even encourages different interests, providing channels for those interests to debate and arrive at compromises. If there is a common good, it is in these compromises of competing interests, not some unitary vision.

◀ *Of course there will always be compromises and standoffs, but the premise of democracy must be the search for a common purpose—a search for choices furthering the interests of us all, not mere trade-offs among competing groups. This difference between us is too important to be left here.*

Democracy and Individuality ★

▶ Let's come back to that because I have another strong objection to the drift of what you're saying.

You seem to want uniformity among people. But democracy depends on diversity, on individuality. In a democracy, some people can aspire to great wealth and others are content with less. In a free enterprise system, the individual's own determination and skills are what matter. You're concerned about the "social good," but not the individual.

It is precisely this diversity in individuality that your vision would scuttle. Your ideas leading to expanded government control would also mean greater uniformity in another sense. In such a society everyone knows that if they want to get anywhere they will have to please the same set of bureaucrats.

◀ *Feeling powerless before faceless economic forces is as great a threat to individuality. As my teenagers project their futures, they're more likely to be asking themselves what qualities will be acceptable to a high-paying employer than to government. Forty percent of a recent Ivy League graduating class were grooming themselves to be investment bankers; surely the structure of economic life is a powerful force for social uniformity, not diversity.*

Individuality doesn't just mean individualism—standing alone. It means developing one's unique gifts, and being able to share them for the enjoyment of oneself and others. Individuality thus flowers the more that society protects everyone's security, everyone's right to earn a living.

Developing genuine individuality also means ongoing encounter with the most diverse ideas, forcing us to reevaluate our own beliefs.[160] In a democratic culture, citizens discuss even many issues that you want us to consider settled, such as the core responsibilities of corporations.

A radical cannot talk for more than five minutes about social reform without using words such as "solidarity" and "collective." . . . Liberals are a bit more subtle . . . [For them] everything has to do with the group. There is the interest group, the workplace group, the large organization, the small-group theory, and so on; the individual just doesn't seem to be of much use . . .

—Benjamin Ward,
The Conservative Economic World View[158]

[I]ndividual differences, which are a source of social energy, are more likely to ripen and find expression if social inequalities are, as far as practicable, diminished.

—R. H. Tawney,
Inequality[159]

► Before we go any further, let me ask you one question. From your many attacks on our society, I'm beginning to think that you believe we don't even have democracy in the United States. Are you really saying this?

> Democracy is a process, not a static condition. It is becoming, rather than being. It can be easily lost, but is never fully won. Its essence is eternal struggle.
> —William H. Hastie[161]

◄ *To me, democracy isn't a "thing" that one "has." It's a set of principles to be continually defended and pushed still further by an active citizenry. We must judge ourselves on the direction in which we are moving. Where more and more people suffer deprivation, can we honestly say we are fulfilling our society's democratic promise?*

► I disagree. Most Americans are doing well. Besides, we cannot determine outcomes. All that we can do is set up fair structures of government. That is democracy. If the outcome is not as we would wish, the fault may well lie in the limitations within human beings, not within the structures themselves.

Summing Up the Dialogue ★

WHAT IS DEMOCRACY?

► A system of government in which citizens freely elect leadership through fair competition.

◄ *A way of life in which citizens work to ensure that*

· *power is accountable to those who must live with the consequences of public decisions*
· *power is so shared that no member of the community is stripped of life's essentials and robbed of dignity.*

HOW DOES DEMOCRACY PROTECT FREEDOM?

▶ By establishing countervailing centers of power, both within government and between the political and economic spheres of life. This protects freedom by preventing the totalitarian concentration of power.

◀ *By infusing the democratic principles of accountability and shared power into both economic and political life, so that all citizens have the opportunity for full development—the essence of freedom.*

WHAT MAKES DEMOCRACY POSSIBLE?

▶ Keeping economic power separate from government so that it can serve as a check on the power of government.

Limiting government's role so that a minority cannot use it against the majority—this means leaving most decisions to the marketplace.

◀ *A wide dispersion of economic power so that*

· *those with the most wealth cannot subvert government for their own ends.*
· *the lives of citizens are not so extremely different that they cannot communicate with one another to arrive at common priorities.*

Both conditions require continuing effort to reduce the role of wealth in campaigns for public office and in participation in public discourse.

SHOULD DEMOCRATIC PRINCIPLES APPLY IN ECONOMIC LIFE?

▶ They already do—in the marketplace we each cast our dollar-votes. But if this means electing bosses in the workplace, no!

◀ *Since citizens' wealth is so unequal, the marketplace is hardly democratic. But the principles of democracy—accountability and the sharing of power so that all citizens are protected—should apply equally in economic as in political life.*

PART SIX

Freedom, Human Nature, and Hope

Freedom: Zero-sum? ★

▶ A defect in your whole line of argument has been your refusal to address the root of the very real conflicts that exist in every society. Your references to the common good gloss over these differences, making it easy for you to portray as some general interest what is really your own version of truth.

Freedom in the real world is, in one sense, like a mathematical equation. If you add to one side, you must subtract from the other.[1] The right that you have been especially advocating, the "right to earn a living," not to mention your advocacy of "affirmative action," obviously detracts from the rights of employers to hire, fire, and pay as they believe is best for their enterprise. In fact, your whole notion of corporate accountability would so diminish the rights of corporations that they could hardly be considered private any longer.

And to the degree that enforcing such rights depends on government bureaucrats and thus on government funds, it requires heavier taxation, diminishing the freedom of every American taxpayer to use her or his income as she or he sees fit, not as you see fit, or the government sees fit.

Your ideas about natural resources protected for the common good is another case of language obfuscating real trade-offs among people. Your demand that government protect wilderness areas, or hold onto public land, means that others who want to develop it are denied the opportunity. In their view, the "public interest" is best served by the much greater wealth to society resulting from their developing these resources.

You mislead people to think that all we have are common interests, or that we would all have the same definition of a "common good."

While trade-offs are inescapable with regard to freedom protected by rights, capitalism's chief virtue is that it eases the

> Whenever either the desire or the need of property increases among men, [and] there is no extension, then and there, of the world's limits. . . . [I]t is impossible for anyone to grow rich except at the expense of someone else.
>
> —John Locke,
> *Essays on the Law of Nature*,
> 1664[2]

inevitable conflicts they generate. Because it is continually generating new wealth, the free market/private property system offers an ever-growing pie. Economically, then, capitalism offers everyone more, diminishing the social conflicts that arise in every society—but more acutely in static societies—over the division of material goods.

◀ *The conflicts you see are obvious. Less obvious is the common ground. Just think for a moment about the priorities of most Americans. Most would choose a well-paid job, a house in a quiet, crime-free neighborhood, clean air, good schools for their kids . . . and on and on. But what makes me able to choose any of these things?*

▶ A lot of hard work and sacrifice on your part.

◀ *Sure, but this isn't enough. My choices hinge on whether opportunities are open to other people, not just me. The more people out of work, the slimmer my chance of getting a well-paid job—simply because the more people unemployed, the lower my wages are going to be. If many jobless people are waiting to take any job, workers can't hold out for higher wages; they know they'll be replaced by others even more desperate. That's simple economics.*

Or take education. I worry a lot about my kids' schooling. Are they being challenged enough? One big drawback is that many of the kids they go to school with come from families whose development is depressed by poverty. So the classroom environment suffers for everyone, and my kids are affected, too. And who will provide a tax base to improve the schools if many families are poor?

Or, more positively, imagine walking through any neighborhood of any city in our country basking in the vibrant street life, with no fear of assault—either psychic or physical—by human misery and deprivation. Such an image can help us grasp the magnitude of what is stolen from us by endemic poverty—and thus the incredible potential to be released by its eradication.

In simple terms, achieving the life I want depends on others achieving the lives they want. This isn't sentimental; it's very practical.

▶ Aren't you denying the reality of competition? Although our productive system is continually generating new wealth, people are competing for the jobs and income available now. Enjoying the freedom that our system offers means that we must also accept that not everyone can do well.

Earlier you stressed how much you believed in finite resources, but now you don't acknowledge the inevitable competition it suggests, since people so enjoy acquiring material comforts and possessions. For most Americans, concern about rights is largely about the right to buy.

◀ *Who could argue? But does our endless accumulation reflect an insatiable acquisitive instinct? Or do we accumulate because of how we think our many "things" will elevate us in the eyes of others—because of a craving for approval, for status?*

Our culture then fosters the wholesale, chronic substitution of this material fix for more creative and interpersonal satisfactions. But how much of this behavior is human nature?

▶ It goes without saying that some people need the approval of others and thrive on satisfying personal relationships, but material desires are unlimited because people see their possessions as extensions of themselves, as a means of self-expression. Thus, we will understandably feel our freedom threatened by others who want the same things we do.

◀ *If we assume that our nature is essentially acquisitive and insatiable, then you're right: freedom must mean the freedom for unlimited consumption.*

But your view of our essence is very recent, only a few hundred years old. Maybe its historical role in pushing people to work hard to overcome scarcity was positive; but certainly in the United States we now have vastly more productive capacity than needed to meet everyone's needs. [5] *Still, we go on operating from the premise of scarcity, unable to see that scarcity will always* exist—*no matter how much we produce—if we believe our material desires to be infinite, and unable to see that our endless drive for greater output is destroying the natural world on which our very survival depends.*

Fortunately, we have another, much older tradition to draw on in understanding what makes us free. In it, our essence is creative more than acquisitive. We realize our essence in devel-

. . . we consent to . . . uniform rules for an [economic] procedure which has greatly improved the chances of all to have their wants satisfied, but at the price of all individuals and groups incurring the risk of unmerited failure. . . .
[The] game of competition in a market . . . means that some must suffer unmerited disappointment.

—Friedrich A. Hayek,
" 'Social' or Distributive
Justice"[3]

. . . and what are the advantages which we propose by that great purpose of human life which we call bettering our condition? To be observed, to be attended to, to be taken notice of with sympathy, complacency, and approbation, are all the advantages which we can propose to derive from it.

—Adam Smith,
*The Theory of Moral
Sentiments*, 1790[4]

oping our unique gifts, be they intellectual, physical, artistic, or spiritual. Freedom is in doing and enjoying these gifts, not in acquiring things. [6]

Freedom is finite and divisible only if it means the right to unlimited accumulation of property—the more for you, the less for me. We are in awful competition. But if freedom means the opportunity to develop our unique gifts, it is infinite and indivisible.

Not only does your freedom to develop not have to limit my expression, but my development in part depends upon yours. How can I deepen my enjoyment of music, for example, unless you, with much greater musical talent, are free to develop your gift? And how can I develop my talent as a writer unless other writers, able to teach and inspire me, have been free to develop their talent? Indeed, how can I sharpen my own thinking without an adversary like you with whom to debate?

Freedom understood as mutually expanding horizons belies the whole notion of zero-sum.

▶ Sounds beautiful; I'm sure you could wax on forever! But let me make two points. First, the greatest achievement of capitalism has been precisely this—not just that it allows people to accumulate property, but that it offers opportunities for all people to develop their capacities.[8] Second, to develop our "innate gifts," as you call them, requires that people have material resources. To develop ourselves and our tastes, sensitivities, and knowledge requires money. Who are you to say that a wealthy family's right to invest in original artwork, or to spend a month a year traveling, isn't an expression of their freedom "to develop"? So thinking in terms of developmental freedom instead of freedom to acquire goods doesn't reduce the essential conflicts among people. If you don't see this, you live in a fantasy world.

◀ I can think of no quality of character, no talent, that requires unlimited wealth to develop. In fact, some who have known unlimited wealth see it as corrupting and demoralizing. [10]

▶ Before going any further, let me tell you what bothers me most. You insist on redefining freedom to suit your ends. To you, guaranteeing that "development needs" are met means expanding everyone's freedom, but such a guarantee is no more than a euphemism for taking from some to give to others. You may argue—and I would disagree—that you have furthered justice, but, please, you can*not* say you have expanded freedom![11]

◄ *Whether one sees in the protection of economic rights an expansion of freedom depends upon where one locates the human essence: is it in our possessions or in the realization of our human gifts?*

Self-Interest Versus Community Interest ★

► So we've peeled off lots of layers, and ultimately we're finding that our differences regarding these many values reflect very real conflicts in our views of what human beings really want—views about "human nature" itself.

If you're saying that our own self-interest can serve broader goals, I would agree—of course. But *you* must agree that the biological sciences now have considerable evidence that selfishness is even in our genes. And in that sense, the market system—mandating decisions based upon a self-interest calculus—best fits our nature.

Since the Seventies, the emerging field of sociobiology has furthered our knowledge of the biological determinants of human social behavior.[13] The theory of the "selfish gene"[14] confirms what has long been known: that we are each, first and foremost, out for our own good.

◄ *The biological sciences have been used since at least Charles Darwin's time falsely to justify your view of ourselves.*

► Darwin showed us that we evolved in a dog-eat-dog world where "survival of the fittest" was the unpleasant truth pushing evolution along. Some may think we can overcome this legacy, but you can't deny its imprint.

Private interest . . . is the only immutable point in the human heart.

—Alexis de Tocqueville, *Democracy in America*, 1835[12]

So far as I am aware, we are the only society that thinks of itself as having risen from savagery, identified with a ruthless nature. Everyone else believes they are descended from gods.

—Marshall Sahlins, *The Use and Abuse of Biology*[15]

◄ Darwin actually insisted that natural selection endowed us with "social instincts," favoring cooperation and mutual aid. [16] But this doesn't contradict the "selfish gene" theory. For in this theory is an irony: "selfish" genes create unselfish organisms!

► How is that?

◄ For genes to survive, the organisms for which they provide blueprints must serve not only their own survival but that of all other organisms with the same genes. This is only too obvious in parents' care for their offspring. But it may also help explain much wider bonds of mutual concern even beyond kinship groups—for what matters is not whether organisms actually share genes but whether they perceive themselves as kin.

With this genetic grounding to our feeling for others' well-being, there's no reason that culture can't build ever broader circles of mutual concern. [18] Human powers of imagination and intellect give us the unique ability consciously to alter who we define as "us." Today many environmentalists argue that our very survival depends on whether we can deliberately enlarge our "family" to include the entire biotic community. [19]

► But we see all around us the most destructive, not positive consequences of such a biologically grounded altruism—the individual's willingness to sacrifice himself or herself for a kin group. It's hardly waning. Just look at the religious wars and racial and ethnic conflicts that if anything seem to be intensifying. If our genetic potential for group solidarity could serve positive ends, surely the world would look very different. We probably wouldn't even be having this debate!

In fact, most human decency toward one another isn't "natural"—it must be created in our malleable early years. We come into this world like little barbarians who must be shaped to accept self-discipline, including consideration for others. [21]

◄ Actually, many, if not most, people who end up as socially destructive—criminals for example—didn't suffer from too little discipline; they themselves were brutalized in childhood. [23] And often what we see as antisocial behavior—such as teen gangs—is itself a distorted cry for social standing when legitimate channels appear blocked.

But I'm not arguing that we are "good" by nature. In fact, it's

As man advances in civilisation, and small tribes are united into larger communities, the simplest reason would tell each individual that he ought to extend his social instincts and sympathies to all the members of the same nation, though personally unknown to him. This point being once reached, there is only an artificial barrier to prevent his sympathies extending to the men of all nations and races.

—Charles Darwin,
The Descent of Man and Selection in Relation to Sex, 1871 [17]

It is thus that man, who can subsist only in society, was fitted by nature to that situation for which he was made.

—Adam Smith,
The Theory of Moral Sentiments, 1790 [20]

[N]early every respectable attribute of humanity is the result not of instinct, but of victory over instinct . . .

—John Stuart Mill,
Three Essays on Religion, 1874 [22]

your insistence again on categorical thinking—we're either good or bad—that's part of our problem. Within human nature is potential both for unspeakable evil and for cooperation.

I'm also arguing that our positive potential lies not only in our powers of reason telling us that we sink or swim together. Deeper still, we have innate feelings toward each other that we repress at great cost to ourselves. Passing a homeless person on the street, I feel myself diminished. If Charles Darwin is right, not only is the dignity of the homeless person hurt, but my instinctive need to help a person in distress is violated. Doing so thus eats at my own dignity and erodes confidence in my society for allowing such suffering amid plenty.

▶ I'm just as concerned as you are about the welfare of others, but a lot of people are probably just annoyed that the homeless are interfering with their enjoyment of public spaces. The point is that, in our society, nothing prevents people who care from acting on their compassion. They *can* do something—they can volunteer at a soup kitchen.

But how can you insist that innate compassion is a dominant trait when, from experiments in academic psychology to today's current violent political conflicts, the evidence everywhere contradicts you? Remember those famous studies from the Seventies, in which subjects in psychological experiments willingly inflicted what they believed were severe electrical shocks on other subjects?[25] That's pretty hard evidence of a lack of feeling for each other.

◀ *Of course I don't deny insensitivity and cruelty. But such studies reveal that much of human behavior depends upon our moral development, whether we've been conditioned to conformity—to just do as we're told—or whether we've developed the confidence to make independent moral judgments.[27] Unfortunately, the very approach you so defend—adherence to the the market and private property as absolutes—undermines confidence in our capacity for just such moral reasoning.*

Plus, one needn't gainsay human potential for evil to acknowledge that how we act depends a great deal on what society rewards, what it expects from us, and thus on what we come to expect from ourselves.

Think about any organization or business you've been part of. When the structure is unclear and unfair, don't people back-

How selfish soever man may be supposed, there are evidently some principles in his nature, which interest him in the fortune of others, and render their happiness necessary to him, though he derives nothing from it except the pleasure of seeing it.

—Adam Smith,
The Theory of Moral Sentiments, 1790[24]

Some men are born without the organs of sight, or of hearing, or without hands. Yet it would be wrong to say that man is born without these faculties. . . . The want or imperfection of the moral sense in some men, like the want or imperfection of the senses of sight and hearing in others, is no proof that it is a general characteristic of the species.

—Thomas Jefferson,
1814[26]

bite and connive? But when the structure is good—clear and fair—people behave very differently.

If we assume the worst, we're sure to get the worst, and we then come to believe the worst. It's a circle.

So, part of the challenge is to open our inner eyes and to take note of the common, even banal daily acts and feelings which reveal our social nature: the daily hour-to-hour satisfactions we receive from being part of a team effort—whether a workplace, school, congregation, family, or partnership. The gratification we get from sacrifice for others and for causes we believe in. The joy we experience in seeing loved ones triumph. The grief and remorse we feel when we let others down. The sometimes overwhelming need for approval from those we respect. All these feelings tie us to each other's fate—yet we often don't consciously register many of these feelings precisely because they are so natural to us. They become like the air we breathe. We register those intense feelings of jealousy, possessiveness, aggressiveness precisely because they're so uncomfortable. And since our culture so presumes we are narrowly self-seeking, it's easy to feel that these negative feelings constitute the only real us.

▶ You're simply glossing over or grossly belittling the powerful drives of greed, envy, possessiveness, and aggression that have always characterized the human condition, in every type of social structure, good and bad.

◀ No, I'm saying that the degree to which they predominate is shaped by society itself. How else to explain the dramatically faster growth and higher rate of violent crime here in the U.S. compared to other Western nations? Americans aren't innately more violent, are we?[30] So we must ask of our society: What does it call forth in us? Does it reinforce the best or the worst?

▶ Certainly I do not undervalue the necessary socializing function of the family and community. Because these institutions are weakened, we do have higher crime rates. But my point is that human nature has always revealed itself as a set of competing propensities—some constructive and some destructive. The sympathetic and cooperative feelings of people are real, but they are hardly dominant, and certainly inadequate to sustain society. So human societies have instituted artificial devices to mold behav-

. . . the sentiments of those, who are inclined to think favorably of mankind, are more advantageous to virtue . . . When a man is prepossessed with a high notion of his rank and character in the creation, he will naturally endeavor to act up to it, and will scorn to do a base or vicious action, which might sink him below that figure which he makes in his own imagination.

—David Hume, "Of the Dignity or Meanness of Human Nature, 1741-42"[28]

Man is biologically predestined to construct and to inhabit a world with others. . . . In the dialectic between nature and the socially constructed world the human organism itself is transformed. . . . man produces reality and thereby produces himself.

—Peter L. Berger and Thomas Luckmann, *The Social Construction of Reality*[29]

. . . As society is composed of individuals, how could society be more immoral than its members? It becomes immoral if its structure is such that moral individuals cannot act in accordance with their moral impulses.

—E. F. Schumacher, "The Critical Question of Size," 1975[31]

ior—the concepts of honor and nobility and the rules of justice and morality among them.[32]

◄ *You see such codes as artificially imposed upon us because you see a line between self-concern and what we feel for others. It's a line that's impossible to draw! Because we are social beings, self-love and love for others are actually facets of one nature. Self-love is a product of lives lived with others. We develop self-esteem only in community. We love ourselves in great measure based on how well we love others and as we believe ourselves worthy of the esteem of others.*

Concern for self and compassion for others might most accurately be conceived as a continuum, or perhaps as an intricate web. At the center is the individual—with concern for self foremost, since our survival depends upon it. That concern dilutes as the web extends from our intimates to more distant associates. But because other people's well-being (from the moods of a spouse to whether a neighbor is out of work) so impinge on our own well-being, and because our self-esteem so turns on others' views of us, we can't separate self-centeredness from selfless concern. It's impossible. [34]

This social basis of the self that Adam Smith described so well in the eighteenth century takes on new meaning as we approach the twenty-first. Our common fate—even with our most distant cousins on far continents and with nonhuman life as well—has now been sealed. Weapons that would obliterate not just an enemy but all life make mutual interest no longer a matter of philosophical speculation.

► But it is much less risky to expect as little as possible from people. Our economic system is based on the notion of individual self-seeking that ultimately, though indirectly, contributes to the whole society's well-being. Our political system is also built on the assumption that our motives are selfish; in setting up competing centers of power and strictly limiting the powers of government, our founders hoped to compensate for our defects.[36]

Our founders had no illusions about human goodness; at least they knew it made no sense—it was just too risky—to build a society on so weak a base.

◄ *Expecting the worst is the riskiest strategy of all! Even the most hard-nosed of our founders believed a republic to be im-*

. . . it is the great precept of nature to love ourselves only as we love our neighbor; or, what comes to the same thing, as our neighbor is capable of loving us.

—Adam Smith,
The Theory of Moral Sentiments, 1790[33]

[Man] is sensible . . . that his own interest is connected with the prosperity of society, and that the happiness, perhaps the preservation of his existence, depends upon its preservation.

—Adam Smith,
The Theory of Moral Sentiments, 1790[35]

. . . *whoever would found a state, and make proper laws for the government of it, must presume that all men are bad by nature.*

—John Adams[37]

possible without a good dose of "civic virtue"—the capacity to incorporate the public interest in our private concerns.[38]

▶ It's only too obvious that people seek both autonomy from each other and power over each other; this desire for control over others is what must be kept in check by a social structure that separates economic and political power and by limited government.

◀ *Because people do often seek unfair power over others, it's your formula that's dangerous. It recognizes only the threat of concentrated political power, but does not challenge those rules that allow economic power to accrue to so few. An economic structure that permits so much control over wealth by a few, and then attaches to property rights (in the form of large corporations) a decision-making authority affecting everybody—all this invites the very abuse of power you fear most!*

I'm suggesting changes to move us toward more, not fewer, checks on power.

▶ But your alternatives would consolidate both economic and political power in the same hands—the greatest threat of all. You can't perceive that threat because you insist on an unrealizable version of "participatory democracy."

◀ *And you rationalize the concentrated political and economic power we have now because you can't conceive of genuine democracy at all.*

▶ According to you, if we can just change our institutions, human beings will change. Your ideas are dangerous because they are utopian and romantic.

◀ *Utopian! What could be more utopian than the notion of a self-regulating market—or, for that matter, a self-regulating political system—in which our needs are met by each of us simply seeking our own gain?*

▶ You refuse to face the facts. However much one can argue the potential for mutual concern, it is weak compared to the individual's basic competitive struggle for survival. Sure, we can put ourselves in others' shoes, but how much easier to be preoccupied with our own private concerns. Yes, it's possible to understand another person's point of view, but our ability at self-deception is even more powerful. In other words, there is truth in much of what you say but our cooperative potential is slight compared to our competitive and aggressive qualities.[42] To deny narrow self-interest as central to human psychology is to court danger. It means trying to make people into something we are not.

◄ *And I'd say that even if you're right and humans have only a sliver of potential for cooperative behavior, given the threats to our planet today, we can't afford not to consciously, actively build on it.*

We can't do that, however, if we stay trapped in your either/ or framework—either let self-interest reign or make people over. Our goal shouldn't be squelching self-interest—hardly! We need changes that will allow more Americans to pursue their interests, including those Americans who are now shut out by poverty and joblessness. But to do so, we'll need to see more clearly how our many legitimate interests are linked with those of others.

I'm worried, for example, about whether my job will be there next year and what would happen if my dad were hit by catastrophic illness. Short of winning the lottery, however, I alone can't buy an end to these anxieties. Pollution-free air is in my self-interest, but by making more income I couldn't improve the air quality. Interest rates increased my mortgage payments, but my influence there is nil. In fact, most of what is in my own interest I can pursue only with others through the political process.

. . . the more realistically one construes self-interest, the more one is involved in relationships with others.
—Bernard Crick,
In Defence of Politics[43]

► But in this political process, you ignore the very real conflicts of interests that do exist, as I have already pointed out. Competition is a fact of life. If you imagine that greater "democracy" in our economic life is instantly going to transform us all into team players, you're dreaming.

◄ *The appropriate goal is meshing self-interest and social ends.*

► That is precisely what capitalism is all about!

◀ *Then that principle should permeate our community and work lives: the greater the individual worker's stake in the enterprise, for example, the higher the productivity benefiting everyone.*

Moral Responsibility and the Market ★

▶ But in all of your emphasis on changing social structures, it's easy to forget that individuals are responsible for their own actions. And some will refuse to accept the obligations that must come with rights. Your vague notion about everyone "participating" in some kind of economic democracy neglects the corresponding obligations that come with it.

With rights come duties. Individuals *earn* the right to participate and wield power in society. They do this through applying themselves to education and pursuing career goals. If they don't—if they drop out, if they don't even bother to learn to read or learn English, if they can't hold down a job—then *they* have made the choice that they don't care enough to earn the privileges a free society offers.

So the biggest danger to society is precisely the human presumptuousness your ideas reflect, the immodest notion that we can create utopia on earth. Not only does it lead to coercion, as I've argued all along, but to carrying along a lot of irresponsible people on the shoulders of others who are more responsible. Either way, freedom is undermined.

◀ *It's the economic rules you're defending that encourage irresponsibility. Do corporate executives have to face the distress caused by their decisions to close plants and invest abroad? The costs fall on the workers and community. Do developers of* high-rent condos have to live with the consequences of a shrinking pool of low-priced housing? They won't have to cope with the homelessness. And in the typical workplace, does the employee have responsibility for improving work procedures? He or she can always say, "I just work here—that's the boss's headache."

In each case, individual actions are separated from their consequences.

On a bigger scale, your willingness always to "let the market decide" means that we citizens are let off the hook. In most cases, that's fine, but some tough moral choices can't be sloughed off—not without great cost to our humanity. Let's forge a better link between reward and responsibility.

▶ But it's precisely your social philosophy that has led to greater irresponsibility—to people blaming society for their problems. Little wonder we see an increase in crime. It's perfectly logical that people feel justified in striking out against society, rather than taking responsibility for themselves. They are responding to a change in the climate of opinion—really since the New Deal—that has shifted the emphasis from individual responsibility to government responsibility. It's a permissiveness that has permeated American social life. To reverse this trend, we must both reduce the functions of government and strengthen the family in its role of instilling values in the young.[45]

◀ Might much of the pathology you attribute to too much permissiveness actually reflect feelings of too little self-direction, too little control over one's own destiny? Anger and self-destruction erupt from a sense of powerlessness.

Besides, you're assigning the family an impossible chore, as long as the underlying ethic of our economic life so encourages irresponsibility. The celebration of economic self-seeking communicates that our worth lies not in our character but in our possessions. So, if you are a defense contractor, why not gouge the taxpayer? Or, why not use insider information to make a killing on Wall Street?[46]

The fact that speculation, not work, means "the rich get richer" degrades the value of work itself. So why not go for the fastest buck—illegally through dealing drugs or legally through dealing in real estate, for instance—rather than pursue the more

. . . Moral action requires an opportunity and a capacity for understanding the consequences of one's actions and for assuming responsibility for those consequences. . . . [T]he structure of American corporate enterprise narrows the domain of moral responsibility to the vanishing point.

Robert A. Dahl,
A Preface to Economic Democracy[44]

arduous task of, say, nursing or teaching, that carries tremendous responsibility but lower pay?

Where decision makers are removed from the impact of their decisions, where the ethic of self-seeking predominates, of course we lose our sense of responsibility to each other.

▶ If you think people can get rich in this country without working, you are nuts. And certainly you can't blame the rules of society themselves because people break them. That's absurd.

Democratic capitalism enforces responsibility to a very demanding taskmaster indeed: the market. No economic unit can profit and prosper unless it efficiently serves the consumers' desires. It constrains and disciplines individual behavior indirectly for the more general welfare, though not directly as you would impose it through government. Democratic capitalism imposes responsibility to an impersonal standard without the dangers inherent in individuals imposing their own standards.

◀ *You assume government assistance dilutes individual responsibility. But government help has permitted many children in poverty to grow into more responsible adults. And in myriad other ways, government is not a means to evade our responsibilities but the tool we need to fulfill our responsibilities to create stable communities and protect the environment.*

A Common Good? ★

▶ Let me clarify. I'm not suggesting that people don't see their interests connected to others. They often do. But it is to others with whom they can identify, who share their particular values and interests. In a multicultural society like ours, there are many, many distinct groupings with varying values—they become competing interests in the real world of economic and political contests. The common good, or the public interest, is what emerges in this healthy competition of interests. Yes, there is a common good if by that you mean personal security, liberty under the law, and hope of increasing prosperity for those who apply themselves. Beyond that, to idealize a common definition of the good is dangerous.[47]

Another basic difference between us is that you perceive government and the political process as vehicles through which people can express their deepest values and I don't. Government throughout history has always been an oppressive force and it always will be. It is society's only legalized form of coercion and force; it will always be threatening.

◄ *But "government" is hardly fixed; history shows it coevolving with society, becoming more responsive as people's aspirations rise.*

► But, as I've said many times now, government officials are just as self-interested as the rest of us; so if your hopes for a "common good" rising above the melee of competing interests rests on government officials, you're really naive. Government officials will always have their own agenda, including perpetuating or enlarging their own piece of the state bureaucracy. So, painting government as a force for good, as you do, misleads and ultimately encourages people to lose their independence.

◄ *If you were right, only despotism would be possible. For what is democratic government without people acting upon what they see as their duties to the whole? Without this, all government transactions would be reduced to bribery and extortion. Even national defense would be impossible. Why wouldn't military officers just sell secrets to the enemy? Indeed, forty years ago spies against the U.S. were politically motivated; by the Eighties, citizens were selling our national security for profit!*

► It's ridiculous to suggest that patriotism depends on some faith in a "common good." Of course citizens feel patriotic and are taught from birth to feel a loyalty to their country. That has nothing at all to do with your notion of a common good that government can express *for us.*

◄ *The dictionary tells us that patriotism means "love of one's country." What is this but pride in what's best about it—in*

Every body of men [including whatever body has the power to legislate and to govern] is governed altogether by its conception of what is its interest, in the narrowest and most selfish sense of the word interest: never by any regard for the interest of the people.
—Jeremy Bentham,
Constitutional Code, 1830[48]

. . . a commonwealth is . . . not any collection of human beings brought together in any sort of way, but an assemblage of people in large numbers associated in an agreement with respect to justice and a partnership for the common good. [Its] first cause . . . is not so much the weakness of the individual as a certain social spirit which nature has implanted in man.
—Marcus Tullius Cicero,
54–51 B.C.[49]

what we as a people have achieved and believe ourselves capable of achieving? It is pride in a common project.

▶ There are just too many competing values in this country for such a concept to have any real meaning—those you state are your own.

◀ *By common good I mean not what we as a people agree on in advance, but the good we seek in common through genuine dialogue.* [50] *Its promise lies in the widely shared values of our diverse people, values that could form the basis of a renewed patriotism as love of country: pride in our society's fairness, with opportunity for all. Pride in our commitment to promote life, so no one is denied the essentials necessary to be a full member of society. Pride in safeguarding our country's magnificent natural beauty.* [51]

Further, unless we can conceive of ourselves as capable of considering the common good, it becomes utterly impossible to take into account the interests of the yet-to-be-born or the interests of nonhuman life.

▶ These noble feelings we, of course, must act upon, as I said, but we can best do so through private channels, not the state. We express our deepest values in personal and group relationships, not through politics and the state.

◀ *What human being can separate the two! The quality of our community, our work lives, our education—very political issues—shape our character that we bring to all our relationships.*

And in much of America's religious tradition, society is understood neither to reflect an externally imposed order, nor to be a product of immutable economic laws; rather, it is our own creation. So as citizens we're responsible for ensuring that it does not violate but reflects our moral values. [53]

While you've accused me of coddling people, my vision actually expects more of people than yours! The many benefits of democracy bring corresponding duties, foremost of which are to protect opportunity for every child's development and to guard the natural world as a home in which we are members, not masters, as a bequest to be passed on, even enriched.

. . . the state [is] a partnership not only between those who are living, but between those who are living, those who are dead, and those who are to be born.

—Edmund Burke,
Reflections on the Revolution in France, 1790[52]

A renewal of economic life depends on the conscious choices and commitments of individual believers who practice their faith in the world. . . . We cannot separate what we believe from how we act in the marketplace and the broader community . . .

—U.S. Catholics Bishops,
Economic Justice for All[54]

Does Capitalism Embody Moral Values? ★

▶ It is socialist societies that try to force people to serve the common good. That such societies have had to resort to coercion and brute force is itself proof that their schemes, like yours, run against human nature.

The market system is much more realistic and therefore less coercive. It reduces the need for compassion and good will as motivating forces behind social improvements.[55] Human beings are limited in their capacity for selflessness. So we want to use it sparingly.

◀ But cooperative feelings don't get "used up." They grow with use! They grow as we experience the heightened self-esteem and the practical advantages of cooperation.[57] And cooperative behavior multiplies: people tend to act more cooperatively when they see others doing it.[58]

▶ Democratic capitalism doesn't deny the existence of the more positive qualities in people, it just doesn't depend on them in economic life. No matter what you say about Adam Smith's views, he underscored that self-interest is the best economic guide.

I know that the market system, or capitalism in general, embodies no lofty principles. But that's precisely what is best about it. It doesn't embody overarching values like "justice" or "equality." Establishing a common set of moral values is the goal of other economic systems, but capitalism is different. Its morality is that it leaves the individual responsible for deciding his or her own morality.[61] Remember the young man I mentioned in the beginning of our talk, the one who'd already had nineteen kids

. . . the requirement of ethical behavior [best] be confined to those circumstances where the price system breaks down. . . . We do not wish to use up recklessly the scarce resources of altruistic motivation . . .

—Kenneth Arrow,
"Gifts and Exchanges"[56]

At first it is of necessity that men attend to the public interest, afterward by choice. What had been calculation becomes instinct. By dint of working for the good of his fellow citizens, he in the end acquires a habit and taste for serving them.

—Alexis de Tocqueville,
Democracy in America, 1835[59]

It is not from the benevolence of the butcher, the brewer, or the baker, that we expect our dinner, but from their regard to their own interest.

—Adam Smith,
The Wealth of Nations, 1776[60]

by the time he was thirty-one, and expected the taxpayer to take care of his children? In the free market economy I'm advocating, he would have to pay for his irresponsibility.

In any case, it's not the role of the political and economic system to call us to live by higher values—for that, humanity has always relied on other means, including religion and tradition.

Capitalism is modest; all it tries to do is establish practical principles to make common life possible. Allowing the market to determine social outcomes impersonally, we can avoid the danger that an authority will impose its definition of the good life or the true nature of human happiness.[62]

◄ *Every society's rules—economic or otherwise—are inescapably moral. In ours, the money value of one's contribution in the market determines one's well-being, so those who suffer most are the very young and the elderly, who now comprise half the poor in America. Logically, can you claim that society shouldn't embody absolute values and then defend the market as the arbiter of value?*

Rules governing economic decision-making are also value-laden. Ours vest in managers (responsible to investors) the sole right, for example, to close and move a plant. These rules carry a clear value statement: that wealth but not work contribution gives people a say.

You do not see these values as values because they are the prevailing ones, so you can label as a moralist anyone who proposes an alternative. This is a particularly insidious form of the tyranny of the majority.

► Cooperation and agreement on moral values is not the aim of capitalism. And this is its strength! Capitalism leaves the realm of the individual person untouched—and private.[64] In that private sphere, it's up to each of us to develop moral virtues.

◄ *You praise the market because it relieves us of moral reasoning. But, as I have said, it is in the exercise of moral choice that we become human, developing what is a uniquely human capacity. In other words, you would shrink an arena in which we can develop a capacity central to our very humanity. So problems like homelessness, species extinction, acid rain pollution all worsen—to me, they're all examples of our abdicating this moral capacity.*

A democratic capitalist society is, in principle, uncommitted to any one vision of a social order. . . . For grave dangers to the human spirit lurk in the subordination of the political system and the economic system to a single moral-cultural vision.

—Michael Novak,
The Spirit of Democratic Capitalism[63]

▶ You do not understand the nature of moral development. While the market system itself does not embody any moral values, it does provide the best structure for people to make moral choices and develop qualities of character themselves. Competition of the marketplace ensures diversity, enabling individuals to select among producers not just on the basis of price and quality of products but on the basis of the firm's ethical behavior. They can, for example, boycott those who discriminate or pollute.[65]

Though capitalism does not embody a moral code, competitive markets automatically weed out crooks, cheaters, and liars. So while competitive markets do not make people moral, they certainly raise the cost of unethical behavior.[66]

Historically a businessperson was understood to be profiting because he or she was honorable. A career in business is good because it develops positive traits of character: diligence, thrift, self-reliance, self-respect, honesty, fair dealing, and so on.[67] It is the competitive element in capitalism that puts one's character to the test. It puts a premium on respect for promises, on self-determination and self-responsibility.[68] In other words, capitalism doesn't embody, but its competitive environment enables these important values to develop.

◀ *Capitalism's own ethic actually defeats the very values you prize! Its narrowing of our values to the single standard of market worth undermines the competitiveness on which capitalism itself is justified. Entrepreneurs seeking only their own gain will undercut competitors, take them over, and pursue any means to free themselves from the discipline of competition.[70] A prosperous market economy actually depends on a culture nurturing values other than market values. Pride in one's work—"workmanship"—isn't a market value; it is appreciation of the creative process itself. Without it, quality suffers.*

Among our more successful trading partners—the Japanese, for example—nonmarket values such as loyalty and group solidarity account for much of their economic success. A typical Japanese manager would reduce everyone's wages before laying off anyone during a downturn—the payoff is in heightened long-term productivity.[71]

▶ The excesses of narrow self-centeredness you describe in our culture reflect the failure of our religious and cultural life. It's always been clear to me that within capitalist societies, freely

Free enterprise is entirely compatible with the highest systems of ethics provided that individuals express those systems in the marketplace.
—Joseph Pichler, "Capitalism in America: Moral Issues in Public Policy"[69]

formed associations, especially the family and religion, are necessary to balance any tendency to excessive individualism.[72] But it's unfair to blame our economic system itself. It should only be judged on whether it produces the goods!

You assume that people's natural sympathies are weak and can be easily eroded. I don't. Our innate sympathies, that you have talked about, soften and make tolerable the inequalities in reward that are necessary to make the market system work.[73] Capitalism doesn't do away with feelings of mutual obligation. It deals only with the economic arena of life, which must be built on self-interest to work.

◄ *But is it possible for people to operate out of sheer economic self-interest during most of our waking hours and still retain a private sphere in which other aspects of our character can flourish? Human beings seek internal unity, and increasingly "economic man" comes to define our whole being. But that doesn't really work either. Americans express increasing discomfort with the ethic of individualism,[75] and a yearning for more connectedness to others.[76]*

At the heart of the problem of establishing a greater sense of community is that capitalism's claim to fairness rests on a loaded premise: anyone who tries can make it. So those that don't make it didn't really try. They therefore don't deserve our sympathy. How can community withstand such judgment?

► Look, when those most underprivileged and up against the worst prejudice—from a George Washington Carver to a Jesse Jackson—can make it and make it spectacularly, surely we must celebrate the openness of our society; it's pride in that openness that binds us together. Besides, your opinions about what Americans "think" or "feel" seem to be based on polls of Americans' attitudes. But can opinion polls really measure anything as profound as human moral judgments? Only in the most superficial way. The "findings" in such polls are as mercurial as fashion, with people often reporting that they feel what the media suggests that others feel. I think it's much more important to see how people act; and you don't find many Americans protesting all the defects you seem to find in our system.

The irony is that it's capitalism's success that has brought on attacks like yours. In fact, the better the system works in providing material abundance and freedom, the heavier the burden it

The principle of self-interest rightly understood is not a lofty one, but it is clear and sure. It does not aim at mighty objects, but it attains without excessive exertion all those at which it aims. As it lies within the reach of all capabilities, everyone can without difficulty learn and retain it.

—Alexis de Tocqueville,
Democracy in America, 1835[74]

. . . pollers of public opinion . . . have been following the will-o'-the-wisp. They have been . . . using statistics . . . [as] a means of being precise about matters of which you will remain ignorant.

—Lindsay Rogers,
The Pollsters, 1949[77]

places on individuals to cope with life's deeper spiritual meaning on their own. Precisely because capitalism frees young people from survival pressures, they can experience life's other limitations, those that people must discover within themselves. And what do they do? Immediately start to attack the institutions that gave them that luxury, the liberty for self-discovery, to begin with![78]

Of course, people will feel alienated in a free society. The alternative would be to remain so closely bound together as to be controlled by others. For many this alienation is unnerving, but it is the price of individual liberty.[79]

Capitalism surely doesn't fragment people into competitors and make cooperation impossible. In this country, people contribute their time and money in voluntary organizations more than anywhere else in the world, certainly more than in nonmarket economies. And volunteer involvement is on the upswing,[80] which belies your notion that people are increasingly distant from each other.

◄ *That Americans are "joiners" just underscores our need to feel connected and useful. But how much are our group leisure pursuits attempts to escape from the frustration and impotence we feel in our work lives and a sense of futility about political involvement?*

► Millions of Americans also volunteer in service organizations trying to help those who are less fortunate. These efforts are also on the increase.

◄ *And many volunteers fear that their efforts aren't adequately meeting even the symptoms, much less getting at the root of problems like homelessness, hunger, or substance abuse. They know that despite their efforts there are* more *poor people today than 20 years ago.*

► Perhaps the most undeniable evidence that capitalism certainly doesn't kill human kindness or dampen fellow-feeling is that we find the staunchest defense of human rights in capitalist countries. This is proof of people's enduring concern for each other in free enterprise economies and our willingness to protect each other.[81] Under which system are more individuals speaking out and taking action against the violation of human rights of their compatriots? Obviously, in the capitalist ones.

◄ *Again, you're comparing what exists under capitalism with totalitarian societies. This is* not *what I've been talking about.*

► I'm not misunderstanding you, I just think you're kidding yourself to suggest that it is possible to veer from capitalism without courting totalitarianism. And if your attack on capitalism held water, doing away with the market should diminish personal alienation and loneliness.[82] Show me a nonmarket economy that has solved these problems. There are none—because alienation and loneliness are inescapably part of the human condition.

◄ *Obviously, when the market is replaced by top-down planning by a few big shots, people will feel alienated. I've never advocated doing away with the market but rather simply putting it in its place, using it as a device to serve our values. And I've hardly advocated more top-down decision-making; I'm saying we have way too much of it within our own system.*

Is Change Possible? ★

► But surely if we humans had the capacity for the changes you advocate, they would have already happened. They haven't. Just where does your more "democratic," "freer," "fairer" society exist?

◄ *Nowhere as a perfected model. But pressure for change in the direction of greater self-determination and economic security as the basis of freedom is evident all over the world. I see it in movements for greater labor participation in the workplace from here to the Soviet Union, for land and credit reform in the Philippines to permit wider access to these essential resources, and here at home in pressure for health care protection as a citizen's right—to name only a few examples.*

▶ How can you seriously propose something that doesn't exist and never has existed? It seems preposterous at the outset.[83]

◀ *You might have posed the same question to Thomas Jefferson or Martin Luther King, Jr.*

To me, it's ironic that one of the greatest contributions of the very capitalism you wish to protect from change was that it allowed people for the first time to perceive their power to make change! Capitalism broke down the authority of tradition, the static conception of each person born into a particular station in life. Dynamism, innovation—this is what characterizes the spirit of capitalism. If true in the way we produce goods, why not in the social order, too?[84]

▶ Wherever anything even close to your vision has been attempted in socialist experiments, it has failed, hurting millions of people in the process. But you refuse to learn from history, which is the first responsibility of anyone advocating social change.

◀ *If you dismiss my views because the Soviet Union or Cuba or China are politically repressive, you've misunderstood all that I've been saying. None has attempted what I advocate, and none had a democratic tradition like ours on which to build.*

▶ But, however much you deny it, your view supposes that we can change human nature. Remaking humanity is not a goal of capitalism.[86] It takes people as they are and democratically allows them to register their wants. It is much less ambitious but much more realistic.

◀ *But capitalism has already remade people's view of their nature! Today's notion that people are driven primarily by economic motives is relatively recent, even considering only the history of so-called civilized societies. Throughout most of human evolution, production and exchange didn't make up a distinct arena of life driven by desire for material gain. These activities were subsumed within a social fabric in which one's community standing was all-important, not one's possessions.*[88]

What's new is our present-day acceptance of market exchange as the norm of human interaction—even to the "surro-

. . . the most serious problem with theories ungrounded in experience is that they can never be tested: unless experience is the proof of the pudding, there is no proof. . . . The fact that no political system has achieved perfect equality will not be taken to prove that . . . such societies are impossible. Once experience is eliminated, anything is possible.
—Jeane J. Kirkpatrick, *Dictatorships and Double Standards*[85]

The liberal conceives of men as imperfect beings. He regards the problem of social organization to be as much a negative problem of preventing "bad" people from doing harm as of enabling "good" people to do good . . .
—Milton Friedman, *Capitalism and Freedom*[87]

The free market is the great destroyer of tradition. It fosters a rootless, restless mode of life. It promotes change for the sake of change. Its ideal

gate" mother renting her womb to give birth to a child she doesn't want to keep!

People aren't static. We are always in the process of changing ourselves and our understanding of our selves. Aristotle believed that slavery was good for both master and slave alike.[90] Less than a century ago, Social Darwinist Herbert Spencer, preaching the innate incapacity of the lower classes, was wined and dined by leading American thinkers. And let's not forget: For most of human history, our nature was believed unfit for political democracy.

If we can document a progression in people's aspiration for and belief in their capacity for self-government, surely we can envision the next steps.

▶ Most Americans *are* satisfied; they feel things are going well in the United States. Commitment to our country and what it stands for is going up—witness the great increase in applications to military service academies and the highest military reenlistment rates since World War II. Americans aren't interested in basic change.[92]

◀ But there is widespread desire for greater fairness. Most Americans believe that the gap between the rich and the poor is too wide.[93] And in overwhelming numbers we want more government effort to end hunger, improve education, and protect the environment.[94] But it's also true that Americans want to believe that whatever one's lot in life, it's deserved,[95] so we tend to blame ourselves for our economic problems, not our society's unfairness.[96]

▶ On the contrary, too many blame society instead of accepting their own responsibility. In any case, the types of changes that you've been proposing are too extreme for most Americans. Instinctively and correctly they are suspicious of any radical change from what has worked so well.

◀ Rather than a radical departure, the direction I am proposing in many ways legitimizes what already exists (the public dimension of corporate property, for example) as well as revives much in the original vision of many of America's founders.

And remember: When our nation was born, its very principles were considered madness. It was America that proved possible what before was deemed impossible—political democracy on a grand scale. So, in suggesting that the next step for Americans is to enlarge our understanding of freedom to include economic citizenship, I am only claiming my American birthright: a belief in change.

▶ It's easy to arrive at beautiful visions as to what could be, but the fact that things are the way they are should itself tell us a lot about what people want and what is possible. The present captures an infinite number of lessons from the past as to what has been tried and what has failed. To ignore those lessons, to believe that you can start anew, is a form of impudence, even arrogance.

◀ But much of what is today and what you have defended throughout our talk is actually quite new, as I just said. The central economic entity of our time—the large corporation—is only a few generations old. Change is inevitable. That we cannot change. We can only ask in what direction are we moving—toward or away from our deepest values?

▶ Americans don't want to change the system because they appreciate that, even with its flaws, capitalism beats all the alternatives. An economic system is either controlled by self-regulating mechanisms without undue human interference, or it is not.

To me your vision means going backward, not forward. It means an elite making decisions. Capitalism represents an advance over such elitism—it overthrew the authority of the Crown and the Church in secular affairs. We don't want to go back to control by another elite.

◀ Of course, I don't either, but your ideas don't mean stasis; they suggest a perilous future. Combine your belief in law and order as virtually the only legitimate function of the state with the mistrust and fear sown in any society generating such extremes of wealth and deprivation as we now have—and where does this combination take us? To a nation increasingly dominated by police functions—a military-driven industry and foreign policy, more police, more citizens behind bars, more privately guarded residences for the rich, more alarm systems and security checks, more fear. It leads us toward a divided society, divided between the few who can live by their wealth and the many unable to live by their work.

. . . liberty is a living thing that passes from one generation to the next. . . . The greatest enemy of a living thing is not its enemies but its friends who wish to cling to its antiquated form.

—Harry Emerson Fosdick, 1935[98]

The Inescapable Trade-offs ★

We are not going to abolish any of those things . . . [war, poverty, discrimination, envy]. If we push them out one window, they will come in through another window in some unforeseen form. . . . That is the history of the human race.

—Irving Kristol,
"The Capitalist Conception of Justice"[99]

▶ You seem to believe that there are real solutions to human problems. Here's another central point on which we differ. There are no solutions, only trade-offs. There *is* no free lunch.

The neat trick of capitalism is that it doesn't require "solving the problem" of human selfishness. It gets people to do what is useful to society by simply looking out for themselves. Because people are not innately self-sacrificing, trying to make them so results in coercion and state control, as we've seen in totalitarian countries. It turns out to be worse than just accepting people as they are.

In other words, every attempt to get rid of social evils entails costs—trade-offs. Trying to discover ultimate solutions to human problems could only be achieved at the intolerably high cost of our freedom.[100]

◀ *Of course there are trade-offs! The challenge is to assess their full costs accurately so that we know exactly what we're giving up for what. Once we appreciate how much we're all hurt by growing hunger and poverty and environmental destruction, I think we could choose better trade-offs.*

▶ But you run up against the one inescapable trade-off in every society—that between equality and freedom. Trying to eliminate poverty and make everyone's situation more equal means limiting the freedom of action of others. Balancing these two values will always be tricky, but most Americans have decided that our present trade-off is about the best one should hope for.

◀ *Equality versus freedom is a misleading formulation. What Americans want isn't equality of outcome but* fairness—*meaning real equality of opportunity. Greater fairness doesn't thwart freedom; it allows greater freedom, as more people have real opportunity and productivity is enhanced.*

But let me make myself absolutely clear on one point. There is a critical trade-off we cannot avoid. It is between two very different understandings of freedom: the freedom of unlimited accumulation, on the one hand, and the freedom of human development on the other. On this, every society must choose.

Sound Processes or Ultimate Goals? ★

▶ At an even deeper level, our differences aren't about which ultimate goals to seek—freedom or equality or what have you. Our differences are about the wisdom of even seeking ultimate goals to begin with. You may deny that you believe in human perfectability, but much of what you say suggests mankind's ability to transcend nearly all human afflictions by taking rational control of our destiny. I think this is dangerous.[101]

It's impossible to develop a system that guarantees people freedom. At best we can establish rules limiting how much power any one person can have and specify the conditions under which those who have power are authorized to act. That's it.[103] Property rights and a free market, for example, aren't ultimates.

◀ *But you have made them precisely that—forcing other values to conform to their design.*

▶ No, they're simply devices conducive to certain values like greater freedom. The processes of the market, private property, and the rule of law can only indirectly contribute to, not guarantee, desired results, and not without unwanted side effects which we must just accept.[104]

Given our present state of fragmented meaning, a pragmatic liberalism is preferable over well-meaning perfectionism.

—Robert Benne,
The Ethic of Democratic Capitalism[102]

The direct attempt to prescribe desired outcomes through collective decisions is impossible and to concentrate enough power to carry out a collective vision is dangerous.[105] All human decisions have unintended consequences. In seeking an illusory "social justice," for example, we destroy the rule of law, as I pointed out earlier.[106]

Individuals can't master the complexity of a social system. No individual is wise enough to make decisions for society, so the best contribution each person can make is to stick to the duties of his or her role—be it business people responding to the market, not their own personal view of social responsibility, or judges adhering to constitutional law, not to their own personal view of distributive justice. These systemic processes, including tradition, should determine outcomes, not individual judgments.

With any other understanding of society, decisions get made for others by surrogate decision makers, based on abstract reasoning detached from the real world or based simply on individual prejudices. But by relying on systemic processes, decisions are safely diffused throughout society and not allowed to fall into the hands of a few.[108] This is the only way to avoid totalitarianism.

◄ *Surely the courage of millions of Americans, stepping outside of their "social roles" in order to change traditions and institutions—to force the end of slavery, to permit unions, to give women the vote, to clean up our rivers—has expanded our freedom and improved our lives. Rather than concentrating power in fewer hands, such changes distribute power more widely as social institutions are made to adapt to the views and needs of more people. These changes move our society in the opposite direction from totalitarianism.*

► But the root of the pain you are trying to address is not in our public policies or institutions—*it is in people.*

Ideological zealots full of their own moral certitude are the greatest danger to constitutional government. Maintaining constitutional freedoms can seem much less important than scoring points for their conception of justice. And when these zealots also pose as disinterested "experts," the danger is compounded.[110] I'm not saying you're one—but you come very close. Once people set out on your route, they will be forever frustrated because the utopia you promise will forever escape them. Like

. . . we do not know how to achieve a given end. We do not know the relationship between the public policies we adopt and the effects these policies were designed to achieve.

—George Stigler,
The Citizen and the State [107]

It is the lot of all human institutions, even those of the most perfect kind, to have defects as well as excellencies—ill as well as good propensities. This results from the imperfection of the Institutor, Man.

—Alexander Hamilton,
The Defence No. 1, 1792–95 [109]

One belief, more than any other, is responsible for the slaughter of individuals on the altars of the great historical ideals. . . . This is the belief that somewhere . . . in divine relation or in the mind of an individual thinker, in the pronouncements of history of science . . . there is a final solution.

—Isaiah Berlin,
Four Essays on Liberty [111]

frustrated religious fanatics, they'll seek to impose their idea of what's right.

◄ *The greatest danger in our society is hardly self-delusion about the possibility of creating the "perfect society"! It's the opposite—feeling so cut off from power to shape our society that we lose any vision of where we are headed as a people.*[112] *This loss violates our very nature, because as human beings, we are creative; being part of making the world better is as much a part of being human as is the pain of disappointment.*

Psychologists confirm that most people have a greater sense of well-being when they contribute to something they care about beyond themselves. In fact, they say, our mental health depends on it.[113]

It is rather the feeling of having no effective voice in shaping public life that is the real danger—one posed in both capitalism and communism. As systems, they share an interest in preventing people's enhanced sense of their own capacities for greater self-government.[115] *Communism may tolerate some participation in the workplace but not in the political arena; capitalism may tolerate some measure of political self-government, but not economic.*

. . . in a world where principles and conduct are unequally mated, men are to be judged by their reach as well as by their grasp—by the ends at which they aim as well as by the success with which they attain them.

—R. H. Tawney,
Religion and the Rise of Capitalism, 1926[114]

Ends or Means? ★

► You couldn't be more wrong. Capitalism fosters economic self-determination through our consumer choices in a free market. But if we agree, and I'm sure we do, that human beings have innate worth, then the most critical question is whether a social order treats human beings as ends or means. In your vision, human beings are reduced to means in achieving some idealized social order.[116]

◄ *No, both capitalism and state-controlled communism justify sacrifice of the individual to a larger social goal. In com-*

. . . market arrangements . . . preserve respect for humans as ends in themselves, as centers of self-transcending freedom.

—Robert Benne,
The Ethic of Democratic Capitalism[117]

munist states, individuals are allowed little voice in choosing leaders because larger political goals are deemed more important. In capitalism, millions go jobless because it's said that without some people unemployed the economy can't function properly.

So we must now go beyond both. Triumphs over slavery, child labor, and the right to organize unions, for example, all reflect a progression in human aspiration to be treated as ends— of innate worth—and never as means. The values I'm outlining here could help take us a step further.

▶ Actually, your vision would reduce us all to pawns of social planners. Democratic capitalism protects the individual's free choice. It doesn't stop anyone from getting a job and developing themselves. In democratic capitalism, the highest value is placed upon the individual—respect for his or her self-direction and initiative.

◀ *No. In capitalism, it's the individual's wealth, not the individual, that has standing. The person without wealth can sleep on the street!*

▶ No, in our system, more than in any attainable alternative, a person is free to earn wealth so he doesn't have to sleep on the street! And we as individuals are all free to help those who need it.

We come to the end of our long talk. I see more clearly now how and why we differ. I see human nature as divided, in internal conflict. This very private struggle to rise above our petty self-seeking, to consider the interests of others, and to make the most of ourselves is the essence of our morality. It's hard. Society can do very little to make it any easier. It *is* the human condition, our curse and our blessing.

◀ *Yes, being human involves pain. But society need not make that pain unbearable by violating our nature—by denying the economic security we need to contribute to community life and by so reducing human ties to market exchanges that we come to deny our own need and caring for each other.*

▶ But it is in the meaning of freedom itself that our visions so diverge, isn't it?

. . . if one demands more of life than life can give, then capitalism is certainly the wrong system. . . . All it gives is a greater abundance of material goods and a great deal of freedom to cope with the problems of the human condition on your own.
—Irving Kristol, "The Capitalist Conception of Justice"[118]

Insofar as human beings want not merely to live but to live well, we are political beings. And insofar as we do not participate in forming the common definition of the good life, to that degree we fall short of the fullest possibilities of the human vocation.
—John H. Schaar, "Equality of Opportunity and Beyond"[119]

◀ *Absolutely.*

▶ For me, the ultimate freedom is in living by my own lights, developing myself and my own morality as I see fit.

◀ *Yes, but what makes this freedom possible? It is the freedom to create with others a society ever more life-giving, ever truer to our deepest values.*

Summing Up the Dialogue ★

IS FREEDOM A ZERO-SUM?

▶ Yes. Expanding some people's rights necessarily means restraining the actions of others, detracting from their freedom. Moreover, income and property are essential to the expression of free choice, but at any given time the supply of wealth is finite. So to enjoy the benefits of democratic capitalism, we must accept that it entails competition in which some win and others lose.

◀ *No. The development of each person's talents contributes to those of others and one's freedom to develop is enhanced the more that opportunities are open to others as well. So freedom conceived as human development is not a zero-sum. Placing a limit on each individual's accumulation, sufficient to ensure that everyone has access to essential resources for development, does not interfere with freedom, for unlimited wealth is not needed to develop any human gift.*

UPON WHAT TRAITS CAN THE ECONOMY BEST BE CONSTRUCTED?

▶ Only upon the presumption of self-interest, the strongest and surest motivator of action. Whether the result of innate sinfulness, or of our evolution in a competitive struggle for survival, the individual's own well-being and success come first. To achieve maximum productive output, the economy must encourage the most self-disciplined and talented by offering unlimited reward and avoiding redistribution of wealth to the less disciplined and less talented.

◄ *Upon human beings' need for work to gain self-esteem by self-support and expression as well as to contribute to a purpose beyond our private pursuits. We are endowed with both self-concern and compassion. The economic structure itself shapes the expression of these innate qualities; what it rewards influences how much we express narrow concern about ourselves or cooperation toward common goals.*

WHAT ECONOMIC STRUCTURE BEST SUITS HUMAN NATURE?

► One in which the institutions of private property and market exchange establish the rules so that individuals can pursue their own goals, ultimately to the benefit of the whole society.

◄ *A structure empowering individuals and communities to determine their values and to choose and adapt economic mechanisms—including the market, private property, and public provision—to serve these values.*

HOW COULD AN ECONOMIC SYSTEM THREATEN HUMAN FREEDOM?

► By allowing individuals to override the impartial rules of the market and property in order to impose their own values upon society, coercing others into their private vision of what's best for society.

By divesting people of their property—the bulwark of freedom—earned with their labor and ingenuity.

By allowing the economy to become controlled by the political process, making economic and political life monolithic rather than counterbalancing.

◄ *By so reducing human interaction to market exchange that it violates each human being's need to be treated as an "end" rather than a "means." Ultimately, this leads to the thwarting and even destruction of life itself, since some individuals, especially children, cannot compete in the market.*

By allowing the market to settle so many choices for us that we are denied critical decision-making arenas in which to develop our moral capacities.

By allowing such consolidation of economic power that its influence compromises the democratic process and some people are made powerless to meet even essential needs.

IS A COMMON GOOD POSSIBLE?

▶ No. The concept of a "common good," or a public interest, is largely an illusion, and it can be dangerous if it is used by those who seek to impose their ideas on others. In a pluralistic society, there are many competing interests, not one unitary vision. Direction emerges out of enlivening competition and compromise among these interests.

◄ *Yes. The common good evolves from genuine public dialogue, leading not just to compromise among fixed interests, but to new and ever-evolving possibilities. Not a goal we know in advance, the common good is the good we seek in common.*

Furthering the common good does not require that we forego self-interest, but rather that we are able to see our own interests linked to those of others. It requires a society that enables citizens to express the very human need to act on our deepest values as well as on our private interests.

DOES CAPITALISM ITSELF EMBODY MORAL VALUES?

▶ No, and it must not. The great virtue of capitalism is that it protects the sphere of the individual. Morality can only be developed by the individual with support from the family and religion. This process is thwarted when society tries to impose its own version of morality.

◀ *Yes, allowing the market to determine individual worth and well-being as well as our treatment of nature is itself a powerful moral statement. By separating individuals from the consequences of their acts, the market encourages moral detachment.*

IS CHANGE POSSIBLE?

▶ The roots of the many evils one might like to change lie not in economic and political institutions. The roots lie in human nature. The economic and political system we have now is probably about the best we can hope for. Indeed, history shows that wherever a more equal society has been attempted it has ended in terrible repression despite the beautiful rhetoric of those behind it.

◀ *Much of what we accept as given today is itself quite new. What I advocate is not a departure but an evolution that draws on the insights of our own nation's founders, insights from which we have strayed. I do not suggest that we chart wholly new ground, but build upon a historical progression in people's aspirations for greater freedom.*

AND OUR DIALOGUE ENDS

And with this exchange, our imaginary dialogue comes to an end.

But I hope it is just the beginning. While my imaginary partner and I have not changed our views, we have built a basis of understanding on which we can better listen. That is the first step.

The next step is for you to take with us. My hope is not that you've taken sides but that you've found yourself arguing with both of us, discovering and sharpening questions that you now feel you must pursue.

My premise is simple: Until we as a people are honestly willing to confront the conflicting understandings of the values shaping American life, we cannot overcome the mounting pain of hunger, poverty, fear, and cynicism that divide us from each other. Only by engaging fearlessly in that dialogue can we begin to heal our nation and together build a politics of hope.

Notes ★

Introduction

1. Robert Bellah et al., *Habits of the Heart: Individualism and Commitment in American Life* (Berkeley, Calif.: University of California Press, 1985).
2. John Stuart Mill, *On Liberty* (New York: Penguin Books, 1982), 99. (Original work published 1859)
3. William Irwin Thompson, *Evil and the World Order* (New York: Harper Colophon Books, 1977), 103.
4. Isaiah Berlin, *Two Concepts of Liberty* (Oxford: Oxford University Press, 1958), 43.
5. The parallel between this view and the modern-day conservative's antipathy to government is striking, even though the "father" of conservatism, Edmund Burke, denied the artificial nature of the state, seeing it as a natural outgrowth of human community.
6. Jeremy Bentham, *An Introduction to the Principles of Morals and Legislation* (New York: Hafner, 1948), ch. 1, sec. 4, 3. (Original work published 1789)
7. R. H. Tawney, *Religion and the Rise of Capitalism* (London: John Murray, 1926), 279–280.
8. John Locke, "The Second Treatise of Civil Government," in *Two Treatises of Government*, ed. Peter Laslett (Cambridge, England: Cambridge University Press, 1960), ch. 5, sec. 37, 312.
9. Adam Smith, *The Theory of Moral Sentiments*, ed. D. D. Raphael and A. L. Macfie (Indianapolis: Liberty Classics, 1982), pt. 2, sec. 2, ch. 3, 85.
10. Ibid. pt. 1, sec. 3, ch. 2, 50.
11. Ibid. pt. 1, sec. 1, ch. 5, 25.
12. Charles R. Darwin, *The Descent of Man and Selection in Relation to Sex* (New York: D. Appleton, 1909), pt. 1, ch. 4, 121.
13. Smith, pt. 2, sec. 2, ch. 3, 88.
14. Ibid., pt. 2, sec. 2, ch. 1, 80.
15. George C. Lodge, *The New American Ideology* (New York: New York University Press, 1986), ch. 7.
16. Smith, *The Theory of Moral Sentiments*, pt. 1, sec. 3, ch. 2, 51.
17. Thomas Jefferson in a letter to Samuel Kercheval, *Thomas Jefferson, Writings*, ed. Merrill D. Peterson (New York: The Library of America/Liberty Classics, 1984), 1401.

Part One

1. Isaiah Berlin, *Two Concepts of Liberty* (Oxford: Oxford University Press, 1958), 7.
2. Thomas Hobbes, *Leviathan*, ed. Michael Oakeshott (New York: Collier Books, 1962), pt. 2, ch. 17, 129.
3. Milton Friedman, *Capitalism and Freedom* (Chicago: University of Chicago Press, 1962), 1–6, 25–26.
4. John L. O'Sullivan, "Introduction. The Democratic Principle—The Importance of Its Assertion, and Application to Our Political System and Literature," *United States Magazine and Democratic Review* 1 (October–December, 1837): 6. Such statements are often used by conservatives to represent the founders' view. See, for example, Richard B. McKenzie, *Bound to Be Free* (Stanford, Calif.: Hoover Institution Press, 1982), 13.
5. Thomas Jefferson, *Thomas Jefferson, Writings*, ed. Merrill D. Peterson (New York: The Library of America/Liberty Classics, 1984), 494.
6. Thomas Paine, *Common Sense and Other Political Writings*, ed. Nelson F. Adkins (New York: Liberal Arts Press, 1953), 4.
7. Jefferson, *Thomas Jefferson, Writings*, 529.
8. Alexander Hamilton, James Madison, and John Jay, *The Federalist Papers* (New York: New American Library), 84.
9. Irving Kristol, *Two Cheers for Capitalism* (New York: New American Library, 1978), 15.
10. Quoted in Andrew Levinson, *The Full Employment Economy* (New York: Coward, McCann, Geoghegan, 1980), 188.
11. Milton Friedman and Rose Friedman, *Free to Choose* (New York: Avon, 1979), 56.
12. R. H. Tawney, *Equality* (London: Allen & Unwin, 1931, 1938, 1952), 260.
13. Thomas Sowell, *A Conflict of Visions* (New York: William Morrow, 1987), 226.
14. *A Call for Action to Make Our Nation Safe for Children: A Briefing Book on the Status of American Children in 1988*, Children's Defense Fund, Washington D.C., 1988, iii. This estimate refers to children under 6 years of age.
15. Ayn Rand, *Capitalism, the Unknown Ideal* (New York: New American Library, 1946), 40.
16. Thurman Arnold, "How They Are Voting," *New Republic* 30 September 1936, cited in Arthur M. Schlesinger, Jr., *The Cycles of American History* (Boston: Houghton Mifflin, 1986), 248.
17. Louis Harris, *Inside America* (New York: Vintage, 1987), 33–38.
18. Henry Shue, *Basic Rights: Subsistence, Affluence, and U.S. Foreign Policy* (Princeton, N.J.: University Press, 1980), 24–25.
19. Montesquieu, *Spirit of the Laws* (New York: Hafner, 1900), vol. 1, 151.
20. Franklin D. Roosevelt, "Annual Message to Congress," 11 January 1944, in *The Public Papers and Addresses of Franklin D. Roosevelt 1944–45*, ed. Samuel I. Rosenman (New York: Harper and Brothers, 1950), 32–44.
21. Andrew Levinson, *The Full Employment Economy*, 194–195. Levinson cites five national polls in which from 59 percent to 93 percent of respondents favored a government-guaranteed right to a job.
22. Roosevelt, "Annual Message," 41.

23. Roger A. Freeman, *The Wayward Welfare State* (Stanford, Calif.: Hoover Institution, 1981), 252.

24. Lawrence M. Mead, *Beyond Entitlement: The Social Obligations of Citizenship* (New York: Free Press, 1986), 72.

25. Robert Lane, "Government and Self-Esteem," *Political Theory* 10 (February 1982): 13.

26. Alfred J. Kahn and Sheila Kamerman, *Not for the Poor Alone* (Philadelphia: Temple University Press, 1975), 153.

27. Michael Novak, *The Spirit of Democratic Capitalism* (New York: American Enterprise Institute/Simon & Schuster, 1982), 48.

28. Paul Tsongas, *The Road from Here* (New York: Alfred A. Knopf, 1981), 135.

29. Friedman and Friedman, *Free to Choose*, 57.

30. Ibid., 83.

31. Richard B. McKenzie, *Bound to Be Free* (Stanford, Calif.: Hoover Institution Press, 1982), 23.

32. We devote about 14 percent to social programs, compared to 20 percent to 34 percent in western Europe and Scandinavia. Ira C. Magaziner and Robert Reich, *Minding America's Business* (New York: Vintage Books, 1983), 16.

33. Nancy Folbre and the Center for Popular Economics, *A Field Guide to the U.S. Economy* (New York: Pantheon, 1987), table 6.2. For details on public employment, see Louis Uchitelle, "In the Work Force, A Reagan Evolution," *The New York Times*, 27 December 1987, sec. E, 5.

34. McKenzie, *Bound to Be Free*, 19.

35. John Adams, "Discourses on Davila," in *Democracy, Liberty, and Property: Readings in the American Political Tradition*, ed. Francis W. Coker (New York: Macmillan, 1949), 465.

36. Folbre, *Field Guide*, table 6.1.

37. Robert Kuttner, *The Economic Illusion* (New York: Houghton Mifflin, 1984), 82.

38. Ibid., 190. In the mid-Seventies the U.S. ranked fourteenth out of seventeenth in taxes as percent of gross domestic product, but eighth in terms of the burden carried by the average production worker.

39. William O'Hare, "The Eight Myths of Poverty," *American Demographics* 8 (May 1986): 25.

40. For an alarming review of the evidence, see Seymour Melman, *Profits Without Production* (New York: Alfred A. Knopf, 1983), 230–231.

41. The increase is given in real dollars. See Office of Management and Budget, *The United States Budget in Brief Fiscal Year 1987* (Washington D.C.: GPO, 1987).

42. Carl Sagan, speech delivered at the Rededication on the 50th Anniversary of the Eternal Light Peace Memorial, Gettysburg, Pennsylvania, July 3, 1988.

43. Total federal employment:

   2 million civilians not working for the military
   1 million civilians working directly for the military
   2.5 million working for firms under military contract to the Pentagon
   2 million in the armed forces

44. In 1981, 71 percent of federal R&D funding was absorbed by the Defense Department, NASA, and military-related expenditures in the Department of Energy. Melman, *Profits Without Production*, 89; see also Seymour Melman, "The 'Key Log' in America's Economic Logjam," *The New York Times* 12 December 1987, opinion page.

45. Kahn and Kamerman, *Not for the Poor Alone*, 172.

46. *The New York Times*, 3 February 1987, 18. The exact estimate is $2.1 billion for the next three years.

47. Michael deCourcy Hinds, "New York Welfare Allowance Rising But Homeless Worries Persist," *The New York Times*, 28 December 1987, 14.

48. Elliott Currie, "Crime and Ideology," *Working Papers* 9 (May–June 1982): 29.

49. James Q. Wilson, "Crime and American Culture," *Public Interest* 70 (Winter 1983): 36–37. For an in-depth conservative argument about crime and society, see James Q. Wilson and Richard J. Herstein, *Crime and Human Nature* (New York: Simon & Schuster, 1985).

50. For a summary of both sides of the argument that weak punishment causes crime, see Elliott Currie, *Confronting Crime* (New York: Pantheon, 1985), 26–28.

51. Ibid., 6, and chs. 4 and 5.

52. *Children in Need* (Washington D.C.: Committee for Economic Development, 1987), ch. 1.

53. Paul Simon, *Let's Put America Back to Work* (Chicago: Bonus Books, 1987), 21.

54. *A Call for Action to Make Our Nation Safe for Children* Children's Defense Fund, vi.

55. Paul A. Samuelson and William D. Nordhaus, *Economics*, 12th ed. (New York: McGraw-Hill, 1985), 217–218, 220, 247–255.

56. For an in-depth discussion of the concept of "wage-led growth," see Samuel Bowles, David M. Gordon, and Thomas E. Weisskopf, *Beyond the Wasteland* (New York: Doubleday, 1983). See also David M. Gordon, "Six-Percent Unemployment Ain't Natural: Demystifying the Idea of a Rising Natural Rate of Unemployment," *Social Research* 54 (Summer 1987): 223–246.

57. Adam Smith, *The Wealth of Nations*, Edwin Cannan, ed., (New York: Random House, 1937), bk. 1, ch. 8, 81.

58. "Sweden's Economy," *The Economist*, 7 March 1987, 21. See also Kuttner, *The Economic Illusion*, 21.

59. Milton Friedman and Rose Friedman, *Tyranny of the Status Quo* (New York: Avon, 1984), 165.

60. A 1978 Gallup Poll found that the median public estimate was that the federal government wastes about 50 percent of all the tax monies it receives. Views of state and local government efficiency were somewhat better. Cited in Paul Blumberg, *Inequality in an Age of Decline* (New York: Oxford University Press, 1980), 224.

61. For a general statement about the failed welfare state, see Kristol, *Two Cheers for Capitalism*, 228–229.

62. Friedman and Friedman, *Tyranny of the Status Quo*, 168.

63. *The Economist*, 295, no. 7395, (25 May 1985): 61.

64. Andrew Levinson, *The Full Employment Economy*, 196–197. Levinson cites a 1976 Potomac Associates Institute study in which from 72 percent to 97 percent of respond-

ents favored public spending for a wide array of social programs. A *Time*/Yankelovich Clancy Shulman poll recorded that from 52 percent to 78 percent of Americans voiced approval for increased government spending on programs to help the elderly, the environment, the homeless, and so on. *Time*, 30 March 1987, 37. See also Harris, *Inside America,* 116–117.

65. Harris, *Inside America*, 117. Over 76 percent and 73 percent of those polled said that they would pay more taxes to fund public schools and day care, respectively.
66. Kuttner, *The Economic Illusion*, 23.
67. Ibid., 24–25.
68. Such programs in Sweden have been estimated to reduce unemployment rates by half. Levinson, *The Full Employment Alternative*, 149. See also Kuttner, *The Economic Illusion*, 176–177, 184.
69. Tamar Lewis, "A Tragedy that Still Echoes, *The New York Times*, 23 March 1986, 10F.
70. *Congressional Record*, vol. 131, no. 26, 6 March 1985. Quoted in Charles Hayes's testimony.
71. Edward I. Koch, "Welfare Isn't a Way of Life," *The New York Times*, 4 March 1988, Opinion page.
72. Kristol, *Two Cheers for Capitalism*, 119.
73. John Stuart Mill, *On Liberty* (New York: Penguin, 1983), 181–182. (Original work published 1859)
74. Charles Murray, *Losing Ground* (New York: Basic Books, 1984), ch. 12.
75. Fred Block et al., *The Mean Season* (New York: Pantheon, 1987), 55.
76. Murray, *Losing Ground*, 9.
77. Kristol, *Two Cheers for Capitalism*, 225.
78. Robert L. Woodson, "The Poor and Conservatives vs. the Poverty Industry," speech to the Heritage Foundation, 13 August 1987.
79. O'Hare, "The Eight Myths of Poverty," 24. As of the mid-Eighties, there were about 32 million people "officially" in poverty and about 12 million recipients of Aid to Families with Dependent Children, what most people think of as "welfare." A total of 19 million received food stamps.
80. Office of Management and Budget, *The United States Budget in Brief, Fiscal Year 1987*, 52–57. Most of the rest goes to veterans and unemployment insurance and to retirement for federal employees and disability, not targeted to the poor.
81. Based on government data compiled by Scott Barancik, Center on Budget and Policy Priorities, Washington, D.C. The exception is Alaska.
82. We devote about 14 percent to social programs, compared to 20 percent to 34 percent in western Europe and Scandinavia. Magaziner and Reich, *Minding America's Business*, 16.
83. Block et al., *The Mean Season*, 37.
84. David Neumeyer, Food Research and Action Center, interview with author, Washington, D.C., 17 April 1988. See also *Increasing Hunger and Declining Help: Barriers to Participation in the Food Stamp Program*, Physician Task Force on Hunger in America, Harvard School of Public Health, May 1986.
85. Ibid., *Increasing Hunger*, 57
86. Marian Wright Edelman, *Families in Peril* (Cambridge, Mass.: Harvard University Press, 1987), 78. Edelman heads the Children's Defense Fund in Washington, D.C.

87. Leonard Goodwin, *Do the Poor Want to Work?* (Washington, D.C.: Brookings Institution, 1972), 68, 112. "Poor people . . . identify their self-esteem with work as strongly as do the nonpoor." Attitudes toward work are directly related to experience—failure in the work world contributes to acceptance of welfare dependency. Similarly, the author points out that "working in jobs that do not pay enough to support their families is likely to . . . discourage them from further work activity."

88. Mead, *Beyond Entitlement*, 36, 40, 49, 50, 72.

89. Michael Harrington, *The New American Poverty* (New York: Holt, Rinehart and Winston, 1984), 21.

90. Freeman, *The Wayward Welfare State*, 254.

91. Ibid., 255.

92. Edward Banfield, *The Unheavenly City* (Boston: Little, Brown, 1968), 47–59. Banfield actually defines a person's class in terms of one's time horizon.

93. In 1986, 41.6 percent of all poor people over the age of fourteen worked. Michael Harrington et al., *Who Are the Poor?* (Washington, D.C.: Justice for All, 1988), 3. See also Sar Levitan and Clifford M. Johnson, *Beyond the Safety Net: Revising the Promise of Opportunity in America* (Cambridge, Mass.: Ballinger, 1984), 44, citing the Bureau of Census, *Money Income and Poverty Status*, 1982, P-60 ser., no. 140 (Washington, D.C.: GPO, 1982), 4.

94. *The New York Times*, 25 October 1982, 1.

95. By net new jobs is meant the difference between new jobs and jobs eliminated. Barry Bluestone and Bennett Harrison, *The Great U-Turn* (New York: Basic Books, 1988), 5. The time periods compared are 1973–1979 and 1979–1986. The poverty line used is $11,000. For an excellent overview, see Gary Loveman and Christopher Tilly, "Good Jobs or Bad Jobs: What Does the Evidence Say?" *New England Economic Review* (January–February, 1988): 46–65.

96. Marvin Kosters and Murray N. Ross, *The Distribution of Earning and Employment Opportunities: A Reexamination of the Evidence* (Washington, D.C.: American Enterprise Institute for Public Policy Research, 1987), 55.

97. Ibid., table 14, 39.

98. Ibid.

99. U.S. Department of Commerce, *Statistical Abstract of the United States 1988*, 108th ed. (Washington, D.C.: GPO, 1988), 375. See also Bluestone and Harrison, *The Great U-Turn*, ch. 3.

100. *Call for Action*, Children's Defense Fund, iii. See also: Edelman, *Families in Peril*, 38; J. Larry Brown, "Hunger in the U.S.," *Scientific American* 256 (February 1987): 41.

101. Ramon G. McLeod, "Low-Pay Jobs May Take the Gain from GAIN," *San Francisco Chronicle*, 22 June 1987, 6. The author calculated costs for the area in which I live, including transportation, child care, and taxes.

102. Mead, *Beyond Entitlement*, 43.

103. David M. Gordon, *The Working Poor: Towards a State Agenda* (Washington, D.C.: Council of State Planning Agencies), 29–30. See also Bennett Harrison, "Welfare Payments and the Reproduction of Low-Wage Workers and Secondary Jobs," *Review of Radical Political Economics* (Fall 1979): 1–16. Harrison writes: "Union membership, the position of the job in the national wage structure, and the local unemploy-

ment rate are always far more important than education and training in explaining the frequency and extent of welfare utilization" (9).

104. Wilson, *The Truly Disadvantaged*, 41–43. See also John D. Kasarda, "The Regional and Urban Redistribution of People and Jobs in the U.S.," paper prepared for the National Research Council Committee on National Urban Policy, National Academy of Science, 1986.

105. Ibid., 26–28.

106. Alvin L. Schorr, "Welfare Reform, Once (or Twice) Again," *Tikkun* (November/December 1987): 17.

107. Wilson, *The Truly Disadvantaged*, figure 3.3. For a full discussion, see chapter 3.

108. *Declining Earnings of Young Men: Their Relation to Poverty, Teen Pregnancy, and Family Formation* (Washington, D.C.: Children's Defense Fund, 1987), 4. Between 1973 and 1986, the real mean earnings of black males twenty to twenty-four years old fell 46 percent.

109. Ibid., 3.

110. O'Hare, "The Eight Myths," 24 Of the 34 million poor, 23 million are white. Only 14 percent of the poor live in poverty stricken areas of central cities.

111. Bluestone and Harrison, *The Great U-Turn*, 126.

112. Mead, *Beyond Entitlement*, ix, 9.

113. R. H. Tawney, *Religion and the Rise of Capitalism* (London: John Murray, 1926), 267.

114. Robert S. McIntyre and David Wilhelm, *Money for Nothing: The Failure of Corporate Tax Incentives 1981–1984* (Washington, D.C.: Citizens for Tax Justice, 1986), 3.

115. Estimates of the size of the "underclass" range from less than a million to as many as 11 million. Isabel Wilkerson, "Growth of the Very Poor Is Focus of New Studies," *The New York Times*, 20 December 1987, 15.

116. Greg J. Duncan, Martha S. Hill, and Saul D. Hoffman, "Welfare Dependence Within and Across Generations," *Science* 239 (29 January 1988): 467.

117. Ken Auletta, *The Underclass* (New York: Random House, 1982), 275.

118. Duncan, Hill, and Hoffman, "Welfare Dependence Within and Across Generations," 467. The median length of receipt is less than four years.

119. Harrison, "Welfare Payments," 1–16.

120. Duncan, Hill, and Hoffman, "Welfare Dependence," 467. Sixty-four percent of young women studied who had been in welfare families received no AFDC during the three-year period of the study. See also Greg H. Duncan, *Years of Poverty, Years of Plenty: The Changing Economic Fortunes of American Workers and their Families* (Ann Arbor: Institute for Social Research, University of Michigan, 1984).

121. Auletta, *The Underclass*, 231. A five-year national study in the late Seventies found that ex-addicts and AFDC mothers benefited most from the subsidized work program and that "benefits exceed the costs" (222). Ex-offenders and young people did less well. Overall, about a third continued in paid jobs after the program ended. Much of the outcome depended on how well managed was the particular site taking part in the national experiment. See chapters 17 and 19. See also note 128 below.

122. Mead, *Beyond Entitlement*, 43.

123. *Business Week,* 12 October 1987, 26–28. Note that one-fifth of all U.S. children are estimated to be poor, but one-fourth of all U.S. children under six.

124. Quoted in Edelman, *Families in Peril,* 51.

125. Harrington et al., *Justice for All,* 4.

126. Robert Greenstein, "Myths and Realities about American Poverty," *Food Monitor* 42 (Fall 1987): 62.

127. *Public Welfare in California,* State of California, Health and Welfare Agency, Department of Social Services, Data Processing and Statistical Services Bureau, Statistical Series PA3-339, calculated from table 11.

128. The study follows the lives of 123 poor children who participated in Headstart programs in Ypsilanti, Michigan. See John Berrueta-Clement, *Changed Lives: The Effects of the Perry Preschool on Youth Through Age 19* (Ypsilanti, Mich.: High Scope Educational C Foundation, 1984). For an excellent evaluation of the impact of the War on Poverty, see Sar A. Levitan and Robert Taggart, *The Promise of Greatness* (Cambridge, Mass.: Harvard University Press, 1976). For a discussion of social programs that do work, see Lisbeth B. Schorr, *Within Our Reach* (New York: Doubleday, 1988).

129. Thomas Sowell, *Knowledge and Decisions* (New York: Basic Books, 1980), 117–18.

130. Ibid., 117.

131. Lester Thurow, *The Zero-Sum Society* (New York: Basic Books, 1980), 24.

132. Quoted in Christian Bay, *The Structure of Freedom* (Berkeley: University of California Press, 1962), 96.

133. Lindsey Gruson, "Life vs. Livelihood at Chrysler Plant," *The New York Times,* 8 July 1987, 10.

134. William Glaberson, "Misery on the Meatpacking Line," *The New York Times,* 14 June 1987, Business section.

135. Charles Lindblom, *Politics and Markets* (New York: Basic Books, 1977), 48.

136. Sidney Lens, "Austria's Quiet Revolution Works," *The Nation* 240, no. 1 (12 January 1985): 15.

137. George Gilder, *Wealth and Poverty* (New York: Basic Books, 1981), 12.

138. Benjamin Ward, *The Conservative Economic World View* (New York: Basic Books, 1979), 50–51.

139. Adam Smith, *The Theory of Moral Sentiments* ed. D. D. Raphael and A. L. Macfie (Indianapolis: Liberty Classics, 1982), pt. 1, sec. 3, ch. 2, 51.

140. For a useful discussion of this issue, see Harrington, *The New American Poverty,* 72–76. If poverty were simply defined as the lowest fifth of the population in income, of course it would always exist; but if it is defined in very real measures such as higher death rates, cross-country comparisons are possible. They demonstrate that it is possible to reduce poverty. The Organization for Economic Cooperation and Development in the early Seventies found, for example, that 13 percent of Americans were poor compared to 3.5 percent of Swedes.

141. William S. Nersesian, M.D., et al., "Childhood Death and Poverty: A Study of All Childhood Deaths in Maine, 1976 to 1980," *Pediatrics* 75 (January 1985): 41–49.

142. J. Larry Brown, "Hunger in the U.S.," 41.

143. For a discussion in a similar vein, see Peter Townsend, *Poverty in the United Kingdom* (Berkeley: University of California Press, 1979).

144. Robert H. Haveman, Victor Halberstadt, and Richard V. Burkhauser, *Public Policy Toward Disabled Workers* (Ithaca, N.Y.: Cornell University Press, 1984), 48. Among eight industrial countries, the U.S. ranked among the lowest in medical care, housing, and other programs for the disabled.

145. Robert L. Woodson, "The Importance of Neighborhood Organizations in Meeting Human Needs," in *Meeting Human Needs: Toward a New Public Philosophy*, ed. Jack A. Meyer (Washington, D.C.: American Enterprise Institute for Public Policy Research, 1982), 140.

146. Robert Nisbet, *Conservatism* (Minneapolis: University of Minnesota Press, 1986), 61–62.

147. Jack A. Meyer, "Private Sector Initiatives and Public Policy: A New Agenda," in Meyer, *Meeting Human Needs*, 6.

148. Tibor R. Machan, "The Petty Tyranny of Government Regulation," in *Rights and Regulation*, ed. Tibor R. Machan and M. Bruce Johnson (San Francisco: Pacific Institute for Public Policy Research, 1983), 287.

149. Edgar Cahn, Southeast Florida Center on Aging, Florida International University, North Miami Campus, TC 320, North Miami, Fla. 33181.

150. Michael Novak, *The Spirit of Democratic Capitalism*, 65.

151. Martin N. Baily and Alok K. Chabrabarti, "Innovation and Productivity in U.S. Industry" Brookings Papers on Economic Activity, no. 2 (Washington, D.C., 1985), 609–632.

152. Harris, *Inside America*, 19. Americans report eight hours more each week spent in work activities than in 1973.

153. For a discussion of the many forces behind the productivity problem, see Melman, *Profits Without Production*. ch. 9; Sam Bowles, David M. Gordon, and Thomas E. Weisskopf, *Beyond the Wasteland* (Garden City, N.Y.: Anchor Press/Doubleday, 1983), ch. 7.

154. See Richard B. Freeman and James L. Medoff, *What Do Unions Do?* (New York: Basic Books, 1984), especially ch. 11. The comparisons controlled for such factors as capital/labor ratios.

155. Between 1960 and 1981, the productivity growth rates in Japan and Germany were among the highest in the industrial world. Yet Japan offers much greater job security than do U.S. corporations, and in West Germany there are many more social welfare protections than in the U.S.

156. Smith, *The Wealth of Nations*, bk. 1, ch. 8, 81.

157. M. Harvey Brenner, *Estimating the Effects of Economic Change on National Health and Social Well-Being*, Joint Economic Committee, U.S. Congress, Washington D.C. Government Printing Office, June, 1984. Brenner finds a particularly clear correlation between increases in unemployment and both cardiovascular mortality and admissions to mental hospitals. Table A, and 55, 56.

158. Quoted in Edelman, *Families in Peril*, 67.

159. For an excellent discussion of the problem, see Sherle R. Schwenninger and Jerry W. Sanders, "The Democrats and a New Grand Strategy," *World Policy Journal*, 3, no. 3. (Summer 1986): 373–374.

160. Novak, *The Spirit of Democratic Capitalism*, 124.

161. Gilder, *Wealth and Poverty*, 12. For a general statement about unintended consequences of reforms, see Sowell, *Knowledge and Decisions*, 108.

162. Friedrich A. Hayek, " 'Social' or Distributive Justice," in *The Essence of Hayek*, ed. Chiaki Nishiyama and Kurt R. Leube (Stanford, Calif.: Hoover Institution Press, 1984), 67–68.

163. Wilson, *The Truly Disadvantaged*, chs. 3 and 4.

164. Donald O. Parsons, *Poverty and the Minimum Wage* (Washington, D.C.: American Enterprise Institute for Public Policy Research, 1980).

165. U.S. General Accounting Office, *Minimum Wage Policy Questions Persist, Report to the U.S. Senate Committee on Labor and Human Resources* (Washington, D.C.: GPO, 1983).

166. Kuttner, *The Economic Illusion*, especially ch. 6.

167. McKenzie, *Bound to Be Free*, 42.

168. Ibid., 116–117.

169. Of course, advocates of this view differ widely in precisely what functions they consider appropriate for government. Here I present a middle ground.

170. Irving Kristol, "Thoughts on Equality and Egalitarianism," in *Income Redistribution*, ed. Colin D. Campbell (Washington, D.C.: American Enterprise Institute for Public Policy Research, 1977), 65.

171. Novak, *The Spirit of Democratic Capitalism*, 48.

172. Kristol, *Two Cheers for Capitalism*, ch. 2. See also Robert L. Woodson, "The Importance of Neighborhood Groups," in Meyer, *Meeting Human Needs*, 134.

173. Friedman and Friedman, *Free to Choose*, xix.

174. Schlesinger, *The Cycles of American History*, 248.

175. Mill, *On Liberty*, 187.

176. *UNESCO Statistical Digest 1986*, UNESCO, London, 1986, 148, 206, 270, 274, 306, 310.

Part Two

1. Adam Smith, *The Theory of Moral Sentiments* (Indianapolis: Liberty Classics, 1982), D. D. Raphael and A. L. Macfie, eds., pt. 1, sec. 2. ch 1, 80.

2. U.S. Congress, Congressional Budget Office, *Trends in Family Income: 1970–1986*. 1988.

3. Ibid., fig 1, xiv; tables 2, 25; figs 17, 37; xx, 26, 27.

4. Robert Benne, *The Ethic of Democratic Capitalism* (Philadelphia: Fortress, 1981), 225, citing Paul Samuelson, *Economics*, 10th ed. (Tokyo: McGraw-Hill Kogakusha, 1976), 85.

5. Lester C. Thurow, *The Zero-Sum Society* (New York: Basic Books/Penguin, 1980), 160.

6. Joseph A. Pechman, *Who Paid the Taxes? 1966–85* (Washington, D.C.: Brookings Institution, 1985), 9–10. See also Frank Levy, *Dollars and Dreams: The Changing American Income Distribution* (New York: Basic Books, 1987).

7. U.S. Congress, Congressional Budget Office, *The Changing Distribution of Federal*

Taxes: 1975–1990. 1987, table B-2, 71. The share going to the top fifth of all families grew from 45.3 percent of total income in 1977 to 49.7 percent in 1988 (calculated with corporate taxes allocated to labor income).

8. Ibid., calculated from table 6 and table 8, 39, 48. The time period is 1977 to 1988; the exact increase was 63 percent. Using what some economists view as a more accurate method for adjusting for inflation, Thomas Byrne Edsall estimates an even greater increase, 74 percent, for the richest one percent. See "The Return of Inequality," *The Atlantic Monthly*, June 1988, 89. The tax rate paid by the poorest decile increased 17 percent, while that of the top one percent decreased 25 percent during the period 1977 to 1988 (table 7, 47).

9. Thomas Sowell, *Knowledge and Decisions* (New York: Basic Books, 1980), 77–78.

10. U.S. Bureau of the Census, *Estimates of Poverty Including the Value of Noncash Benefits: 1985* (Washington, D.C.: GPO, 1986), table 1, 16.

11. In 1960, the official poverty line was 54 percent of the median income; by 1979, it was only 38 percent. Michael Harrington, *The New American Poverty* (New York: Holt, Rinehart and Winston, 1984), 73. According to U.S. Bureau of the Census, *Money Income and Poverty Status of Families and Persons in the U.S., 1986* (Washington, D.C.: GPO, 1986), tables 1, 2, 6, incomes of families of over 46 million Americans fall below half the median. But by the official count, only 32 million Americans are below the poverty line.

12. Sowell, *Knowledge and Decisions*, 77.

13. Robert Nozick, *Anarchy, State, and Utopia* (New York: Basic Books, 1974), 160.

14. Ibid., 238.

15. Milton Friedman and Rose Friedman, *Free to Choose* (New York: Avon, 1979), 136.

16. William Greider, *Secrets of the Temple: How the Federal Reserve Runs the Country* (New York: Simon & Schuster, 1987), 456–457.

17. Office of Management and Budget, *The United States Budget in Brief, Fiscal Year 1987* (Washington, D.C.: GPO), 81. About 20 percent of government bonds are held by individuals; the rest by banks, insurances companies, and other institutions in which the returns go primarily to better-off individuals.

18. Jeff Faux, "Reducing the Deficits," *Briefing Paper* (Washington, D.C.: Economic Policy Institute, 1987), 6. Between 1977 and 1988, this came to $129 billion, an average annual loss of over $1,400 for most families, but a $13,000 average gain to those in the top 10 percent. Projections based on data from the U.S. Congressional Budget Office study, *The Changing Distribution of Federal Taxes: 1975–1990*, cited above.

19. Robert Kuttner, *The Economic Illusion* (Boston: Houghton Mifflin, 1984), 39.

20. Ibid., 18, citing a study by Michael Kinsley in *The New Republic* analyzing the sources of wealth of the 400 richest Americans. See also Lester Thurow, "A Surge in Inequality," *Scientific American* 256 (May 1987): 30.

21. World Bank, *World Development Report 1984*, Washington, D.C., table 28. For data comparing after-tax income among countries, see Ira C. Magaziner and Robert B. Reich, *Minding America's Business* (New York: Vintage Books, 1982), exhibit 12.

22. "Executive Pay Goes Sky-High," *U.S. News & World Report*, 29 April 1985, 61. For Japan's figure, see TRB from Washington, *The New Republic*, 14 May 1984, 41.

23. Until the early Eighties, the rate of poverty among the elderly was higher than for the

population as a whole and was reduced mainly by government assistance, primarily Medicare and Social Security. Data on net wealth by age group suggest that among families headed by older Americans differences are greater than for families headed by those in their thirties and forties. "Survey of Consumer Finances, 1983: A Second Report," *Federal Reserve Bulletin* (December 1984): 863.

24. U.S. Congress, Congressional Budget Office, *The Changing Distribution of Federal Taxes*, appendix B, table B-2.

25. Quoted in Bertram Gross, *Friendly Fascism* (Boston: South End Press, 1980), 94.

26. U.S. Congress, Congressional Budget Office, *The Changing Distribution of Federal Taxes*.

27. In 1985, the effective tax rate of the lowest decile was 21.9 percent; the top decile, 25.3 percent. In Pechman, *Who Paid the Taxes? 1966–85*, 67. The most regressive tax is the sales tax. Families in poverty pay five times more of their income in state sales and excise taxes than do the richest families. See *Nickels and Dimes: How Sales and Excise Taxes Add Up in the 50 States*, Citizens for Tax Justice and the Institute on Taxation and Economic Policy, Washington, D.C., 1988, 4.

28. Adam Smith, *The Wealth of Nations* (New York: Random House, 1937), bk. 5, ch. 2, pt. 2, 777.

29. Peter Peterson, "No More Free Lunch for the Middle Class," *The New York Times Magazine*, 17 Jan. 1982, 41.

30. Terry L. Anderson and Peter J. Hill, *The Birth of the Transfer Society* (Stanford, Calif.: Hoover Institution Press, 1970), chs. 1 and 7.

31. Roger Friedland and Jimmy Sanders, "The Public Economy and Economic Growth in Western Market Economies," *American Sociological Review* 50 (1985): 421–37.

32. "No Business Like War Business," *The Defense Monitor*, 16, no. 3. (1987), 6. Stocks of military contractors were 60 percent above commercial stocks between 1975 and 1985.

33. John Hospers, "Free Enterprise as the Embodiment of Justice," in *Ethics, Free Enterprise and Public Policy: Original Essays on Moral Issues in Business*, ed. Richard T. de George and Joseph A. Pichler (New York: Oxford University Press, 1978), 76.

34. Friedrich A. Hayek, *The Constitution of Liberty* (London: Routledge & Kegan Paul, 1960), 94.

35. Irving Kristol, *Two Cheers for Capitalism* (New York: New American Library, 1978), 176. See also "A Capitalist Conception of Justice" in de George and Pichler, *Ethics, Free Enterprise and Public Policy*, 59.

36. Seymour Melman, *Profits Without Production* (New York: Alfred A. Knopf, 1983). See also Mark Green and John F. Berry, *The Challenge of Hidden Profits* (New York: William Morrow, 1985).

37. Smith, *The Theory of Moral Sentiments*, 86.

38. Quoted by Robert Kuttner, "Growth With Equity," *Working Papers*, 8, no. 5 (September–October 1981): 32.

39. Benne, *The Ethic of Democratic Capitalism*, 229. See also George Gilder, *The Age of Enterprise* (New York: Simon & Schuster, 1984).

40. Sowell, *A Conflict of Visions* (New York: William Morrow, 1987), 86. Here and in

other quotes I use from this book, Sowell is summarizing a philosophical tradition, one that he himself no doubt identifies with, judging from views expressed in his other works. See, for example, Sowell, *Knowledge and Decisions*, 75.

41. Eric Schmuckler et al., "The 400 Richest People in America," *Forbes*, 26 October 1987, 106.

42. Patricia O'Toole, *Corporate Messiah* (New York: William Morrow, 1984), 32.

43. Peter Passell, "Executive Pay: Is It Too High?" *The New York Times*, 27 April 1988, sec. C2. See also Robert S. McIntyre and David Wilhelm, *Money for Nothing: The Failure of Corporate Tax Incentives 1981–1984* (Washington, D.C.: Citizens for Tax Justice, 1986), 9.

44. Estimate refers to real purchasing power. "Where Bosses Are Paid Most," *The Economist*, 6 June 1987, 71. U.S. top executives are by far the highest paid in the world. With stock options added in, the U.S. executive typically makes over 40 percent more than the next highest paid, the Swiss.

45. George Will, "In Defense of the Welfare State," *The New Republic*, 9 May 1983, 25.

46. Bayard Rustin, "From Protest to Politics: The Future of the Civil Rights Movement," *Commentary* 39, no. 3 (February 1965): 25–31.

47. Daniel Yankelovich, *New Rules* (New York: Bantam Books, 1982), 35, 36.

48. In 1986 only 20 percent of college freshmen came from families making less than $20,000 a year, down from 40 percent in 1980. Robert Kuttner, "The Patrimony Society," *The New Republic*, 11 May 1987, 20.

49. Faux, "Reducing the Deficits," table 6.

50. Jim Hightower, "Where Greed, Unofficially Blessed by Reagan, Has Led," *The New York Times*, 21 June 1987, opinion page.

51. James K. Stewart, *Theft by Employees in Work Organization* (Washington, D.C.: National Institute of Justice, 1983), foreword, 21.

52. U.S. Congress, Congressional Budget Office, *The Changing Distribution of Federal Taxes*, table 6, 39. The bottom eight deciles experienced in average family income in real dollars between 1977 and 1988. A related study that adjusts for family size records a deline in real income for the bottom 40 percent and only a small gain for the bottom 60 percent. See Stephen Rose and David Fasenfest, *Family Income Changes in the Eighties* (Washington, D.C.: Economic Policy Institute, 1988).

53. Sowell, *A Conflict of Visions*, 130.

54. George Gilder, speech delivered to the Symposium on Catholic Social Teaching and the American Economy, University of Notre Dame, December 1983.

55. Irving Kristol, "Thoughts on Equality and Egalitarianism," in *Income Redistribution*, ed. Colin D. Campbell (Washington, D.C.: American Enterprise Institute for Public Policy Research, 1976), 39.

56. David Ricardo, *On the Principles of Political Economy and Taxation* (London: John Murray, 1817), 190.

57. Historically, savings rates have not declined when taxes for the wealthy were raised. See A. M. Okun, *Equality and Efficiency: The Big Trade-Off* (Washington, D.C.: Brookings Institution, 1975), 98–100.

58. Robert Kuttner, "Growth with Equity," 37.

59. McIntyre and Wilhelm, "Money for Nothing," 7.

60. Sweden, for example, enjoys twice the savings rate of the U.S. Kuttner, *The Economic Illusion*, 70–72.

61. Ibid., 69–71, 75–82. See also Kuttner, "Tax Policy and Capital Formation in the U.S. and Europe: Reconciling Growth with Equity," *Tax Notes*, 19 April 1982, 163–180.

62. People making over half a million dollars a year get 70 percent of their income from investments. Nancy Folbre, The Center for Popular Economics, *A Field Guide to the U.S. Economy* (New York: Pantheon Books, 1987), figure 1.3.

63. Faux, "Reducing the Deficits," table D, 17, based on *National Income and Product Accounts*, table 2.1.

64. David Morris, "Marx's '84 Issue," *The New York Times*, 3 September 1984, opinion page.

65. Friedman and Friedman, *Free to Choose*, 15.

66. For more information on community development funds, write to the National Association of Community Development Loan Funds, 151 Montague City Rd., Greenfield, Mass. 01301.

67. George Gilder, speech delivered to the Symposium on Catholic Social Teaching and the American Economy, University of Notre Dame, December 1983. See also Gilder, *Wealth and Poverty* (New York: Basic Books, 1981) 245.

68. Bertrand de Jouvenel, *The Ethics of Redistribution* (London: The Syndics of the Cambridge University Press, 1952), 40–41.

69. Robert Nisbet, *Conservatism: Dream and Reality* (Minneapolis: University of Minnesota Press, 1986), 54.

70. Estate and gift taxes contribute less than one percent to federal revenues. Office of Management and Budget, *The United States Budget in Brief, Fiscal Year 1987* (Washington, D.C.: GPO), table 3. Today a couple can leave $1.2 million completely tax free, according to Cynthia Hutton, "Keeping It All in the Family," *Fortune 1988 Investors' Guide*, 111.

71. Milton Friedman, *Capitalism and Freedom* (Chicago: University of Chicago Press, 1962), 164.

72. Nisbet, *Conservatism*, 52. Here Nisbet is summarizing the conservative view on inheritance.

73. Thomas Jefferson in a letter to John Adams, *Thomas Jefferson, Writings*, ed. Merrill D. Peterson (New York: The Library of America/Liberty Classics, 1984), 1306.

74. Kristol, *Two Cheers for Capitalism*, 207–209.

75. Tax cuts for the wealthy cost the treasury about $60 billion annually in fiscal years 1988 and 1989. Robert S. McIntyre, "The Populist Tax Act of 1989," *The Nation*, 2 April 1988, 462. The deficit is roughly $150 billion.

76. Nozick, *Anarchy, State, and Utopia*, 243.

77. Robert E. Lane, "Government and Self-Esteem," *Political Theory* 10 (February 1982): 8–9.

78. Quoted in James Sterba, *Justice: Alternative Perspectives* (Belmont, Calif.: Wadsworth Publishers, 1980), 126.

79. Nozick, *Anarchy, State and Utopia*, 241.

80. Daniel Bell, *The Coming of the Post-Industrial Society* (New York: Basic Books, 1973), 453.

81. Jennifer Hochshild, *What's Fair? American Beliefs about Distributive Justice* (Cambridge, Mass.: Harvard University Press, 1981) and Robert E. Lane, *Political Ideology* (New York: The Free Press of Glencoe, 1962).

82. Norman Podhoretz, "The Intellectuals and the Pursuit of Happiness," *Commentary*, 55, no. 2 (February 1973): 7.

83. Robert Nisbet, "Where Do We Go From Here?" in Campbell, *Income Redistribution*, 183.

84. Bell, *Post-Industrial Society*, 451.

85. Kristol, *Two Cheers for Capitalism*, 165.

86. Friedman and Friedman, *Free to Choose*, 14.

87. Sowell, *A Conflict of Visions*, 125.

88. Irving Kristol, "About Equality," *Commentary* 54, no. 5 (November 1972): 46.

89. Lester C. Thurow, "Equity, Efficiency, Social Justice, and Redistribution," in *The Welfare State in Crisis* (Paris: Organization for Economic Co-operation and Development, 1981), 140. The difference in earnings between the top and bottom quintile of fully employed white males is 5 to 1, but for everyone else, it is 27 to 1.

90. Benne, *The Ethic of Democratic Capitalism*, 225.

91. See Christopher Jencks et al., *Inequality: A Reassessment of the Effect of Family and Schooling in America* (New York: Basic Books, 1972). Sons of families in the top fifth income bracket have earnings on average 75 percent higher than those coming from the bottom fifth. See also, Samuel Bowles and Valerie I. Nelson, "The Inheritance of IQ and the Intergenerational Reproduction of Economic Inequality," *Review of Economics and Statistics* 56 (February 1974): 39–51.

92. Adam Smith, *The Wealth of Nations* bk. 1, ch. 2, 15.

93. See note 21.

94. Seymour Martin Lipset, "Social Mobility in Industrial Societies," *Public Opinion*, 5, no. 3 (June/July 1982): 43, citing Robert M. Hauser et al., "Temporal Change in Occupational Mobility: Evidence for Men in the United States," *American Sociological Review* 40 (June 1975): 280.

95. *The New York Times*, 27 October 1988, A18.

96. Sowell, *A Conflict of Visions*, 88–89, 200, and ch. 6.

97. Ibid., 226.

98. Jeane J. Kirkpatrick, *Dictatorship and Double Standards* (New York: Simon & Schuster and the American Enterprise Institute, 1982), 15.

99. Sowell, *A Conflict of Visions*, 72–73.

100. John H. Schaar, "Equality of Opportunity and Beyond," in *Equality*, ed. J. Roland Pennock and John W. Chapman (New York: Atherton Press, 1967), 248.

101. J. Larry Brown, "Hunger in the U.S.," *Scientific American* 256, no. 2 (February 1987): 37–41. Estimate on percentage of children under six who live in poverty is from Children's Defense Fund, Washington, D.C.

102. Daniel Moynihan, "How Has the United States Met Its Major Challenges Since 1945?" *Commentary*, 80, no. 5 (November 1985).

103. Irving Kristol, "The Capitalist Concept of Justice," de George and Pichler, *Ethics, Free Enterprise and Public Policy*, 58.

104. Nozick, *Anarchy, State and Utopia*, 238. The "floor of decency" is my term, not Nozick's.

105. James S. Fishkin, *Justice, Equal Opportunity, and the Family* (New Haven, Conn.: Yale University Press, 1983), 155–157.

106. *Writings of James Madison*, ed. Gaillard Hunt (New York: Putnam & Sons, 1900–1910), vol. 6, 86.

107. For a provocative discussion of the appropriate role of money, see Michael Walzer, *Spheres of Justice* (New York: Basic Books, 1983).

108. C. B. Macpherson, *Democratic Theory: Essays in Retrieval* (Oxford: Clarendon Press, 1973), 55.

109. Ibid., 75.

110. June 1965, Address, Howard University.

111. Nathan Glazer, *Affirmative Discrimination: Ethnic Inequality and Public Policy* (New York: Basic Books, 1975), 62–63. Also Morris B. Abram, "Affirmative Action: Fair Shakers and Social Engineers," *Harvard Law Review* 99 (1986): 1315.

112. According to U.S. Bureau of Labor statistics, for example, blacks comprise 10 percent of the adult population. However, only 3 percent of lawyers are black, while 34 percent of all cleaners and "servants" are black.

113. U.S. Department of Commerce, *Statistical Abstract of the United States 1988*, 108th ed. (Washington D.C.: GPO, 1988) table no. 231, 139.

114. Gary Becker, "Productivity Is the Best Affirmative Action Plan," *Business Week*, 27 April 1987, 18.

115. Urban League report using U.S. Census Bureau data, *San Francisco Chronicle*, 25 July 1987, sec. A.

116. For example, the proportion of black faculty members in 1983 was only 4 percent, a drop from 1977. *The Chronicle of Higher Education*, 10 February 1988, A12.

117. James E. Ellis, "The Black Middle Class," *Business Week*, 14 March 1988, 63.

118. Richard B. McKenzie, *Bound to Be Free* (Stanford, Calif.: Hoover Institution Press, 1982), 54.

119. Blacks represent 32 percent of all felony arrests in the United States but 48 percent of U.S. prisoners. Joan Petersilia, The National Institute of Corrections, U.S. Department of Justice, *Racial Disparities in the Criminal Justice System* (Santa Monica, Calif: Rand, 1983), xiii. New York's 1985 rate of black imprisonment was, at 776 per 100,000 population, 50 percent higher than South Africa's and 10 times higher than for U.S. whites. Jim Murphy, *A Question of Race: Minority/White Incarceration in New York State* (Albany, N.Y.: Center for Justice Education, 1987). See *The Death Penalty* (New York: Amnesty International Publications, 1987), which documents racial disparity at each step of the judicial process. It reports that fifty-three of fifty-eight prisoners executed over a nine-year period had killed whites, even though blacks and whites are victims of homicide in roughly equal numbers (183).

120. Richard Posner, *The Economics of Justice* (Cambridge, Mass.: Harvard University Press, 1981), 374.

121. *Affirmative Action to Open the Doors of Job Opportunity: A Policy of Fairness and Compassion That Has Worked*, A Report of the Citizens' Commission on Civil Rights, Washington, D.C., 1984, 140–146.

122. Ibid., 143. Johnson & Johnson was responding to a survey on the impact of affirmative action.

123. Abram, "Affirmative Action," 1319.

124. For a similar line of reasoning, see Richard A. Wasserstrom, "Racism, Sexism, and Preferential Treatment: An Approach to the Topics," *UCLA Law Review* 24 (1977): 581, 620–621.

125. McKenzie, *Bound to Be Free*, 54; Sowell, *Conflict of Visions*, 79.

126. Randall Kennedy, "Persuasion and Distrust: A Comment on the Affirmative Action Debate," *Harvard Law Review* 99 (1986): 1337.

127. Glazer, *Affirmative Discrimination*, 197.

128. Currently three-quarters of those polled favor affirmative action for women and minorities (a finding that Louis Harris considers one of his most underreported). Louis Harris, *Inside America* (New York: Random House, Vintage, 1987), 191.

129. Kennedy, "Persuasion and Distrust," 1329.

130. *Affirmative Action to Open the Doors of Job Opportunity*, 130–146.

131. Sowell, *Knowledge and Decisions*, 300.

132. Ellis, "The Black Middle Class," 64.

133. Jim Schachter, "Unequal Opportunity," *Los Angeles Times*, 17 April 1988, sec. IV, 1, 5.

134. Kennedy, "Persuasion and Distrust," 1331.

135. Thomas Sowell, "Black Progress Can't Be Legislated," *Washington Post*, 12 August 1984, sec. B, 4.

136. Ira Glasser, "Affirmative Action and the Legacy of Racial Injustice," in *Affirmative Action: Eliminating Racism*, ed. Phyllis A. Katz (New York: Plenum, 1988), 341.

137. Glenn C. Loury, "Beyond Civil Rights," *The New Republic*, 7 October 1985, 25.

138. Sowell, *Knowledge and Decisions*, 300. See also James P. Smith and Finis Welch, "Affirmative Action and Labor Markets," *Journal of Labor Economics* 2, no. 2 (1984): 269–295.

139. *Affirmative Action to Open the Doors of Job Opportunity*, 123.

140. Richard A. Posner, "The DeFunis Case and the Constitutionality of Preferential Treatment of Racial Minorities," in *The Supreme Court Review 1974*, ed. Philip B. Kurland (Chicago: University of Chicago Press, 1975), 13–15.

141. *Affirmative Action to Open the Doors of Job Opportunity*, 163, citing Marcus M. Alexis, "The Effect of Admission Procedures on Minority Enrollment in Graduate and Professional Schools," in *Working Papers: Bakke, Weber and Affirmative Action* (New York: Rockefeller Foundation, 1979). 52–71.

142. *Affirmative Action to Open the Doors of Job Opportunity*, 165.

143. Ellis, "The Black Middle Class," 64.

144. Nozick, *Anarchy, State, and Utopia*, 32–33.

145. Alexander Bickel, *The Morality of Consent* (New Haven, Conn.: Yale University Press, 1975), 133.

146. Allan P. Sindler, *Equal Opportunity: On the Policy and Politics of Compensatory Minority Preferences*, (Washington, D.C.: American Enterprise Institute, 1983), 12.

147. Lester C. Thurow, "The Leverage of Our Wealthiest 400," *The New York Times*, 11 October 1984, Opinion page. The piece refers to 400 individuals and 82 families identified by *Forbes*.

148. Kristol, *Two Cheers for Capitalism*, 167–168.

149. J. R. Pole, *The Pursuit of Equality in American History* (Berkeley: University of California Press, 1978), 26–37. In South Carolina, including the slaves, 90 percent of the population was unpropertied.

150. George Gallup, Jr., "Americans Believe There's More Poverty than U.S. Says," *San Francisco Chronicle*, 11 February 1985, 10.

151. Jean Jacques Rousseau, *On the Social Contract with Geneva Manuscript and Political Economy*, Roger D. Masters, ed. (New York: St. Martin's Press, 1978), bk. 1, ch. 9, 221–222.

152. Quoted in Nisbet, *Conservatism*, 67.

153. "No Business Like War Business," 6. Weapons manufacturing is almost twice as profitable as comparable commercial business.

154. Kirkpatrick, *Dictatorships and Double Standards*, 15.

155. Nozick, *Anarchy, State, and Utopia*, 158–159.

156. Friedrich A. Hayek, " 'Social' or Distributive Justice," in *The Essence of Hayek*, ed. Chiaki Nishiyama and Kurt R. Leube (Stanford, Calif.: Hoover Institution Press, 1984), 69–70.

157. Sowell, *A Conflict of Visions*, 56–57.

158. Kristol, *Two Cheers for Capitalism*, 126.

159. Sowell, *Knowledge and Decisions*, 370.

160. Kristol, "Thoughts on Equality and Egalitarianism," 42.

161. Sowell, *Knowledge and Decisions*, 330.

162. Nozick, *Anarchy, State, and Utopia*, 164.

163. Ibid., 163.

164. Jean Jacques Rousseau, *The Social Contract*, bk. 2 (Indianapolis: Hackett, 1983), 46.

165. Friedrich A. Hayek, *The Road to Serfdom* (Chicago: University of Chicago Press, 1944), 79.

Part Three

1. Nancy Folbre and the Center for Popular Economics, *A Field Guide to the U.S. Economy* (New York: Pantheon, 1987), figure 1.8. Data from *Federal Reserve Bulletins* refer to all nonbanking corporations. For a comprehensive study of concentration, see Edward S. Herman, *Corporate Control: Corporate Power* (New York: Cambridge University Press, 1981), especially ch. 6.

2. F. M. Scherer, *Industrial Market Structure and Economic Performance* 2d ed. (Chicago: Rand McNally, 1980), 67.

3. Benjamin Ward, *The Conservative Economic World View* (New York: Basic Books, 1979), 29.

4. Yale Brozen, "The Corporate Merger: Erosion of Competition or Expanding Horizons," *The Sovereign Citizen* (Fall 1983) (The Institute for American Values, Nichols College, Dudley Massachusetts), 14, citing the work of Prof. Sam Peltzman in note 10 below.

5. William M. Shepherd, "Causes of Increased Competition in the U.S. Economy, 1939–1980," *Review of Economics and Statistics* 64 (November 1982): 613.

6. George Gilder, *Wealth and Poverty* (New York: Basic Books, 1981), 37–38.
7. Scherer, *Industrial Market Structure and Economic Performance*, 67.
8. Frances Moore Lappé, *Diet for a Small Planet*, 10th anniversary edition (New York: Ballantine Books, 1982), pt. 3, ch. 2, 140–158. See also ibid., chapter 6 for a discussion of the pricing strategies of oligopolies; chapter 14 for a discussion of the role of advertising.
9. Henry Simons, *Economic Policy for a Free Society* (Chicago: University of Chicago Press, 1948), 72.
10. Sam Peltzman, "The Gains and Losses from Industrial Concentration," *The Journal of Law and Economics* 20 (October 1977): 229–263.
11. Ralph K. Winter, Jr., "Advertising and Legal Theory," in *Issues in Advertising: The Economics of Persuasion*, ed. David G. Tuerck (Washington, D.C.: American Enterprise Institute for Public Policy Research, 1978), 24.
12. Walter A. Adams and James W. Brock, *The Bigness Complex* (New York: Pantheon, 1986), especially pt. 2.
13. Lee Iacocca, speech to the American Bar Association Annual Meeting, August 10, 1987.
14. Alan Greenspan, "Antitrust," in Ayn Rand, *Capitalism: The Unknown Ideal* (New York: New American Library, 1962), 59.
15. Ibid., 59.
16. Dominick T. Armentano, *Antitrust and Monopoly* (New York: John Wiley & Sons, 1982), 3.
17. Judge Abram Chayes, "The Modern Corporation and the Rule of Law," in *The Corporation in Modern Society*, ed. Edward Mason (Cambridge, Mass.: Harvard University Press, 1959), 28.
18. Irving Kristol, *Two Cheers for Capitalism* (New York: New American Library, 1979), 54.
19. Milton Friedman, *Capitalism and Freedom* (Chicago: University of Chicago Press, 1962), 15.
20. Kristol, *Two Cheers for Capitalism*, 26.
21. Milton Friedman and Rose Friedman, *Free to Choose* (New York: Avon, 1979).
22. See Frances Moore Lappé and Joseph Collins, *World Hunger: Twelve Myths* (New York and San Francisco: Grove Press/Food First Books, 1986).
23. Paul A. Samuelson, "Modern Economic Realities and Individualism," in *Individualism: Man in Modern Society*, ed. Ronald Gross and Paul Osterman (New York: Dell, 1971), 196.
24. Friedman, *Capitalism and Freedom*, 21.
25. From "On the Road Again," in the album "Sonny and Brownie," A&M Records, 1973.
26. The civil service employs 18 percent of the total population but 25 percent of all blacks, although blacks comprise 12 percent of the population. Government employment has been the principle route for minorities to enter the middle class. Lester Thurow, "Equity, Efficiency, Social Justice, and Redistribution," in *The Welfare State in Crisis* (Paris: Organization for Economic Co-operation and Development, 1981), 143–144.
27. Friedman, *Capitalism and Freedom*, ch. 7.
28. Ben H. Bagdikian, *The Media Monopoly* (Boston: Beacon Press, 1987), 148.

29. Robert Benne, *The Ethic of Democratic Capialism* (Philadelphia: Fortress Press, 1981, 135.

30. Ibid., 134.

31. Simons, *Economic Policy for a Free Society*, 71.

32. Winter, "Advertising and Legal Theory," 19.

33. Quoted in Bagdikian, *Media Monopoly*, 149.

34. Frances Fox Piven and Richard A. Cloward, *The New Class War* (New York: Pantheon Books, 1982), 9.

35. Bagdikian, *The Media Monopoly*, 231.

36. Friedman and Friedman, *Free to Choose*, 5.

37. Kristol, *Two Cheers for Capitalism*, x.

38. Joseph Schumpeter, *Capitalism, Socialism and Democracy* (New York: Harper & Row, 1975), 67.

39. Michael Lerner, *Surplus Powerlessness* (Oakland, Calif.: Institute for Labor and Mental Health, 1986), 48–49.

40. Louis Harris, *Inside America* (New York: Vintage, 1987), 17.

41. Benne, *The Ethic of Democratic Capitalism*, 127.

42. *Financing and Delivering Health Care: A Comparative Analysis of OECD Countries* (Paris: Organization for Economic Cooperation and Development, 1987), table 18, 55.

43. The United States is the only Western country without a national health plan. In infant survival rates, the U.S. ranks near the bottom among industrial countries. Even U.S. whites, a subgroup with relatively better access to medical care, do not compare favorably with many other industrial countries. Ira C. Magaziner and Robert B. Reich, *Minding America's Business* (New York: Vintage, 1983), 19–20. In longevity rates, ten countries surpass the U.S. *Financing and Delivering Health Care*, table 9, 37.

44. Ruth Marcus, "Constitution: Wasn't That an Old Iron Ship?" *Washington Post*, 2 March 1987. Three-quarters of those surveyed support such an amendment.

45. Adams and Brock, *The Bigness Complex*, 54,

46. Ibid., 44.

47. Simons, *Economic Policy for a Free Society*, 59–60.

48. For a useful critique of "mergermania," see Mark Green and John Berry, *The Challenge of Hidden Profits: Reducing Corporate Waste and Bureaucracy* (New York: William Morrow, 1985), ch. 4.

49. Brozen, "The Corporate Merger," 15–16.

50. Samuel Bowles and Richard Edwards, *Understanding Capitalism* (New York: Harper & Row, 1985), 194–195.

51. Judith H. Dobrzynski, "A New Strain of Merger Mania," *Business Week*, 21 March 1988, 126. Although *Business Week* is more hopeful about upcoming mergers, it reports that seven out of ten mergers that took place in the Sixties and Seventies failed, with the combined value of the two companies worth less than the two had been separately; profits often decline. See also Green and Berry, *The Challenge of Hidden Profits*, ch. 4; A. M. Louis, "The Bottom Line on Ten Big Mergers," *Fortune*, 3 May 1982, 84–89.

52. Ben Wattenberg, *The Good News Is that the Bad News Is Wrong* (New York: Simon & Schuster, 1984), 259.

53. See, for example, Seymour Melman, *Profits Without Production* (New York: Alfred A. Knopf, 1983). See also Center for Defense Information, "No Business Like War Business," *The Defense Monitor* 16, no. 3 (1987): 4–5. "Six major aerospace firms are dependent on the government for at least 60 percent of their sales . . . In the absence of effective competition in the military industry, the profit motive gives companies the incentive to sell as many weapons at as *high* a price as possible."

54. Adams and Brock, *The Bigness Complex*, 331, citing a General Accounting Office study.

55. Robert S. McIntyre and David Wilhelm, *Money for Nothing: The Failure of Corporate Tax Incentives 1981–1984* (Washington, D.C.: Citizens for Tax Justice, 1986), 3.

56. Barry Commoner, "A Reporter at Large: The Environment," *The New Yorker*, 15 June 1987, 52.

57. *San Francisco Chronicle*, 3 April 1984, 3, quoting the Insurance Institute for Highway Safety.

58. Gus Tyler, "What Do Unions Really Do?" *Dissent* 27, no. 4 (Fall 1980): 471. See also Seymour Melman, *Profits Without Production*, 168–169. The U.S. machine tools industry slowed investment in new technology after the mid-Sixties because transferring tools and techniques abroad was more profitable, and managers turned to profit-making by "cost pass-along" to customers instead of by improving efficiency. See also Byung Yoo Hong, *Inflation Under Cost Pass-Along Management* (New York: Praeger, 1979). For a conservative answer, see Peltzman, "The Gains and Losses from Industrial Concentration."

59. Green and Berry, *The Challenge of Hidden Profits*, 166.

60. Chalmers Johnson, speech before the Foreign Correspondents Club, Tokyo, 17 December 1982, quoted in ibid., 166–167.

61. Sale, *Human Scale*, 252.

62. Quoted in Barry M. Mitnick, *The Political Economy of Regulation* (New York: Columbia University Press, 1980), 109.

63. Chris Welles, "Is Deregulation Working?" *Business Week*, 22 December 1986, 52.

64. Richard B. McKenzie, *Bound to Be Free* (Stanford, Calif.: Hoover Institution Press, 1982), 39.

65. Ibid., 37.

66. Ibid., 27.

67. Ibid., 28.

68. Susan J. Tolchin and Martin Tolchin, *Dismantling America* (Boston: Houghton Mifflin, 1983), ch. 7.

69. Lee Iacocca, speech to the American Bar Association Annual Meeting, August 10, 1987.

70. Jeane J. Kirkpatrick, *Dictatorships and Double Standards* (New York: Simon & Schuster and the American Enterprise Institute, 1982), 204.

71. Abraham Lincoln, address at the Sanitary Fair, Baltimore, 1864. Quoted in Sidney Hook, *The Structure of Freedom* (Stanford, Calif.: Stanford University Press, 1962), 11.

72. McKenzie, *Bound To Be Free*, 35–37.

73. Ibid, 50.

74. Ibid., 35.

75. Adam Smith, *The Wealth of Nations*, 4, ed. Edwin Cannan (New York: Random House/Modern Library, 1937), vol. 2, bk. 4; ch. 9, 651.

76. McKenzie, *Bound to Be Free*, 43–44.

77. Tolchin and Tolchin, *Dismantling America*, 237.

78. E. Lynn Miller and Mary Elizabeth Pennypacker, *The New York Times*, 4 March 1988, letter to the editor. Miller and Pennypacker are authors of *Decommissioning Nuclear Power Plants*. For a discussion of the broad issue of government in planning, see George C. Lodge, *The New American Ideology* (New York: New York University Press, 1986), 291–292.

79. Garrett Hardin, "The Tragedy of the Commons," *Science* 162 (13 December 1968): 1243–1248.

80. Richard L. Stroup and John A. Baden, *Natural Resources: Bureaucratic Myths and Environmental Management* (Cambridge, Mass.: Ballinger, 1983), 18–20.

81. Thomas Sowell, *Knowledge and Decisions* (New York: Basic Books, 1980), 125–126.

82. For the debate on privatization of public lands, see George M. Johnston and Peter M. Emerson, eds., *Public Lands and the U.S. Economy: Balancing Conservation and Development* (Boulder, Colo.: Westview Press, 1984).

83. Stroup and Baden, *Natural Resources*, 124.

84. Ibid., 14. For an introduction to this overall analysis, see: Richard Posner, *The Economics of Justice* (Cambridge, Mass.: Harvard University Press, 1985).

85. Quoted in Gordon Lee, "What If the Government Held a Land Sale and Hardly Anybody Showed Up," *National Journal* 14, no. 39 (25 September 1982): 1630.

86. Stroup and Baden, *Natural Resources*, ch. 2.

87. Ibid., 47.

88. Ibid., 123 ff.

89. Ibid., 102.

90. A General Accounting Office study concluded that the Forest Service lost $1.2 billion on timber sales from 1982 through 1986. Thomas A. Barron, "Mismanaging Public Lands," *The New York Times*, 29 February 1988, Opinion page.

91. Samuel P. Hays, *Conservation and the Gospel of Efficiency* (Cambridge, Mass.: Harvard University Press, 1959).

92. A. M. Freeman, Robert Haveman, and Allen Kneese, *The Economics of Environmental Policy* (New York: John Wiley & Sons, 1973), 23.

93. Stroup and Baden, *Natural Resources*, 50.

94. Mark Sagoff, "At the Shrine of Our Lady of Fatima or Why Political Questions Are Not All Economic," *Arizona Law Review* 23 (1981): 1291. See also Sagoff, *The Economy of the Earth* (New York: Cambridge University Press, 1988).

95. William F. Baxter, *People or Penguins: The Case for Optimal Pollution* (New York: Columbia University Press, 1974), chapter 4.

96. Stroup and Baden, *Natural Resources*, 97.

97. J. H. Dales, *Pollution, Property and Prices* (Toronto: University of Toronto Press, 1968).

98. Stroup and Baden, *Natural Resources*, 87.

99. Mark Sagoff, "Economic Theory and Environmental Law," *Michigan Law Review* 79 (June 1981): 1398.

100. Stroup and Baden, *Natural Resources*, 86.
101. Commoner, "A Reporter at Large: The Environment," 52.
102. Mark Sagoff, "Do We Need a Land Use Ethic?" *Environmental Ethics* 3 (Winter 1981): 303.
103. Commoner, "A Reporter at Large: The Environment," 59.
104. Ibid., 51–52.
105. Ibid., 60, quoting former General Motors executive John DeLorean.
106. David Glasner, *Politics, Prices, and Petroleum: The Political Economy of Energy* (Cambridge, Mass.: Ballinger, 1985), 47.
107. Ibid., 61.
108. Tropical hardwood prices have been going up at a modest annual rate of roughly 3 percent to 6 percent for almost two decades, with prices varying in response to demand in the industrial world.
109. James Wessel with Mort Hantman, *Trading the Future* (San Francisco: Institute for Food and Development Policy, 1983), chapter 7.
110. Glasner, *Politics, Prices, and Petroleum*, 40.
111. Anthony Scott, *Natural Resources: The Economics of Conservation* (Toronto: Toronto University Press, 1955), 97.
112. Frederick Hayek, *The Constitution of Liberty* (Chicago: University of Chicago Press, 1960), 369–370.
113. Glasner, *Politics, Prices, and Petroleum*, 62.
114. Julian Simon, *The Ultimate Resource* (Princeton, N.J.: Princeton University Press, 1981), 33.
115. Ibid., 47.
116. Ibid., 151.
117. Glasner, *Politics, Prices, and Petroleum*, 40.
118. Simon, *The Ultimate Resource*, 48–49.
119. Peter H. Raven, *The Global Ecosystem in Crisis* (Chicago: The John D. and Catherine T. MacArthur Foundation, 1987), 15.
120. Aldo Leopold, *A Sand County Almanac* (New York: Sierra Club/Ballantine Book, 1966), xix.
121. Simon, *The Ultimate Resource*, 152–153.
122. World Commission on Environment and Development, *Our Common Future* (New York: Oxford University Press, 1987), pt. 2.
123. J. Baird Callicott, *In Defense of the Land Ethic* (Albany: State University of New York Press, 1988) (on press).
124. Simon, *The Ultimate Resource*, ch. 9.
125. Stroup and Baden, *Natural Resources*, 25.
126. Ibid., 25.
127. Adam Smith, *The Wealth of Nations*, 492–493.
128. Stroup and Baden, *Natural Resources*, 63, 67.
129. Amory B. Lovins and L. Hunter Lovins, "Electric Utilities: Key to Capitalizing the Energy Transition," *Technological Forecasting and Social Change* 22 (1982): 155.
130. Richard Morgan, Tom Riesenberg, and Michael Troutman, *Taking Charge: A New*

Look at Public Power (Washington, D.C.: Environmental Action Foundation, 1976), 22–24.

131. Alan Durning, "Setting Our Houses in Order," World Watch (May/June 1988): 32–33, citing Howard Geller of the American Council for an Energy-Efficient Economy.

132. John Ise, "The Theory of Value as Applied to Natural Resources," American Economic Review 1 (June 1925): 284–291.

133. McKenzie, Bound to Be Free, 84–85.

134. Amory B. Lovins and L. Hunter Lovins, Brittle Power: Energy Strategy for National Security (Andover, Mass.: Brick House, 1982), ch. 1.

135. Stroup and Baden, Natural Resources, 47.

136. Ibid., 41.

137. Arthur F. Bentley, The Process of Government, quoted in Mitnick, The Political Economy of Regulation, 109.

138. John Baden and Richard Stroup, "The Environmental Costs of Government Action," Policy Review 4 (Spring 1978): 25.

139. Stroup and Baden, Natural Resources, 51.

140. Friedman, Capitalism and Freedom, 13.

141. Karl Polanyi, The Great Transformation (Boston: Beacon Press, 1944, with Rinehart & Co., 1957), 140–141.

142. Sagoff, "Do We Need a Land Use Ethic?," 305.

143. Charles Schultz, The Public Use of Private Interest (Washington, D.C.: Brookings Institution, 1977), 17–18.

144. Sowell, Knowledge and Decisions, 100.

145. Friedman, Capitalism and Freedom, 22–24.

146. Benne, The Ethic of Democratic Capitalism, 143.

147. Charles Higham, Trading with the Enemy: An Exposé of the Nazi-American Money Plot 1933–1949 (New York: Delacorte Press, 1983), xv, chs. 3 and 6.

148. Arthur M. Okun, Inequality and Efficiency: The Big Trade-Off (Washington, D.C.: Brookings Institution, 1975), 119.

149. William Glaberson, "Behind Du Pont's Shift On Loss of Ozone Layer," The New York Times, 26 March 1988, Business section.

Part Four

1. Richard McKenzie, Bound to Be Free (Stanford, Calif.: Hoover Institution Press, 1982), 99.

2. John Locke, "The Second Treatise of Civil Government," in Two Treatises of Government, ed. Peter Laslett (Cambridge, England: Cambridge University Press, 1960), ch. 9, sec. 124, 368–369.

3. Through the Middle Ages it was understood that the function of the state was to protect property with its attendant social and political privileges—to preserve the existing ruling group. The power of the state and the power of property were not perceived as separate. Only in later liberal theory was it supposed that the state could protect property, as distinct from the privileges of the ruling class. Richard Schlatter, Private Property: The History of an Idea (London: Allen & Unwin, 1951), ch. 4.

4. J. L. Hammond and Barbara Hammond, *The Village Labourer* (New York: Augustus M. Kelley, 1967), chs. 2 and 5.

5. McKenzie, *Bound to Be Free*, 100–101. For a historical overview of American perspectives on the relationship of property to freedom, see *Democracy, Liberty, and Property: Readings in the American Political Tradition*, ed. Francis W. Coker (New York: The Macmillan Co., 1949).

6. Adam Smith, *The Wealth of Nations*, book 5, ed. Edwin Cannan (New York: Random House, 1937), bk. 5, ch. 1, pt. 2, 674.

7. John Taylor, "Construction Construed, and Constitutions Vindicated," in *Democracy, Liberty, and Property: Readings in the American Political Tradition*, ed. Francis W. Coker (New York: Macmillan, 1949), 497.

8. Thomas Jefferson in a letter to the Rev. James Madison in *Thomas Jefferson, Writings*, ed. Merrill D. Peterson (New York: The Library of America/Liberty Classics, 1984), 841.

9. John Adams in *The Works of John Adams*, vol. 9, ed. Charles Francis Adams, (Boston: Little, Brown, 1854), 376–377.

10. Alexander Hamilton, James Madison, and John Jay, *The Federalist Papers* (New York: New American Library, 1961), 472.

11. Quoted in Clinton Rossiter, *Seedtime of the Republic* (New York: Harcourt, Brace & World, 1952), 75.

12. "Survey of Consumer Finances, 1983: A Second Report," *Federal Reserve Bulletin* (December 1984): 863–864.

13. Ibid.

14. John Taylor, "Construction Construed," 497.

15. Milton Friedman and Rose Friedman, *Free to Choose* (New York: Avon, 1979), 58.

16. In 1950, two-thirds of American families could buy a home spending no more than a quarter of their income in mortgage payments; by 1981, only one-tenth could. *Jobs with Peace Campaign Report* 2, no. 1 (Winter 1988): 1. In 1949, 14 percent of a thirty-year-old man's salary was needed to make mortgage payments on an average house; by 1985, 44 percent. Robert Kuttner, "The Patrimony Society," *The New Republic*, 11 May 1987, 18.

17. Estimate by economist Sam Bowles, University of Massachusetts, Amherst; telephone communication, July 1, 1984.

18. "Survey of Consumer Finances," 864. Considering financial wealth alone, 55 percent of all families have zero or negative net worth; including real estate, 20 percent do. (863)

19. Charles Lindblom, *Politics and Markets* (New York: Basic Books, 1977), 49–50.

20. James Fenimore Cooper, from "On Property," in *The American Democrat*, in Coker, *Democracy, Liberty, and Property*, 511.

21. Patricia O'Toole, *Corporate Messiah: The Hiring and Firing of Million-Dollar Managers* (New York: William Morrow, 1984), 31–42.

22. Abraham Lincoln, address to the Sanitary Fair, Baltimore, 18 April 1864, quoted in John Bartlett, *Bartlett's Familiar Quotations*, 15th ed. (Boston: Little, Brown, 1980), 523.

23. C. B. Macpherson, "Liberal-Democracy and Property," in *Property: Mainstream and Critical Perspectives*, ed. C. B. Macpherson (Toronto: University of Toronto Press, 1978), 199–207.

24. John Stuart Mill, *Principles of Political Economy* (New London: Colonial Press, 1900), vol. 1, bk. II, ch. 2, section 1, 213.

25. George Gilder, *The Spirit of Enterprise* (New York: Simon & Schuster, 1984), 257.

26. Thomas Sowell, *Knowledge and Decisions* (New York: Basic Books, 1980), 126.

27. Locke "The Second Treatise of Civil Government," in John Locke, *Two Treatises of Government*, ed. Laslett, ch. 5, sec. 37, 312.

28. *Coppage* v. *Kansas*, 236 U.S. 1 (1915).

29. William Tucker, "Where Do the Homeless Come From?" *National Review*, 25 September 1987, 32–43.

30. Jeremy Bentham, *The Works of Jeremy Bentham, Principles of the Civil Code*, ed. John Bowring (New York: Russell & Russell, 1962), vol. 1, pt. 1, ch. 11, 312.

31. For discussion and references, see Frances Moore Lappé and Joseph Collins, *World Hunger: Twelve Myths* (New York: Food First Books/Grove Press, 1986), ch. 6.

32. Adrienne Koch, *Jefferson and Madison: The Great Collaboration* (New York: Alfred A. Knopf, 1950), 78–79.

33. Thomas Jefferson in a letter to James Madison, in *Thomas Jefferson, Writings*, 841–842.

34. Benjamin Franklin, "Queries and Remarks Respecting Alterations in the Constitution of Pennsylvania," in Coker, *Democracy, Liberty, and Property*, 90. See also Page Smith, *Dissenting Opinions* (San Francisco: Northpoint Press, 1984), 39.

35. Thomas Jefferson in a letter to James Madison, 1789, *Thomas Jefferson, Writings*, 959. See also Richard K. Matthews, *The Radical Politics of Thomas Jefferson: A Revisionist View* (Lawrence: University of Kansas Press, 1984), ch. 2.

36. Thomas Jefferson in a letter to James Madison, *Thomas Jefferson, Writings*, 959.

37. See, for example, Marty Strange, *Family Farming: A New Economic Vision* (San Francisco/Lincoln: Food First Books/University of Nebraska Press, 1988), 50–51, 54–55, 274–275. Strange argues that young farmers inheriting land should be required to pay for the land by farming it, preventing some from inheriting so much wealth that they can easily outbid their neighbors for additional land, thereby over time becoming a landed aristocracy.

38. John Adams, "A Defence of the Constitutions of Government of the United States of America," in Coker, *Democracy, Liberty, and Property*, 464.

39. Adams, "Discourses on Davila," in ibid., 465.

40. G. Andrew Bernat, Jr., *Farmland Ownership and Leasing in the United States*, 1982 (Washington D.C.: U.S. Department of Agriculture, 1987), 4.

41. John Stuart Mill, *The Principles of Political Economy*, vol. 1, bk. 2, ch. 1, sec. 3, 205–206. Emphasis added.

42. "Survey of Consumer Finance, 1983," Federal Reserve Bulletin (September, 1984), table 13, 689.

43. Jeff Faux, "Reducing the Deficits," in *Briefing Paper* (Washington, D.C.: Economic Policy Institute, 1987), table D, 17, based on *National Income and Product Accounts*, table 2.1.

44. For a useful discussion, see C. B. Macpherson, *Democratic Theory: Essays on Retrieval* (Oxford: Clarendon Press, 1973), 21 ff.

45. Christopher Jencks et al., *Inequality: A Reassessment of the Effect of Family and Schooling in America* (New York: Basic Books, 1972), 6.

46. Friedman and Friedman, *Free to Choose*, 15.

47. For more information, contact the Center for Economic Organizing, Washington, D.C.

48. "Where's the Wealth?," *Dollars and Sense* no. 105 (April 1985): 9. The share of Americans owning stocks has been declining.

49. William Robbins, *American Society: A Sociological Perspective*, 2d ed. (New York: Alfred A. Knopf, 1960), 182–184.

50. "Will Money Managers Wreck the Economy?" *Business Week*, 13 August 1984, 88. See also Paul I. Blumberg, *The Megacorporation in American Society: The Scope of Corporate Power* (Englewood Cliffs, N.J.: Prentice-Hall, 1975), 95.

51. Robert J. Larner, *Management Control and the Large Corporation* (New York: Dunellen Publishing Co., 1970), table 1, 12. Larner estimated that 84 percent of the top 200 largest nonfinancial corporations were management-controlled in 1963. See also "The Macho Men of Capitalism," *Business Week*, 1 October 1984, 58. Here ITT's Harold Geneen himself admits that corporate boards are incapable of reigning in management chiefs.

52. View of economist Arthur Laffer, discussed in John Judis, "Corporate Raiders Are Speeding Decline," *In These Times*, 26 June–9 July 1985, 3.

53. "Will Money Managers Wreck the Economy?," 86–93.

54. Robert B. Reich, "Corporation and Nation," *The Atlantic Monthly*, 261, no. 51 (May 1988): 76–81.

55. "Public Power Costs Less," *Public Power* 39, no. 3 (May–June 1981): 14–16.

56. Henry Simons, *Economic Policy for a Free Society* (Chicago: University of Chicago Press, 1948), 51.

57. Svetozar Pejovich, "Basic Institutions of Capitalism and Socialism," in Pejovich, ed., *Philosophical and Economic Foundations of Capitalism* (Lexington, Mass.: Lexington Books, 1983), 1.

58. Terry Anderson and Peter J. Hill, *The Birth of the Transfer Society* (Stanford, Calif.: Hoover Institution Press, 1980), 5.

59. "U.S. Steel's Debt-shrouded Future," *Business Week*, 18 October 1982, 154–155; "U.S. Steel's Get-Tough Policy," *Business Week*, 30 August 1982, 74.

60. George C. Lodge, *The New American Ideology* (New York: New York University Press, 1986), 219.

61. The 20,000 member Mondragon federation of cooperatives in the Basque region of Spain is one example. See Part V for further discussion of worker ownership.

62. Sweden's labor market boards, involving both local and national participation, help corporations avoid layoffs by funding retraining of workers and other assistance. Sweden also requires corporations to set aside a portion of profits for job-creating expenditures during economic downturns. See Part V for more discussion.

63. Robin Williams, *American Society: A Sociological Perspective* (New York: Alfred A. Knopf, 1960), 181.

64. Quoted in Arthur Selwyn, *The Supreme Court and American Capitalism* (New York: The Free Press, 1968), 50–55. This decision was part of what were called the Granger cases. The leading case permitted a state commission to protect farmers by establishing a maximum storage rate that grain elevators could charge. Between 1890 and World War I, the doctrine behind these rulings was replaced by one in which property had a

foundation in natural law, superseding society's authority to protect the commonweal. John P. Roche, "Entrepreneurial Liberty and the Fourteenth Amendment," *Labor History* 4 (Winter 1963): 3–31.

65. Quoted by Lodge, *The New American Ideology*, 209.
66. Locke, "The Second Treatise of Civil Government," ch. 5. Passages from the beginning of this chapter have sometimes been used to argue that Locke believed that no one was entitled to more property than one could use and no more than left "enough, and as good" for others. But it becomes clear in the rest of the chapter that Locke believed that because the earth's bounty is virtually limitless, unfettered accumulation is justifiable and doesn't harm others—once money had been established as a store of value. (Locke abhorred the spoilage of hoarded perishables, but money, he reasoned, allowed people to avoid spoilage by simply accumulating wealth in currency.)
67. Macpherson, "Liberal-Democracy and Property," in Macpherson, *Property*, 199–207.
68. John Paul II, *On Social Concern*, Encyclical Letter 2, 30 December 1987, 86.
69. As recently as the nineteenth century, "private enterprise" referred to individual proprietors, not to corporations. James Willard Hurst, *The Legitimacy of the Business Corporation in the Law of the United States, 1780–1970* (Charlottesville: The University Press of Virginia, 1970), 49.
70. Irving Kristol, "On Corporate Capitalism in America," in *The American Commonwealth*, ed. Nathan Glazer and Irving Kristol (New York: Basic Books, 1976), 126–127.
71. Henry C. Simons, *Economic Policy for a Free Society* (Chicago: University of Chicago Press, 1948), 34.
72. Ronald E. Seavoy, "The Public Service Origins of the American Business Corporation," *Business History Review* 52 (Spring 1978): 30–60. Hurst, *The Legitimacy of the Business Corporation*, 15.
73. See, for example, Adolf A. Berle, Jr., and Gardiner Means, *The Modern Corporation and Private Property* (New York: Macmillan, 1933). Berle and Means describe how stockholders gradually lost power, 139 ff. See also Creel Froman, *The Two American Political Systems: Society, Economics, and Politics* (Englewood Cliffs, N.J.: Prentice-Hall, 1984), especially chapter 5.
74. Ralph Nader and Carl J. Mayer, "Corporations Are Not Persons," *The New York Times* April 9, 1988, opinion page.
75. Nancy Folbre, *A Field Guide to the U.S. Economy* (New York: Pantheon Books, 1987), table 1.8. The top 100 firms control 61 percent of the total assets of nonfinancial corporations. Based on data from *Fortune Magazine* and the Federal Reserve.
76. Prediction of Judd Polk, senior economist at the U.S. Chamber of Commerce, quoted in Harry C. Boyte, *The Backyard Revolution* (Philadelphia: Temple University Press, 1980), 188–189.
77. Robert A. Dahl, *Dilemmas of Pluralist Democracy* (New Haven: Yale University Press, 1982), 184.
78. Irving Kristol, "Capitalist Conception of Justice," in *Ethics, Free Enterprise and Public Policy: Original Essays on Moral Issues in Business*, ed. Richard T. de George and Joseph A. Pichler (New York: Oxford University Press, 1978), 64–65.
79. A paraphrase of Michael Novak, *Forbes*, 26 March 1984, 213.
80. Lay Commission on Catholic Social Teaching and the U.S. Economy, *Toward the*

Future: Catholic Social Thought and the U.S. Economy: A Lay Letter, American Catholic Committee, 127 East 35th St., New York, N.Y. 10016, 1984. (The conservative Catholic businessmen's response to a draft of the Catholic bishops' letter on the U.S. economy, *Justice for All.*)

81. Irving Kristol, *Two Cheers for Capitalism* (New York: New American Library, 1979), xi.

82. Ira C. Magaziner and Robert B. Reich, *Minding America's Business: The Decline and Rise of the American Economy* (New York: Vintage Books, 1982). Exhibits 1–15 provide data showing more equal income distribution and greater social benefits in most other Western industrial countries compared to the United States.

83. See, for example, Howard Zinn, *A People's History of the United States* (New York: Harper Colophon Books, 1980); Richard Owen Boyer and Herbert M. Morais, *Labor's Untold Story*, 3d ed. (New York: United Electrical, Radio and Machine Workers of America, 1975).

84. R. H. Tawney, *Equality* (London: Allen & Unwin, 1952), 265.

85. For discussion of this thesis, see Frances Moore Lappé, Rachel Schurman, and Kevin Danaher, *Betraying the National Interest* (New York and San Francisco: Grove Press/ Food First Books, 1987).

86. Quoted in Robert Pear, "The Main Civil Liberty: A Right Not to Starve," *The New York Times,* 18 July 1984. Shattuck was formerly with the American Civil Liberties Union.

87. Milton Friedman, *Capitalism and Freedom* (Chicago: University of Chicago Press, 1962), 9.

88. Thomas Jefferson, quoted in Lawrence Goodwyn, *The Populist Moment* (New York: Oxford University Press, 1978), frontispiece.

Part Five

1. Bernard Crick, *In Defence of Politics* (Baltimore: Penguin, 1964), 56.

2. Joseph Schumpeter, *Capitalism, Socialism and Democracy*, 3d ed. (New York: Harper and Brothers, 1950), 271.

3. Ruth Marcus, "Constitution: Wasn't That an Old Iron Ship?" *Washington Post*, 2 March 1987, 37.

4. Robert Nisbet, "Public Opinion," in *The American Commonwealth*, ed. Nathan Glazer and Irving Kristol (New York: Basic Books, 1976), 166–170. Nisbet makes only the general point here; I added the affirmative action example.

5. Ibid., 166.

6. Schumpeter, *Capitalism, Socialism and Democracy*, 291.

7. George Will, *Statecraft as Soulcraft: What Government Does* (New York: Simon & Schuster, 1983), 16.

8. Alexander Hamilton, James Madison, and John Jay, *The Federalist Papers* (New York: New American Library, 1961), 301.

9. Thomas Jefferson in a letter to James Madison, *Thomas Jefferson, Writings*, ed. Merrill D. Peterson (New York: The Library of America/Liberty Classics, 1984), 882.

10. Physician Task Force on Hunger, *Hunger Reaches Blue Collar America* (Cambridge, Mass.: Harvard School of Public Health, 1987), 1.

11. John Dewey, "Liberty and Social Control," *Social Frontier* (November 1935): 41.
12. C. B. Macpherson, *Democratic Theory: Essays on Retrieval* (Oxford: Clarendon Press, 1973), 51.
13. C. B. Macpherson, *The Political Theory of Possessive Individualism* (New York: Oxford University Press, 1962), 129, 134.
14. Richard B. McKenzie, *Bound to Be Free* (Stanford, Calif.: Hoover Institution Press, 1982), 22.
15. John Bowring, ed. *The Works of Jeremy Bentham, Constitutional Code*, vol. 9, (New York: Russell & Russell, 1962), bk. 1, ch. 9, 47.
16. For a useful discussion of the evolution of our conception of democracy, see Macpherson, *Democratic Theory*, 79.
17. Richard K. Matthews, *The Radical Politics of Thomas Jefferson: A Revisionist View* (Lawrence: University of Kansas Press, 1984), ch. 5.
18. James MacGregor Burns, *The Vineyard of Liberty* (New York: Vintage, 1983), 62.
19. Schumpeter, *Capitalism, Socialism and Democracy*, 290–291.
20. For an excellent introduction to this understanding of democracy, see the following by Harry C. Boyte: *Backyard Revolution* (Philadelphia: Temple University Press, 1980); *Community Is Possible: Repairing America's Roots* (New York: Harper & Row, 1984); (with Sara M. Evans) *Free Spaces: The Sources of Democratic Change in America* (New York: Harper & Row, 1986).
21. S. M. Miller et al., "The Emerging American Progressive Ideology," *Social Policy* 17, no. 4 (Spring 1987).
22. The Commonwealth Agreement is a partnership between the Baltimore Public Schools, the Greater Baltimore Committee, and BUILD, a multiracial, church-based organization.
23. Thomas Jefferson in a letter to John Adams, *Thomas Jefferson, Writings*, 1380.
24. Leland B. Yeager, "Is There a Bias Toward Overregulation?," in *Rights and Regulation: Ethical, Political, and Economic Issues*, ed. Tibor R. Machan and M. Bruce Johnson (San Francisco: Pacific Institute for Public Policy Research; Cambridge, Mass.: Ballinger, 1983), 106.
25. Ibid., 105.
26. Robert Lane, "Government and Self-Esteem," *Political Theory* 10 (February 1982): 7–8.
27. Ibid., 8, citing Alexander Szalai, ed., *The Use of Time* (The Hague: Mouton, 1972), 577, 579.
28. Yeager, "Is There a Bias Toward Overregulation?," 100, 104–107.
29. Samuel Huntington, "The Democratic Distemper," in *The American Commonwealth*, ed. Nathan Glazer and Irving Kristol (New York: Basic Books, 1976), 37.
30. Yeager, "Is There a Bias Toward Overregulation?," 108.
31. Benjamin R. Barber, "The Undemocratic Party System: Citizenship in an Elite/Mass Society," in *Political Parties in the Eighties*, ed. Robert A. Goldwin (Washington, D.C.: American Enterprise Institute for Public Policy Research, 1980), 34–49.
32. John H. Schaar, "Equality of Opportunity, and Beyond," in *Equality*, ed. J. Roland Pennock and John W. Chapman (New York: Atherton, 1967), 245.
33. William Greider, *Secrets of the Temple* (New York: Simon & Schuster, 1987), 50–51.
34. Ibid., 51.

35. Bruce Stokes, "Self-Help in the Welfare State," in *Rethinking Liberalism*, ed. Walter Anderson (New York: Avon, 1983), 97. Two-thirds of Americans have come to this conclusion, twice the proportion of a decade ago. According to Daniel Yankelovich, *New Rules* (New York: Bantam, 1982), in 1977, 60 percent of Americans agreed that "the people running the country don't care what happens to people like me" (93).

36. Richard A. Posner, "The DeFunis Case and the Constitutionality of Preferential Treatment of Racial Minorities," in *The Supreme Court Review 1974*, ed. Philip B. Kurland (Chicago: University of Chicago Press, 1975), 27.

37. See, for example, C. B. Macpherson, *Democratic Theory*, 79 ff; Samuel Bowles and Herbert Gintis, *Capitalism and Democracy* (New York: Basic Books, 1986), especially ch. 5; Benjamin Barber, *Strong Democracy: Participatory Politics for a New Age* (Berkeley and Los Angeles: University of California Press, 1984), ch. 8.

38. Barber, *Strong Democracy*, 136–137.

39. Mary Parker Follett, *The New State*, quoted in Bertram Gross, *Friendly Fascism* (Boston: South End Press, 1980), 364.

40. Information from Jerry Jenkins, Citizen Participation Coordinator, St. Paul, Minn., 4 April 1988.

41. Peter L. Berger, *The Capitalist Revolution* (New York: Basic Books, 1986), 73.

42. Robert Benne, *The Ethic of Democratic Capitalism* (Philadelphia: Fortress, 1981), 96.

43. Ibid., 79; Milton Friedman, *Capitalism and Freedom* (Chicago: University of Chicago Press, 1962), 16.

44. Milton Friedman and Rose Friedman, *Free to Choose* (New York: Avon, 1979), xvii. Emphasis in original.

45. The total cost of campaigns for all public offices in the U.S. doubled in the four years before 1980, reaching almost a billion dollars. Ben H. Bagdikian, *The Media Monopoly* (Boston: Beacon Press, 1987), 192.

46. My estimate is based on these facts: Roughly one-fourth of all senators are millionaires even without considering their salaries, personal residences, or investments in blind trusts; and enormous holdings are disguised by being listed under the broad value category, "$250,000 or more." See Jeffrey L. Sheler, "Congress's Millionaires—A Thriving Breed," *U.S. News & World Report* 98 (3 June 1985): 35–36.

47. Nancy Lammers, *Dollar Politics*, 3d ed. (Washington, D.C.: Congressional Quarterly, 1982), 15, 83–84.

48. Ibid., 82–83.

49. Jean Cobb, "The Power of the Purse," *Common Cause Magazine*, 14, no. 3, (May/June 1988): 15.

50. David Adamany, "PAC's and the Democratic Financing of Politics," *Arizona Law Review* 22 (1980): 580.

51. Ben J. Wattenberg, *The Good News Is that the Bad News is Wrong* (New York: Simon & Schuster, 1984), ch. 43.

52. Quoted by Philip Stern in *The Best Congress Money Can Buy* (New York: Pantheon, 1988), 77.

53. Testimony of Fred Wertheimer, President of Common Cause, on Campaign Finance Reform and Federal Election Campaign Amendments of 1987, before the Subcommittee

on Elections of the Committee on Administration of the U.S. House of Representatives, 14 July 1987.

54. Khayyam Zev Paltiel, "Campaign Finance: Contrasting Practices and Reforms," in *Democracy at the Polls*, ed. David Butler et al. (Washington, D.C.: American Enterprise Institute for Public Policy Research, 1981), 154–171.

55. Michael Pinto-Duschinsky, *British Political Finance 1830–1980* (Washington, D.C.: American Enterprise Institute for Public Policy Research, 1981), ch. 9.

56. William Pfaff, "The Shame of U.S. Political Campaigns," *San Francisco Chronicle*, 4 July 1984.

57. Stern, *The Best Congress Money Can Buy*.

58. *Buckley* v. *Valeo*, 424 U.S. 1, 19 (1976).

59. Ibid.

60. G. Warren Nutter, "Income Redistribution," in *Income Redistribution*, ed. Colin D. Campbell (Washington, D.C.: American Enterprise Institute for Public Policy Research, 1976), 44.

61. Adamany, "PAC's and the Democratic Financing of Politics," 581–582.

62. James S. Fishkin, *Justice, Equality, Opportunity and the Family* (New Haven, Conn: Yale University Press, 1983), 166.

63. For a general discussion of these issues, see Eve Pell, *The Big Chill* (Boston: Beacon, 1984). Until a new law superseded the McCarran–Walter Immigration Act on January 1, 1988, the United States systematically barred foreigners on the basis of their political views. As of this writing, the State Department is proposing an amended immigration bill that would exclude those "whose entry could cause potentially serious adverse foreign policy consequences." To keep abreast of related issues, see *First Principles*, newsletter of the Center for National Security Studies, 122 Maryland Ave., N.E., Washington, D.C. 20002.

64. Bagdikian, *The Media Monopoly*, 4, 21. Here Bagdikian says 29 corporations remain, but elsewhere he has reported that by 1988, the number had dropped to 26.

65. Ibid., 4.

66. Ibid., 26.

67. Ibid.

68. *San Francisco Chronicle*, 21 May 1985.

69. A classic discussion of the problem is Grant McConnell, *Private Power and American Democracy* (New York: Vintage, 1966).

70. Alexandra Allen, "Blow Away the Foul-Air Lobby," *The New York Times*, 11 June 1988, Opinion page.

71. *Labor*, 17 October 1941, quoted in Gross, *Friendly Fascism*, 359.

72. Robert Nozick, *Anarchy, State, and Utopia* (New York: Basic Books), 272.

73. Ibid.

74. *Olmstead* v. *United States*, 277 U.S. 479 (1928), quoted by Friedman and Friedman, *Free to Choose*, frontispiece.

75. Friedman, *Capitalism and Freedom*, ch. 1.

76. Quoted by Carl Sagan, speech at the Rededication on the 50th Anniversary of the Eternal Light Peace Memorial, Gettysburg, Pennsylvania, July 3, 1988.

77. "No Business Like War Business," *The Defense Monitor* 16, no. 3 (1987): 6.

78. Most modern-day thinkers in the Liberal tradition would not do away with regulation altogether. Instead, they would greatly scale it back. See, for example, Irving Kristol, "A Regulated Society?," *Regulation* 1 (July–August 1977): 12; R. A. Hayek, *Law, Legislation, and Liberty*, vol. 3 (Chicago: University of Chicago Press, 1979) 62.

79. Thomas R. Dye and John W. Pickering, "Government and Corporate Elites: Convergence and Differentiation," *Journal of Politics* 36, no. 4 (November 1974): 905. Most of these individuals are from the corporate sector; only a few hundred are elected. See also Thomas R. Dye, *Who's Running America?*, 2d ed. (Englewood Cliffs, N.J.: Prentice-Hall, 1979). Dye also states that 100 corporations control over half the nation's manufacturing (239).

80. Charles Lindblom, *Politics and Markets* (New York: Basic Books, 1977), 356.

81. Charles Francis Adams, ed., *The Works of John Adams*, vol. 9 (Boston: Little, Brown, 1854), 378.

82. Irving Kristol, *Two Cheers for Capitalism* (New York: New American Library, 1978), 107.

83. "Survey of Consumer Finances, 1983, *Federal Reserve Bulletin* (September, 1984) Table 13, 689.

84. Robert J. Larner, *Management Control and the Large Corporation* (New York: Dunellen Publishing Co., 1970), table 1, 12. Larner estimates that 84 percent of the 200 largest nonfinancial corporations were under management control in 1963. See also Paul I. Blumberg, *The Megacorporation in American Society: The Scope of Corporate Power* (Englewood Cliffs, N.J.: Prentice-Hall, 1975), ch. 5.

85. John Judis, "Corporate Raiders Are Speeding Decline," *In These Times*, 26 June–9 July 1985, 3.

86. Jim Hightower, "Where Greed, Unofficially Blessed by Reagan, Has Led," *The New York Times*, 21 June 1987, Opinion page. Ray Marshall, *Unheard Voices: Labor and Economic Policy in a Competitive World* (New York: Basic Books, 1987), 110.

87. Louis Harris, *Inside America* (New York: Vintage, 1987), 259.

88. Walter Adams and James W. Brock, *The Bigness Complex* (New York: Pantheon, 1986), ch. 4. See also Kirkpatrick Sale, *Human Scale* (New York: Coward, McCann & Geoghegan, 1980), 314.

89. This estimate from George C. Lodge, *The New American Ideology* (New York: New York University Press, 1986), ch. 9. Just 100 firms control over 60 percent of industrial assets. Nancy Folbre and the Center for Popular Economics, *A Field Guide to the U.S. Economy* (New York: Pantheon, 1987), table 1.8.

90. James Willard Hurst, *The Legitimacy of the Business Corporation in the Law of the United States*, 1730–1970 (Charlottesville: The University Press of Virginia, 1970), 97.

91. T. K. Quinn, *Giant Business: Threat to Democracy* (New York: Exposition Press, 1953), 145.

92. Estimate in 1978 by Murray Weidenbaum, in Machan and Johnson, *Rights and Regulation*, 5.

93. Quoted by Joel Seligman, "Free Speech in the Workplace," *The Nation*, 27 November 1976, 564.

94. John B. Judis, "Corporate Raiders are Speeding Decline," *In These Times*, 26 June–9 July 1985, 3.

95. Lodge, *The New American Ideology*, 291–292.

96. Ibid., 261–262.

97. Henry Simons, *Economic Policy for a Free Society* (Chicago: University of Chicago Press, 1948), 58.

98. This technique, along with a commitment to retrain and relocate displaced workers, has been used successfully in Sweden to keep unemployment at half or even a third of levels here.

99. For more information from those working toward this goal, contact the Center for Economic Organizing, Washington, D.C.

100. George C. Lodge, *The American Disease* (New York: Alfred A. Knopf, 1984), 293.

101. R. H. Tawney, *Equality* (London: Allen & Unwin, 1952), 194.

102. Richard B. McKenzie, *Fugitive Industry: The Economics and Politics of Deindustrialization* (San Francisco: Pacific Institute for Public Policy Research; Cambridge, Mass.: Ballinger, 1984), 99.

103. Lodge, *The New American Ideology*, 248, 250.

104. See, for example, Boyte, *The Backyard Revolution*, 64–65. Also, for a survey of community-controlled organizations helping shape local economic priorities, see "Economic Experiments," *National Catholic Reporter*, 28 August 1987, 8–13.

105. Peter Applebome, "Changing Texas Politics at its Roots," *The New York Times*, 31 May 1988, A10.

106. Peter Clavelle, "A City Supports Worker Ownership: Burlington, VT," *Changing Work* (Spring 1986): 12–15.

107. F. A. Hayek, "The Use of Knowledge in Society," *American Economic Review* 35 (September 1945): 519–530.

108. Technically, the state constitutional amendment bars nonfarm corporations from using the corporate form to own farmland. For information, contact the Center for Rural Affairs, Walthill, Neb. 68067.

109. Adams and Brock, *The Bigness Complex*, 373. The authors suggest that no mergers of the biggest (billion-dollar) firms be permitted by the FTC unless they demonstrate materially how the public needs would be better served.

110. Armen A. Achian and Harold Demsetz, "Production, Information Costs, and Economic Organization," *American Economic Review* 62, no. 5 (December 1972): 777.

111. Thomas Sowell, *A Conflict of Visions*, 166. The word "not" is obviously intended but missing in the first sentence of the second paragraph.

112. See, for example, Mark Green and John F. Berry, *The Challenge of Hidden Profits* (New York: William Morrow, 1985). For developments in workplace democracy in the United States, see the publication *Workplace Democracy*, 111 Draper Hall, Amherst, Mass. 01003.

113. Seymour Melman, *Profits Without Production* (New York: Alfred A. Knopf, 1983), 71.

114. Adam Smith, *The Wealth of Nations*, ed. Edwin Canaan (New York: Modern Library/ Random House, 1937), bk. 4, ch. 9, pt. 3, 700.

115. *People and Productivity: A Challenge to Corporate America* (New York: New York Stock Exchange, Office of Economic Research, 1982), 32. For a good introduction to

the issue and effect of workplace democracy, see John Simmons and William J. Mares, *Working Together* (New York: Alfred A. Knopf, 1983).

116. *People and Productivity*, 35, citing a Department of Commerce study which found a statistical correlation between employee ownership and profitability, other things being equal: Michael Conte and Arnold S. Tannenbaum, "Employee-Owned Companies: Is the Difference Measurable?" *Monthly Labor Review* (July 1978). See also Corey M. Rosen et al., *Employee Ownership in America: The Equity Solution* (Lexington, Mass.: Lexington Books/D.C. Heath, 1985), 2–3. For more information on employee ownership, contact the National Center for Employee Ownership, 426 17th St., Suite 650, Oakland, Ca., 94612.

117. John Stuart Mill, *Principles of Political Economy* (London: The Colonial Press, 1900), vol. 2, bk 4, ch. 7, sec. 6, 295.

118. Marshall, *Unheard Voices*, 163.

119. Friedrich A. Hayek, *The Constitution of Liberty* (Chicago: University of Chicago Press, 1960), 277.

120. Yankelovich, *New Rules*, 41, citing Robert P. Quinn and Graham L. Staines, *1977 Quality of Employment Survey*, Survey Research Center of the Institute for Social Research (Ann Arbor: University of Michigan, 1979).

121. Nozick, *Anarchy, State, and Utopia*, 251.

122. Rosen, *Employee Ownership*, 49, 51.

123. Ibid., 51. See also Corey Rosen and Michael Quarrey, "How Well Is Employee Ownership Working?," *Harvard Business Review*, Special Report no. 87511 (September–October 1987).

124. Mill, *Principles of Political Economy*, vol. 2, bk. 4, ch. 7, sec. 6, 280–281.

125. Nozick, *Anarchy, State, and Utopia*, 255–261.

126. Thomas Jefferson, First Inaugural Address, *Thomas Jefferson, Writings*, 493.

127. Lane, "Government and Self-Esteem," 7.

128. Michael Lerner, *Surplus Powerlessness* (Oakland, Calif.: Institute for Labor and Mental Health, 1986), chapters 2 and 3.

129. Simmons and Mares, *Working Together*, 16, citing a 1976 poll by Peter Hart Associates.

130. *Oakland Tribune*, 25 February 1985.

131. Schumpeter, *Capitalism, Socialism and Democracy*, 83.

132. Here I'm referring to the Mondragon federation of over one hundred cooperatives. So well have they been adapting production to a changing economy that when Spain faced 20 percent unemployment in the 1980s, these cooperatives laid off virtually no one. See, for example, William Foote Whyte and Kathleen King Whyte, *Making Mondragon: The Growth and Dynamics of the Worker Cooperative Complex* (Ithaca, N.Y.: ILR Press, Cornell University, 1988). For information related to U.S. initiatives, contact the Industrial Cooperative Association, 249 Elm St., Somerville, Mass. 02144.

133. Quoted in Andrew Levinson, *The Full Employment Economy* (New York: Coward, McCann & Geoghegan, 1980), 80–81.

134. Quoted in Adams and Brock, *The Bigness Complex*, 313.

135. Melman, *Profits Without Production*, 183.

136. "Japan's Edge in Auto Costs," *Business Week*, 14 September 1981, 92–93.

137. Richard B. Freeman and James L. Medoff, *What Do Unions Do?* (New York: Basic Books, 1984), especially ch. 11. For a useful discussion of the debate about unions and productivity, see Marshall, *Unheard Voices*, ch. 5.

138. Kuttner, *The Economic Illusion*, 147.

139. Cited in Marshall, *Unheard Voices*, 124.

140. Simons, *Economic Policy for a Free Society*, 145.

141. Daniel Yankelovich et al., *Work and Human Values*, Aspen Institute for Humanistic Studies, September 1983.

142. Marshall, *Unheard Voices*, 129, 176.

143. "Pan Am Forces Out 2 Top Officers," *The New York Times*, 22 January 1988, 29.

144. Gus Tyler, "What Do Unions Really Do?" *Dissent*, 27, no. 1 (Winter 1980): 474.

145. Tawney, *Equality*, 15–16.

146. Robert A. Dahl, *A Preface to Democratic Theory* (Chicago: University of Chicago Press, 1956), 134.

147. Norman Cousins, *The Pathology of Power* (New York: W. W. Norton, 1987), ch. 10.

148. Harris, *Inside America*, 35, and Daniel Yankelovich, *New Rules* (New York: Bantam, 1982), 36.

149. One-third report this view. Citing a study by University of Houston political scientist James Gibson. Other findings: Since the McCarthy era, the percentage of Americans who believe that they cannot freely express their views has doubled to 20 percent. Fifty-four percent say that citizens probably or definitely should not be allowed to criticize the Constitution. *San Francisco Chronicle*, 12 September 1987, 5.

150. For an eloquent discussion of these issues, see Bowles and Gintis, *Democracy and Capitalism*, especially ch. 5; Robert A. Dahl, *A Preface to Economic Democracy* (Berkeley: University of California Press, 1985), 94–110.

151. Will, *Statecraft as Soulcraft*, 152.

152. Quoted in Marshall, *Unheard Voices*, 160.

153. For further discussion, see Macpherson, *Democratic Theory*, 68.

154. Robert A. Dahl, "On Removing Certain Impediments to Democracy," *Political Science Quarterly* 42 (Spring 1977): 8.

155. Sale, *Human Scale*, 379–380.

156. Helen Ginsburg, *Full Employment and Public Policy: The United States and Sweden* (Lexington, Mass.: D. C. Heath and Co., 1982), 78. The gap in voter participation between the top third by income and the bottom third reached 40 percentage points in the Eighties, up from 25 points in the Sixties. Thomas Byrne Edsall, "The Return of Inequality," *The Atlantic Monthly*, June 1988, 93.

157. Smith, *The Wealth of Nations*, bk. 5, ch. 1, pt. 3, 734–735.

158. Benjamin Ward, *The Conservative Economic World View* (New York: Basic Books, 1979), 5.

159. Tawney, *Equality*, 49.

160. Barber, *Strong Democracy*, 190.

161. Quoted in Gross, *Friendly Fascism*, 359.

Part Six

1. Paraphrase of remarks by Judge Robert Bork during the congressional hearings considering his nomination to the Supreme Court, 1987.

2. John Locke, "Is Every Man's Own Interest the Basis of the Law of Nature? No," in *Essays on the Law of Nature*, ed. W. von Leyden (Oxford: Oxford University Press/Clarendon, 1954), 211.

3. Friedrich A. Hayek, " 'Social' or Distributive Justice," in *The Essence of Hayek*, ed. Chiaki Nishiyama and Jurt R. Leube (Stanford, Calif.: Hoover Institution Press, 1984), 71–72.

4. Adam Smith, *The Theory of Moral Sentiments*, ed. D. D. Raphael and A. L. Macfie (Indianapolis: Liberty Classics, 1982), pt. 1, sec. 3, ch. 2, 50.

5. According to economist Benjamin Ward, "Our current population could be maintained at a decent, 'American' standard of living with the use of well under half of our current output." Benjamin Ward, *The Radical Economic World View* (New York: Basic Books, 1979), 35.

6. For a discussion of freedom in this vein, see C. B. Macpherson, *Democratic Theory: Essays on Retrieval* (Oxford: Clarendon Press, 1973), especially 20–21, 62–63, and Macpherson, *The Life and Times of Liberal Democracy* (New York: Opus Books, Oxford University Press, 1977), 47–67.

7. *Whitney* v. *California*, 274 U.S. 357, 375 (1927).

8. Milton Friedman, *Capitalism and Freedom* (Chicago: University of Chicago Press, 1962), 169.

9. Michael Novak, "The New Science," *National Review*, 17 July 1987, 58.

10. See, for example, Lewis H. Lapham, *Money and Class in America: Notes and Observations on Our Civil Religion* (New York: Weidenfeld & Nicolson, 1988).

11. Isaiah Berlin, *Two Concepts of Liberty* (Oxford: Oxford University Press, 1958), 10, especially the lengthy footnote.

12. Alexis de Tocqueville, *Democracy in America*, ed. Francis Bowen and Phillips Bradley (New York: Alfred A. Knopf, 1960), 1, 246.

13. E. O. Wilson, *Sociobiology* (Cambridge, Mass: Harvard University Press, 1975).

14. Richard Dawkins, *The Selfish Gene* (New York: Oxford University Press, 1976).

15. Marshall Sahlins, *The Use and Abuse of Biology* (Ann Arbor: University of Michigan Press, 1976), 100.

16. Charles R. Darwin, *The Descent of Man and Selection in Relation to Sex* (New York: D. Appleton, 1909), ch. 4.

17. Ibid., 124.

18. According to E. O. Wilson, *Sociobiology: The New Synthesis* (Cambridge, Mass.: The Belknap Press of the Harvard University Press, 1975), sociobiology recognizes two types of altruism: kin selection and reciprocal altruism. The first is a willingness to sacrifice with no expectation of return. The second is of the "I'll scratch your back if you'll scratch mine" variety (117, 120). Wilson sees the second type of altruism as malleable, writing that "the precise location of the dividing line between ingroup and outgroup is shifted back and forth with ease." Wilson, *On Human Nature* (Cambridge, Mass: Harvard University Press, 1978), 163. But even the first-order altruism appears malleable, in my view. Evidence of culture "fooling" our identification of kin abounds,

allowing us to experience the kin-selection variety of altruism even toward those with whom we obviously share no genes—with adopted children, for example. Or consider those who risk their lives as volunteer combatants—the Lincoln Brigade, for instance—because they so share the ideals of the other combatants that they appear as "brothers," though they may have little culture and few genes in common.

This discussion benefits from insights of environmental philosopher J. Baird Callicott, University of Wisconsin, Stevens Point. See Callicott's *In Defense of the Land Ethic* (Albany: State University of New York Press, 1988).

19. See, for example, Aldo Leopold, *A Sand County Almanac* (New York: Ballantine Books, 1966) and J. Baird Callicott, ed., *Companion to A Sand County Almanac* (Madison: University of Wisconsin Press, 1987). Also Holmes Ralston, III, *Philosophy Gone Wild: Essays in Environmental Ethics* (Buffalo, N.Y.: Prometheus Press, 1986).

20. Smith, *The Theory of Moral Sentiments*, pt. 2, sec. 2, ch. 3, 85.

21. Thomas Sowell, *A Conflict of Visions* (New York: William Morrow, 1987), 150.

22. John Stuart Mill, *Three Essays on Religion* (London: Longmans, 1885), 46.

23. Doctors interviewing fourteen of the thirty-seven male juveniles on death row found that during childhood all had suffered head injuries and twelve of the fourteen had been physically abused as children. *Science News*, 31 October 1987, 287. For a discussion of research on the link between parenting and subsequent criminal behavior, see Elliott Currie, *Confronting Crime* (New York: Pantheon, 1987), 201–210.

24. Smith, *The Theory of Moral Sentiments*, pt. 1, sec. 1, ch. 1, 9.

25. Stanley Milgram, *Obedience to Authority: The Experimental View* (Boston: Houghton Mifflin, 1974).

26. Thomas Jefferson in a letter to Thomas Law, *Thomas Jefferson, Writings*, ed. Merrill D. Peterson (New York: The Library of America/Liberty Classics, 1984), 1337–1338.

27. For a discussion of human moral development, see Lawrence Kohlberg, *The Psychology of Moral Development: Essays on Moral Development*, vol. 2 (San Francisco: Harper & Row, 1984), especially ch. 7. See also Elliot Turiel, *The Development of Social Knowledge* (New York: Cambridge University Press, 1983), ch. 9.

28. David Hume, *Essays, Literary, Moral, and Political* (London: Alexander Murray and Son, 1870), Essay 10, 46.

29. Peter L. Berger and Thomas Luckmann, *The Social Construction of Reality* (Garden City, N.Y.: Anchor/Doubleday, 1967), 183.

30. Elliott Currie, "Crime and the Conservatives," *Dissent* 34, no. 4 (Fall 1987): 427–437. By the late Seventies, per capita male deaths by criminal violence were ten to twenty times greater in the United States than in seven other Western countries plus Japan.

31. E. F. Schumacher, "The Critical Question of Size," *Resurgence* (May–June 1975), 20.

32. Sowell, *A Conflict of Visions*, 22.

33. Smith, *The Theory of Moral Sentiments*, pt. 1, sec. 1, ch. 5, 25.

34. See Smith, *The Theory of Moral Sentiments*, especially 22, 25, and 317. The philosophy of Adam Smith is often used to bolster the case that individual self-interest best explains human behavior and is an adequate base for a sound economic system. Andrew Skinner (see his introduction to *The Wealth of Nations*, New York: Penguin Classics, 1986, especially pages 26–27) and, in much the same vein, Thomas Sowell (*A Conflict of Visions*, 20–22) argue that Smith thought of human nature in terms of two compet-

ing "propensities"—those which are "selfish" and those which are "social." According to Skinner, Smith says that "fellow feeling" and the need for approval dispose man to society but are not sufficient to sustain it. So man must establish sources of control—rules of justice and morality. Sowell calls these rules "artificial" (22). To the contrary, Smith conceived our "moral sentiments" such as fellow-feeling and justice as based in (1) universal human feelings, (2) our innate capacity, therefore, to imagine ourselves in someone else's position, (3) our need for the approval of others, and (4) our need to feel that that approval is deserved. Thus, for Smith, fellow-feeling and self-love are inextricably interwoven.

Smith writes that justice is "not left to the freedom of our own wills" (178). This contrasts sharply with Sowell's notion of artificial conventions to control and subdue man's narrowly egotistic nature. Even Skinner points out that, for Smith, rules of justice evolve, not from a recognition of their utility but out of "fellow feeling." And Skinner acknowledges that in Smith justice and morality are expressions of man's nature.

For the best summary of Smith's moral philosophy, I suggest an essay written just after his death by his close associate, Dugald Stewart, and presented in 1793. In summarizing Smith's view, Stewart underlines Smith's belief in innate human sympathies and the social basis of the self. See Dugald Stewart, "Account of the Writings and Life of Adam Smith, L.L.D." in Adam Smith, *Essays on Philosophical Subjects* (Indianapolis: Liberty Classics, 1982), 265ff.

35. Ibid., *Theory of Moral Sentiments*, pt. 2, sec. 2, ch. 3, 88.
36. See, for example, James Madison in *The Federalist Papers*, no. 51 (New York: The New American Library, 1961), 320–325, and John Adams, "A Defence of the Constitutions of Government of the United States of America," in *Democracy, Liberty, and Property*, ed. Francis W. Coker (New York: Macmillan, 1949), 121–132.
37. John Adams, quoted by Clinton Rossiter, *Conservatism in America*, 2d ed., rev. (New York: Vintage, 1962), 111.
38. For a provocative discussion of our founders view of human nature, see Gary Wills, *Explaining America: The Federalist* (Garden City, N.Y.: Doubleday, 1981), especially 188–192.
39. James Madison, *The Writings of James Madison*, ed. Gaillard Hunt (New York: G. P. Putnam, 1900–1910), vol. 5, 223.
40. Cited in Robert A. Dahl, *A Preface to Democratic Theory* (Chicago: University of Chicago Press, 1956), 8.
41. R. H. Tawney, *Equality* (London: Allen & Unwin, 1952), 211.
42. See, for example, Robert Ardrey, *The Territorial Imperative* (New York: Atheneum, 1966) and Conrad Lorenz, *On Aggression* (New York: Harcourt, Brace and World, 1966). For a response, see Ashley Montague, ed., *Man and Aggression*, 2d ed. (New York: Oxford University Press, 1973).
43. Bernard Crick, *In Defence of Politics* (Baltimore: Penguin, 1964), 25.
44. Robert A. Dahl, *A Preface to Economic Democracy* (Berkeley: University of California Press, 1985), 98–99.
45. Milton Friedman and Rose Friedman, *The Tyranny of the Status Quo* (New York: Avon, 1983), 134–136.

46. For an excellent discussion of the impact of market values on human interaction, see Barry Schwartz, *The Battle for Human Nature* (New York: W. W. Norton, 1986).

47. Irving Kristol, *Two Cheers for Capitalism* (New York: New American Library, 1979), 166–167.

48. Jeremy Bentham, *Constitutional Code*, in *The Works of Jeremy Bentham*, ed. John Bowring (New York: Russell & Russell, 1962), bk. 9, ch. 15, 5.

49. Marcus Tullius Cicero, *The Republic*, trans. C. W. Keyes, vol. 1, xxv, 41, The Loeb Classical Library edition (Cambridge, Mass.: Harvard University Press, 1928), 65.

50. Robert Bellah and William Sullivan, "The Common Good," *Tikkun* 3, no. 3 (July/August 1988): 92.

51. See, for example, Louis Harris, *Inside America* (New York: Vintage Books, 1987). Also Barry Sussman, "A Final Poll of Opinions—My Own," *Washington Post*, 19 January 1987, national edition. Sussman notes that after 10 years as director of polling he is most struck by "a set of unifying values, concerns and goals that constitute what I like to think of as a people's agenda." They include concern about the environment and opportunity for the poor.

52. Edmund Burke, *Reflections on the Revolution France*, ed. J. G. A. Pocock (Indianapolis: Hackett, 1987), 84–85.

53. *Economic Justice for All: Pastoral Letter on Catholic Social Teaching and the U.S. Economy* (Washington, D.C.: National Conference of Catholic Bishops, 1986), especially 33–40. Over a dozen other religious bodies have produced statements about the individual's responsibility to help ensure that the social order embodies ethical values.

54. Ibid., xiv–xv.

55. Charles L. Schultze, "The Public Use of Private Interest, *Harper's*, May 1977, 45.

56. Kenneth Arrow, "Gifts and Exchanges," *Philosophy & Public Affairs* 1 (Summer 1972): 354–355.

57. For a popular review of a number of academic studies on the greater effectiveness of a cooperative instead of a competitive approach in educational and other settings, see Alfie Kohn, "How to Succeed without Even Vying," *Psychology Today* 20 (September 1986): 22–28.

58. Derek Stuart Wright, *The Psychology of Moral Behaviour* (Harmondsworth, England: Penguin, 1971), 133–139.

59. Alexis de Tocqueville, *Democracy in America*, ed. J. P. Mayer (Garden City, N.Y.: Doubleday, 1969), 512.

60. Adam Smith, *The Wealth of Nations*, ed. Edwin Cannan (New York: Modern Library/Random House, 1937), bk. 1, ch. 2, 14.

61. For a discussion of this point, see Michael Novak, *The Spirit of Democratic Capitalism* (New York: American Enterprise Institute/Simon & Schuster, 1982), 65 ff.

62. See Kristol, *Two Cheers for Capitalism*, x, 56, and Irving Kristol, "Capitalist Conception of Justice," in *Ethics, Free Enterprise and Public Policy: Original Essays on Moral Issues in Business*, ed. Richard T. de George and Joseph A. Pichler (New York: Oxford University Press, 1978), 66–67.

63. Novak, *Spirit of Democratic Capitalism*, 67–68. See also Robert Benne, *The Ethic of Democratic Capitalism* (Philadelphia: Fortress Press, 1982), 212.

64. Ibid., Novak, 50–55, 65.

65. Joseph Pichler, "Capitalism in America: Moral Issues in Public Policy," in de George and Pichler, *Ethics, Free Enterprise and Public Policy*, 27.

66. Svetozar Pejovich, "Basic Institutions of Capitalism and Socialism," in *Philosophical and Economic Foundations of Capitalism*, ed. Svetozar Pejovich (Lexington, Mass.: Lexington Books, 1983), 4.

67. Kristol, *Two Cheers for Capitalism*, 81.

68. Pejovich, "Basic Institutions of Capitalism and Socialism," 3.

69. Pichler, "Capitalism in America," 37.

70. Robert A. Dahl, *Dilemmas of Pluralist Democracy: Autonomy vs. Control* (New Haven, Conn.: Yale University Press, 1982), 153.

71. *People and Productivity: A Challenge to Corporate America* (New York: New York Stock Exchange, Office of Economic Research, 1982), 18.

72. Peter L. Berger, *The Capitalist Revolution* (New York: Basic Books, 1984), 113.

73. Kristol, "Capitalist Conception of Justice," 60–61.

74. de Tocqueville, *Democracy in America*, vol. 1, 122–123.

75. Robert Bellah et al., *Habits of the Heart: Individualism and Commitment in Everyday Life* (Berkeley and Los Angeles: University of California Press, 1984), 290.

76. From 1973 to 1980, the percent of Americans expressing a "hunger for community" grew from 32 percent to 47 percent. Daniel Yankelovich, *New Rules: Searching for Self-Fulfillment in a World Turned Upside Down* (New York: Bantam 1982), 48, 93.

77. Quoted by Robert Nisbet, "Public Opinion versus Popular Opinion," in *The American Commonwealth*, ed. Nathan Glazer and Irving Kristol (New York: Basic Books, 1976), 187.

78. Kristol, *Two Cheers for Capitalism*, xi.

79. Novak, *The Spirit of Democratic Capitalism*, 53.

80. Yankelovich, *New Rules*, 10.

81. de George, "Moral Issues in Business," in de George and Pichler, *Ethics, Free Enterprise and Public Policy*, 12.

82. Ibid., 12.

83. Kristol, *Two Cheers for Capitalism*, xiii.

84. Robert Dahl and Charles Lindblom, *Politics, Economics and Welfare* (New York: Harper and Brothers, 1953), 7.

85. Jeane J. Kirkpatrick, *Dictatorships and Double Standards* (New York: Simon & Schuster and the American Enterprise Institute for Public Policy Research, 1982), 10, 17 ff.

86. Benne, *The Ethic of Democratic Capitalism*, 154.

87. Friedman, *Capitalism and Freedom*, 12. Here Friedman uses the appellation "liberal" as I have in this book. See the introduction for further discussion.

88. Karl Polanyi, *The Great Transformation* (Boston: Beacon Press, 1944, with Rinehart & Co., 1954), 46ff, 249.

89. Christopher Lasch, *The New Oxford Review* (October 1987): 25.

90. *Politics* in *The Basic Works of Aristotle*, ed. Richard McKeon (New York: Random House, 1941), bk. I, ch. 5, 1132–1133.

91. Thomas Jefferson in a letter to Samuel Kercheval, *Thomas Jefferson, Writings*, 1401.

92. *Time*, 24 September 1984, 12, 16. A 1984 Yankelovich survey for *Time* reported that 71 percent of whites and half of nonwhites feel that things in the U.S. are going well.

93. Gallup poll, cited in *San Francisco Chronicle*, 11 February 1985. Sixty percent of the respondents reported that they feel income and wealth should be more evenly distributed.

94. Harris, *Inside America*, 116, 174–175, 248–249.

95. Robert E. Lane, *Political Ideology* (New York: The Free Press of Glencoe, 1962), 73, 79.

96. Michael Lerner, *Surplus Powerlessness* (Oakland, Calif.: Institute for Labor and Mental Health, 1986). See also Richard Sennett and Jonathan Cobb, *The Hidden Injuries of Class* (New York: Vintage, 1973).

97. Quoted in Russell Kirk, *The Conservative Mind* (Chicago: Henry Regnery Co., 1953), 41.

98. Harry Emerson Fosdick, *The Power to See It Through* (New York: Harper and Brothers, 1935), 102.

99. Kristol, "The Capitalist Conception of Justice," 69.

100. Thomas Sowell, *A Conflict of Visions*, ch. 2.

101. Peter Berger, *Facing Up to Modernity* (New York: Basic Books, 1977), 59–60.

102. Benne, *The Ethic of Democratic Capitalism*, 212.

103. Sowell, *A Conflict of Visions*, 92–93.

104. Ibid., 36–37. See also Thomas Sowell, *Knowledge and Decisions* (New York: Basic Books, 1980), pt. 1.

105. Hayek in Nishiyama and Leube, *The Essence of Hayek*, chs. 5 and 14.

106. Sowell, *A Conflict of Visions*, 201.

107. George Stigler, *The Citizen and the State* (Chicago: University of Chicago Press, 1975), 24.

108. Sowell, *A Conflict of Visions*, 56–57, 93, 113.

109. Alexander Hamilton, *Selected Writings and Speeches of Alexander Hamilton*, ed. Morton J. Frisch (Washington, D.C.: American Enterprise Institute, 1985), 390.

110. Sowell, *Knowledge and Decisions*, 370.

111. Isaiah Berlin, *Four Essays on Liberty* (New York: Oxford University Press, 1968), 167.

112. For a discussion of the rise in Americans' sense of alienation from power, see Harris, *Inside America*, 33.

113. For an introduction and excellent bibliography to the debate on human motivation, see Michael A. Wallach and Lise Wallach, *Psychology's Sanction for Selfishness* (San Francisco: W. H. Freeman and Co., 1983).

114. R. H. Tawney, *Religion and the Rise of Capitalism* (London: John Murray, 1926), 285.

115. Branko Horvat, *The Political Economy of Socialism* (Armonk: M. E. Sharpe, 1982), especially pt. 1.

116. Friedrich A. Hayek, *The Road to Serfdom* (Chicago: University of Chicago Press, 1944), 25.

117. Benne, *The Ethic of Democratic Capitalism*, 173.
118. Kristol, "Capitalist Conception of Justice," 69.
119. John H. Schaar, "Equality of Opportunity and Beyond," in J. Roland Pennock and John W. Chapman, eds., *Equality* (New York: Atherton Press, 1967), 245–246.

Index

Ability(ies):
  development of individual's, 86, 87, 97
  freedom for, 14–15, 239–40, 241, 263
  wealth related to, 91–92
Absolutism, 6
Achian, Armen A., quoted, 220
Acid rain, 209, 254
Accumulation, limits on, 96–97
Acquisitiveness, *see* Income; Possessions; Property
  rights
Adams, John, quoted, 30, 167, 173, 212, 245
Advertising, 120, 125–27
Affirmative action, 194, 237
  versus reverse discrimination, 97–106
Agee, James, quoted, 48
Agriculture, 149, 171–72, 218, 219
  farmland, 170, 173–74
Aid to Families with Dependent Children, *see*
  Welfare
Airline industry, 135
Alcoholism, treatment of, 32
Alternative worldview, 11–17, 17*n.*
  see also Liberal worldview; *individual issues and values*
Anderson, Terry, quoted, 178
Antisocial behavior, 241
Aristocracy, 85

Aristotle, 12, 260
Arnold, Thurman, quoted, 26
Arrow, Kenneth, quoted, 253
Australia, 51
Austria, 34, 185, 205
Automobile industry, 133–34, 147, 225
Autonomy, 7, 246

Babbitt, Irving, quoted, 109
Baden, A., quoted, 151, 154
Bagdikian, Ben, quoted, 208
Bakke case, 99
Banks, 175–76
Barber, Benjamin, 16
  quoted, 202
Benne, Robert, quoted, 265
Bentham, Jeremy, 15
  quoted, 7–8
Bell, Daniel, quoted, 88
Benne, Robert, quoted, 92, 125–26, 156, 263
Bentham, Jeremy, quoted, 171, 197, 251
Bentley, Arthur F., quoted, 135, 154
Berger, Peter L., quoted, 202, 244
Berlin, Isaiah, quoted, 7, 21, 264
Bickel, Alexander, quoted, 106
Biological sciences, 9, 241

Blacks, 124
   affirmative action versus reverse discrimination, 97–106
Block, Fred, et al., quoted, 41
Brandeis, Louis D., 209, 210, 240
Brooks, Gail L., quoted, 105
Brozen, Yale, quoted, 132
Buddhism, 11
Bureaucracy, 62, 154, 237, 251
Bureau of Land Management, 142
Burke, Edmund, quoted, 252, 260
Burlington, Vermont, 217
Burns, Arthur, 134
   quoted, 73–74
Burns, James MacGregor, 198
Bush, George, quoted, 93

Callicott, J. Baird, quoted, 151
Campaign financing, 203–6
Capitalism, 4, 54, 80, 83, 110, 187, 188, 203, 212, 221, 250
   change and, 259
   civil liberties and, 184–85
   conflicts eased by, 237–38
   gap between rich and poor and, 70
   meshing of self-interest and social ends in, 247
   mobility of capital, 224
   moral values and, 253–58
   value of the individual in, 265–66
   see also Market, the
Capital mobility, 224
Carter, Jimmy, 204
Catholic Church, 1986 bishops pastoral letter, 198
CBS Records, 177
Central Intelligence Agency (CIA), 207
Chamber of Commerce, U.S., 224
Change, possibility of, 258–61
Charity, 52–54, 257
Chayes, Judge Abram, quoted, 121
Child abuse, 32
Child care, 41, 47, 96, 130–31
Chile, 185
Children living in poverty, see Poverty

China, 11, 88, 108, 185
Chisholm, Betty, quoted, 224
Chlorofluorocarbons, 151, 158
Chrysler Corporation, 50, 121
Cicero, Marcus Tullius, quoted, 251
Citizen movements, 198
Citizen participation in democratic process, 198–202, 229–30
   apathy and, 199, 200
   campaign financing, 203–6
   voter turnout, 201
Citizenship, 62–63
Civil rights, 197
   freedom of the press, 207–8
   freedom of speech, 206
   the market, property, and, 184–87
Civil service jobs, 124
Clean air legislation, 209
Clean Water Act, 146
Closed entry, 120
College education, 36
Common Cause, 204
Common good, 24, 237–38, 250–52
   self-interest versus, 241–48, 253
Communism, 11, 60, 188, 265
   individual sacrificed to larger social goal in, 265–66
   political parties and, 193
   state control over the economy, 4, 210, 215, 218
Communities Organized for Public Service, 217
Community development loan funds, 83
Community involvement, 201–2
Community needs, corporate responsiveness to 215–18, 219
Community planning, 217, 218
Competition:
   free media and, 208
   in the marketplace, 119–21, 132, 133, 218– 239, 255
      concentrated power and, 119–21
      deregulation and, 135–36
      international, 129, 177, 225
Confucianism, 11
Conservation, see Environment

Consumer, 211–12, 221, 250, 265
  treadmill, 22–23
Continental Illinois, 121
Contributions, campaign, 203–6
Control Data Corporation, 102
Coolidge, Calvin, quoted, 126
Cooper, James Fenimore, 169
"Corporate raiders," 176–77
Corporations, 182–83, 211–19, 261
  advertising by, 120, 125–27
  birth of, 182
  community needs and, 215–18, 219
  control of the media, 208
  economic responsibility of, 36–37, 213–14, 215,
    237
  efficiency, size, and profits of, 131–34
  foreign owners of U.S., 177
  legal rights of, 183
  payment for pollution, 145–48, 215–16
  planning by, the government and, 179
  power of, 188, 201, 209, 210, 212, 214, 246
  shareholders of a, 37, 168–74, 176, 177,
    213–14, 221, 223
  taxes on, 46–47, 133, 168, 209, 228
  see also Market, the; Work; Workers
Cortes, Ernesto, Jr., quoted, 217
Crick, Bernard, quoted, 191, 247
Crime, 249
  poverty and, 32–33
  violent, 244
Cuba, 185
Culture of democracy, 227–30

Dahl, Robert A., 16
  quoted, 183, 228, 229, 249
Darwin, Charles, 9, 13, 241–42, 243
  quoted, 242
Dawkins, Richard, 9
Day care, see Child care
Defense Department, U.S., 134
Defense spending, 31–32, 36, 58, 74–75,
  109
Deficit, federal, 72, 85
Demand, 129

Democracy, 61–64, 186, 193–234
  accountability of government in, 193
  checks and balances in, 195
  citizen participation in, 198–202, 203–6
  culture of, 227–30
  defining, 193–96, 197, 232
  democratic economic system, possibility of,
    211–19
  differences in wealth as threat to, 107
  dispersion of power in, 195
  economic rights and, 196–97
  individuality and, 231–32
  participatory, 201, 246
  popular opinion and, 194
  power in a, 194–95, 197–98, 210
  relationship of political and economic life in a,
    155–57, 202–11, 216–17, 229–30
  as representative government, 193, 194, 198
  special interest groups in a, 154, 199, 201–2,
    204–5, 209
  summary of the dialogue, 232–34
  unions in a, 225–27
  in the workplace, 216, 220–25, 229
Demsetz, Harold, quoted, 220
Dependency, 45, 47, 49, 54
Deregulation, 135–36, 219
Descartes, René, 8–9
Development of individual talents, 86, 87, 97
  freedom for, 14–15, 239–40, 241, 263
Dewey, John, quoted, 196
Dignity, 94
Discrimination, affirmative action versus reverse,
  97–106
Diversity and democracy, 231–32
Dole, Robert, quoted, 205
Doubleday, 177
Dow Chemical, 183
Drugs, 46, 257

Economic responsibility of corporations, 36–37,
  213–14, 215, 237
Economic security, 27–31, 196, 218, 231, 237, 258
  freedom and, 27–32, 50–51, 55–58, 261
  free speech and, 187

Economic security (*cont.*)
  risk-taking, and the work ethic, 55–58
  see also Job security; Market, the; Work
Economic sphere, *see* Market, the
Education:
  preschool, *see* Preschool programs
  public, 41, 46, 63–64, 94, 96, 238, 260
Egalitarianism, "slippery slope" of, 89–90
Eisenhower, Dwight, 210
  quoted, 210
Elections, 193
El Salvador, 185
Energy resources, 217–18
  government and, 152–55
  market and, 152–55
  public utilities, 153, 177–78
Entitlements, 27–31, 45
  see also specific programs
Environment, 209, 237, 260
  acid rain, 209, 254
  citizen movements to protect the, 198
  making polluters pay, 145–48, 215–16
  market and resource depletion, 148–49
  market prices and resource use, 142–45
  the market, property rights, and, 141–42
  resources for future generations, 149–51
  toxic wastes, 133, 228
Environmental Protection Agency, 136, 183
Envy, 87–89
Equality:
  fairness, and freedom, 107–10
  trade-offs between freedom and, 262–65
Equality of opportunity, 93–97, 262
  affirmative action versus equality of
    opportunity, 97–106
Equality of outcome, 93–97
Equitable Life Assurance, 102
Ethics, 228
  see also Morality
Exclusive use of property, 170, 178, 180

Fairness, 67–115, 262–63
  affirmative action or reverse discrimination,
    97–106

egalitarianism, "slippery slope" of, 89–90
envy and, 87–89
equality, and freedom, 107–10
equal opportunities or equal outcomes,
    93–97
gap between rich and poor, 69–71, 73, 92
hope and, as incentives, 79–80
incentives for the rich, 80–81
inequalities and self-esteem, 86–87
of inheritance, 72–73, 84–85
of the market, 75–76
of redistribution of income, 71–75, 85, 89–90,
    108–9
responsibility for inequalities, 91–92
reward for sacrifice and risk, 82–84
summary of dialogue on, 113–15
what works, 76–78
who decides what's fair?, 110–12
  see also Justice
Family, role of, 249, 256
Farming, *see* Agriculture
Fascism, 185
Fathers and child support payments, 48–49
Federal Bureau of Investigation (FBI), 207
Federal Housing Authority, 85
Federal Register, 137
Federal Reserve, 71–72, 134, 201
Finland, 205
Firestone, 177
Follett, Mary Parker, quoted, 202
Food and Drug Administration, 136–37
Food stamps, 41, 48, 70
Forbes, 107
Ford, Gerald, quoted, 24
Forest management, 142
Forest Service, 143
Fosdick, Harry Emerson, quoted, 261
France, 34
Franklin, Benjamin, 173
  quoted, 45, 173
Freedom, 21–66, 111, 248, 266–67
  acquisitiveness and, 11
  as autonomy, 7
  to develop unique talents, 14–15, 239–40, 241,
    263

economic security and, 27–32, 50–51, 55–58, 261

entitlements and rights, 27–31

fairness, equality, and, 107–10

government responsibilities and, 46–51

income and, 21–23

individual responsibilities and, 39–45, 50

from interference and to do what one wants, 21–26

market's efficiency and, 119–61

privacy and, 54–55

property, power, and civil liberties, 165–90

summary of dialogue on, 64–66

trade-offs between equality and, 262–63

zero-sum?, 237–41

Freedom of the press, 207–8

Freedom of speech, 206

Freeman, A. M., quoted, 143

Freeman, Roger A., quoted, 42

Friedman, Milton, 17, 122
  quoted, 24, 34, 71, 121–22, 127, 155, 175, 187, 203, 259

Friedman, Rose, quoted, 24, 34, 71, 127, 175, 203

General Dynamics, 228

General Motors (GM), 134, 221

Gilder, George, quoted, 119

Glas, Joseph P., 157

Glazer, Nathan, quoted, 101

Governing elite, 194, 195, 198
  wealth of, 203

Government:
  and/or the market, 155–57
  communist, see Communism
  democratic, see Democracy
  deregulation, 135–36, 219
  economic security and, 27–32, 50–51, 55–58, 196–97
  entitlements and rights, 27–31
  as expression of our social nature, 13, 23
  interference of, 25, 26, 109, 110
  price of neglect, 32–35
  property rights as protection against power of, 165–68

protective function of, 23, 26, 27, 31–32, 57, 124, 153, 209–10

as provider or rule setter, 35–38

in the public interest, 24, 251

regulation and the market, 134–40, 203, 211, 214–15, 219

responsibilities of, and freedom, 46–51

responsiveness of, 27

risks of unintended consequences of programs of, 59–60

role in a free society, 61–64

size of, 30–35, 62
  limited, 23, 24, 26, 61, 197, 199–200, 209, 249

suspicion of, 9

as a threat, 251

use of resources and, 152–55

Grand Canyon, 44

Great Britain, 205–206

Greenhouse effect, 151

Greenspan, Alan, quoted, 120

Habits of the Heart (Bellah), 5

Hamilton, Alexander, quoted, 167, 264

Handicapped, aid to the, 61

Hanke, Steven, quoted, 142

Harvard Business School, 216

Hastie, William H., quoted, 232

Haveman, Robert, quoted, 143

Hayek, Friedrich A., quoted, 75–76, 111, 112, 239

Hazardous wastes, 37–38, 133, 228

Headstart program, 33, 48

Health care, see Medical care

Hewlett-Packard, 102

Hill, Peter J., quoted, 178

Hobbes, Thomas, 7, 13, 15
  quoted, 23

Holmes, Oliver Wendell, quoted, 87

Homeless, 32, 243, 249, 254, 257

Homestead Acts, 85

Hope as incentive, 79

Housing, 46, 72, 168, 171, 172, 248–49
  homeless, 32, 243, 249, 254, 257
  segregated, 124

Human being as ends or means, 265–67
Human nature:
    possibility of change in, 258–61
    self-interest and, 241–48, 253
    ultimate goals and, 263–65
Human rights, 257
Hume, David, quoted, 244
Humphrey, Hubert, quoted, 223
Hunger, 194–95, 230, 257, 260
Huntington, Samuel, quoted, 199
Hyatt-Clark, 221

Iacocca, Lee, 73
    quoted, 120
Incentives, 77–78
    hope and fairness as, 79–80
    for the rich, 80–81
Income:
    freedom and, 22–23, 24
        taxes on, 24–25
    redistribution of, 71–75, 85, 89–90
    see also Fairness
Individuality, democracy and, 231–32
Individual responsibility, freedom and, 39–45, 50
Inequality, see Fairness
Inflation, 34, 72, 179
Inheritance, 72–73, 84–85, 173
Interest rates, 71–72
Interference, 25–26, 109
    of government, 25, 26, 109, 110
International competition, 129, 177, 225
Interstate Commerce Commission, 135
Investment, 80–81, 82–83
Irrigation, water for, 154
Italy, 218

Japan, 56, 80, 140, 177, 218, 225, 255
Jefferson, Thomas, 16, 27, 173, 174, 197, 230
    quoted, 15, 23, 85, 166, 173, 188, 195, 198,
        223, 243, 260
Jencks, Christopher, et al., quoted, 174
Job security, 226
    see also Economic security

Job training and retraining, 41, 44
John Morrell & Company, 50
Johnson, Chalmers, quoted, 134
Johnson, Lyndon B., quoted, 97
Johnson and Johnson, Inc., quoted, 99
John II, Pope, quoted, 181
Jouvenel, Betrand de, quoted, 83
Judeo-Christian tradition, 8
Justice, 13–14, 67, 245
    see also Fairness
Justice Department, U.S., 105

Kahn, Alfred J., quoted, 32
Kamerman, Sheila, quoted, 32
King, Martin Luther, Jr., quoted, 57
Kirkpatrick, Jeane J., quoted, 93, 110, 138, 159
Kneese, Allen, quoted, 143
Kristol, Irving, quoted, 95, 111, 122, 185, 213,
    262, 266

Lane, Robert, quoted, 28
Lasch, Christopher, quoted, 259–60
Lay Commission on Catholic Social Teaching and
    the U.S. Economy, quoted, 184
Leisure time, 128, 129
Leopold, Aldo, quoted, 150
Lerner, Abba, quoted, 37
Lerner, Michael, quoted, 129
Liberal worldview, 4, 7–11, 17, 17n.
    biological sciences and, 9
    dichotomy in, 9
    Judeo-Christian tradition and, 8
    see also Alternative worldview; individual
        issues and values
Lincoln, Abraham, quoted, 138, 169
Lindblom, Charles, quoted, 51, 168, 212
Lobbyists, 199, 204–5, 209
Local Ownership Project, Burlington, Vermont,
    217
Locke, John, 180, 181
    quoted, 9–10, 165, 171, 237
Lodge, George, 216
    quoted, 14

Low-birth-weight babies, 32
Luckmann, Thomas, quoted, 244

McGee, Brownie, 124
Macham, Tibor, quoted, 53
McKenzie, Robert, quoted, 30, 139, 197
MacNaughton, Donald S., quoted, 179
Macpherson, C. B., 16
  quoted, 96, 196
Madison, James, quoted, 24, 96, 195, 246
Majority opinion, 193, 194
Market, the, 9, 13, 119–61, 167, 200
  competition in, *see* Competition
  corporate payment for pollution, 145–48,
    215–16
  democratic economy, possibility of, 211–19
  democracy in the workplace and, 220–25
  economic rights and, 195–96
  efficiency, size, and profits, 131–34
  fairness of the, 75–76
  government and/or, 155–57, 202–3, 211
  government and resource use, 152–55
  as individual choice, 121–23
  interests and principles, 157–58
  media access and, 207
  moral responsibility and, 248–50
  personal prejudice and, 123–25
  in political life, 193
  prices and resource use, 142–45
  property, and civil liberties, 184–87
  property, and the environment, 141–42
  regulation and, 134–40, 203, 214–15, 219
  relationship to political sphere of, 155–57,
    202–11, 229–30
  resource depletion and, 148–49
  resources for future generations and, 149–51
  self-interest and, 245
  success of, 128–31
  summary of the dialogue, 158–61
  voluntary choice and, 125–26
  see also Capitalism
Marriage rate, 45
Mason, George, quoted, 246
Mead, Lawrence M., quoted, 44, 47

Media:
  control of the, 207–8
  political power and, 206
Medicaid, 41, 48
Medical care, 94, 96, 218
  market system and, 130
  as a right, 130, 131, 194, 196, 258
  welfare and, 41, 42, 46, 48
Medicare, 30, 35
Mellon, Andrew, quoted, 77
Membership, rights of, 14, 55, 95
Mergers, 132, 133, 135, 224
Military budget, *see* Defense spending
Military-industrial complex, 210
Mill, John Stuart, quoted, 5, 40, 63, 170, 174,
  221, 222, 242
Minimum wage law, 59
Minorities:
  affirmative action versus reverse discrimination,
    97–106
  interests of, *see* Special interest groups
Mobil Oil, 206–7
Monetary policy, 201
Money, *see* Income; Possessions; Property rights
Monopoly, 119, 120
Montana, 198
Montesquieu, quoted, 27
Morality, 9, 228, 244, 245
  capitalism and, 253–58
  moral responsibility and the market, 248–50
Mortgage interest deduction, 72
Moynihan, Daniel, quoted, 94

NASA, 134
National debt, *see* Deficit, federal
National security, *see* Government, protective
  function of
Natural resources, *see* Environment
Nature Conservancy, 143–44
Nebraska, 218, 219
Nepotism, 99, 124
Netherlands, 185
News media, *see* Media
Newton, Isaac, 10–11

Nicaragua, 185
Nisbet, Robert, quoted, 52–53, 84, 194
Norway, 34
Novak, Michael, quoted, 58, 240, 254
Nozick, Robert, 15
    quoted, 71, 86, 112, 209
Nuclear weapons, 31–32
Nutter, G. Warren, quoted, 206–7

Occupational Safety and Health Agency, 136
Oil industry, 153, 209, 215
Okun, Arthur M., quoted, 156
Opinion polls, 256
Orwell, George, 54
Ozone layer, 151, 158

Pacific Lumber Company, 142–43
Paine, Thomas, quoted, 23
Pakistan, 185
Pan Am, 227
Participatory democracy, 201, 246
Partnerships, 213
Patman, Wright, quoted, 201
Patriotism, 251–52
Pension funds, 175, 176, 216
Pentagon, see U.S. Defense Department
Permissiveness, 249
Personal philosophy, 6, 16–17
Petrochemical industry, 146–47
Philippines, 171–72, 258
Physician Task Force on Hunger, quoted, 195
Pichler, Joseph, quoted, 255
Pickens, T. Boone, quoted, 215
Polanyi, Karl, 16
    quoted, 155
Policymaking:
    corporate advertising to influence, 127
    special interest groups and, 154, 199, 201–2,
        204–5, 209
    see also Democracy
Political Action Committees (PACs), 204–5, 209
Political parties, 193
Political process, see Democracy

Pollution, 151
    corporate payment for, 145–48, 215–16
    see also Environment
Populism, 88
Posner, Richard, quoted, 98–99, 201
Possessions:
    importance of, 9, 239, 241, 263
    see also Property rights
Poverty, 38, 94, 238, 250, 254, 257
    crime and, 32–33
    gap between rich and poor, 69–71, 73, 94, 129,
        260
    governmental responsibilities and, 46–49
    individual responsibility and, 39–45
    price of neglect, 32–35
    private charity to relieve, 52–54, 257
    redistribution of income, 71–75, 85, 89–90,
        108–9
    as relative concept, 51–53
    see also Fairness; Rich; Welfare
Power, 264
    in communist society, 210
    concentrated, the market and, 119–21
    of corporations, 188, 201, 209, 210, 212, 214,
        246
    in a democracy, 194–95, 197–98, 210
    property rights and, 165–68
    of the rich, 84–85, 96, 107, 207
Prejudices, the market and individual, 123–25
Preschool programs, 33, 48, 49, 96
Press, freedom of the, 207–8
Prices, market, and resource use, 142–45
Privacy, freedom as, 54–55
Proctor & Gamble, 120, 229
Productivity, 34, 56, 79, 119, 128, 226–27, 255
Property ownership, voting rights and, 212
Property rights, 9–10, 13, 14, 95–96, 165–90, 197,
        246, 263
    decision making and its consequences, 175–79
    exclusive and inclusive, 180–81
    incentive to production, 170–72
    limited or unlimited?, 172–74
    the market, and civil liberties, 184–87
    the market, and the environment, 141–42
    market prices and resource use, 142–45

private enterprise, 182–84
  as protection against state power, 165–68
  right to the fruits of one's labor, 169–70
  separateness of economic and political life,
      187–88
  state ownership, 177–78, 179
  summary of the dialogue, 189–90
  see also Possessions
Proprietorships, 213, 214
Protestant ethic, 8, 14
Prudential Insurance, 219
Public interest, see Common good
Public opinion, 194, 207, 256

Quinn, T. K., quoted, 214

Rand, A. Barry, quoted, 102
Rand, Ayn, quoted, 26
Rath Packing Company, 222
Reagan, Ronald, 204, 230
  quoted, 96
Reagan administration, 228
Recycling, 156
Redistribution of income, 71–75, 85, 89–90
Reed, Rex, quoted, 229
Regulation:
  the market and, 134–40, 203, 211, 214–15,
      219
  see also Deregulation
Religion, 254, 255, 256
Representation, 29
  see also Democracy
Representative government, 193, 194, 198
Reverse discrimination versus affirmative action,
      97–106
Rewards, see Fairness
Ricardo, David, quoted, 80
Rich, the, 167–68, 174, 240
  ability related to wealth, 91–92
  envy of, 87–89
  gap between poor and, 69–71, 73, 92, 129, 260
  government by the, 203
  power of the, 84–85, 96, 107, 207

redistribution of income, 71–75, 85, 89–90,
      108–9
  taxes and, 70, 72, 80, 83
  see also Fairness; Poverty
Right(s), 194–96, 257
  civil, see Civil rights
  duties associated with, 248, 252
  entitlements and, 27–29
  governmental responsibilities and, 46
  medical care as a, 130, 131, 194, 196, 258
  property, see Property rights
Risk-taking:
  investment and, 82–83
  security, and the work ethic, 55–58
  wealth and, 91–92
Rockefellers, 207
Rogers, Lindsay, quoted, 256
Roosevelt, Franklin, 27
  quoted, 27
Rousseau, Jean-Jacques, quoted, 108–9, 112
Rustin, Bayard, quoted, 79

Sacrifice, self-, 242
Sagoff, Mark, 16
  quoted, 144–45
Sahlins, Marshall, quoted, 241
St. John de Crevecoeur, 167
St. Paul, Minnesota, 202
Samuelson, Paul A., quoted, 123, 225
San Antonio, Texas, 217
Savings, 81
Savings and loan industry, 138
Scandinavia, 34, 56, 185
Schaar, John H., quoted, 94, 200, 266
Schlesinger, Arthur M., Jr., quoted, 62
Schools, see Education
Schultz, Charles, quoted, 156
Schumacher, E. F., quoted, 244
Schumpeter, Joseph, quoted, 128, 193, 224
Scott, Anthony, quoted, 149
Segregation:
  in housing, 124
  laws, 100
Self-centeredness, 8

Self-determination, 258
Self-discipline, 241
Self-esteem, 245, 253
  affirmative action and, 102–3
  inequalities and, 86–87
Self-interest, 253, 257, 262
  versus community interest, 241–48, 253
"Selfish gene," theory of, 241, 242
Senior citizens:
  aid to, 61, 70
  poverty among, 41
Shattuck, John, quoted, 187
Shue, Henry, quoted, 27
Sigler, Andrew, quoted, 213
Simon, Julian, quoted, 150
Simons, Henry, quoted, 120, 126, 131–32, 178,
    182, 216, 226
Single-parent families, 59
  living in poverty, 40, 44–45, 48–49
Small businesses, loans to, 36
Smith, Adam, 12, 16, 245, 253
  quoted, 12, 13–14, 34, 52, 56, 67, 74, 77, 92,
    139, 152, 166, 220–21, 230, 239, 242, 243,
    245, 253
Social Darwinism, 9, 260
Socialism, 175, 187, 217, 259
Social Security, 30, 31, 70, 74, 106
Sociobiology, 9, 241
Solar heating, 152
South Africa, 157, 185
South Korea, 185
South Shore Bank, 83
Soviet Union, 31, 88, 185, 218
Sowell, Thomas, 15
  quoted, 48, 77–78, 80, 93
Spain, 225
Special interest groups, 154, 199, 201–2, 204–5,
    209
Speech, freedom of, 206
Spencer, Herbert, 260
Spousal abuse, 32
Standard Oil, 157
Steinbeck, John, 69
Stigler, George, quoted, 264

Stock ownership, 37, 168, 174, 176, 177, 213–14,
    221, 223
Stroup, Richard L., quoted, 151, 154
"Supply-side" economics, 77
Supreme Court, 99, 100, 204
  quoted, 171, 206
Surrogate mothers, 259–60
Survival, right to, 195–96
Sweden, 35, 78, 179
Switzerland, 78

Takeovers, corporate, 215
Talents, development of unique, 86, 87, 97
  freedom for, 14–15, 239–40, 241, 263
Taoism, 11
Tawney, R. H., 16
  quoted, 9, 25, 45, 185, 216, 227, 231, 246, 265
Taxation, 31, 35, 46–47, 74, 83
  of corporations, 46–47, 133, 168, 209, 228
  freedom and, 24–25, 26, 237
  on gifts and estates, 84, 85
  investment and, 80–81
Tax codes, 36
  benefiting the rich, changes in, 70, 72, 80
Tax Reform Act of 1986, 209
Taylor, John, quoted, 166, 168
Television, political power and, 206
Terry, Sonny, 124
Third World, 185–86
Thompson, William Irwin, quoted, 6
Thoreau, Henry David, quoted, 50
Thurow, Lester, quoted, 50, 107
Tobin, James, quoted, 225
Tocqueville, Alexis de, quoted, 241, 253, 256
Totalitarianism, 185, 187, 195, 203, 258, 262
Toxic wastes, 37–38, 133, 228
Trade deficit, 225
Trade-offs between equality and freedom, 262–65
Trade unions, 225–27
Tradition, 254
Transfer payments, government, 70, 73, 74
"Trickle-down" economics, 77
Tsongas, Paul, quoted, 27

Tyler, Guy, quoted, 227
Tyranny, 194, 195, 203
  of economic powerlessness, 196

Unemployment, 27–28, 33, 34, 37, 42, 59, 179,
    196, 238, 266
  benefits, 36, 50, 51, 224
Unions, 225–27
United Kingdom, 34, 35, 36, 48, 60, 205–6
U.S. Catholic Bishops, quoted, 252
U.S. Defense Department, 134
U.S. Employment Service, 42
U.S. Justice Department, 105
USSR, *see* Soviet Union
Utility companies, 153, 177–78
Utopianism, 248, 264–65

Voter turnout, 201
Voting rights, 212

Waite, Chief Justice, quoted, 179
Ward, Benjamin, quoted, 231
Wealthy, *see* Rich, the
Welfare, 39–41, 43–44, 46, 47, 62, 224
Welfare state, 60
West Germany, 34, 36, 56, 140, 185, 205

Will, George, quoted, 78, 194, 229
Wilson, E. O., 9
Wolin, Sheldon, 16
Women:
  affirmative action versus reverse discrimination,
    97–106
  unequal pay for, 98, 124
Wood, General Robert E., quoted, 215
Work, 8, 14, 47, 128–29, 249–50
  affirmative action versus reverse discrimination,
    97–106
  in a democratic corporation, 216, 220–25, 229
  expansion of job market, 36, 41
  low-paying jobs, 42, 43–44, 112, 129, 187
  see also Economic security; Workers
Worker(s):
  -owners, 83, 179, 221–25
  productivity, *see* Productivity
  responsibility of, 37, 221–25, 229, 258
  turnover, 226
  unions, 225–27
Work ethic:
  decline in, 80–81
  Protestant, 8, 14
  security, risk-taking, and the, 55–58
Workplace, democracy in the, 216, 220–25, 229

Yeager, Leland B., quoted, 199

About the Author ★

Frances Moore Lappé's first book, *Diet for a Small Planet*, has been credited with launching a nutrition revolution. Published in 1971, it has sold over 3 million copies. In 1975 she and Joseph Collins founded the Institute for Food and Development Policy based in San Francisco. In 1977, together they wrote *Food First: Beyond the Myth of Scarcity*. This book fundamentally shifted the international debate about world hunger to a political and economic framework by examining the actual root causes of the issue. With her colleagues, Lappé has written numerous other books, including *World Hunger: Twelve Myths*, and *Betraying the National Interest*, as well as articles that have appeared in a wide array of publications.

In 1985 Lappé and her children, Anthony and Anna Lappé, collaborated on the book *What to Do After You Turn Off the TV*, a personal guide for enriching family life. Lappé lectures regularly and appears often on radio and television.

For "vision and work healing our planet and uplifting humanity," Frances Moore Lappé and the Institute for Food and Development Policy were honored in Sweden with the presentation of the 1988 international Right Livelihood Award, often called the "Alternative Nobel Prize."

About the Institute for Food and Development Policy: ★

The Institute, also known as Food First, is an education-for-action center addressing the underlying economic and political causes of hunger and poverty. With 20,000 members and a staff of sixteen, it publishes books, classroom curricula, action guides, and audio-visual materials that are used in over fifty countries in more than twenty languages.

With the publication of *Rediscovering America's Values,* the Institute launches a new educational effort. The Institute believes that the deepening problems of hunger, homelessness, welfare, and low-paying jobs are not at base economic questions; they reflect fundamental value choices that we as a people are making. Our social values have meaning, however, and can serve as guides to effective action only as we gain confidence in them through genuine dialogue. To help Americans reclaim our social values, to ignite new hope that public policies can reflect our deepest values, the Institute thus seeks to stimulate dialogue on America's values in all walks of life—from the classroom, to the newsroom, to the halls of Congress.

To learn more about the Institute's work, please write to:

Institute for Food and Development Policy
145 9th Street
San Francisco, California 94103

An Invitation from
Frances Moore Lappé ★

Writing *Rediscovering America's Values* opened the door to many exciting developments. I'll explain—with the hope that you will want to join with me.

Throughout the 1980s I became increasingly distressed by the debasement of politics. Nothing less was needed—I became convinced—than a profound renewal of our democracy—democracy not as merely a set of fixed institutions but as a way of life actively engaging citizens.

So in 1990, with Paul M. Du Bois, I cofounded a new organization—the Institute for the Arts of Democracy. Our action program we call Building Citizen Democracy. We're working with leading educators to develop tools for teaching democracy by "doing democracy." We're developing networks of leaders in the fields of community organizing, the media, workplace democracy, and political practice.

If you, too, are frustrated by the sad state of public life and want to take part in promising community-based developments revitalizing our democracy, please write to us. We'll be delighted to send you membership and program information:

Building Citizen Democracy
145 Ninth Street
San Francisco CA 94103